8—

#40267

AF327555

Books by Kenneth Jerold Comfort

Power, Politics and the Ego

(FIRST EDITION 1998, ISBN 0-9659144-0-2)
(SECOND EDITION, *REVISED*, 2003, ISBN 0-9659144-2-9)

The Ego and the Social Order

(2000, ISBN 0-9659144-1-0)

The Ego and the Pursuit of Happiness

(2003, ISBN 0-9659144-3-7)

Ego Ontogenesis and Human Behavior

(2004, ISBN 0-9659144-4-5)

*National Security Policy and the Development
of Tactical Nuclear Weapons: 1948-1958*

(FIRST EDITION 1970)
(SECOND EDITION 2004, *REVISED*, ISBN 9659144-5-3)

THESE BOOKS ARE PUBLISHED BY THE PUBLIC ADMINISTRATION
INSTITUTE OF NEW YORK STATE, INC.

The above listed volumes can be ordered through your bookstore or by mail from The Public
Administration Institute of New York State, Inc, PO Box 74, Cohoes, New York 12047, or by
telephone 1-(518)-2 35-7921.

EGO ONTOGENESIS
AND HUMAN BEHAVIOR

By

Kenneth Jerold Comfort

The Public Administration Institute
of New York State, Inc.
Cohoes, New York

Published in the Year 2004

Ego Ontogenesis and Human Behavior

ISBN 0-9659144-4-5

First Impression 2004

Manufactured in the United States of America
by Acme Bookbinding, Charleston, Massachusetts

For Harold Dean Comfort, Jr.

Preface

This is the fourth in a series of volumes in which the author developed his theory of human political behavior which began with his study of political psychology. In writing the first of the four volumes, *Power, Politics and the Ego*, the author immediately discovered that in the absence of a theory of psychology which could explain political behavior, one would have to be developed in order to illuminate the nature of political behavior. In developing a theory of political behavior, the author soon came to rely upon concepts of ego psychology, which had the necessary scope to address such an all-encompassing topic as political behavior. In subsequent volumes, the author gravitated away from political behavior to human behavior exclusively, which the current volume epitomizes.

The theory of human behavior presented in this volume is based upon the ontogenesis of the ego—the ego's coming into being—which evolves from the individual's first perception of its own existence continuing throughout the course of life, passing through a series of stages ending with the individual's ultimate demise. At each stage, the ego encounters profound trauma to which it responds adaptively by modifying its structure and adding new means of dealing interactively with its environment, carrying these modifications forward through successive stages.

This theory concerns the social environment of the ego as much as it does the ego itself, insisting that the effect of the ego upon its environment is as much a shaping force upon the latter as the latter is upon the former. The individual ego in its ontogenesis creates the social environment, and the social environment in turn impacts the ego, which shapes its ontogenesis in an iterative process which determines the ego's form and functioning and what it becomes at each stage of ontogenesis.

The author has striven to keep the use of technical terms to a minimum, but new concepts emerging from the theory presented here have necessitated the use of terms not widely shared by all readers. To assist the reader, a glossary of terms describing the way they are used in this volume has been included in the appendix.

TABLE OF CONTENTS

APPENDIX

1

THE EGO

The Primordial Period

The human ego is that function of the organism which experiences the organism's existence and guides the organism's behavior with the aim of reducing the tension which the ego experiences variously by obviating or defeating the source of tension producing stimuli or by seeking and finding access to tension reducing stimuli. For example a hot and humid day may function as a source of ego tension producing impinging stimuli, and a cool breeze on a hot and humid day may function as a source of ego tension reducing stimuli. The ego might guide behavior so that the individual seeks a place on a hillcrest or at the seashore where cool breezes are known to waft.

Ego tension is the ego's awareness of disquiet which may range in intensity from the slightest unease to total panic. The greater the severity, of the tension, the stronger the impulse to get rid of it. The sources of tension producing impinging stimuli may be external to the ego or within it. They may arise from within the ego in the form of thoughts which are disturbing such as ideas or memories. They may arise from within the organism but from outside the ego produced by impingements of physiological functioning such as hunger and thirst. Or they may arise from without the organism in the form of stimuli produced by drugs ingested, injected or inhaled which impact the brain of which awareness is transmitted to the ego. They may take the form of physical or social conditions which impinge upon the organism such as threat of physical harm, or deprivation, or direct impact upon the ego's integrity by threatening the ego's very capacity to reduce tension.

Some impinging stimuli are sensate, physically impacting the body in conscious awareness. Other stimuli are insensate or silent such as those which are accompanied by no sensation such as the secretion of hormones, or the rise and fall of blood sugar levels which the ego may mistakenly attribute to physical objects. For example sexual desire may be attributed to the sight of a sexual object rather than to the silent impingement of testosterone. And hunger many be attributed to the sight of food rather than to low blood sugar.

The human organism may be thought of as existing in an envelop of impinging stimuli which disturbs it and provokes responses aimed at removing the affects of the disturbance. The responses arise within the organism impelled by physiological functioning to interact with the impinging stimuli to obviate or defeat them, and the ego is aware of those responses which are sensate and the decision making process which determines what those responses are.

Much of the physiological activity of the organism is insensate, and the ego is unaware of it until and unless it becomes sensate in the form of pathology. This activity of receiving impinging stimuli and responding to them is the essence of human behavior, with the exception of certain responses which do not require decision making on the part of the organism and are termed reflex responses. Much ego-guided human behavior responds to aims not understood by the ego because they have not been analyzed by the ego so that the ego is unaware of their purpose. These aims are established as a concomitant of ego ontogenesis, and will be described in the pages to come.

The ego is not an organ, but owes its existence to the functioning of the brain. The brain is the seat of decision making in the human organism and the evaluator of the stimuli which impinges upon the organism. Whether or not the ego is merely a witness to the organism's evaluation of impinging stimuli and decision making about obviating or defeating ' tension producing stimuli, the ego nevertheless tends to perceive itself as the evaluator and the decision maker.

The will is a function of the brain, which is experienced by the ego as an ineluctable driving force compelling it to act with the aim of defeating tension producing stimuli. The ego experiences the tension increase from impinging stimuli, and it experiences the act of determining the source of the tension producing impinging stimuli and the decision to act with the aim of defeating the tension producing impinging stimuli. And the ego experiences the compelling force, the will, emanating from within to defeat the tension producing impinging stimuli. The ego not only experiences these phenomena but perceives them as functions of the ego itself.

Whether or not the ego actually possesses free will, it nevertheless perceives itself as possessing free will. There are moments, however when individuals experience indecisiveness and a lack of volition to take action, but such moments for most individuals tend to be infrequent and brief. It is the normative experience of the human individual that it is willful and that it is the decider of its behavior and that it is capable of fending for itself. How the human organism became the way it is is a subject of study of many branches of science. The subject of the present enquiry is the ego itself, which is the seat of that part of the organism which is aware of itself and is a witness to the organism's decision making and activity to deal with impinging stimuli.

Ego Ontogenesis

The ego does not surface into awareness full-blown but comes into being over time. It is relatively simple when first perceived by the organism, but becomes increasing complex during its ontogenesis. The ontogenesis of the ego does not cease until the death of the organism when the process is occluded. The ego of the individual who perishes at age fifteen will be less complex and different in numerous ways than it would become if the same individual did not perish until age twenty-five. If the same individual did not die until age forty-five, the ego would be still more complex and different. If he did not die until age sixty-five, further complexity and differences would have evolved. The ontogenesis of the ego—its coming into being—is continuous until the ego ceases at death.

TRAUMATA AND EGO ONTOGENESIS

The ontogenesis of the ego results from adjustments made by the ego to tension producing stimuli as the ego guides behavior to defeat tension producing stimuli. Such tension producing stimuli are vast in number, and each stimulus precipitates an ego response and adjustment. But it is the major traumata which produce the definitive shaping effect upon the structure and functioning of the ego.

The Oral Stage

The first major traumata is the severation of weaning. But the ego experiences lesser traumata prior to weaning and is changed by them in lesser ways. They function as harbingers of the trauma of weaning because they warn the infant ego that it interacts with an external agent which it only vaguely comprehends and with which it experiences less than perfect accord. The first severation of import which the ego experiences is birth itself, but the ego's interaction with its surround tends to be relatively smooth because of intense parental care-giving which softens the abruptness of the severation.

Many other occasions which foreshadow the severation trauma of weaning follow in the form of the parent's leaving the infant alone for periods of time and coming to the infant's care when it cries for relief from tension producing stimuli such as excretory wetness and boredom. When the severation of weaning does occur, the infant ego has been forewarned by portents that severation might occur so that when the infant ego tries to make sense of it when it happens it is able to comprehend the significance of the occurrence, if only vaguely at first.

Weaning does not occur all at once but is a process of transition from gaining nourishment from the breast or bottle while in the enfolding arms and against the warm contours of the parent to gaining nourishment from utensils while in a sitting position out of contact with the body of the parent. The length of the weaning process is partly a function of the time consumed by the infant ego in accepting it and learning to take nourishment in the new way.

Because the weaning process is tension producing in the severest degree, the infant ego responds by guiding behavior to resist weaning. The parent intersperses periods of proffering the cup or spoon with periods of breast or bottle-feeding. The infant tends to cling more fiercely to the breast or bottle and to suckle more determinedly, recognizing the intense pleasure that suckling gives and its great value to the infant. The infant ego experiences resentment, and may bite the nipple or pummel the breast in anger. The infant ego may guide behavior to push away the cup, the spoon or the bowl, to cast them from the highchair tray or fling them to the floor. If the infant does not actually do these things he may nevertheless experience the anger or the wish to do them.

The Severation Trauma of Weaning

Weaning is the first severe trauma experienced by the ego because it severs the ego's principal cathexis, or bond, to its external agent of absolute dependence, the parent or primary caregiver. Weaning is experienced as abandonment and helplessness. As weaning progresses, the infant ego begins to recognize that what it vaguely suspected—that it is absolutely dependent upon an external agent which can extend or withhold tension reducing support—that the infant ego itself is not absolute in its power to control tension reducing and tension producing stimuli which gives it pleasure or unpleasure and that the inconstancy of the external agent is itself a severe tension Producing stimulus. To deal with the tension increase produced by the inconstancy of the external agent, the infant ego guides behavior to strengthen the cathexis to the external agent and the capacity to manipulate the external agent upon which its security from tension producing stimuli is absolute.

The first ego mechanisms are born as a tension reducing response to weaning in the form of identification and introjection. Identification is suggested to the infant ego as a reaction to discovering its separateness from the external agent with which it formerly experienced itself as a whole. Through identification it can attempt to maintain the wholeness which it experienced before the cathexis severation of weaning. The infant ego reasons that if it were the same as the external agent, then it would not inflict unpleasure upon itself by being inconstant.

To strengthen the effect of identification the infant ego also introjects the external agent to make itself and the external agent one and the same as if severation never occurred. Introjection is suggested by the suckling process—the taking in of something external as the taking in of the milk from the breast or bottle which is the essential tension reducing activity of nursing.[1] The ego will resort to the mechanisms of identification and introjection repeatedly throughout the course of life to deal with tension producing stimuli produced by the severing of cathexes to external objects.

The Ego Narcissism Deficit

Narcissism—The ego's cathexis itself, or self-love—is extended by the infant ego to the external agent of absolute dependence as a concomitant of identification and introjection. The infant ego reasons that if it is one and the same with the external agent, its cathexis to itself must also cathect to the external agent of which it perceives itself as a part. The self-love extended to the parent is perceived as a partial loss of the love which the infant ego attaches to itself, establishing a deficit of narcissism. It thereafter craves a return of the narcissism extended to the parent, which tends to come in the form variously of parental cuddling of the infant, effusive baby talk, kisses and stroking and smiling attention. Throughout the course of life the individual craves a return of infantile narcissism in various forms of indulgence such as effusive praise, kissing and stroking, primacy in the attention of others and various expressions of esteem and devotion.

---

[1] Suggested by **Ruth Monroe,** *Schools of Psychoanalytic Thought.* New York: The Dryden Press, Inc., 1955.

The Ego Power Deficit

Before the trauma of weaning the infant ego perceived itself as omnipotent. Upon each occasion when it experienced the unpleasure of tension increase and wished that the pleasure of tension reduction would return, its wish was almost always promptly fulfilled. That it was the ministrations of the external agent of the caring parent that caused the displacement of unpleasure with pleasure and not simply the result of the infantile wish created the illusion for the infant ego that it could have what it wanted simply by wishing for it.[2] As weaning progresses and the infant ego begins to perceive its absolute dependence upon an external agent, it comes to a realization that it is not all-powerful. The infant ego had no concept of power before weaning, but its loss of the illusion of power resulting from weaning engenders the concept of power which in retrospect the infant ego had had only the illusion of having possessed before weaning.

The infant ego craves the restoration of the experience of omnipotence in order to reduce the deficit of power lost as a consequence of weaning. The continuing presence of the power deficit serves as tension producing stimuli to the ego throughout the course of life which it continually guides behavior to reduce. The power deficit is experienced each time the ego wishes for what it is unable to obtain or is reminded of its weakness. The reduction of ego tension is always temporary because ego deficits are permanent, and awareness of them invariably returns to increase tension anew which the ego will resume guiding behavior to reduce.

Ego Surety

Ego surety is critical for the ego's guidance function. The ego's surety is its belief that it understands reality and how to deal with it affectively, that it can accurately recognize the sources of tension producing stimuli and determine an effective means to deal with them. Perceptions of surety arising from immediate sense perception tend to be widely shared across ages, cultures and history. That fire burns, that water quenches thirst and that the ingesting of food reduces hunger are realities accepted by the vast majority of people in all cultures throughout history. But the Christian perception that the God which the Christians worship created the world is a surety not shared by Hindus, Muslims and Buddhists, and was accepted only by Jews prior to the first century A.D. The more remote from immediate sense perception that the perception of reality is, the more abstract the conclusions about reality are and the more disparate they become and unlikely to be shared by a majority of individuals.

---

[2] Also, see **Ruth Monroe,** loc cit.

It is in the nature of the human ego that it must believe in the accuracy of its perception of surety in order to guide behavior to reduce tension and concomitant unpleasure which the will impels it to do. Even when its conclusion regarding a surety perception involves many levels of abstraction above and beyond immediate sense perception, its belief in the accuracy of that surety perception is as strong as if it involved immediate sense perception. For example, devout Christians believe that their God exists even though they cannot perceive Him with their senses.

Ego Worth

The experience of worth becomes important to the infant ego as a consequence of weaning. Perceiving the importance of the parent to its tension reduction need, the infant ego begins to crave testaments of the infant's importance to the parent. The value given to the infant by the parent reduces ego tension for the infant ego produced by the decathexis or abandonment experienced by the infant ego as a consequence of weaning. The infant ego reasons that if the parent values me as I do the parent, then the parent will continue to cathect me and take care of me. It is the first use of projection by the ego—the attribution to an external object of a propensity possessed by the ego. Thereafter, the infant ego craves and seeks praise from the parent as an expression of worth.

Worth and narcissism wishes become fused in the filial desires of the infant ego because each contributes to the reduction of ego tension produced by the need for each. The stroking of the infant by the parent, the kisses and effusive baby talk betoken in the same parental act both the infant's value to the parent and the parent's love for the infant. Ego tension produced by the narcissism deficit and by filial decathexis fears are reduced simultaneously. The ego's desire to receive expressions of worth continue throughout the course of life as does the desire for a return of narcissism which is often accomplished in the same act by a parentified external object.

Resolution of the Severation Trauma of Weaning

The trauma of weaning tends never to be fully resolved. Nevertheless, the infant ego eventually adapts to weaning and learns to accept the cup, spoon and bowl as the means to gain tension reducing nourishment as it also learns to forego the breast or bottle and the nipple, but not without leaving behind residual behavior manifesting the incomplete resolution of the weaning trauma. The severation trauma residue is unique for each individual, but in many ways similar for all individuals. That residue is composed of techniques of tension reduction which had to be abandoned but clung to in part as the struggle to reject weaning was lost. For example the suckling pleasure, no longer required to ingest nourishment, continues to seek expression in such behaviors as sucking the thumb or the pacifier. The pleasure of physical contact with the external agent of parent continues as the child climbs upon the parent's lap to snuggle close as he did when nursing at the breast or bottle. Messiness in the highchair continues in the form of spilling food and smearing it about, and tends not to cease even after the child is allowed to take his nourishment at the adult dining table where dawdling and messiness tend to persist. These residual behaviors are tension reducing because they enable the infant ego to manifest the resentment and rejection of the trauma of weaning which continues to be less than fully resolved and productive of ego tension.

The Severation Trauma of Toilet Training

Frequently the toilet training process begins before weaning has been completed so that the infant ego is impacted by yet another severe cathexis severation shock before it has finished coming to terms with the severation trauma of weaning.[3] Much as the parent is motivated to wean the infant because of the ego tension produced for the parent by the continuation of nursing, so is the parent subjected to increasing ego tension as the child's practice of voiding and evacuating into its diaper continues. Not only do these practices of the infant burden the parent with increasingly unpleasant childcare tasks, but the failure of the child to make progress toward the eventual achievement of self-dependence impinges upon the parent's ego worth. The failure of the child to demonstrate progress toward maturity at a rate established as a societal norm exposes the parent to the feared disesteem of his peers and consequent diminished ego worth.

The severation of weaning leaves the child with diaper-changing and clean-up as the principal mode of cathexis to the parent. In the vaguely discerned perception of the child, who has not yet acquired object constancy,[4] the nursing parent and the diaper-changing parent are not clearly perceived as the same parent. Object constancy is the capacity of the infant to perceive the parent or other object as continuing even when out of the infant's sight rather than to perceive the parent or object as no longer existing when it is out of the infant's sight. The infant ego begins to relate to the diaper-changing parent as it did to the nursing parent, bringing some of the same behaviors to bear upon an entirely different set of cir-

---

[3] See **Ruth Monroe**, loc. cit.

[4] **Mahler, Margaret S.; Pine, Fred; and Bergman, Anni**. *The Psychological Birth of the Human Infant: Symbiosis and Individuation*. New York: Basic Books, Inc., 1975.

cumstances. As the nursing infant gazed reassured into the loving face of the nursing parent, it now gazes into the face of the diaper-changing parent, in both circumstances to reduce the ego tension cathexis severation fear. As the nursing infant took pleasure in the contact with the soft and reassuring body of the parent, the diaper-changed infant takes pleasure in the touch of the parent in the cleaning of the buttock and genital area, which has an erotic component.

The Derivative Relatedness
Transference Devolution Process

It is in response to the trauma of toilet training that the derivative relatedness transference devolution process begins to form. In dealing with the severation trauma of toilet training, the infant ego transfers to the anal stage parent its relatedness to the oral stage parent who is succeeded by the former. Relatedness is the proclivity of the ego to act toward and expect from an external object of cathexis predictable tension producing or tension reducing treatment or mixture of tension producing and tension reducing treatment to which the ego becomes accustomed and tends to interact predictably.

The transference of relatedness is a practice of the ego aimed at redirecting to another cathexis object the relatedness previously established toward an object of cathexis related to earlier. This disposition of the ego is spurred by its impulse to obviate or to reduce tension produced by impinging stimuli by using the least tension producing means perceived by it to be at its disposal in the given circumstances. Consequently, the ego transfers to the anal stage parent its relatedness to the oral stage parent which is the least tension producing action it perceives it can take to reduce the tension produced by the toilet training severation trauma.

The parent of toilet training is interacted with by the infant as it had interacted with the parent of weaning. Stated another way, the anal stage infant ego employs the same techniques and strategies to reduce the tension caused by toilet training that it used to deal with the tension which had been produced by weaning. This behavior guidance practice of the ego devolves from one stage of ego ontogenesis to the succeeding stage, taking in its train the complex of relatednesses and dependent behaviors of one stage to the next stage cascading forward throughout the course of life.

Because each successive stage of ego ontogenesis is in its circumstances invariably in some way different from the preceding stage, the ego tends to modify—as little as possible—the techniques and strategies it had used before to adapt to the new circumstances. Consequently, the ego's response to each trauma of its ontogenesis, although largely similar, is in various ways different from previous ones, adding to the ego's armamentarium of tension reduction techniques.

The infant's voiding and evacuating in its diapers is tension producing for the parent because the task of cleaning up after the infant is a chore. Furthermore, the parent is eager to promote his own ego worth by keeping his offspring's development apace with societally expected norms. Consequently the parent is eager to complete toilet training, which cannot be accomplished until the infant has attained sphincter control, which is dependent upon physiological development. But sphincter control, when it has developed, gives the infant ego an additional technique to those employed to defeat weaning, namely the capacity to time bowel evacuations and bladder voiding to the consternation of the parent.

Much as the infant ego resisted weaning by biting the nipple, it now resists toilet training by "biting" with the contracted sphincter to delay voiding and evacuation, and then at the parent's distress, releasing the body wastes at times inconvenient for the parent, creating a mess as it did with its food during the weaning process. Thus, the infant ego uses the techniques employed to resist weaning and adds to those techniques new techniques made possible by sphincter control with similar results in the form of messiness and inconvenience for the importuning parent.

Just as the techniques employed by the infant ego during weaning continue to be used in modified form to deal with the impingement of toilet training, so do the techniques used to resist toilet training continue to be used, after being added to the techniques used to resist weaning, to deal with subsequent tension producing stimuli. The techniques called upon by the ego to deal with tension producing stimuli emanating from major severation traumata, it also employs to deal with tension producing stimuli emanating from the less severe impinging stimuli encountered in everyday living.

Resolution of the Severation
Trauma of Toilet Training

As it eventually accepted the cup and the spoon during weaning, the ego guides behavior to accept the practice of voiding and evacuating in the facilities for this purpose taught by the parent as the norm of the society of which the parent is a member and is training the child to become a member. The tension increase experienced by the child from continuing resistance to toilet training becomes greater than the tension increase experienced by using toileting facilities imposed by the parent. The patent displeasure of the parent at the infant's toileting accidents in which it soils its underclothing tends to increase ego tension for the infant, in particular the tension produced by the ego worth deficit which is exacerbated by parental disapproval. The infant accepts the toileting practices imposed by the parent but without relinquishing all of the behaviors it had developed to resist toilet training. These residues of toilet training resistance tend to persist throughout the remaining course of life.

Techniques added to the infant ego's tension reduction armamentarium derived from weaning, such as suckling, crying and messiness, are joined by such toilet training techniques as timed holding onto or retaining, and expelling or discarding. Later during the course of life, by means of the derivative relatedness transference devolution process, infantile suckling and crying devolve into such tension reducing behaviors as kissing, oral sex, excessive eating and the like and plaintive protesting, begging and haranguing from infantile crying through successive modifications of the original tension reducing behavior to deal with changing tension producing circumstances emanating from later stages of ego ontogenesis.

Derivative behaviors devolving from anal stage tension reduction techniques might include retentive behaviors such as collecting objects upon which the ego places value which might include money, works of art, antiques, books, baseball cards, and even common string and rubber bands. Derivative behaviors devolving from anal stage tension reduction techniques in resisting toilet training such as expelling urine or feces at times inconvenient for the parent may take the form of activities dealing with fecal matter or urine such as finger painting, cooking sauces and gravies, brewing liquids such as beer, tea, coffee, wine and whiskey. It might involve such tension reducing behaviors as hosing the garden with water or putting out fires by choosing the career of fireman. It must be kept in mind that a given behavior tends to result from the ego's aim of reducing tension from more than one source simultaneously so that preparing food which resembles fecal matter such as, say, sausages not only reduces unresolved toilet training tension but also reduces ego tension produced by hunger.[5]

The Severation Trauma of the Oedipus Conflict

The Oedipus conflict is precipitated by changed circumstances in the infant's life which include greater intellectual and empathic prowess, the

---

[5] For a discussion of the Freudian concept of over determination, see for example the note on page 212, Part III, vol. II. **Sigmund Freud**. *The Standard Edition of the Complete Writings of Sigmund Freud*. Edited by **James Strachey**. London: The Hogarth Press, 1971. Also see vol. 3 Pages 131, 216 & 294: vol. 4 Pages 149, 219n 283-4, 292-3, 306-8, 309n & 330; vol. 5 Page 480; vol. 6, Page 61n; vol. 7 Pages 31n, 47, 53, 60 & 83; vol. 8, Page 163; vol. 9 Pages 51-2 & 85; vol. 13 Page 100; vol. 17 Page 56 & vol. 18 Page 216

emergence of capacities for object constancy and for individualizing the parents and increased expectations of the parent for the child's self-dependence development. In the child's perception, the parent trifurcates from a generalized parent in which the child relates in much the same way to both parents to a separate recognition of the father, the mother and the generalized parent. Before, as the child began to individualize its parents it might inadvertently refer to its mother as "Daddy," and to its father as "Mommy." Before the parents were individualized, the infant ego tended to relate to either parent in the same way, interacting similarly with either parent.

The emergence of the new trifurcated parent severs the infant ego's cathexis to the former generalized parent. The infant ego gradually comes to distinguish between mother and father and to relate to each differently as well as sometimes to relate to both parents together as the former generalized parent. Each parent conveys to the child an expectation that the child will begin the tension producing process of eventually gaining self-dependence. For example the child may be expected to begin learning to dress himself with parental assistance and to amuse himself without constant parental attention.

The Oedipus conflict is an element of the Oedipus complex proposed by Sigmund Freud which was suggested to him by the story of the Greek King Oedipus in the Sophoclean drama of the same name. In the Sophoclean tragedy, Oedipus unwittingly kills his father and marries his mother for which he suffers great remorse. Audiences tend to experience tension increase from their own early childhood experiences of guilt toward the same sex parent because of rivalry for preferment with the opposite sex parent. As King Oedipus suffers from the horror of what he has done, even though he was not aware at the time that the man he killed was his father and that the woman he married was his mother, and in self-imposed retribution blinds himself. The audience members experience tension reduction vicariously through identification with characters in the play and from a sense of satisfaction that rectitude has been restored in filial-parental relationships and that in their own lives they have escaped the tragedy of Oedipus.

As the infant ego begins to individualize its parents it comes to relate differently to the same sex parent than it does to the opposite sex parent. Observing the special relationship between the parents from which the infant is excluded, the experience of envy and jealousy is born which continues throughout the remaining course of life in relation to a succession of persons and circumstances in which the ego perceives itself variously as left out, subordinated, denied or decathected. At moments when the infant ego relates to its parents as to the generalized parent, the propensity for individualizing the parent is obviated, and the infant experiences stronger filial-parental cathexis, which is tension reducing. In child-rearing practices, the acting together by parents toward their child tends to be more successful in eliciting a desired response from the child because the child enjoys the tension reduction experience of strengthened cathexis to the generalized parent. But when the child relates to a parent individually, it experiences tension increase and tends to act to reduce the tension in ways which manifest the Oedipus conflict. The trauma of severation from the generalized parent tends to be re-experienced by grown children whose parents are divorced or have a troubled marriage and who each plead with the child to take his side against the other parent. The grown child is better equipped than the infant to tolerate severation from the generalized parent.

When relating to the individualized opposite sex parent the Oedipal child seeks to insinuate himself into the special relationship he observes between his parents with the aim of gaining preferment with the opposite sex parent. The cathexis he had experienced in relation to the generalized parent with its elements of identification, introjection and worth he tends to transfer to the opposite sex parent with mounting intensity. The special bond tends to contain erotic components with concomitant exhilarating sensations in erogenous zones of the body.

However, when relating to the individualized same sex parent, the child ego often experiences rivalry, invidiousness, derogation and discrimination. The child's filial hostility is projected onto the same sex parent, and the child comes to fear retribution from the same sex parent for the child's usurpation of the parent's special relationship with the opposite sex parent. The fear of parental retribution precipitates a reaction formation which intensifies the child's hostility toward the same sex parent, provoking still greater filial fear in an ever spiraling magnitude which becomes so intense that the means adopted by the child to deal with the resulting ego tension is to suppress awareness of not only the rivalry and fear of the same sex parent but as well the desire for preferment with the opposite sex parent.

As a consequence of individualizing the parent and relating to each parent differently, the cathexis to the generalized parent is severed, which is experienced as great trauma. The tension reduction experience provided by relatedness to the generalized parent deserts the infant ego and is displaced by the misguided hopes and fears of the Oedipus conflict. Although the ego will continue to relate to the generalized parent, the intensity of the cathexis will diminish, and relatedness to each individualized parent will become ascendant. The child will frequently attempt to separate the parents to pit them against each other in the hope of achieving some aim which both parents together would deny, but when the parents unite to forestall that aim, the child is again confronted by the generalized parent and tends to yield to it. More often, the child will approach each parent individually in ways which are suffused with behavioral residues of the imperfectly resolved Oedipus conflict.

Narcissism and the Oedipus Conflict

The narcissism deficit trifurcates so that the Oedipal child seeks a return of narcissism not only from the generalized parent but also from each individualized parent. From the opposite sex parent the child tends to seek demonstrations of love which contain the element of preferment in which the child hopes to experience special importance tinged with eroticism in the opposite sex parent's regard for him. In later childhood the child may engage in behaviors aimed at gaining special admiration from the opposite sex parent. The little boy climbs high in the tree, or executes summersaults in the grass, or runs fast and jumps high hoping to attract the admiration of his mother. By showing off, he hopes the mother will favor him with admiration not sought from his father in this way. To seek admiration from his father, he is likely to act in ways which imitate his father so as to show that he is like his father. To gain the special affection of her father, the little girl may become coquettish by climbing upon his lap and flirting with him. Such behaviors are intended to gain not only the love of the parent, and thus a return of the narcissism extended to the parent, but also erotic regard from the opposite sex parent.

Power and the Oedipus Conflict

The Oedipal child continues to be dependent upon the parent for its power and tends to summon its parent's intervention whenever it wishes to exercise power to some purpose for which power is needed. For example, in conflict with a sibling or playmate in which he is losing, the Oedipal child may cry for his parent to come to his rescue and employ parental power to force the solution he seeks in the dispute because his personal power is insufficient to enable him to get his way. Without recognizing it, the Oedipal child is totally dependent upon the parent for food, shelter and other necessities of physical survival.

To get its way when the parent demurs, the child may invoke various techniques it acquired in dealing with the traumata of weaning and toilet training such as angry or plaintive crying which may escalate into tantrums manifested in the flinging about of playthings or household objects, not unlike the tipping over of its bowl or cup or deliberately dropping its spoon to the floor during weaning, and deliberately messing its diapers or undergarments as it did during toilet training. By the time of the Oedipus conflict, the child will have gained power over some aspects of its life as for example locomotion in crawling or toddling to where it wishes to go and in manipulation so that it can grasp and use objects for play and amusement.

Ego Worth and the Oedipus Conflict

The Oedipus conflict is especially tension producing for the child's ego worth deficit. Before the onset of the Oedipus conflict, the ego guided the child to seek approval from the generalized parent—a simpler task. After the child ego has individualized the parents and encountered the Oedipus conflict, the task of gaining parental approval becomes complex. In pursuing approval from the same sex parent, the Oedipal child is confronted with the task of ingratiating a parent with whom he also competes for preferment with the opposite sex parent. In his attempts to please the parent with whom he competes, the Oedipal child stirs his own fears of parental retribution which may compel him to fail at the very aim at which he is struggling to succeed. It is not unusual to find an individual struggling unsuccessfully throughout life to gain the admiration of the very same sex parent with whom as a child he perceived himself in competition.

To the extent he is able to reduce the ego tension produced by these circumstances by means of suppression, he is able to obviate the tension by being unaware of the origins of his unpleasure. But as he fails at tasks aimed at gaining the admiration of the same sex parent, he disappoints both himself and the same sex parent. Personal tragedies are commonplace such as the son who fails academically in pursuing training to follow professionally in his father's footsteps. To succeed academically would please his father and earn paternal approval, but at the same time the child mistakenly fears that his success would challenge the father's own success and precipitate devastating paternal retribution. Such a pattern was started during the strategy adopted to resolve the Oedipus conflict by deferring to the same sex parent and followed the child through ego ontogenesis in school and later in academe so that he safely avoids surpassing the same sex parent by failing at what he is doing to earn the approval of the same sex parent. The child's ego worth deficit is greatly exacerbated by such failure. Such is the tragedy of the Oedipus conflict.

A female Oedipal child can suffer a similar fate in competition with her mother. Not wanting to provoke maternal retribution because of her filial competition, she will condemn herself to fail at aims intended to equal or surpass those of her mother, which if she succeeded at them she would gain maternal approval and appease her ego worth deficit. Take the example of the daughter of a beautiful, poised and socially successful woman who after suppressing her Oedipal fears, grows up to be plain, awkward and socially feckless. By not grooming and beautifying herself, she simultaneously defers to her mother mistakenly to avoid maternal retribution, but earns her mother's disapproval for failing to achieve a comeliness in which her mother can vicariously take pride. In her adult life, her lack of comeliness and social poise exacerbates her ego worth deficit. Having suppressed her filial-maternal competitiveness during the resolution of the Oedipus conflict, she is unaware of why she is unable to be attractive and may mistakenly attribute her uncomely appearance to the bad luck of not having been born with good looks.

The filial fear of maternal retribution was a misperception of the Oedipal child brought forward through the derivative relatedness transference devolution process in which at each stage of ego ontogenesis she interacted with cathected others such as parents, play peers and school authorities with deference to assure their acceptance of her while actually provoking their disesteem by her uncomely appearance. The behavioral residue of the unresolved Oedipal conflict established a strategy of dealing with decathexis tension by deference and competitive failure in relation to cathected-to others which ironically put her cathexis to them at risk because of her unprepossessing qualities. The ego's suppression of the Oedipus conflict tends to be carried forward from one stage of ego ontogenesis to the next so that the child, and later the adult, fails to recognize its misperception of a non-existent parental threat. Successful psychotherapy may unearth such a misperception from its state of suppression and afford the sufferer a measure of relief.

The Superego and the Oedipus Conflict

The superego emerges as the primary tension reduction means to deal with the Oedipus conflict. The superego forms as the child ego adopts a tension reduction strategy of capitulating totally to the parent to end fears of retribution and decathexis from the same sex parent. The child gives up the competition with the same sex parent for preferment with the opposite sex parent, thus removing the tension producing conflict with the same sex parent. Thereafter, the child ceases to perceive the opposite sex parent as an object from which preferential treatment is sought over the same sex parent and as an object of eroticism. Romantic inclinations toward the opposite sex parent are abandoned to re-emerge in adolescence toward a surrogate parentified opposite sex object such as an opposite sex age peer.

The child also relinquishes conflict with the parent in all matters in which the child perceives itself in disagreement with the parent. From that time forward until adolescence, in the child's perception the parent almost always knows best. This is a period during which the child's intellectual capacities and curiosity grow so that it welcomes parental explanations of phenomena that the child perceives in reality. The propensity to enquire of the parent the meaning of what it perceives in the world about it becomes strong because of curiosity, and the child tends to ask many questions about what it sees and hears and to deposit the explanations given by the parents and parental surrogates such as teachers into its rapidly growing store of knowledge.

Of particular importance to ego ontogenesis is the propensity of the Oedipal child to accept the parent's teachings about right and wrong conduct. The ego craves understanding of how it should guide behavior in the treatment of others and how it should expect to be treated by others. Acts of hostility toward the parent become taboo, and this posture of taboo is transferred to other parentified entities so that acts of hostility are condemned as wrong unless they are justified by exceptions to rules established by society proscribing hostile behavior toward others. During the time which follows the establishment of the superego, whenever the child engages in hostile behavior toward anyone, and particularly toward play peers, a supervising adult such as parent or teacher will chastise the child and shame him into desisting from hostile behavior. The resolution of the Oedipus conflict is made possible by the establishment of the superego which ends flagrant Oedipal hostility.[6]

Rectitude and the Oedipus Conflict

The concept of rectitude emerges from the resolution of the Oedipus conflict. In its acceptance of filial hostility as wrong and worthy of punishment, which becomes a staple of the superego, the child ego extends this perception to parentified others including play peers. Through projection, the Oedipal child becomes concerned about the way it is treated by others, and the concept of morality is given birth, although dimly perceived. The force of morality on individual behavior arises from the superego, which chastises the ego when it contemplates hostility toward others, precipitating ego fear of parental retribution and decathexis. Such ego-guided morality is the salvation of the weak in society vis-à-vis the strong and is the foundation of the science of ethics. The parentification of societal organizations, institutions and their functionaries creates a matrix of superego guardians which surrounds the potentially errant ego and impinges upon it with the tension producing threat of retribution should it transgress.

The superego arises from the ego's reaction formation to its misperception of having an unchecked license to precipitate retribution. The superego prevents the ego from going too far, in the child's mistaken expectation, and putting itself into danger of eliciting overwhelming vengeance from a parent angered by the child's usurpation of the same sex parent's prerogatives. The Oedipal child projects his own jealously and anger onto the same sex parent which he believes will precipitate a terrifying desire for vengeance in the same sex parent as it would in him. To obviate its propensity to anger the

---

[6] See **Blos, Peter.** *On Adolescence, A Psychoanalytic Interpretation.* New York: The Free Press, A Division of Macmillan Publishing Co., Inc., 1966. **Blos, Peter** *The Adolescent Passage: Developmental Issues.* Madison, Connecticut: International Universities Press, 1989 and **Sarnoff, Charles.** *Latency.* London: Jason Aronson, Inc., 1989.

parent, the Oedipal ego establishes a reaction formation to its own unlicensed predilections in the form of the superego which thereafter controls the ego by inflicting the tension producing experience of guilt when its unbridled predilections might cause it to provoke vengeance from an offended parent, or later in the course of life, from an offended parental surrogate such as teacher, employer or functionary of the criminal justice system.

The experience of guilt is itself a reaction formation to the fear of provoking retribution for going too far and offending the authority of a vengeful parent, and later such vengeful parentified authorities as clergy, teachers, employers, law enforcement officers and criminal justice officials and saints and deities. Having been established by the ego during the amnesia period[7] of early childhood, the superego tends to continue in force throughout the remaining course of life to prevent the ego from going too far in satisfying those tension reduction propensities which violating such taboos as incest would effect. The Ten Commandments given to Moses serve as an example of fundamental superego proscriptions and prescriptions immanent in institutions erected by society to reinforce the superegos of its members.

Surety and the Oedipus Conflict

The surety deficit is engendered by the experience of weaning which subjects the infant ego to the discovery that what it believed about reality— that whatever it wanted it could have merely by wanting it—was profoundly incorrect. This discovery sets the ego upon a lifelong search for knowledge of reality to reduce the tension of the surety deficit by overcoming ignorance. Until his very last breath, the individual tends to remain piqued by curiosity about unanswered questions.

Rectitude is much more than ethical behavior. It has to do with the harmonious synchronization of ego-guided behavior with reality. Rectitudinous behavior is behavior which conforms to reality. The ego which guides behavior to conflict with reality will sooner or later come to grief, and it is the function of the superego to limit behavior from coming into conflict with reality and to obviate or defeat tension producing stimuli, which it can only accomplish in harmony with reality. It is patent that a society whose members are in sustained open conflict with each other will produce great tension increase for its members. Therefore, reality dictates that limitations upon hostile behavior of a society's members is exigent to the well being of all.

Morality attempts to find and to enforce rules of conduct which maintain peace while being fair to everyone. But this is an impossible task because principles of fairness will not be universally agreed upon. In the ab-

---

[7] Autobiographical memory begins at about age four or five. Before that the individual tends to have only fragments of memories.

sence of accepted universal principles of reality, first principles upon which a system of ethics can be logically erected are unknown. Only by agreement can principles of reality and of ethics be established by which a society will abide, and such principles perforce are not absolute. The rules of fairness have to be agreed upon by the population in general and inculcated into the superegos of enough members of society that their imposition of those rules will be sufficient to enable them to prevail over the objection of those who do not accept the rules.

As a concomitant of resolving the Oedipus conflict, the child ego accepts the parents' explanation of reality, usually without question. The child ego's lack of knowledge together with the persistence of its curiosity and its desire to accept the teachings of its parent impel the child ego to accept virtually wholesale and with little protest the knowledge of reality offered by the parent. This absorbed knowledge includes facts about the nature of reality as well as prescriptions and proscriptions about both right and wrong behavior as well as about wise and unwise behavior.

The Id and the Oedipus Conflict

The Id is created as a defense against the tension producing assaults of the superego. The superego subjects the ego to the pain of guilt for its transgressions against its prescriptions and proscriptions, and tends actually to obviate many of those transgressions so that they do not exceed mere contemplation of them. The id emerges as an invented object of projection to take the blame for the ego's indiscretions or contemplated indiscretions.[8] The ego declares to the superego that "it" or the id made me do it or wants me to do it—meaning to transgress against superego prescriptions and proscriptions. By this projection, the ego hopes to absolve itself of desires and behaviors aimed at tension reduction but that are anathema to the superego. Incest, filial hostility, usurpation of parental preferment, envy—these are the tension reducing wishes of the child ego for which the id is erected to take the blame. The child experiences these dangerous wishes and feels helpless to control them. By projecting them onto the id, the child ego is able to claim innocence and reduce the ego tension which the wishes occasion.[9] As

---

[8] For a discussion of the id. See **Bettelheim, Bruno.** *Freud and Man's Soul.* New York: Alfred A. Knopf, 1983.

[9] The Freudian concept of the id differs in that Freud regarded the id as the seat of drives and impulses which it was the task of the ego and superego to control. The present author attributes the id to a creation of the ego and not the repository of drives. (See Bruno Bettelheim, op cit) The latter the present author attributes to brain functioning arising from phyllogenetically inherited impulses devolved through evolution from earlier forms of life.

ego ontogenesis proceeds, the concept of the id diminishes in importance. By the time of young adulthood, the ego all but abandons the id defense, and tends to recognize its own complicity in behavior condemned by the super-ego, or projects its guilt onto other persons, groups or phenomena rather than onto the id.

Ego Mechanisms

By that point in ego ontogenesis at which the Oedipus conflict is re-solved, a number of important mechanisms have been created by the ego employed to reduce tension when other means would produce greater ten-sion. Ego mechanisms have in common their tendency to conflict with real-ity so that eventually they fail in their use. They tend to be temporary solu-tions to dealing with sources of tension producing stimuli which will not lastingly succumb to their application. Mechanisms employed by the ego tend to be self-deceiving in that they are illogical and misguiding. They are invariably created by the ego's attempt to deal with a source of ego tension newly impinging which is insuperable, usually the severance of the child from the external object of absolute dependence.

Once created, an ego mechanism tends to remain in the ego's armamen-tarium throughout the remaining course of life to be used at times when im-pinging stimuli must be defeated by the least tension producing means which the ego perceives to be at hand. Mechanisms are based upon illogical reason-ing and protect the ego from tension producing stimuli impinging from sources in reality. Eventually the mechanism fails, and ego tension returns to which the ego responds by a renewed effort to resolve the conflict with reality or to apply the mechanism again to deal with the tension. Suppression is a mechanism which often is repeatedly reapplied to tension producing imping-ing stimuli which returns again and again to keep the stimuli away from awareness.

Because only impinging stimuli of which the ego is aware produces ten-sion, how is it that the ego is able to respond to tension increase from many stimuli simultaneously? The answer lies in the rapidity with which percep-tions of reality enter and leave the attention of the ego, so like the juggler who keeps several objects in the air simultaneously but touching only one of them at a time, the ego keeps several perceptions of reality in ready reach of his attention at the same time while focusing on each separately. For exam-ple, the individual at his place of employment may attend to a perception of a task before him that he is working on, and also upon a perception that he is hungry and eager for lunch time to arrive, as well as contemplating a leisure activity planned for the evening and also on a problem he is having with his children, all at the same time—each of these items focused upon for brief periods but repeatedly so that he can attend to all of them during the same time frame by interleaving each of the them with the others rapidly like the juggler. For example each time an object of suppression reappears, the ego simply suppresses it anew so that the ego is relieved of conscious awareness of and the unpleasure which attention to it would bring. If awareness returns with such great force that he cannot suppress it he will be forced to deal with it in the context of reality and to suffer great and painful tension increase.

The first tension reducing mechanisms which the ego creates are formed in the ego's response to weaning and are suggested by perceptions with which the ego is familiar. Identification is suggested by the ego's wish to return to the status quo ante in which it perceived itself and the external agent of parent as one and the same, and introjection is suggested by imbibing the milk from the breast or bottle by taking it in.[10] Identification and introjection, if they were real and not merely mechanisms, would restore the status quo and end the tension producing severation trauma which weaning inflicts. The mechanisms of identification and introjection are frequently summoned by the ego throughout the remaining course of life to deal with tension producing stimuli. The list of objects with which the ego identifies and the list of objects it introjects is immense and include such diverse objects as one's parent, sibling, school, employer, favorite sports team, home town, nation and religion.

The ego mechanism of projection is suggested by the spitting out of food or drink urged upon the infant during weaning. Being spit upon is regarded as a disgusting and offensive insult by almost everyone who has been or imagines being subjected to it. This mechanism devolves into verbal spitting out of offensive words to others who are objects of one's anger or fear. It may come to involve the use of epithets, derision and sarcasm. It often becomes fused with the practice of expelling fecal matter or urine in conjunction with anger towards an external object and is manifested in imprecations toward others involving reference to these repugnant body wastes.

The ego often combines projection with other mechanisms in its tension reduction efforts. For example, projection is combined with reaction formation to form the superego. The Oedipal child projects its filial hostility onto the same sex parent by mistakenly assuming that the same sex parent entertains competitive and hostile concerns about the Oedipal child and would destroy him as the child wishes to destroy the same sex parent. The filial fear begets a reaction formation of hostility as a protection against the misperceived threat from the same sex parent. The superego takes form as a resolve to suppress all hostility and rivalry vis-à-vis the same sex parent after which the ego is no longer aware of Oedipal rivalry for preferment with the opposite sex parent, fear of the same sex parent and eroticism toward the opposite sex parent.

---

[10] **Ruth Monroe**, loc cit.

Suppression

Suppression is a form of forced forgetting or removing from attention the perception of something which is intensely tension producing. It is the refusal to think about something that is tension producing. Because reality always returns, the act of suppression must be repeated interminably each time the thought of what is suppressed returns to awareness. The ego develops a practice of suppressing thoughts which might trigger the re-emergence of the original suppressed thought. Stated differently, memories which might stimulate recall of suppressed thoughts are themselves suppressed to prevent a train of thought which would lead to the original suppressed thoughts.

The ego learns to avoid reminders of suppressed thoughts. In everyday experience, the individual will tend to stay away from places or things which would remind him of suppressed thoughts. The mere contemplation of going to such a place or taking up such a thing produces unpleasant awareness which is tension producing and thus provokes avoidance to obviate the tension. An example might be the individual's unwillingness to visit a certain house or room, or travel to a certain town or city, or wear a certain style of clothing because even the contemplation of going to or doing any of these things stimulate a negative experience such as fear, anger or depression—these experiences being reminders of tension producing suppressed thoughts.

For example, an individual may refuse to wear clothing of a certain color, say green, because it offends his ego ideal which has rejected green as an acceptable color for clothing. The color green may remind the individual of the practice of his father wearing green clothing and thus evoke childhood feelings of filial hostility and fear of paternal retribution. In resolving the Oedipus conflict, the child rejected his aim of competing with his father for preferment with his mother, an experience which was depressing and tension producing.

To reduce the tension from memories of this experience, the ego guides behavior to suppress these thoughts. To enforce the suppression, the ego also guides behavior to reject green clothing which is a reminder of the father at the time of the Oedipus conflict suppression. To protect from such reminders the ego guides behavior to form in the ego ideal a dislike of green clothing. Thenceforth, thoughts of wearing green clothing like his father during the suppression of the Oedipus conflict is depressing because it contravenes his ego ideal. The mere sight of or thought of green prevents the suppressed thought from reappearing, and memory of the Oedipus conflict remains out of awareness.[11]

---

[11] Sigmund Freud conceived an unconscious mind, which apparently in his view operated almost as if it were a parallel mind working independently of and guiding the conscious mind. One imagines brain functioning in which (continued on next page)

Sublimation

The mechanism of sublimation is created as a consequence of the process by which the toilet training trauma is resolved. The infant ego's predilection for body wastes lingers even after he has developed a reation-formation of repugnance for them. Consciously, he finds feces and urine to be revolting, but his former liking for them continues in his thoughts which frequently present themselves notwithstanding his suppression of those thoughts. To aid in the continued suppression of these predilections, he adopts ways to sublimate fecal and urinary matter by associating them with acceptable objects. Such awareness permits him to continue to enjoy these objects by using suppressed reminders of them. Thus, the creation of culinary delights allows a chef or cook to enjoy working with substitute feces while not recognizing his relatedness to foods as substitute feces or urine. Sausages and sauces might function in this way for a particular ego. Other substances which may serve as reminders of body wastes might include oil paints, modeling clay, beer, or similar objects openly accepted by society as worthy, and are sublimations of fecal matter and urine.

Continuations

The suppression of cathected objects and of tension reducing practices of the primordial period of ego ontogenesis before the emergence of autobiographic memory leaves residues of those experiences which continue into later periods of ego ontogenesis as suppressed vestiges. Because they are suppressed they continue to affect behavior without the ego's awareness of their origins. Kissing, cigarette smoking and drinking from a beer bottle may serve as continuations of the suckling experience first enjoyed when nursing. Spitting and cursing may serve as continuations first experienced when resisting weaning.

Collecting as in hobbies or amassing money, or stubborn resistance to a tension producing imposition may be continuations left from the infantile resistance to toilet training. Modeling with clay or repeatedly rewriting a re-

---

patterns of stimuli moving circuitously across synapses produces thoughts which guide behavior independently of a conscious mind operating through different pathways and across different synapses at the same time producing different thoughts which guide behavior at odds with the unconscious thoughts. While the present author acknowledges the incalculable debt owned to Sigmund Freud by the science of psychology, he is unpersuaded that parallel minds operate independently of and at odds with each other in the same brain.

port or work of fiction may be continuations of the joy experienced in touching feces and the resistance to letting them go which the infant was chastised and forbidden to do during toilet training. Masturbation, erotic interest in the opposite sex, courting, off color jokes and reading or writing romantic literature are examples of continuations of the Oedipus conflict experience.

Reaction formations might include Puritanism or modesty about sex. Continuations may persist throughout the remaining course of life as tension reducing behaviors which assist the ego to deal with the unresolved vestiges of major severation traumata. It is important to note that each of the continuation behaviors cited above do not function as a continuation behavior each time it occurs. Sometimes a kiss is perfunctory and not impelled by eroticism. At times, the drinking of beer from a bottle may occur because no other drinking vessel is available. Occasionally, an individual may rewrite his report because he discovered that he omitted important material. But just as often these behaviors may be continuations induced by the practice of keeping tension producing primordial memories suppressed which engaging in tension reducing continuation behaviors enable the ego to accomplish. Continuations persist throughout the course of life and tend to be reshaped by the ego over time as new circumstances impinge upon old residues remaining from severation traumata.

The Latency Period

The suppression of the Oedipus conflict ends the primordial experience of the ego and marks the beginning of autobiographical memory. Of primordial life, the ego tends to remember little more than fragments of experience, but with the beginning of the latency period, the ego is able to begin constructing the story of the individual's life with a considerable degree of continuity from that time forward. The latency period is a major outcome of the resolution of the Oedipus conflict. The infant ego comes to accept it's exclusion from the special relationship between the parents, and struggles to restore its cathexis to the generalized parent.

While residues of Oedipal behavior continue, the child ego experiences greater comfort from relating to the generalized parent which is possible only when relatedness to the individualized Oedipus conflict parent is kept in a state of suppression. Consequently, upon occasions when the infant ego is tempted to interact with a parent competitively or in the pursuit of preferment or eroticism, a fear of retribution impinges which produces ego tension which tends to be quickly reduced by a return to the suppression of Oedipal urges. In this way, Oedipal urges tend to be kept at bay, and the ego experiences a period of the greatest peace and equanimity it will enjoy during the entire course of life.

2

THE EGO AND BEGINNING OF POST-PRIMORDIAL LIFE

The Latency Period

The suppression of the Oedipus conflict, which coincides with the end of primordial life, ushers in the latency period in which memory of experience begins to maintain continuity, and the individual begins to perceive his life as if it were a story which he is living and which he could relate to others, albeit at first falteringly. Thenceforth, whatever experience the ego is aware of which is tension producing or tension reducing, or associated with tension producing or tension reducing experience, particularly the experience of ego ontogenesis, it will be able to store in memory forever and will be able to recall when reminders point to it. It should be noted, however, that experience to which the ego is indifferent because it is insufficiently tension producing or tension reducing to provoke lasting interest will likely be forgotten.

Memories of experiences which were suppressed during primordial life tend to remain suppressed in post primordial life and can be understood only through deduction from experience in post-primordial life. Specific information about the ego's ontogenesis prior to the suppression of the Oedipus conflict can be known only when deduced. Consequently, those who are not persuaded by theoretical constructs aimed at explaining primordial experience through analysis of post-primordial experience will likely remain unpersuaded. However, there are cases in which former skeptics became persuaded after undergoing a measure of psychoanalytic therapy.

The latency period lasts some six to ten years beginning with the formation of the superego and the resolution of the Oedipus conflict at about age four to six and ends with the onset of puberty at about age ten to fourteen, varying from one individual to the next. The latency period tends to be experienced as a long and memorable stretch in the lives of most people, it being longer than all of the years the individual has lived up until the time the latency period begins. The tension producing thoughts of the Oedipus conflict, being suppressed, disturb the latency ego relatively little but remain latent until the onset of puberty when they erupt anew into expressed filial-parental conflict regarding such matters as sex, rivalry, power, worth, surety and narcissistic gratification.

Meanwhile, during latency the parent-child relationship is at its most benign and often tends to be a joy for both parent and child. Such filial-parental conflict as there is tends to focus more upon self-dependence issues such as the child's willingness to take on chores of self care—his person, his belongings, his sleeping quarters, his school work—and upon chores of helping his family such as cleaning and maintaining the family ménage and upon deportment—how the child should conduct himself in relation to peers and adults. But the latency child is unlikely to challenge parental power, preferment, authority and surety.

Parentification

Parentification is a process in which the ego transfers relatedness to the parent to non-parent objects. The practiced interactions between parent and child, the expectations the child has vis-à-vis the parent, the ways in which the child treats the parent tend to be transferred to other objects which are perceived as like the parent in certain special ways. For example when the four-to-six year old child begins to attend preschool or kindergarten the person of the female teacher seems much like the mother. The teacher is authoritative, dictatorial and dominating, and may at time manifest kindness and protectiveness and at other times rebuke and admonishment, like the parent. The seeming omniscience, prescience and omnipresence of the parent appear to the child to have been transferred to the teacher or delegated by the parent to the teacher.

The ego engages in parentification to reduce the tension produced by its dependence upon and subjection to the object parentified much as the ego was dependent upon and subject to the actual parent. All of the issues of narcissism, power, worth and surety existing between the child and the parent take up residence in the relationship between the child and the parentified object. Much as the child ego glorifies the parent so that by identification the child ego indirectly glorifies itself, so it transfers the propensity of filial adulation to the parentified object. Normatively the child tends to adore his teacher and to exalt and glorify him or her, and to take pride in being his or her pupil.

Filial Ambivalence

Filial ambivalence—the simultaneous affection and hostility experienced toward the parent—is also transferred by the child to parentified objects. Filial ambivalence emerged as a consequence of weaning as the child ego discovered that the external agent upon which it relied absolutely to defeat tension producing stimuli and to furnish tension reducing stimuli was inconstant, at times extending parental protection and affection and at other times withholding these benefits, provoking a reaction formation of filial hostility to parental inconstancy. The child ego at times regards the parent as protector for which it bestows filial affection, and at other times regards the parent as tormentor in response to which the child ego responds with filial hostility.

Filial ambivalence, born of the severation trauma of weaning, continues in the child-ego's relation to the parent of toilet training when at times the child experiences affection for the parent when the parent is perceived as beneficent and at other times experiences fear and hostility toward the parent who is perceived as maleficent, withholding tension reducing beneficence or inflicting the tension producing imposition of toilet training upon the child. During the Oedipus conflict experience, filial ambivalence individualizes the two parents, at times relating positively to the same sex parent and at times relating negatively to the same sex parent and at times relating positively to the opposite sex parent and at other times relating negatively to the same sex parent. The child-ego also continues to relate alternately positively and negatively toward the generalized parent.

An important outcome of the trifurcation of the formerly generalized parent during the ascendancy and resolution of the Oedipus conflict is the ego's propensity to bifurcate displaced filial ambivalence, which is a tension reducing process by which the ego selects one moiety of a parentified pair to relate to as beneficent and the other moiety of the parentified pair to relate to as maleficent. For example, a child may perceive his teacher and the school principal as a parentified pair with, say, the teacher perceived as kind and solicitous and the principal as punitive and demanding. The pairing of these two objects of filial displacement may have been provoked by school rules that students are detained in the principal's office if caught misbehaving on the school grounds, while the teacher continues to be seen as kindly and supportive.

They are paired because both are perceived as powerful authorities of the school, one the obverse of the other. The beneficent teacher serves as an object upon which the child-ego can displace the identification and introjection first aimed at the beneficent parental moiety, and by glorifying the teacher can vicariously enjoy ego worth-enhancing pleasure which glorification affords. The maleficent school principal serves as an object of projected hostility as the feared moiety of the parental pair upon which filial hostility can be safely projected because it would not likely provoke dangerous retribution from the actual parent.

Displaced filial ambivalence becomes a tension reducing mechanism extensively employed by the ego throughout the remaining course of life. Examples of its use are legion with respect to such parentified pairs as one's own nation and the enemy nation, one's own sports team and the adversary sports team, one's own school or college and a rival school or college, one's own church and a church whose doctrine conflicts with that of one's own church. To be parentified, an object must be perceived as powerful and threatening or powerful and protecting, but few objects tend to be parentified if they are perceived as simultaneously both threatening and protecting. Typically, only the parent ever tends to be perceived in this way, although exceptions may occur in cases of a particularly closely related-to individual such as an older sibling or grandparent or spouse upon which substantial dependence has been transferred. Sometimes it may be seen in the relationship between a tormentor and a victim as in the case of a prisoner of war over whom the tormentor has nearly absolute control.

The pleasures of Latency

During latency the child grows out of infancy into a "little person," the boy seeming like a miniature male adult and the girl seeming like a miniature female adult. Often parents dress up their latency children in attire which resembles adult attire, the boy wearing a little suit and the girl wearing a dress imitative of adult fashions. Parents who are disposed to do so are able to develop camaraderie with their latency children, playing with them at games, indulging in hobbies with them, traveling with them to interesting places, enjoying outings with them and above all teaching them, inculcating them with the parent's visions of surety and rectitude.

It is at this time that the child learns about religion, morality and the nature of reality and absorbs the parent's beliefs and values about all manner of things such as politics and prejudices, whom to admire and whom not to admire, and how people should conduct themselves. The parent tends to relive vicariously though his latency child his own latency childhood, and to plan for his child's future as he had once dreamed of his own future. For the parent of the latency age child, his offspring appears to offer him a new chance to compensate for his own failed dreams by directing his child along the path he took or should have taken. This propensity of the parent often comes to grief during his child's adolescence if the child chooses the parent's dream to rebel against in establishing his own separate identity.

Narcissism and Latency

The latency ego's narcissism deficit is more easily appeased than at any time during the course of life following weaning. Through the identification with, introjection of, idealization and glorification of the parent the child ego vicariously reduces the tension of the narcissism deficit. At times when he suffers a loss of narcissistic gratification, he may intensify his glorification of the parent to enhance the parent's attractiveness so that he may vicariously enjoy the parent's endearing qualities as if they were his own.

Because parental relatedness trifurcates as a concomitant of the Oedipus conflict, filial identification and introjection trifurcates so that the same sex parent becomes the object of identification and introjection of extended narcissism. The love, or return of narcissism, which the child seeks from the opposite sex parent tends to have a tincture of eroticism fused with romanticism. Romanticism is a form of defensive affection in which eroticism is disguised as idealized affection free from eroticism. In romantic tales of medieval knights battling in a joust while wearing the colors of a female chosen to admire, typically the wife of a higher ranking noble, illustrate the essence of romantic love. Like the little boy in the throes of the Oedipus conflict, frightened of incurring the wrath of the father with whom he competes for the affection of his mother, the knight can love the idealized untouchable lady without incurring the wrath of the lady's powerful husband.

Ego Worth and Latency

To reduce ego worth deficit tension, the latency age ego tends to glorify the same sex parent in order to elevate that parent's worth so as to enjoy the tension reduction provided vicariously by identification with and introjection of the same sex parent. Children on the playground and in the neighborhood can be heard boasting of the admirable qualities of their same sex parent. The little boy might boast that his dad can beat up your dad, attesting the power of his father which he vicariously shares through identification.

It is during latency that the child ego comes to experience for the first time the glory or the shame in the society of his peers of being the child of his parent. If his parent is held in high esteem by the child's peers because of the parent's social status, accomplishments or other admiration assets, then the latency child enjoys reflected glory and the pleasure of decreasing ego worth deficit tension. His own ego worth reflects that of his parent. If the parent is held in mediocre or low esteem by the latency child's peers, the child's own worth may be correspondingly affected.

This is the point in the course of life that the child begins to perceive the existence of social status and what his place in society is likely to be when he reaches adulthood. He can begin to accept and to adapt to the inevitability of his future status or resolve to struggle to achieve higher status. These are the circumstances in which the seeds of social mobility are sewn which fuels rivalry and competition in society for status and worth. The parent who himself failed to achieve satisfactory social status in his own life will likely begin either to inculcate social ambition or acceptance of their existing social status in his own child during the latter's latency age struggle. If the child perceives his parents to occupy a high status, he may simply come to enjoy that high status in relation to his latency age peers and become concerned to maintain it or to burnish it in his own adulthood.

Power and Latency

As with narcissism deficit tension, so it is with power deficit tension, the latency age ego resorts to identification with and introjection of the parent to reduce the tension of the ego power deficit. The latency child perceives his personal power as puny compared with that of his parent, but so long as he arrogates to himself his parent's superior power he can reduce the tension of his impotence. He depends upon the parent's power for everything—for shelter, food, clothing, protection from physical danger and from intimidation by others. He may provoke others, then run to his parent for protection. The parent may tell him to stand up to the bravado of intimidating play peers or neighborhood bullies, or may sooth his diminished ego worth resulting from conflict with more powerful antagonists.

As the latency child begins to assess his power relative to that of others, he also begins to develop techniques with which to respond to the power of others exerted against him. These techniques were given their initial shape by the ego during its primordial struggles, particularly with the Oedipus conflict, and they tend to vary among individuals. They may include responding to force with force, or finessing the intimidator by ruse or manipulation, or by beating a retreat. The techniques employed will tend to form the practices followed during the remaining course of life.

Surety and Latency

Latency is the period during the course of life in which the ego absorbs a greater amount of information and values than during any other. Whatever the parent conveys to him, or is conveyed by parental surrogates to whom the parent has delegated parental authority such as teachers and clergy, the child introjects with little doubt as to its validity. Any doubt the child may entertain about a parentally imposed idea resurrects tension from the suppressed Oedipus conflict whose resolution established the latency period initially. Such doubt evokes fear of parental retribution, and the thought tends to be quickly suppressed anew.

It is during latency that the child ego first begins to appreciate the existence of the deity or of deities. Before latency, whatever the parent taught about religious beliefs impressed the child but little—his parent being his only deity. But as the parent teaches the latency age child that he himself depends upon and defers to a deity, the child begins to sense the weakness of the parent as an object of his dependence and transfers filial relatedness to the deity which was proffered to him by his parent. Thereafter the child looks to the deity for help in matters which the child believes the parent is unable to give.

The curiosity of the latency child, fostered by his increased intellectual capacity to wonder about what he beholds around him, seeks answers from his parent. He begins to assemble a store of knowledge based upon what he believes his parent believes. He may sometimes mistakenly attribute parental beliefs to ideas which he extrapolates from other beliefs articulated by his parent. For example, parental religious views based upon a religious commandment such as that enjoining covetousness may mislead the latency child into believing that his parent does not envy those who have greater material possessions or attractiveness assets than he. Normatively, it will not be until the onset of puberty that the child-ego will begin emphatically to doubt information, ideas and values of the parent.

Latency and Rectitude

Rectitude, the concept of right and wrong behavior, is born during the resolution of the Oedipus conflict and the emergence of the superego as the infant ego struggles with its fear of and hostility toward the opposite sex parent. Rectitudenous behavior conforms to reality, and reality suggests to the ego that hostility exerted toward a more powerful adversary may invite retributive destruction. By adopting the parent's pronouncements about what constitutes right and wrong conduct, the ego will refrain from guiding the child's behavior to act out hostile wishes toward the same sex parent which the child fears might invite retributive destruction from the parent.

Rectitudinous behavior, then, is restraining oneself from acting with hostility toward another, and overcompensating one's hostile wishes by displacing them with expressions of courtesy and pretenses of affection. Thus, routine interactions between individuals are filled with affected expressions of courtesy and affection. The handshake or bow, the disingenuous smile, the perfunctory words of praise form the little courtesies of common social intercourse. Such politesse is considered appropriate even though perceived as not truly sincere. It protects against provocative action which might elicit a hostile response. It is the mark of civilized discourse.

Rectitudinous behavior is inculcated by the parent in his latency child who tends to absorb it with little questioning, and although the child may at times forget to practice it he will nevertheless tend readily to do so when reminded. By the time the child reaches puberty, normatively he has absorbed his parent's teachings about acceptable conduct and has learned to practice it. When he enters adolescence, he finds that his age mates are practicing a measure of polite conduct, and he is grateful for the training which helps him fit into and be accepted into the society of others. The degree of polite conduct and the particular form it takes in adolescence is strongly shaped by the practices established in the particular culture and socioeconomic class to which the adolescent belongs.

Latency and Curiosity

Pent up curiosity craves satisfaction during latency. With his increased intellectual capacity and capacities for locomotion and manipulation, the latency child wants to know the "why" of nearly everything he sees, hears and handles. The school may help him with its systematic teaching of knowledge and skills required by society in the formal transmission of the cultural past to the future. But the latency child's interests tend to go far beyond those which the school can satisfy. The child is keenly interested in exploring his world, both geographically and socially. He wants to see other places than his own house and garden and other people than his family and siblings. The school grounds are a good place to begin this exploration, but they are not enough. With his new play peers he ranges afield to other places in the community, all too often to places which skirt danger which his parent would abhor. With his friends, he may venture to the shopping mall, to the park, to the riverbank, to abandoned buildings and to the residences of children of whom his parent may disapprove. Should the parent discover these adventures, he may be frightened for his child and take corrective measures.

Latency and Mastery

The degree of mastery gained and displayed by the latency child is substantial. During primordial life, the child learned to manipulate the parent by means of crying and the timing of bodily waste elimination. During the struggle with the Oedipus conflict and its resolution, he learned the strategy in dealing with his parents of divide and conquer, to pit his parents one against the other. These techniques he expands upon during latency and learns to apply them to others as well as to refine them in dealing with his parents. Crying ripens into articulate speech with which parents variously are deceived, cajoled and flimflammed into acceding to the child's wishes. The timing of elimination evolves into alternate extending and withholding obedience and resistance. All of these techniques and strategies as well as numerous others are mastered and applied successfully not only in dealing with the parent, but also in dealing with parentified objects and with play peers.

The latency child also tends to display substantial increase in self dependence capabilities. Demonstration of mastery in such acts as dressing himself, performing his own toileting, taking nourishment at the adult dining table, performing chores and performing school work normatively reflect latency age accomplishment. In most societies the latency child can read and write at least with limited skills, can reckon numbers and successfully play at games with complicated rules and requiring the use of equipment such as balls, bats and clubs. The latency child also begins to display a degree of mastery over the knowledge of his society having come to understand the roles and functions of teachers, clergy, police, firemen, shopkeepers and bus and tram drivers.

Latency and Counter Manipulation Behavior

Counter manipulation techniques were first learned in reaction to toilet training. The parent manipulates the child—literally manhandles the child—to the potty chair and later to the adult toileting facilities. The parent, anticipating an impending bowel movement or bladder voiding may upon occasion pick up his child and take it to the bathroom. With the advent of sphincter control, the child learns to time eliminations so as to counter-manipulate the parent— to foil the parent's attempt to manipulate him to the toilet.

Counter manipulation behavior is aimed at reducing ego tension by defeating the effort of the perceived source of the impinging stimuli—the parent or parentified entity—to subject the ego to tension increase which the decathexis of toilet training imposes. The irony of counter manipulation behavior is that it is by its nature self-injurious. The child who defeats his parent's effort to toilet train him may spend periods of time in the discomfort of soiled clothing. The child who toddles defiantly away from his parent may tumble down the stairs, painfully injuring himself.

Latency age counter manipulation behavior tends to be manifested in resistance to self-dependence training. The child refuses to wear his goulashes, but gets his feet wet, which is uncomfortable. He refuses to tidy his room, then cannot find the equipment he needs to play games with his friends. Or he refuses to do his schoolwork, suffers embarrassment at recitation, falls behind in school and is relegated by schoolyard society to the company of those with lower status. Counter manipulation behavior is commonplace but is manifested in a variety of ways by different latency age children, depending upon which tension producing requirements imposed by the parent the child fortuitously chooses to resist.

Latency and the Pursuit of Happiness

Happiness depends upon the success attained in reducing ego tension, and happiness during latency especially depends upon reducing tension produced by the tension sources peculiar to latency. The requirement for establishing a place for himself in the family group is a major source of tension for the latency age ego.

The Family Group as a Source of Tension

The family may be complex with numerous siblings and extended family members, and if it is a recombined family with step-parents and step siblings and half brothers and half sisters it is an even more complex society in which the latency child must find a social place. Whatever the composition of the family, the latency child will find himself in a rank order of precedence with the older members having more seniority and therefore normatively more power and privilege than the younger members. Older siblings will serve as objects of parentification for younger members, and the latency child may both be the object of a younger child's displaced filial ambivalence and also be the displacer of filial ambivalence upon an older child or extended family member.

Precedence, preferment and the privileges of seniority are implanted in the ego during the latency age familial struggle and tend to endure throughout the remaining course of life. Seniority emerges as a factor of when the individual enters the family, birth order being a major determiner of seniority. Normatively, particularly in traditional families, the father is the head of the family and its most powerful and privileged member with the mother as second in command and in privilege. The latency child's displaced filial ambivalence may bifurcate so that he will relate to one family member as a beneficent parental surrogate and to another member as a maleficent parental surrogate. Thus, the Oedipus conflict will tend to impel behavior in relation to other family members shaped by vestiges of the suppressed Oedipus conflict. Such behavior may take the form of quarrelsome rivalry and hostility toward the family member who is related to as a surrogate maleficent same sex parent, and warm camaraderie toward the family member related to as the beneficent same sex parent.

Factions tend to emerge in large families in which displaced parentified relatedness occurs. The rank order in which the latency child finds himself in the family, the way power is exerted upon him and privilege rationed out to him because of his rank, and the way in which he adapts to these conditions, strongly shapes the strategy and tactics he comes to use in interacting with the world in which he makes his way. His sense of where he fits into a social milieu is largely established in this way, and happiness in the present and in the future depends upon it. If he is relatively pleased by his place in the social scheme, he will know a measure of happiness. If not, he will experience ego tension increase and a measure of unhappiness which he will strive to overcome by advancing himself, or will submit to and accept his place. In the latter case, he may attempt to reduce ego tension by finding a social milieu into which he is able to fit comfortably. Social groups of like-minded individuals tend to form in this way.

Latency age boys tend to shun the company of latency age girls as they struggle to establish their masculinity in emulation of their father. Latency age girls may feel that boys are unfairly given preferment, but typically seek each other's society in which they assess the desirableness of boys they know, emulate their mothers by fantasizing about their futures as women, wives and mothers and compare ideas about how to make themselves attractive in dress, grooming and manner. When latency children succeed in these pursuits, they tend to experience happiness, or to the extent they fail, experience unhappiness.

Latency children tend to seek status among their peers as a means to reduce the ego tension produced by the vestiges of suppressed Oedipal rivalry. Oedipal rivalry tends repeatedly to threaten to reemerge from its suppressed state, producing ego tension increase which the latency child seeks the means to reduce. By displacing filial ambivalence upon play peers, the latency child is able to deflect the tension of emergent Oedipal impingement. Rivaling others among his play peers for status and preferment among his latency society reduces the tension of the re-emergent Oedipal impingement.

The latency child greatly deplores his small size and puny strength relative to adults. Those boys who are larger and stronger tend to enjoy greater status among their peers because they possess the assets of greater size and strength, and they tend to dominate the peer society, other things being equal. A few months of difference in age may span a significant growth in size, knowledge and skills during latency. Being older becomes a status asset, because the older child is more experienced and more accomplished than the younger child and often looked to for guidance in group activities. The small child longs to grow larger and may suffer diminished ego worth because of his size. He will choose means to cope with the tension produced by his small size. Fantasies in which he is large and powerful may be resorted to. Or he may become scrappy and pugnacious to play peers to over-compensate for his small size, or he may take up weight lifting or other forms of athleticism in the hope of overcoming the derogating effects of his small size.

The latency girl seeks status through grooming and attractiveness like adult women, whom latency girls seek to emulate. Normatively the girl who is older and regarded as pretty possesses a natural advantage in status assets and tends to dominate her female peer society much as the older, physically large and strong latency boy normatively dominates his male peer society.

Happiness for the latency child requires social acceptance among peers and the possession of the status assets required to achieve it.

Accomplishment is an important tension reducer for the latency child. The latency child not only perceives the smallness of his size relative to adults, but he is acutely aware of the greater accomplishment of the adult. The adult knows more and can do more. In almost every area of capacity, the adult exceeds the child, contributing to the child's experience of relative inferiority. Accomplishment by the child even when it fails to bring him abreast of the adult reduces the ego tension of inferiority and contributes to his happiness.

Playing with toys which emulate adult equipment, tools and trappings and even using actual adult paraphernalia is a means adopted by the latency child to reduce the ego tension of filial inferiority and to sustain his faith in his future adult parity. Thus, the little girl may want to help mother with cooking or sewing by actually using kitchen equipment and the sewing machine. She may raid her mother's closet and dress up in her mother's clothing and play at being an adult. The little boy may expropriate his father's tools to construct a toy or a doghouse. The latency boy may seek such playthings as toy trucks, trains and guns, then take up games which emulate adult activities. Having access to such toys or being able to simulate them is important to the happiness of the latency child.

Latency and Self -Dependence

The imperative of achieving self-dependence progress is both tension producing for the latency child as well as tension reducing. The greater his self-dependence, the greater his independence because independence is possible only to the extent the child can take care of himself without the direct intervention of the parent. The parent of the latency child is both eager and anxious to see his child make self-dependence progress. The parent is eager because he wants to enhance his own ego worth through gains of his child, which he can boast about to his friends, and the parent is eager because he wants to escape tension producing childcare burdens which his offspring's self-dependence advancement would enable him to do. The parent is anxious because his child's self-dependence failures would reflect negatively upon the parent's ego worth as well as extend the childcare burden which the parent hopes will diminish.

The parent hopes to see his child do well in school, which reflects well upon the parent's persona and so that his child will one day be able to gain a livelihood. The parent also hopes that his child will become adept at making friends and at attracting the admiration of members of the opposite sex. The child must be able to do well socially if he is to enjoy the support of others in his pursuit of place and economic success. The child must be able to attract members of the opposite sex if he is eventually to be able to marry well and to establish a family which produces grandchildren to perpetuate the memory of the parent beyond the parent's demise. The parent wants to see his child take on chores and be able to tolerate the carrying out of unpleasant tasks which survival and success depend upon.

The child tends to be both eager and reluctant to take up these challenges. He is reluctant because they are tension producing, but at the same time he is eager because they elicit the admiration of the parent and reduce the tension of the ego worth deficit. Moreover, accomplishment is a testament to his growing personal power which reduces the tension of the ego power deficit. Accomplishment also demonstrates mastery which the latency child is eager to realize.

Economic Skills and Latency

Both parent and child want to see the child manifest knowledge and skills which demonstrate progress toward gaining the capacity one day to derive a livelihood from the society of which he is a member. This means doing well in school, which is a primary determiner of future employment and social status. Pursuing his education is the latency child's principal responsibility. Consistently doing homework attests to progress toward academic success. Progress also means successfully taking on small tasks for financial reward such as running errands for pay or performing other small, remunerated services for neighbors or shopkeepers. The ability of the child to save money rather than to spend all that comes into his hands demonstrates a potential for success in a society whose economy is based upon invested savings and is typically viewed as gratifying by the parent.[1]

The latency child begins to anticipate the career he will take up when he becomes an adult, and the career he contemplates tends to be selected more to reduce the ego tension experienced during latency rather than the ego tension he will experience when he actually takes up a career in adulthood. The little boy may see his future self in an exciting and adventurous role such as pirate, cowboy, astronaut or circus performer rather than in a role which he might actually fill in adulthood such as factory worker, businessman, lawyer or physician. The little girl may imagine herself in fantasy as opera singer or famous movie actress rather than as a housewife and mother, or office worker or assembly line worker, although many will assume the latter, being more accepting of the reality in which they live.

---

[1] Savings can be invested either in financial instruments or in meeting the expenses of education or training for remunerative employment.

Displaying a proclivity for doing better than his peers esteems the child in the eyes of the parent. Demonstrating competitive superiority in school by out-shinning class mates in academic grades and achievement awards gratifies the ambitious parent who is relieved that his child will be able to make his way in the economy from which all must extract a living. Demonstrations of leadership by being popular with and attracting a following among peers is viewed by parents as harbingers of future social success as well as economic success. Evidence of social independence in the ability to accept social slights without being weakened and to continue afterward with apparent confidence and effectiveness is gratifying to the parent.

Latency and Physical Capacity

Self-dependence capacity is demonstrated in displays of physical skills and abilities by the latency child. It is in latency that the child's locomotor, manipulative and acrobatic skills begin to flower dramatically. The child craves to run, jump, whirl about, climb, tumble and ride toys which accelerate his mobility, all of which attests his possession of the physical capacities which betoken a successful future. Carnival rides such as Ferris wheels, bumper cars, roller coasters, whirligigs and merry-go-rounds beckon the latency child with almost irresistible attraction. Among toys aimed at latency children are tricycles and bicycles, scooters and skates—all of which give them mobility accompanied by thrilling sensations of wind and motion. The child of latency at last is not compelled merely to plod along on short legs, but can abbreviate time and space with celerity, and streak past adults as if leaving them standing still. The latency child who is disabled or physically underdeveloped and unable to enjoy these physical sensations is fatefully denied these pleasures and is compelled to look for happiness in other experiences and often finds it there.

Latency and Training for Citizenship

Training for citizenship tends to begin in earnest during latency which, because of the recently formed superego, is the first time in the course of life that the ego conceives of right and wrong behavior and is able to understand rules established to regulate human interaction. Citizenship in the broadest meaning of the term has at its base the interacting with others peacefully according to practices which obviate hostile social contact. Above the base are groups of individuals united by special interests such as being members of the same family, sharing the same social aims, or formal objectives. Above the array of groups are entities intended to organize society to accomplish

·formal specialized functions such as law enforcement, education, public safety, and to facilitate economic activity. Above these organizations are governing bodies which possess the sovereign power of the state within which society organizes itself to compel adherence to its rules by errant members. Such organizations include legislative bodies to design social rules and executive bodies to execute and enforce the rules enacted by the legislative bodies.

Under the dominance of the parent and obedient to the parentally imposed superego, the latency child, with little questioning, absorbs the values and knowledge conveyed by his parent including political values and political party identification, and is thus trained for citizenship by the parent reflecting the parent's vision of what is appropriate citizenship behavior. All manner of citizenship behavior is conveyed to and absorbed by the latency child from his parent including what passes for civil discourse, citizenship responsibility, and how and to what extent to participate in governing. The parentification of governmental institutions tends to emerge at this time, and these institutions—governmental agencies, branches of government, political parties, campaigning and elections, the constitution—all tend to become visible to the latency child and to be related to by him as he perceives his parent relate to them.

It is the onset of puberty and the profound physiological changes in the body and the equally profound changes in societal attitudes toward the child which brings the latency period to a close.

3

ADOLESCENCE

Adolescence is a period in the course of life which spans the years between the end of latency and the beginning of young adulthood. In primitive societies, adolescence may be a very short period because the demands of adulthood tend to be imposed very quickly upon the child by a society living close to the margin which cannot spare the luxury of extending to the child a long period of training for adulthood. In highly educated industrial societies with market economies and a requirement for relatively high skills in its population, the luxury of a long period of training for adult responsibilities tends not only to be afforded by society but forced upon its adolescent children to prepare them for life in a highly complex and technically accomplished society. The period allocated to adolescence is not determined so much by physiological factors as it is by societal requirements.

Adolescence is precipitated by the onset of puberty which severs the child from the parents of latency. The Oedipus conflict, which lay dormant during latency, erupts anew under the impulse of puberty. Puberty engenders not only physiological changes, including the development of organs of human reproduction and dramatic growth in size and strength, but also new and more demanding expectations for the post-latency child by parents and society.

The adolescent rather quickly learns that he is expected by his parents and by society to choose a career from which he can obtain a livelihood as either a breadwinner or spouse of a breadwinner, find a mate and form a family. The negative consequences of failure would be greatly diminished ego worth and a lack of the tension reducing pleasures and privileges which accrue to adults. The more complex technically the society is in which the adolescent must find his way, the greater and more formidable the challenge he tends to perceive himself faced with. Long years of education and training stretch out before him which eats into the time he can allot to the pursuit of tension reducing pleasures as he did during latency. During adolescence he must progressively give up time for pleasure and increase the time devoted to choosing and pursuing a career. In a complex, technical society, the variety of careers from which the adolescent may choose is vast and may continue to expand even after he has made his choice. From a career of homemaker to that of high ranking public official, from starting a small business to becoming head of a vast corporation, from a career in a variety of professions to being a technician or a tradesman in any of a multiplicity of fields, from a career in the arts to a career in professional sports, or if nothing else he may find himself in the career of unskilled laborer—the range of choices is extensive. From this multiplicity of options the adolescent must make his choice, and if he is unable to choose, he will nevertheless drift into one career or another because no one in society is permitted to avoid the obligation of pursuing a career without being called a shirker or perceived as disabled.

Adolescence and Narcissism

During adolescence the ego's search for narcissistic gratification expands beyond the parent, play peers, teachers and other caregivers to parentified entities such as adolescent society itself, its leaders, high school teachers and salient societal institutions such as the school, the church, the state and the government, to important personages such as elected officials, and to heroes of fiction, entertainment and sports and to the deity or deities. The adolescent ego craves recognition from a wider public than play peer society of neighborhood and playground. Athlete heroes of high school sports, prom queens, debate champions and leaders of social cliques, or their counterparts in non-Western societies, become objects of envy, admiration and parentification whose approval and friendship is sought for narcissistic gratification by members of rank and file adolescent society, and the occupants of these lofty venues are the recipients of the narcissistically gratifying approbation of their admirers. To be one of these cynosures or accepted into the society of these cynosures is deeply craved by members of adolescent society to appease the ego tension produced by the narcissism and worth deficits.

To be accepted or lionized, the adolescent ego is driven by the tension of the narcissism and worth deficits to strive to fit into the adolescent social milieu by demonstrating his acceptance of its values. Toward this end the adolescent tends to conform to whatever standard he is able to detect as prevailing in the adolescent society. Because of the transitory nature of adolescence, standards and vogues tend to be fleeting because there is no enduring touchstone which adolescents can rely upon for guidance, except in highly traditional societies. Consequently, fashions in clothing, life styles, teenage argot, what the "in" thing is, social leadership attributes and attractiveness assets are continually changing, leaving the adolescent in a perpetual quandary as to what he should do to make his way in adolescent society. Eventually, as he enters young adulthood and is confronted by its more enduring demands, the perplexities of adolescence tend to be overtaken by more urgent importunities of young adulthood.

Adolescence and Power

The ego power deficit experienced by the latency child is greatly reduced for the adolescent, who has suddenly gained substantial growth in size and strength so that his perceived inferiority to his parent diminishes. He begins to experience an acceleration of his progress toward achieving parity with his parent. The adolescent boy who has undergone a growth spurt compares himself with his father in size and strength and in knowledge and intelligence and finds himself drawing abreast of his parent. He gradually begins to resent having to submit to his father, who appears to fail to recognize the growing parity of his son in both physical and intellectual prowess. There are fantasies about having a confrontation with the father if the latter continues to refuse to yield to the son. The adolescent continues to depend upon his parents' power to deal upon his behalf for the physical necessities of survival such as food and shelter.

Normatively the father, who may remember when he was an adolescent, perceives the son as overestimating his prowess and continues to protect the resentful son from dangerously overreaching himself. The father may remember how his own parent had suddenly grown wiser after he the father had found himself moving from adolescence into the treacherous waters of adulthood. The son may preen before other adolescent females, but he will continue to be very careful about competing with his father for the attention of his mother.

The adolescent girl begins to perceive herself as drawing abreast of her mother in sexual attractiveness and in intelligence. The gaining of pulchritude as her figure fills out and in light of her youthful freshness, she may be led to believe that she could compete successfully with her aging mother in attracting male admirers. She may experiment by tentatively flirting with the same men she sees her mother chatting up at social gatherings, in the shopping mall and on the street. But she will tend to be very cautious about competing with her mother for her father's attention.

The adolescent tends also to extend the reach of his increased power to objects beyond the family which he parentifies as he comes to regard himself as deserving of new respect from adult neighbors, from the parents of his play peers, from teachers, shopkeepers and employers. He may become impudent towards any of these entities if he perceives them as failing to recognize his new importance. Adolescents who have automobiles or motorcycles may drive their vehicles with a degree of recklessness which annoys adults, cutting in and out of traffic, leaving behind the more cautious adult drivers. The automobile or motorcycle gives the adolescent greater manifest power than he has ever exercised, and displaying that power in audacious driving may be a great reducer of the ego power deficit tension with which he has long been burdened. Line-jumping at supermarket queues, at cinema box offices, pushing his way through crowds of adults in marketplaces, in shopping malls and on sidewalks is typical of the brashness of adolescents with their newly found sense of power. The adolescent who has obtained gainful employment working in the company of adults may show off his new power by working faster and harder at the tasks required by the job, showing up the adults whose experience in life has taught them to proceed at a more sustainable pace.

Adolescence and Surety

The adolescent may become a know-it-all when around adults, especially in the presence of his parents, flexing his newly acquired "intellectual muscle." The adolescent is amazed at how little his parent knows of the world and of how to do things. He is often quick to educate his parent by informing his parent from his fund of newly found knowledge, turning the tables upon the parent who had been educating him only a short time ago before he became an adolescent. From peers, from the communications media, from school, he has suddenly gleaned a wealth of information which he gratuitously bestows upon his hapless parent, as if the parent had never attended school nor read newspapers. The parent is seen as old fashioned and out of touch, and the adolescent seldom hesitates to inform the parent of his backwardness.

Adolescence and Rectitude

As it is with surety, so it is with rectitude—the adolescent thinks he knows best. Awash in adolescent society with its lack of enduring standards to serve as signposts and rebelling against parental authority, the adolescent tends to take his cue about right and wrong behavior from the prevailing views of his peer society. Especially salient in the adolescent's estimation is the unfair advantage which the prerogatives arrogated by adults to themselves give to the parent's generation. They have much more money than adolescents, and they tend to be in charge everywhere and unwilling to be guided by the views of adolescents.

The adolescent looks about and sees much that is unfair and much that needs to be done to correct the unfairness. Poor persons should be better treated. Schools should be improved, and so should streets and roads. Businesses should place the public good above profit. Civic improvements should be made immediately, and because adults have the money and are in charge, they should get busy and do the right thing sooner rather than later. The adults should listen to and heed the adolescents because their vision is fresh and forward-looking, but the adolescent seems endlessly impeded by the reactionary posture of the adult generation. Wherever the adolescent finds himself, adults tend to be suppressing his enthusiasm and thrust for improvement. It is the young people which the adolescent sees as striving to correct the wrongs of the world in the face of a complacent adult generation. It tends not to occur to the adolescent that costly improvements which the adolescents urge would have to be paid for by the adult generation upon whom the main tax burden falls and not upon the adolescents who still live under their parents' roof and sit at their parents' dining table.

Certain elements of surety and rectitude tend to be left by most adolescents to the major institutions of society. For example, the church and theology continue to be left to the clergy whose theological pronouncements generally go unchallenged by adolescents. However, a portion of adolescents who are children of devout parents will even challenge the church, as a means of filial rebellion. This is the point in the course of life when atheism may be born in the mind of an adolescent rejecting the religion of his parent in the course of individuating and establishing his separate identity.

It is also the point in the course of life in which zealotry may be born in the adolescent struggling to establish his separate and unique identity by demonstrably surpassing the piety of his parent to demonstrate that he is different from his parent without offending his parent and risking parental decathexis by rejecting his parent's religion. It is the birth of the "holier than thou" posture often seen in passionately religious adolescents and young adults. Ironically, the adolescent and young adult also hopes to reduce the ego tension of his worth and narcissism deficits by fostering the admiration and love of his parent through his zealotry for his parent's religion.

As for interpersonal morality, the adolescent struggles with inculcated precepts of the sort represented by the Biblical ten commandments, and will tend to look for and find hypocrisy in the conduct of his parent and in adults of his parent's generation, especially at times when he is reprimanded for his own youthful excesses. Morality in conduct with his peers will tend to mimic the morality which the adolescent perceives in the conduct of his parents and their adult friends among themselves and in relation to society generally. Neither hypocrisy nor generosity of spirit tend to be omitted in the conduct of adolescents and their parents with members of their respective peer societies.

A major issue of morality with which adolescents struggle is that of sexual conduct. Newly exposed to the heightened importunities of sexual and reproductive urges, adolescents tend neither to have attained the defenses of their parents and their parents' generation from sexual importunities nor have available the ego tension relief opportunities from sexual tension enjoyed by their parents. When the sexual mores of society are strict, the adolescent superego is strengthened by the behavior of the adult society which the adolescent observes around him. Widespread condemnation of divorce, adultery, fornication, prostitution, vulgar language and pornography helps the adolescent impose limitations upon his own sexual behavior. But looser proscriptions against sexual activity, a high divorce rate, widespread fornication, adultery, and pornography, especially when they are depicted as socially acceptable by popular entertainment, vitiates the resolve of the adolescent to obey the sexual dictates of his superego and enables him to excuse sexual license in his own behavior.

The degree of moral rebuke in society of sexual license also affects adolescent sexual behavior after the fact of sexual promiscuity leading to pregnancy. Teenage boys abandoning the babies they sire to the care of the teenage girl they impregnated and the increased social acceptability of unwed motherhood enable the adolescent to indulge sexual and reproductive urges with but little fear of negative consequences, which tends to lead to increased incidence of single parent adolescent families dependent upon society for sustenance which they cannot provide for themselves. Parents who wish to see continence in their adolescent children sometimes find themselves all but helpless in the midst of widespread sexual license.

Mastery and Adolescence

The intellectual capacities of adolescents grow dramatically in parallel with their growth in physical size and strength. The many things they could not do during latency because of their small size and lack of strength and intellectual capacity now become possible. The secondary school adolescent may truly become an athlete in track and gymnastics. In all manner of physical activity, in work and in play, he excels beyond anything he was able to do during his latency years. After he has attained his adolescent growth spurt, he can take his place along side adults in places of gainful employment or in performing household chores. Thus, to gain mastery, he need' but practice the skills he readily acquires in commonplace adult tasks.

The adolescent is also able to acquire expertise in chosen fields of endeavor by specializing in a technology or the acquisition of a skill which other persons, including both adolescents and adults, have not chosen. Thus, the adolescent may become an automobile mechanic, a computer operator, an aviator, a long distance truck driver, a carpenter or master of any of a myriad of specialties which are mastered only by specialists. The adolescent may master his academic work, becoming knowledgeable in fields of learning with mastery equivalent to that of rank and file members of adult society.

In interpersonal relations, the adolescent's degree of mastery tends to be weaker. In his pronouncements about politics and economics, he may not be taken as seriously by adults as he is in the quality and productivity of his work in the factory or the field, in the shop and or in household chores. In the display of empathy regarding the concerns of others, in the degree of urbanity evident at social gatherings and in the amount of acumen he demonstrates in understanding the motives and actions of adults, the adolescent still tends to be wanting, and typically must await young adulthood before his polish gains its desired luster. The skills at which the adolescent most desires to acquire mastery—attracting a mate and gaining a livelihood—in many cases continues to elude him throughout most of his adolescent years.

Adolescent Individuation, the Superego and the Ego Ideal

After gaining size, strength and intellectual capacity, the adolescent begins to individuate from his parent much as the toddler individuated from his mother after gaining a capacity for locomotion. The superego, created partly as the indispensable condition for resolving the Oedipus conflict, intensifies during adolescent individuation, not only in the tension and unpleasure it afflicts upon the ego but also the pain it gives to others as the adolescent projects the tension producing imperatives of his superego on to others as a means to reduce the unpleasure to which it subjects him.

The Oedipus conflict resurges during adolescence because of the child's greater parity of power with the parent and equally great diminution of inferiority to and fear of the parent. After his growth spurt, the adolescent's fear of filial decathexis is greatly mitigated, and his filial rivalry returns in force. He often stands up to the same sex parent with contradiction, perversity and outright defiance, but filial rivalry for the favor of the opposite sex parent tends to be displaced on to peers of the opposite sex, with the reaction formation of incest taboo tending to stem the adolescent's entertaining of sexual thoughts aimed at the opposite sex parent.

The ego ideal, which absorbed many of the values inculcated by the parent during latency, surges during adolescence as the child struggles to establish his identity separate from his parent and unique in the world. Possessing a unique identity is indispensable to the individual if he is to fend for himself without requiring protective intervention by his parent or by parental surrogates. To be on one's own, to take care of oneself, to do as one pleases, one must have a sense of self-dependence and of independence and above all a degree of separateness from all others. This condition requires a sense of uniqueness for which a unique identity is indispensable.

The ego ideal, incipient at the resolution of the Oedipus conflict and the birth of the superego and fostered during latency, begins to acquire its lasting shape during adolescence. The ego ideal is composed of everything needed to defend against every source of tension producing impinging stimuli which the ego is capable of imagining and to gain access to every source of tension reducing stimuli which the adolescent imagines he would want at his disposal. Thus, contained in the ego ideal are attributes of comeliness, strength, social popularity, the possession of admiration assets, superior skills, knowledge and abilities, high intelligence to show off to others and to deal with threats, and also the imperatives of the superego inculcated by the parent.

The ego ideal indeed idealizes all that it contains, thus accounting for the lofty posture of superiority presented by the adolescent which aims at the highest standards of human aspiration, above the manifest behavior of members of the adult generation who appear to the adolescent to have abandoned their ideals. The ego ideal is a reaction formation to the years of tension producing inferiority experienced by the ego during the latency years when the child was small, weak, bewildered, fearful of his parent yet wholly dependent upon his parent. Now he can compete again as he had during the years of the Oedipus conflict but without the profound fear of decathexis.

The adolescent superego which contains the array of inculcated parental values which the adolescent ego accepted to retain the filial-parental cathexis and disdain for those parental values which the adolescent ego rejected in the process of establishing a separate identity, becomes a weapon against the parent and the members of the parent's generation. The adolescent calls them to task for failing to manifest in their behavior the values which they taught their children during latency. The adolescent believes that he manifests those values in his own conduct but that his parents and their generation often do not. The many foibles and imperfections, great and small, of which the parent and the parent's generation are found guilty tends to elicit shouts of astonishment and derision from adolescents, who regard themselves as superior to adults, whom they regard as hypocritical and feckless.

Parallel with the development of the ego ideal are the ego real and the ego actual. The ego real is perceived as the ego as it really is rather than as ideal because the ideal is unachievable. In the self-perception of the ego, it vacillates between the ideal and the real. When it perceives itself as ideal, ego tension diminishes, and when the ego demonstrates great accomplishment toward the ideal as in the case of a major triumph in performance or mastery or receiving acclaim by others, the reduction of tension is so great and rapid as to give the ego a heady feeling of exhilaration. But when the adolescent ego fails at its aim of achieving the ideal, it may experience tension increase, unpleasure and depression.

Because the ego never assesses accurately where it is on the continuum between the ideal and the real, it often perceives the ego actual as ascendant. The ego actual is neither the ideal nor the real, but the true state of the ego. The ego actual is not knowable, but rather is an abstraction. Reality for the ego is the experience of fluctuating between the ideal and the real, and when the ideal is ascendant the ego experiences tension reduction and pleasure, and when the real is ascendant the ego experiences tension increase and unpleasure.

For the adolescent in a peer society highly critical of its members, swings between the ideal and the real tend to occur frequently during daily existence. To catch sight of his reflection in a shop window and find himself wanting, to receive a lower than hoped for grade on a school examination, to find himself weighing a pound heavier on the bathroom scales than his ideal weight, to experience a social slight because a peer across the room did not return a greeting with as much enthusiasm as thought appropriate, to be forced by parents to wear a garment not fully conforming to peer society fashion—any of these experiences may give ascendancy to the ego-real and plunge the adolescent into depression which he or she struggles to conceal from family and friends.

Adolescence and Curiosity

Suddenly finding himself in a much wider world, the adolescent becomes intensely curious about what he finds in that world. High on the list is sex. Whether to engage in sex, how to perform sex, whether performing sex is right or wrong and whether the consequences of performing sex are damaging and dangerous are all questions which the adolescent wonders about and tends to consult his peers to satisfy his curiosity. He is averse to seeking explanations from his parents about sex because doing so would provoke Oedipus conflict tension, and parents are reluctant to initiate sexual discussion with their adolescent children because it would vicariously provoke Oedipus conflict tension in them and might give rise to tension producing questions from their child about the parents' own sexual behavior.

The adolescent tends to learn about sex from informal sources such as teenage peers, pornography, and fragments of information conveyed by the communications media. Societally authorized delivery of information to adolescents about sex and reproduction and the particulars of what constitutes permitted and prohibited sexual conduct tends to be lacking because of institutionalized embarrassment and disagreement about what teenagers should be told and the fear of provoking prohibited sexual activity in children simply by talking to them about sex.

The adolescent tends to be curious about how to earn a livelihood sufficient to support a family and how to attract a mate. He becomes intensely curious about how his parent was able to gain an income and to become married, and he wishes to enquire of his parents about acquiring these capacities. But even after his parent has explained these phenomena, the adolescent tends to continue to be puzzled. It is one thing to be told how to do these things, but it is another to understand exactly how to do them oneself.

Throughout adolescence the teenager continues to puzzle over how he will be able to attract a mate and provide for a family when he becomes an adult, and he struggles to position himself to be able to do these things when he becomes an adult. For some adolescents, achieving adulthood becomes ever allusive, and adolescent years extend far into young adulthood years and for some even into middle age without the individual ever discovering how to attract and provide for a mate.

Many adolescents also become curious about the nature of reality, about the origins of life, about where the universe came from, and about other cosmic questions provoked by their formal education in science or by philosophical discussions overheard among adults. They tend to begin to seek answers from teachers and books and from religious authorities. For some, their curiosity leads to the questioning of the answers to such questions opined by authorities.

Ego Mechanisms and Adolescence

Adolescence is the period in which ego mechanisms come into large-scale use for the first time. The preceding latency period placed fewer stringent demands upon the ego so that the practice of using mechanisms tended to be less urgent. While latency is not without its tension producing imperatives, less is expected of the latency child and forgiveness for failures tends to be more readily given. The mechanisms created during earlier epochs of ego ontogenesis are called upon to deal with the impinging stimuli particular to adolescence. The impulse to reduce sexual tension produced by the impinging stimuli of secreted hormones places the adolescent in the way of severe unpleasure which the deprivation of sexual release imposes. The parentally inculcated and socially corroborated prohibitions against behavior aimed at reducing sexual tension—masturbation and sexual intercourse— erect insuperable barriers to the satisfaction of sexual tension. Widespread masturbation and fornication nevertheless occur with the latter tending to be less widespread than the former. These behaviors, which are aimed at reducing sexual tension, paradoxically produce superego tension which is equally painful. Ego mechanisms are summoned liberally and repeatedly to reduce the tension of superego guilt. Suppression of thoughts about past masturbation or fornication tends to be heavily relied upon when rationalization and the denial that masturbation or fornication is wrong fail to reduce superego tension. But the imperatives of the superego are never far from awareness and repeatedly reassert themselves to be denied, rationalized and suppressed anew.

The pain of superego guilt tends to be distributed unevenly over the adolescent population so that some suffer sexual guilt with much greater severity than do others, but few escape it totally. The result is the presence in society of widespread judgmentalism toward those unfortunate enough to be publicly exposed for sexual misconduct. Judgmemntalism reduces ego tension by enabling the judgmentalist to project his guilt for his own sexual misconduct, or his wish to engage in acts of sexual misconduct, on to others, or his wish to reduce the ego tension caused by sexual deprivation because of remaining chaste by displacing his own hostility toward superego imperatives on to those who violate those imperatives.

The adolescent summons the support of ego mechanisms to reduce the tension of ego ideal failures which repeatedly beset him. Denial, rationalization, sublimation, projection, identification, introjection and displacement are often called upon. Rationalization is often resorted to by the adolescent when doubts about his comeliness beleaguer him or shortcomings in academic or other areas of achievement occur. Projection is called upon by the adolescent ego to rid itself of tension producing guilt for failures to demonstrate moral virtue at times when his resolve weakens. Identification with and introjection of superior entities such as heroes of fiction, sports and entertainment are valuable for boosting ego worth when self-esteem is flagging. The displacement of filial feelings on to idealized parental surrogates may assist the adolescent ego to reduce decathexis tension when rejection by peers is experienced. During adolescence, the ego tends to refine the use of mechanisms already in hand rather than to create new ones.

Adolescence and Choosing a Career

The adolescent experiences great tension produced by societal expectations which impel him to choose a career. Choosing a career in life is an indispensable precursor in establishing a unique identity separate from that of being merely the child of the parent. The heterosexual child has already in significant degree modeled himself upon the same sex parent, which adds to the difficulty of establishing an identity separate from the parent. But the adolescent ego is strongly guided in choosing a career by the desire to please the parent because parental approval is essential to gaining worth and narcissistic gratification. Ego worth, as well as narcissistic gratification, emanate from parental approval and admiration for the child. Consequently, parental preference in career choice is extremely important to the child. Whatever career in life he chooses, the adolescent hopes that his parent will approve of it and admire him for it. But in choosing a career the adolescent must depart in some measure from the preference of his parent if he is to distinguish himself from his parent. The result is that career choice is a function of acceding to parental preferences while at the same time rejecting parental preferences. This paradox is accomplished by rejecting the career choice most admired by the parent, and instead choosing a career less well admired by the parent.

The son may reluctantly enter his father's business or take up his father's trade or profession but lack sufficient passion to do well at it because he experiences a loss of identity which vitiates his resolve to succeed. Or, the son takes up the father's career choice with great intensity to surpass the father, thus appeasing his father's career choice preference while distinguishing himself from his father by surpassing his father. Or the son may take up his father's career but harbor a fear of provoking paternal hostility by surpassing the father, and consequently do poorly to obviate feared paternal hostility.

The same may be done by a daughter in responding to her mother's career choice for her, and surpass her mother as home maker or society matron or in a profession to maintain her separate identity without risking maternal decathexis, or do poorly at emulating the mother to avoid maternal recrimination for exceeding the mother's success. The adolescent is compelled to search for a career which he is capable of performing the tasks associated with it, while eliciting parental approval and avoiding parental jealousy without submerging his identity to that of the parent.

It is remarkable how the son or daughter in adulthood follows in the footsteps of his or her parent at least in some important respect which the parent would be expected to admire. The son who hunted or fished with his father takes up hunting and fishing as important hobbies in his life. The daughter of a mother who was fond of social entertaining takes up social entertaining as an important activity in her life. The son whose father enjoyed repairing and driving automobiles becomes an automobile aficionado. The daughter whose mother was skilled at sewing becomes a seamstress who proudly sews her own clothes.

It is unusual for an adult to follow a career for which he believes his parent would not admire him. The shape given to career choice by the adolescent because of his desire to earn parental admiration or to avoid parental disapproval cannot be overestimated. The child tends to make this choice with little recognition that he has made the choice because of strong parental influence, but rather tends to believe that his choice was made independently. Even when the adolescent chooses to follow directly in his parent's footsteps, he tends not to be aware that he did so to experience heightened ego worth through parental approval. Yet when the adolescent chooses a career path never spoken about or little discussed by his parent, he tends to believe the parent would admire him for it.

But, in establishing his separate identity, the adolescent tends to choose a career different from one preferred most by the parent and settles upon a different career but one which he believes that his parent will nevertheless admire. For example, the son who refuses to make a career in his father's hardware store nevertheless becomes a hardware salesman. The daughter who refuses to become a homemaker like her mother nevertheless becomes a high school home economics teacher. By such a choice, the child is able to rebel against the parent without alienating the parent, while simultaneously earning parental admiration and increased ego worth.

Derivative Behavior in Adolescence

Derivative behavior initiated in primordial life continues into latency and from there into adolescence, but modified by the particular impingements of adolescent experience. Derivative behavior is produced by the derivative relatedness transference devolution process during ego ontogenesis in which the relatedness of the ego to an object including its response pattern to tension producing impingements perceived as emanating from the related-to object is adjusted and adapted for use in a later circumstance during ego ontogenesis in a procession which leads to a series of subsequent modifications of the original relatedness and response pattern so that at later stages the original relatedness and response pattern is reshaped to suit the later circumstances.

For example, the technique of crying as an instrument of power used by the newborn eventually becomes verbal complaining in the child and later still in the adult responding to parentified others becomes more creative and imaginative verbalizations which may include satire, derision and caustic wit as it is reshaped from one circumstance to the next to respond to changing tension reduction requirements. The adolescent may employ the verbal technique of playing upon the parent's vanity to get his way with his parent by telling his parent things he believes will please his parent such as reporting his achievements at school or other activities such as sports at which he believes his parent hopes he will excel.

The technique of the untimely withholding and releasing of bowel or bladder products during primordial life becomes during latency the withholding of behavior pleasing to the parent such as eating the parent-proffered food or cleaning up after himself as the parent urges to get his way and at other times pleasing the parent by eating the food proffered and cleaning up after himself to earn the parent's favor in support of the child's tension reduction aim such as obtaining permission to stay up late to watch a television program or scan the internet past bed time.

In adolescence, such parent-pleasing behavior as doing homework in a timely fashion or performing household chores affectively may be used to manipulate the parent into granting permission to date a boy of whom the parent disapproves as the adolescent struggles to reduce the ego tension produced by the need to develop social skills which will help her one day find a mate. Also, from the begging and pleading techniques resorted to during latency, the adolescent child begins to develop more sophisticated verbal stratagems such as playing one parent off against the other to achieve his tension reduction aim.

Parentification in Adolescence

The use of parentification intensifies during adolescence as the spectrum of objects of parentification expands. As the adolescent struggles to individuate and to establish a separate and unique identity he looks beyond the family and his parent for objects to which to relate. The adolescent may parentify admired or feared age peers, secondary school teachers, school administrators, officials of government, and especially figures in professional sports, popular entertainment and heroes and heroines depicted in fiction, in motion pictures and in television dramas. The adolescent becomes aware of political figures such as mayors, governors and presidents and tends to parentify them, relating to them as benevolent parental surrogates or as malevolent parental surrogates as the fortuity of tension reduction needs present themselves.

Displaced Filial Ambivalence

In the struggle to diminish the strength of his relatedness to his parents and consequent dependence upon his parents, the adolescent seeks malevolent parentified objects upon which to project his own perceived failings and upon which to displace filial hostility. At the same time, he looks also for objects upon which to displace idealized filial affection. Adolescent boys may be found idolizing the sports coach at secondary school, and the adolescent girls may be discovered idolizing one of their secondary school teachers. These idolizing behaviors enable the teenager to shift a portion of his filial relatedness from the actual parent to a surrogate parent and thereby reduce his dependence upon his actual parent as an object of introjection and identification. The adolescent can begin to model himself upon this idolized extra-familial individual and thereby diminish his dependence upon his actual parent for identity. The idolized parental surrogate may be only the first in a series of idolized parental surrogates, which stretches throughout the remaining course of life into old age.

It is the practice of the ego to relate to objects of ambivalence in bifurcated pairs in which each member of the pair is related to as one moiety of displaced filial ambivalence, either benevolent or malevolent. For example, the adolescent ego may relate to his teacher as a benevolent parental surrogate, and to the school principal as a malevolent parental surrogate, with the teacher and the principal perceived as a bifurcated parentified pair. When the adolescent ego relates to the teacher as benevolent, it automatically searches for a malevolent counterpart, and if the adolescent experiences a negative encounter with the principal, the principal may serve fortuitously as the other moiety of the bifurcated pair.

Counter manipulation Behavior in Adolescence

Counter manipulation behavior tends to be self-injurious. It emerged during primordial experience when the toddler began to resist the decathexis of toilet training by the untimely elimination of body wastes made possible by the development of sphincter control. The child learned about manipulation from the experience of being forcibly taken to the potty during the imposition of toilet training, that he could manipulate the parent so as to resist the decathexis of toilet training by the untimely elimination of his wastes, and through the derivative relatedness transference devolution process counter manipulation behavior was carried forward into latency and adolescence.

During adolescence, derivative counter manipulation behavior took the form of the alternate pleasing and displeasing of the parent and parental surrogates in ways that tended to be self-injurious. Counter manipulation behavior tends to be self-injurious. The infant who soils his clothing by releasing body wastes to resist the decathexis of toilet training, or who suffers constipation because he holds his bowels too long in an effort to defeat his parent's toilet training aim causes unpleasure for himself. Wearing soiled clothing subjects the child to unpleasant wetness and chafing, and holding the bowel too long subjects the child to painful constipation. These are self-injurious behaviors.

By means of the derivative relatedness transference devolution process, self-injurious counter manipulation behavior comes into many tension reduction uses during the course of life. The withholding of feces devolves into the withholding of help to others such as family and friends or the withholding of superior job performance to an employer. The former may bring about the loss of one's friends and the good will of one's family members, and the latter may bring about the loss of one's employment. These counter manipulation withholding techniques may produce a net tension increase in that while they reduce tension by resisting the impositions of family, friends and one's employer, they produce greater tension increase because of their negative consequences.

The Id During Adolescence

The id begins to diminish in importance during adolescence as the child begins to perceive himself as more powerful and capable of confronting the world about him. His practice of blaming the id for his own failures comes into conflict with his growing belief that he is the determiner of his own fate. He cannot logically both believe in his own empowerment at the same time that he blames the id for his failings. By the time the individual reaches full adulthood, he largely gives up the practice of blaming some uncontrolled force within him for his own bad behavior. "It made me do it" ceases to be used to reduce superego tension produced by a failure of the ego to guide behavior in conformance with reality.

The Adolescent and the Larger Society

It is during adolescent individuation that the individual sorties deeply into the world beyond the ménage. The greater power bestowed upon the adolescent because of his substantial growth in physical size, strength an intellectual capability combined with his desire to individuate and to begin his search for a career, tends to cause the adolescent to become discontented with restrictions which would limited him to the familial precincts. The search for a mate is enough to impel the adolescent to seek districts beyond the ménage.

The adolescent will affect the larger society by his successes and failures at learning to socialize in ways supportive of society while achieving the importunities imposed upon him by society of establishing a career, of acquiring the ability to make a livelihood for himself and the family he will create, of finding a mate, begetting and providing for his children and functioning as a responsible citizen.

The adolescent must successfully individuate if he is to become a self-dependent individual. This requires him to establish his identity separate from that of his parent and unique in the world. In the process of individuating, the adolescent will come into conflict with his parent and with established institutions and organizations in society. These institutions and organizations and their functionaries will be parentified and related to variously as malevolent parental surrogates and as beneficent parental surrogates, the former disruptive of the status quo and the latter supportive of the status quo.

Malevolent parental surrogates tend to become targets of the adolescent's filial rebellion and are selected fortuitously as the adolescent finds himself in need of such a target. The resurgence of the Oedipus conflict tends to bring about a reassertion of filial hostility and competitiveness' which has to affect of intensifying filial rebellion and injecting competitiveness into the dynamic of human interaction in the society of which the adolescent is a member. As a rebel, the adolescent, whose views tend to continue into young adulthood, tends to be the change agent of society in all manner of societal concerns and practices from styles of clothing, music preferences, choice of entertainment and life style to preferences in economic systems, forms of government, political parties and candidates for public office. Because the adolescent is the predecessor to the young adult, and the young adult is the offspring of adolescence, the ego's propensities established during adolescence are extended into young adulthood and shape both the young adult and the society which the young adult occupies.

4

YOUNG ADULTHOOD

Young adulthood begins when adolescence ends, which is the point in the course of life when the individual first becomes aware that he is expected to take up adult responsibilities as defined by his society. In contrast to adolescence, which begins rather abruptly at the onset of puberty, adulthood tends to come on slowly as a transition from childhood to adulthood. Adulthood comes much sooner in primitive societies than in industrial societies, the former having little tolerance for a long period of adolescence.

The severation trauma of young adulthood is brought about by the changed expectations which the parent and society have for the adolescent and the changed expectations which the adolescent has for himself. Having reached his full physical size and intellectual capacity, he demands that he be accorded the privileges of an adult at the same time that society demands that he assume the responsibilities of an adult. Thus, the young adult demands that he be permitted to have a mate and be accorded full adult status, and society demands that he be able to provide a livelihood for himself and his mate and that he marry and establish a family. Hence, the time for experimentation in social interaction and choosing a career, in acquiring basic social and economic skills and in finding a mate is over.

The freedom to roam and seek adventure are gone but not easily relinquished. Carefree days become few in number, and the taking up of adulthood burdens becomes all but inescapable. If he has not completed his training for a career, he must hurry because he is expected to provide his own livelihood and the livelihood of a mate and of his own family. If the young adult is female, she is expected to find a husband, bear and rear children. She may also be expected to enter the workforce and produce income to help support the young family. If she pursues a prestigious career, she finds herself severely burdened not only with the demands of such a career but also with all of the demands placed upon other young adult women. The young adult who has not put away his childhood playthings will find himself pressured to do so quickly. Henceforth, he or she will dream of the carefree days of adolescence, of play and adventure, and from time to time strive to recreate these conditions which he or she enjoyed in his or her former status. Advertisers, product salesmen, manufacturers of retail goods, purveyors of narcissistic services such as restaurants, resorts, entertainments and vacations will appeal to the young adult's fantasies about the carefree life in the hope of getting him or her to part with some of his or her earnings in exchange for commercially dispensed narcissistic gratifiers. The young adult will be tempted by these blandishments, but little able to afford them.

Taking up the responsibilities of providing for a family normatively is highly tension producing. Obtaining employment or starting a business or pursuing a trade or profession may be extremely difficult when economic conditions are poor and tend to be challenging even when economic conditions are favorable. Often debt is incurred to purchase a residence and an automobile if the young adult lives in suburbs or village, and if he or she resides in the inner city, finding an affordable apartment which is capable of reducing the ego tension of the deficits of narcissism and worth may subject the young adult to considerable dissatisfaction and unpleasure.

The young adult tends to look to the future with hope for greater affluence and better times as the principal means to appease his current discontent. Meanwhile, children are born, unpaid bills accumulate and there is no money to purchase the self-indulgences wanted to appease the narcissism deficit. Leisure activities needed to reduce ego tension experienced because of life's struggles have to be low in cost and tend to consist of such inexpensive pastimes as playing parlor games or listening to recorded music with young adult friends who are subject to the same conditions of life, and taking one's family on picnics in the park and visiting museums.

Narcissism in Young Adulthood

The narcissism deficit tends to be exacerbated for most young adults because of their penury. Self-indulgences requiring the expenditure of money are but rarely enjoyed, and the newly married young adult couple with their newborns must depend upon each other for narcissistic gratification or they may commiserate with peers subject to the same conditions. This is the time when the neonate needs to experience the lavishing of parental warmth and approval, and young parents need to praise each other for their procreative accomplishment. The dreaming of future luxuries will have to suffice for the present although grandparents and family friends may occasionally bestow an item of luxury upon the young parents. They will content themselves with the advantages of youth such as good health, fit physical condition, bursting energy, a long life ahead of them and dreams of a more affluent future.

Power and Young Adulthood

For the young adult, power is at low ebb. The power of adolescence which takes the form of physical strength, high energy, physical health and youthful good looks does not serve the young adult as well as it did the adolescent. The adolescent needed power to attract social acceptance from adolescent peers and to gain status in adolescent society, to attract a mate, to gain the admiration of others who valued these attractiveness assets and to acquire education or training for financial success in the economy.

But in young adulthood, these instruments of power, while helpful, are not enough to succeed in an economy which requires financial power. In a money economy, one must have money, or the capacity to obtain money, to have the power necessary to succeed in the adult society. In the absence of inherited wealth, which is the condition of the vast majority of young adults, financial power tends to be lacking because the young adult has not had enough time to establish himself in a business, a career or a trade with sufficient success to become affluent.

Even if the young adult has inherited wealth, he must find a way to occupy his time which elicits respect from his peers. The inheriting of wealth in and of itself is not enough to accomplish this aim. The young adult with inherited wealth may find himself competing in the job market with those not having inherited wealth for the occupations the latter need for their economic survival. In a society which admires work, inherited wealth will not excuse idleness in the pursuit of ego worth.

As with the narcissism deficit during young adulthood, so it is with the power deficit, the individual is left to deal with ego tension by dreaming of better times ahead, of struggling to make progress toward those better times, of fantasizing about the future, of cultivating patience and industry towards the day when he will have financial power and be able to enter the marketplace and purchase the ego worth assets he craves to obtain status and narcissistic gratification. Those who are not able to summon the patience and the industry to traverse this period of their lives but instead squander the time or resort to criminal activity to obtain money to gratify their deficits of narcissism, power and worth put themselves at risk of failure to achieve these benefits when they reach middle adulthood.

Ego Worth and the Young Adult

In the pursuit of ego worth, the young adult is frustrated by not being able to enter the marketplace with financial power in order to purchase what middle age adults are normatively able to acquire in the way of ego worth assets. He tends to fall back upon what supported him during adolescence and to cultivate an image which reflects his expected future success. Thus, he talks about his promotion opportunities at his place of employment, or his future successes in his profession or trade or the future success which he expects to achieve in his business.

To show that he is making social progress, he may seek the company of successful middle age adults by socializing where they socialize, by seeking to be sponsored for membership in a social club at a junior level, or to seek a middle age patron through sycophancy. He employs the attractiveness assets he used in adolescence which continue in young adulthood such as youthful comeliness, vigor and strength to curry favor with those who can help him. To the extent he perceives himself as succeeding in these pursuits, he will enjoy a reduction in ego worth deficit tension. If he is not making social progress, but is drifting without purpose other than indulging in leisure pursuits, he will likely sense that something is wrong about what he is doing which will undermine the experience of pleasure which he is seeking. In those cases in which the young adult is without ambition and has no propensity for sacrificing current pleasures to future gains in power, worth and status and is content to follow this path throughout the remaining course of life, the sacrifice of current pleasures would not be a sacrifice worth making.

Surety and Young Adulthood

The surety issues which occupied so important a place in the preoccupations of the adolescent tend to be displaced by more urgent concerns. While the young adult continues to care about the many rebellious values he took up during adolescence in clothing styles, choice of leisure pursuits, arcane adolescent argot, peculiar music, idealized social values, political party identification, religious views and numerous others, his dedication to them tends to be supplanted by the more urgent needs of making progress in his career, succeeding economically, paying bills, looking after his children and providing for their welfare. While the former are not relinquished, the priority which they hold for the young adult is forced downward on his list of concerns.

During adolescence he needed to rebel against parental values to establish a separate and unique identity in order to individuate and create his ego ideal. In young adulthood, his identity and ego ideal become immersed in creating and providing for his family more than it does in rebellious posturing. Therefore, while the adolescent rebellion remains, it tends to be overshadowed by the young adult's obligations to his newly created family, the pursuit of his career and the need to generate financial power as the basis of his identity and ego ideal. Thus, while the young adult remains fixed upon his new path of being a family man or woman, provider for and care-giver to young children, he or she nevertheless tends to remain interested in the radical issues of adolescence, but cannot relinquish adult responsibilities to indulge in them again.

However, if his rebelliousness is compatible with his career, he may be able to indulge it while fulfilling his new role. For example, if he rebelled against parental political values, he may enter the risky career of politician which may enable him to attend to both concerns. Or if his rebelliousness was aimed at old fashioned business practices, he may launch a business career as an innovator. If he enters the clergy or the profession of educator, he may rebel against "outmoded" religious or teaching practices. He will attempt to combine his radicalism with his family responsibilities in fashioning his identity and ego ideal. He may continue to wear rebellious adolescent clothing styles and listen to rebellious adolescent music, but when difficult choices are confronted, he is likely to place career and family above continued adolescent rebelliousness.

The young adult, who thought he knew more than his parent when he was an adolescent, now begins to respect his parent's knowledge once more. He wonders how his parent got through the difficulties of starting and providing for a family, of launching a career and becoming financially successful. He looks upon his parent with new respect for having accomplished what he the young adult is only now setting out to accomplish.

Rectitude and Young Adulthood

The superior rectitudinous propensities established in adolescence continue into young adulthood but in diminished form. In adolescence, the young person had criticized his parent's generation for perceived failures to do their moral duty in paying the costs of better schools, public conveniences, paved streets, parks, exemplary fire and police protection and other public amenities and necessities. He perceived his parents' generation as lacking rectitude. They seemed to him as not always honest in their dealings, not always charitable towards others or dutiful in their citizenship obligations, and he might scold his parents for their failings of rectitude. But in young adulthood after taking up the burdens of adult responsibilities like those born by his parents, his carping tends to soften. While not relinquishing his rectitudinous ideals, he comes to allow room for a degree of failure in himself and in his parents. Rectitude becomes an ideal pursued more than achieved, and he begins to look upon the fault-finding adolescent generation following upon his own generation as immature and overweening.

Curiosity in Young Adulthood

Having become informed about his world through formal education, through the public communications media, and through association with adult mentors, the intensity of the young adult's curiosity lessens. Partly satisfied, his curiosity nevertheless continues, and he seeks answers to the many questions he encounters in young adult life, as well as questions regarding the nature of the society, the world and the universe. He is aware that much is known about which he has not informed himself. He is left to decide whether to pursue more knowledge through formal education, the reading of books or the public communications media, or to concentrate his concerns on how to make a livelihood, how to get ahead and how to deal with his family and circle of friends and acquaintances.

He may take up a hobby about which curiosity piques his interest. From the arcane of fishing and hunting, automobile racing or vehicle maintenance, from photography or bird watching, from computers and electronics—depending upon which hobby he takes up—his curiosity will tend to be focused upon it more than elsewhere. The great questions of human existence, of the meaning of life, of the limits of the universe, the origin of the big bang and the ultimate destiny of the human race will continue their presence among his concerns but take a back seat to the quotidian problems of how to pay his bills, advance his career, deal with the perversity of his spouse and cope with child-rearing difficulties.

Mastery in Young Adulthood

The physical and intellectual capabilities of the individual arrive at their mature state during young adulthood. The individual will continue to expand the reach of his intellectual and physical capabilities through practice, acquisition of knowledge and the attainment of skills, but by young adulthood his biological equipment has achieved its epigenetic completion. The young adult is normatively better equipped than at any earlier time to exploit the possibilities of his capacities. Capacities for acrobatics, locomotion, manual manipulation and manipulation of others tend to be at their peak.

The young adult tends to achieve mastery in those areas of need which importune him most. These tend to be the needs imposed upon the young adult by his biology and by the society of which he is a part. Controlling the external world through control of the parent becomes control of the external' world through control of parentified others such as spouse and offspring, or institutions such as employer, or functionary such as supervisor. He gains mastery of the tasks contained in his employment, and in dealing with threat from whatever source. Success in the economy, finding a place in society, gaining status, worth and power, satisfying narcissism, succeeding at a profession or trade—these are areas in which the young adult pursues mastery.

Individuation in Young Adulthood

While the importance of individuation as a source of tension producing stimuli is never greater than during adolescence, the magnitude of its importance begins to diminish during young adulthood. The young adult burdened with a spouse and family to provide for and a career to pursue has a better concept of who he is than when he was an adolescent. However, to the extent that he failed to solidify his identity during adolescence, he will continue to grapple with it during young adulthood. The burdens of career and family responsibilities will continually remind him of who he is, but if he suffers from doubt about these identity determiners which have taken over his life, then he may suffer the consequences of having an identity in the perception of others which he does not want for himself.

Careers are chosen to win favor and worth by eliciting parental approval and by eliciting the approval of parentified others. But if the career of husband or wife, father or mother or bread winner is not perceived as enough to elicit the parental approval, or if the young adult drifted into such a career after being diverted from an earlier chosen career whose purpose was to gain the admiration and approval of parents and parentified others, the young adult may experience a loss of ego worth and unremitting ego worth deficit tension. He always has before him the contrast between the identity he sought and the identity he drifted into.

The young adult who had longed for a career high in status and difficult to achieve such as famous entertainer, sports hero, celebrated author, cinema star, high government official, prize winning scientist, astronaut and the like—and many more choose such vaunted roles than achieve them—then he is subjected to a double source of tension producing stimuli emanating from the disparity of the identity he never achieved and the identity he settled for. However, the human ego normatively is sufficiently resilient that the great majority of individuals are compelled to settle for an identity other than the one they had longed for nevertheless come to terms with the identity which settled upon them and enjoy at least a modicum of ego worth.

Most adults became something other than what in adolescence they had dreamed of becoming. Even those who found their way into a high status career may earlier have dreamed of a different high status career and now find themselves dissatisfied. The deficits of narcissism and worth are permanent and can never be fully satisfied for more than brief periods. The traumata of primordial cathexis severation create permanent deficits of cathexis severation. As a consequence, even the most successful achiever is left at the apex of his accomplishment with an experience of emptiness—with a sense of, "Is this all there is?"

Counter Manipulation in Young Adulthood

The counter manipulation propensities of primordial life continue through derivative relatedness transference devolution to adapt and modify in response to new circumstances imposed by succeeding stages of ego onto-genesis into forms which correspond to young adult experience. Indi-viduation ego tension, being less importunate than during adolescence, will in young adulthood tend to be manifested in ways harmful to relationships within the young adult's newly created family, with persons and organiza-tions associated with his career and with his social life.

With his spouse, counter manipulation behaviors transferred from ado-lescence may be imposed upon the spouse with the result that the spouse withholds the affection desired by the counter manipulating young adult, or worse still, may even manifest hostility in the marital relationship. For ex-ample, the biting of the nipple during weaning may have devolved into withholding the products of elimination during toilet training, and mani-fested itself in the new forms of fussy eater and constipation during latency.

During adolescence it may have devolved into withholding compliance to parental self-dependence demands in the form of failure by the adolescent to tidy his room and to perform effectively household chores assigned by the parent and to do well in school. This stubbornness may have devolved in young adulthood into the withholding of testaments of spousal affection and support in the willing performance of familial responsibilities, eliciting re-sentment in the perturbed spouse. At his place of employment or business, his counter manipulation behavior may irritate the employer or the custom-ers of his business and may cause the loss of employment or loss of busi-ness. Counter manipulation behavior may lead to the loss of social friends by irritating them. In all of these examples, the counter manipulator has in one way or another injured himself by his counter manipulating behavior.

Filial Ambivalence in Young Adulthood

The bifurcated filial ambivalence behavior patterns established during adolescence continue into young adulthood, but partly in modified form. As the individual's preoccupation with objects important to his ego ideal such as the school, the church, the government and the nation are supplanted by objects important to his career, the family he has formed, his children and spouse, the objects of filial ambivalence change accordingly. He may relate to his employing organization as a benevolent parental surrogate with which he identifies, and from that identification he buttresses his ego ideal, while he relates to his supervisor as a malevolent parental surrogate whose disre-spect injures his ego ideal. His demanding supervisor may elicit a re-experiencing of the filial rivalry and fear which had reemerged with the on-set of adolescence and continued into young adulthood.

An object tends to elicit filial ambivalence whenever the ego is filified by an object of relatedness. A spouse who makes demands which reminds the young adult ego of similar importunities placed upon him by the same sex parent of childhood may find himself or herself responding as if to a ma-levolent parental surrogate, evoking a hostile response like that with which he or she responded to the same sex parent in childhood. Such responses could strain the marital relationship. Contrariwise, the spouse may upon another occasion act favorably in a way which reminds the young adult ego of occasions when the same sex parent bestowed a measure of affection, thus eliciting a relatedness to the spouse as to a benevolent parental surrogate, strengthening the marital relationship. Later, when the young adult reaches middle age, filial ambivalent relatednesses to societal institutions and their functionaries will again become particularly salient because of the renewed interest the ego takes during middle age in societal concerns after the individual has successfully traversed young adulthood and established himself in terms of power, wealth, social place and social status.

Ego Mechanisms and Young Adulthood

By young adulthood the ego has acquired a sizable panoply of tension reducing mechanisms to defend against the many sources of tension producing stimuli which impinge upon the ego. *Identification*, which was established by the primordial ego in reaction to the severation of weaning, was aimed at defeating the severation of weaning by unifying the infant ego with the external object of parent upon whom the infant was nearly totally dependent for the reduction of tension producing stimuli and for access to tension reducing stimuli. By the time of young adulthood, the mechanism of identification is heavily relied upon to solidify the cathexis to parentified others such as spouse, offspring and employing organization. The young adult perceives the external world through the eyes of his or her spouse as if each of the marital pair is one and the same individual. Married couples tend to grow to look alike in appearance in degree and style of personal grooming, choice of leisure activities, food preferences and the like. While there continues to be differences between them, the similarities they grow into can be striking.

Introjection, which was also established to defeat the decathexis tension produced by weaning, involves the figurative "taking in" of the parent by the ego, much as the infant took in the mother's milk while suckling at the breast or bottle. Introjection aimed at defeating the severation of weaning by continuing, if only figuratively, to take in the mother's milk, is intended to preserve the infant-mother cathexis. In young adulthood, each spouse introjects the other while each identifies with the other. In their embraces, the marital pair strive to engulf each other as if to become one. During their marital years, they acquire much together from the marketplace in the form of tension reducing assets such as their residence, furnishings, automobile and leisure paraphernalia. If they come to a parting because of separation or divorce, they may experience great difficulty dividing between them the acquisitions of their marital years because their acquisitions are introjected by each of the marital pair, and decathecting from each item revives the tension producing unpleasure of the original primordial infant-parent severation traumata caused by weaning, toilet training and the Oedipus conflict.

The ego mechanism of *projection* tends to arise from the experience of the spitting out of unwanted food or drink introduced into the infant's mouth during the weaning process. The infant ego learns that it can force back out the food or drink inserted by the parent to try to defeat weaning which is highly tension producing because it severs the filial-parental cathexis mode of suckling at the breast or bottle. When the ego begins to experience the dangerous filial hostility and competitiveness toward the same sex parent during the Oedipus conflict, it seeks to reduce the tension producing fear by projecting its hostility and competitiveness upon the id, which the ego creates for that purpose. By blaming the id, the ego absolves itself of culpability and the threat of parental retribution.

The mechanism of projection continues to be employed in the shifting of blame for the ego's own failings and dangerous hostilities on to external targets such as persons, groups, organizations and institutions in the ego's environment. In particular, projection becomes an often resorted to mechanism to deflect the ego tension produced by superego failings. By the time of adulthood, projection is often used to deal with the ego tension of guilt experienced because of failure to adhere to the imperatives of the superego. The commonplace behaviors of jealousy, hostility, sexual lust, peculations and peccadilloes forbidden by the superego which impinge upon the ego because of superego chastisement are commonly reduced by projecting the blame upon suitable external objects fortuitously selected for this purpose. In adulthood, such objects tend to include disliked neighbors, objectionable fellow workers, obnoxious members of one's social group, detested other groups, organizations and institutions such as rival sports teams, other religions and other nations. Detested members of society often serve as objects of projection such as criminals, welfare cheats, homeless persons and anyone seen as not contributing his fair share to the commonweal.

The mechanism of *transference* is created by the ego to assist in the suppression of the Oedipus conflict. By transferring dangerous or forbidden relatednesses toward the parents such as hostility toward and competitiveness with the same sex parent for preferment with the opposite sex parent, the ego temporarily rids itself of the ego tension produced by these dangerous filial relatednesses. By transferring these forms of relatedness to objects other than the actual parents, the latency ego can continue to enjoy the tension reducing pleasure of luxuriating in the experience of hostility toward the same sex parent and lust toward the opposite sex parent without experiencing the ego tension of fear. Surrogates for the same sex parent serve as objects of projected hostility, and surrogates for the opposite sex parent serve as objects of displaced lust. The psychoanalytic therapist becomes an object of transference for his patient and uses the knowledge gained by analyzing the transference to help his patient.

Surrogates for the latency child might include kindly nursery or kindergarten opposite sex teachers as beneficent parentified entities, and forbidding teachers as maleficent parentified entities. The latency ego will tend to project filial hostility upon the latter and displace affection upon the former. The mechanism of *displacement*, a complement to the mechanism of projection, is initially created to reduce the ego tension produced by the Oedipus conflict. By attributing, or displacing, to a sibling, extended family member or teacher perceived as benevolent, the latency child can continue to experience filial lust aimed at a safe target rather than upon the opposite sex parent directly which would bring him into dangerous conflict with the same sex parent. Filial displacement of dangerous eroticism toward the opposite sex parent facilitates the ego's effort to suppress the Oedipus conflict upon which the latency period follows. The ego is unaware of its displacement behavior and if it became aware of it, the displacement would fail because it would compel the return of realty.

Suppression is a key mechanism to resolving the Oedipus conflict. To reduce the intolerable tension produced by Oedipal rivalry and fear of provoking parental hostility, decathexis and worse, the Oedipal relatedness to the parents is suppressed, meaning that it is forced out of awareness. The act of suppression must be repeated each time thoughts and reminders of Oedipal fear and rivalry impinge. The result is the repeated forcing out of awareness the thoughts and reminders of the Oedipal conflict as on-going practice. The reader can gain a grasp of this process simply by taking a moment to try to imagine having sexual intercourse with his opposite sex parent. With lightening speed, most readers will suppress this image because of their deep revulsion for it. This is how suppression works to keep Oedipal wishes and fears at bay. As for the fear of harm at the hands of the same sex parent, it tends to be relieved partly by the eventual maturity of the adult mind whose judgment tells it that the parent does not wish to harm him and by the projection of the Oedipal fear on to surrogate maleficent parentified entities.

But suppression of filial hostility toward the same sex parent can be grasped by taking a moment to imagine inflicting great harm upon the same sex parent such as striking him or her with a lethal instrument. Such an image is intolerable, and it will tend to be immediately suppressed. However, the reader may know of someone in his life such as a detested supervisor, an enemy of the nation such as a Hitler or a Mussolini, a scheming rival at one's place of employment or the owner of an unfairly competing business, in relation to whom the reader can summon at least a fleeting image of inflicting a great blow upon this person that one cannot imagine inflicting upon one's same sex parent even at a moment of great anger toward the parent. Superego chastisement may be evoked by thoughts of inflicting physical harm upon almost anyone, but the thought of inflicting physical harm upon one's parent can hardly be entertained even for a moment and is immediately forced out of awareness, meaning that it is suppressed. Patricide and matricide occur only occasionally, being relatively rare notwithstanding the feelings of filial hatred which from time to time rise up in the thoughts of a son or daughter.

In adulthood, suppression becomes an often-employed mechanism to banish tension producing thoughts which importune the ego. Superego failures, disappointments, depressive thoughts and the like arising from the frustrations produced by impediments to achieving the aims of young adulthood often evoke the mechanism of suppression to remove sources of tension producing realities from awareness. Because reality tends to return, the employment of suppression must be used repeatedly against a continuing source of ego tension.

The mechanism of *reaction formation* is evoked by the ego's attempt to reduce the tension produced by the Oedipus conflict. Fear of parental retribution tends to elicit the reaction formation of filial hostility in response to the terror which fear of parental retribution gives rise. Reaction formation functions to defeat impinging stimuli by confronting the source of those stimuli with greater apposing stimuli. Thus, hostility is a reaction formation to fear when it aims to crush the provoker of fear. Revulsion is a reaction formation to an object of forbidden lust which defends against the dangers of filial eroticism. Reaction formation is initially created to protect the infant from its desire to play with and eat its fecal products. When the feces are perceived as repugnant, the infant will eschew them. In young adulthood, reaction formation often occurs in the form of hostility toward the threat of competition by a rival or a threat of retribution by, say, a parentified supervisor, teacher or law enforcement official who is perceived as malevolent.

The ego mechanism of *overcompensation* arises from the ego's strategy of protecting itself from a source of impinging stimuli by creating a bulwark of defense so formidable that the impinging stimuli are perceived as having no chance to inflict harm. Overcompensation may have been created to defeat the weaning process by the infant's refusal to give up the nursing bottle or breast even after it had become satiated. By guiding behavior to continue to suckle beyond satiety, the ego creates a parental expectation that nursing must continue and not be cut off, with the result that completion of the weaning process and the decathexis it occasions is delayed

Later after the weaning ego has guided behavior to accept the cup and the spoon, it may continue to guide behavior to overeat as a means to retain the new filial-parental cathexis so as to reduce the tension produced by the fear of another severance experience. The infant grows fat from the excessive ingestion of nourishment, and may cry uncontrollably if the nourishment is taken away. During toilet training, the infant ego guides behavior to withhold bowel evacuation and bladder voiding to stave off the terror of cathexis severance. Constipation and bladder infection may result from this form of overcompensation.

As a consequence of filial guilt arising from the Oedipus conflict, the infant ego may guide behavior to manifest great filial hostility to overcompensate as protection from the terror of feared parental retribution. Thus, the infant may become hostile toward the same sex parent, and in its toddler years hit at the parent, throw tantrums and physically resist parental control. During the latency years, the child ego may guide behavior so that the child overcompensates by being overly compliant to parental supervision, and displays little initiative and self-reliance. During adolescent individuation the overcompensating child may fail to individuate successfully for lack of initiative and self-reliance. Over-compliance and submissiveness may follow such an individual throughout adulthood and deprive him of the fullness of life.

Fantasy is a mechanism heavily relied upon during latency to enable the ego to reduce the tension produced by the reality of the individual's many limitations of size, power, strength, worth, mastery, narcissistic gratification and by the individual's general inadequacy. The latency child fantasizes about all of these concerns, and enjoys fiction which supports its fantasy. Thus, the latency child may identify with images in fantasy and fiction such as heroes and heroines which enable him to overcome the ego tension produced by his many perceived deficiencies. Fantasy tends to be resorted to throughout the life of nearly every individual in order to surmount in reverie the deficiencies he perceives in himself, in his unfulfilled wants and accomplishments and in his failed aims.

Denial is a mechanism which is as often relied upon as suppression. Everyone tends to be able to recognize denial when it is used by someone else, but is seldom able to recognize it when one uses it himself. Denial is a refusal to recognize some aspect of reality because of the tension producing stimuli which emanate from that reality. Denial is employed to defeat the tension of superego guilt. It is employed to deflect misperceptions of reality which subvert one's concept of surety. Denial is used to remove the tension increase caused by various instances of personal failure. The latency child denies his lust for the opposite sex parent, and the individuating adolescent denies that he hates his same sex parent. The young adult denies that he mistreats his spouse or offspring or that he does not give his employer full due.

Sublimation is a mechanism which permits the ego to guide behavior in ways which enables the individual to indulge in otherwise forbidden activities. For example, the cook who prepares gravies, sauces, pureed vegetables and sausage links may be indulging in a sublimated way his infantile wishes to handle his feces. The feces the infant was forbidden to handle during toilet training, the adult can now handle in actualized form by sublimating them as foodstuffs. Repugnance for gravies, sauces, pureed vegetables and sausage links may be a reaction formation to an infantile desire for them. The adult may sublimate his infatuation for a member of the opposite sex by worshiping him or her from afar having sublimated him or her as too lofty to be approachable and misses his or her opportunity for a desired liaison.

Rationalizing is one of the most common mechanisms employed by the human ego and like denial, while it is not easy to recognize it in one's own behavior, it tends to be easily recognized in the behavior of others. One may rationalize superego guilt by projecting it on to others. One may rationalize failures in one's performance by alluding to external interference. One may rationalize an inadequacy of personal power by misattributing it to sickness. One may rationalize loss of worth by alleging fortuitous impediments. And one may rationalize failures of mastery by citing unwarranted intrusions.

The ego is a fecund engenderer of tension reducing mechanisms of which the foregoing are but a few common ones. Mechanisms are by nature self-deceiving because they defy logic and have the power to deflect the tension produced by the impingement of reality for only a limited period because reality always returns to defeat the mechanism or to compel a reapplication of the mechanism or the application of a different mechanism or an acceptance of reality. When mechanisms fail altogether and the sources of tension producing impinging stimuli are unrelenting, the individual may suffer great and persistent ego tension and neurosis.

Ego Ideal, Persona and Self Image in Young adulthood

The ego ideal shaped during adolescence tends to become less anxiety-producing in young adulthood, although the young adult is not free of ego ideal anxiety. The ego ideal is composed of attributes perceived as needed to defeat all tension producing stimuli which the ego imagines itself exposed to in the present and in the future. Normatively, the young adult tends to be less insecure than the adolescent and therefore less dependent upon the ego ideal to cope with tension producing stimuli.

However, the ego ideal is a permanent fixture of the ego, and its importance varies with changes in the ego's perceived vulnerability. During adolescence, ego vulnerability tends to be perceived as high, while during young adulthood, ego vulnerability tends to be perceived as less formidable although as continuing to exist nevertheless. The individual who failed during adolescence to establish an adequate ego ideal will bring this impediment with him in his transition to young adulthood where it will continue to burden him.

For the young adult, the ego ideal will contain capacities for successfully pursuing his chosen career, for establishing and providing for his family, for acquiring status and for making a place for himself in society. And it will contain the imperatives of the superego. These are attributes of his self-image, and his persona is the self-image he presents to society.

Young Adulthood and Derivative
Relatedness Transference Devolution

An examination of the derivative relatedness transference devolution of oral, anal and Oedipal severation conflict from weaning to young adulthood will illuminate the nature of the process. The oral severation episode has a suckling phase and a biting phase, the latter emerging after the infant has acquired teeth and can bite the nipple in an effort to reduce ego tension by defeating the severation of weaning. Both suckling and biting may serve as tension reducing continuations which persist throughout the course of life. The tension reduction behavior of suckling at the breast may continue after weaning in such infantile behaviors as sucking fingers or a pacifier. The continuation of biting might operate in the form of chewing objects which the infant puts into its mouth such as toys or buttons. In toddlerhood, oral behavior may be manifested variously in sucking on candy or on eating utensils. The oral biting continuation may occur in such behaviors as masticating chewing gum, and hard candy or in adulthood, chewing tobacco.

During latency, the various forms in which oral stage tension reduction continuations are manifested expand greatly and include such behaviors as kissing and sucking at drinking straws. The oral biting continuation may devolve into verbal behaviors such as uttering foul language learned from schoolmates. In adolescence, oral sucking may devolve further into verbalizations such a sweet-talking or singing to an object of affection such as one's pet or a girlfriend or a boyfriend, while oral biting may devolve into criticism and deprecation aimed at disliked objects.

By young adulthood, oral behavior will have devolved into a greater' variety of more adroit continuations. Oral sucking continuations may devolve into such mouthings as poetry intended to beguile a lover, and oral biting may devolve into negative utterances such as sarcasm and epithets aimed at disliked persons. In various tension reduction behaviors of the young adult in family relationships, at his business or employment, in leisure activities and in social interaction, oral continuations may operate to his advantage or disadvantage. He can respond to the actions of family members with pleasant utterances or with caustic derision. He may respond to customers or colleagues with good humor or foul temper and to social friends with pleasant camaraderie or with peevishness. Each of these oral sucking or oral biting continuations will tend to affect the success or failure of his aims.

An examination of the ego's response to the derivative relatedness transference devolution of anal stage severation traumata also may illuminate the process. The severation of toilet training confronts the infant ego with a tension increase experience not wholly dissimilar to what it has already experienced in weaning, and the ego casts about for a means to reduce the tension increase of toilet training. The tension reduction techniques employed in the effort to defeat weaning are still being employed in the struggle against weaning—specifically crying, physically struggling against the coercive manipulations of the parent, biting the nipple, spitting out the food and drink forcefully introduced into the mouth. These techniques, being fortuitously available, are called upon again by the infant ego who cries, struggles against being forcibly taken to the toilet, but biting the nipple serves to suggest the technique of biting down upon the column of feces and the stream of urine with the sphincter to hold it back, a capacity provided by the advent of sphincter control, and spitting out the food and drink forcefully introduced into the mouth morphs into the projecting of the feces and urine from the body into one's clothing at times inconvenient for the parent.

The toilet training process contains both an expulsive phase and a retentive phase depending upon the development of sphincter control. Prior to the development of sphincter control, feces and urine are excreted willy nilly as untrammeled biological processes. The diaper is filled with excretory matter that is removed by diaper changing which tends to be experienced by the infant ego as highly pleasurable. Continuations will reflect tension reducing pleasant experiences arising from the sensations of the diaper change with memories of the odor of feces and urine, the erotic sensations on the buttocks and genitalia as they are wiped clean by the wash cloth, the smiling face of the parent hovering overhead as he or she changes the diaper. Expelling feces and urine are pleasing experiences not dissimilar to spitting out unwanted food and drink during weaning. The toddler enjoys throwing objects such as food and toys and eating utensils.

At all ages, the release of feces and urine tends to be a tension reducing pleasant experience which may be eagerly sought when bowel or bladder pressure importunes. However, the infant will also remember the unpleasure of diapers filled with waste which may subject him to unpleasant wetness and chafing. And the ego's repugnance for excretory wastes, a reaction formation to reduce the tension of feared parental decathexis because of the child's coprophiliac propensities, will continue in the form of aversion for fecal and urinary odors and places where bowel evacuation and bladder voiding are carried on. Normatively, human beings have an aversion to abiding in toilets or cleaning or repairing them. Such an aversion is a common continuation of the ego's reaction formation to the infantile pleasure in his bodily wastes.

Continuations from the Oedipus conflict experience are many and tend to involve interpersonal relations and relatednesses to societal entities. The infant ego tends to confront the Oedipus conflict severation with the techniques fortuitously available from the weaning and toilet training. Crying, struggling physically against parental manipulation which excludes the child from the private parental relationship, crying becomes whining petulance, the biting the nipple of the behavior employed to resist weaning the biting or clenching of the sphincter employed to resist toilet training becomes verbalized as angry complaining in struggling against Oedipus conflict rejection by the marital pair seeking privacy. Spitting out food and drink in the struggle against weaning and projecting out the urine and feces at inconvenient times for the parent during the infant ego's resistance to toilet training becomes the hurling of objects such as toys during the resistance to the parental pair's privacy from which the child is excluded and from the child's attempts to expropriate the preferment of the opposite sex parent from the same sex parent.

The Conscious Mind and the Unconscious Mind

One of the most difficult ideas to accept from the Freudian thesis is the concept of an unconscious mind fully structured and operating independently of and parallel to the conscious mind, of which the conscious mind is totally unaware, with the unconscious mind shaping and determining the content in part of the conscious mind, and determining the ego's guidance of the individual's tension reduction behavior.

The concept of the unconscious mind is unnecessary to a theory of psychology based upon the ego's unawareness of all of the factors which determines the tension reduction guidance it gives to the individual. The individual cannot possibly be aware of every thought or stimulus which affects it because it can be aware of only one thing at a time, even if for a fraction of a second. If the ego were to remember everything which it ever experienced it would have to devote a similar amount of time to remembering what happened in the past that was expended when it originally lived the experience. This would be impossible.

However, the conscious mind can take the time necessary to analyze patterns of its behavior to discover which ideas from the past it is acting upon. But only a small proportion of all behaviors can be analyzed at a given time because the time required to effect the analysis of all behavior is prohibitive. However, analyzes of patterns of behavior—but not the remembering of all past behavior—can be accomplished so that the conscious ego will be able to identify these patterns and attempt to avoid them when they may be tension producing or seek them when they are tension reducing. For example, the average individual knows better than to rob a bank because he might be caught and incarcerated. He does not have to take the time to think about it because not robbing banks is an established pattern for him. Also, the average individual knows to seek shelter when dark clouds accompanied by thunder and lightning are approaching. The ego's ability to recognize patterns of its behavior is highly efficient in allowing the ego to guide behavior to avoid tension-producing patterns of behavior and to utilize tension reducing patterns of behavior.

But the conscious mind may be unaware of the filial hostility it displaces upon a parentified malevolent object of relatedness because it has not analyzed the factors which would disclose this reality. The Oedipus conflict from which filial fear and hostility arose occurred during primordial life before the ego began to experience autobiographical memory. In post primordial life, the ego can know what happen during its primordial life only by means of deduction from the evidence of post primordial experience which requires an analysis which few are likely to make. Consequently, the practice of relating with filial hostility toward the feared parent is displaced from the same sex parent of primordial experience upon parentified objects whose awesome and authoritative presence elicits parentification which is composed of equivalent tension producing stimuli and the ego's response to that stimuli in a pattern experienced by the ego vis-à-vis the parent during primordial life.

Parentification is elicited in post-primordial life because of the ego's subordination to and dependence upon the parentified object to which filial-parental relatedness occurs. Behavior which some theorists believe is guided by instructions from an unconscious mind rather is likely to be behavior which is guided by set patterns previously established in the ego but not understood in the present because they have not been analyzed to show how they were established. That which is called unconscious guidance is either guidance by unanalyzed patterns of behavior not recognized because they have not been analyzed and understood by the ego, or it is guided by biologically precipitated stimuli such as sexual lust (testosterone) and hunger (lowered blood sugar).

For example, if an individual repeatedly antagonizes his teacher or supervisor, analysis which retraces the concatenation of transferences of ego ontogenesis may disclose that he relates to the teacher or supervisor as he did to his same sex parent early in the latency period, an experience which he has suppressed but which can be remembered. The original experience of filial hostility during the Oedipus conflict occurred during primordial life and cannot be re-experienced. But the filial fear and hostility experienced during latency points to the same mental state from which it originated in primordial life. By allowing himself to think about his filial hostility if only for a moment before suppressing it anew, he may be able to recognized the filial fear and hostility which he routinely suppresses and transfers to the teacher or supervisor where it finds expression and reduces the ego tension initiated during primordial life by the Oedipus conflict and carried forward in life by the relatedness transference devolution process.

A step-by-step explanation of the process by which primordial conflict experience and the ego's response to the experience is transmitted to post-primordial experience and shapes the ego's response to post-primordial experience which elicits a response similar to the primordial response can be illustrated by the following example of a response to the Oedipus conflict.

The first step in the process involves the primordial ego experiencing a reaction formation of filial hostility in response to a fear that it has enraged the same sex parent by guiding behavior to compete with him or her for preferment with the opposite sex parent. In the second step in the process, the primordial ego suppresses its perception of this experience to rid itself of the tension it produces. The third step in the process is the establishment of the superego to eradicate and prevent future filial competition and hostility from occurring, allowing the ego to enter the latency period of relative filial-parental peace.

Thereafter during latency, filial competition, hostility and fear resurface from time to time from their suppressed state caused by the inevitable return of reality in response to which the latency ego invariably suppresses it anew. But when the latency ego is confronted by a threat which it perceives as sufficiently similar to the primordial parental threat, the ego tends to perceive the post-primordial threat as if it were the same as the parental threat experienced during primordial life.

It is a propensity of the human ego to experience a new threat as if it were the same as a similarly configured threat experienced in primordial life. An object which presents such a threat in post-primordial life will tend to have a configuration which conforms closely in the ego's perception. An individual or other entity such as a group or organization which is perceived as powerful, authoritative and demanding and upon which the ego perceives itself significantly dependent that it may resemble the primordial parent sufficiently so as to present a threat will tend to elicit primordial relatedness from the post-primordial ego. The response pattern established by the ego during primordial life is called upon anew to deal with a similar tension producing situation by applying techniques already in its armory of responses to such situations.

In adulthood, the individual may relate to his teacher or supervisor with filial hostility because the teacher or supervisor interacts with him in such a way that memories of the tension producing filial fear and hostility of latency resurfaces which is immediately suppressed anew to reduce the ego tension it produces. To sustain the suppression, the filial fear and hostility is displaced upon the teacher or supervisor to which the adult ego relates as to the same sex parent of the primordial Oedipus conflict.

The Young Adult and His Family

Normatively, it is during young adulthood that the individual mates and forms his family. The young adult male has to find and woo a female, and the young adult female has to find and attract a male suitor. They marry, form a family, beget and rear children. This experience is different for the male than it is for the female.

The Young Adult Male

From the time he reaches puberty, the young adult male experiences an incessant sexual lust precipitated by hormone changes which occurred during adolescence and impels him to search for females with whom he can engage in acts of sexual intercourse or to search for suitable males if he is homosexual. The testosterone level for the young adult female normatively is lower than for the male, causing a disparity in the intensity of sexual lust experienced by males and females. It is an ironic truism that the young adult male seeks sexual intercourse without marriage, and the young adult female seeks marriage without sexual intercourse. But the normative outcome of the sexual aspect of their lives is that men by and large must marry to have an opportunity for the regular reduction of sexual tension, and women who marry are obliged by the constraints of marriage to engage in sexual intercourse with their marital partners even at times when they prefer not to.

The laws and mores of his society place limitations upon the young adult male's behavior aimed at repeatedly satisfying the sexual lust which he continually experiences. Masturbation is a major source of sexual tension reduction, but masturbation tends to be a palliative more than a true satisfier of sexual tension and does not obviate the young adult's male's craving for a female sex partner. In societies with strict rules for the satisfaction of sexual lust, intercourse with his marital partner will tend to be the young adult male's only hope of providing for the reduction of sexual tension on a regular basis.

While adultery is an option widely engaged in, adultery is risky and often leads to legal separation or divorce which produces a net tension increase and concomitant unpleasure. In less strict societies, the young adult male may have options short of marriage for appeasing his sexual lust such as fornication with prostitutes or willing female sexual partners outside of marriage, or living with a female who is willing to engage in sexual intercourse without marriage or commit adultery. For most, even in a relaxed society, the young adult male's main reliance for the continuous reduction of sexual tension will be intercourse with his marital partner.

Courting and Sex

Men tend to prefer to have sex with many partners, while women tend to prefer to limit their sexual partner to one male to whom they are married. Although this paradigm tends to be uppermost in women's minds, female promiscuity is too commonplace to permit the paradigm to be a universal reality. Young adult males succeed often enough at fornication to sustain their hope of reducing sexual tension without marriage and the availability of willing women is great enough to reward the young adult males' efforts at promiscuous intercourse. Ultimately, however, the young adult male is driven into marriage to reduce the frustration of insufficient sexual reward for his effort.

The frequency of the young adult male's sexual success and the availability of accommodating women is a function of the social mores of his society which tend to fluctuate in response to many factors affecting society such as economic prosperity or lack of it, the presence of war or of peace and the stringency with which tradition limits sexual behavior in the given society. The degree of sexual license prevailing at a given time waxes and wanes in waves of permissiveness and intolerance. Consider the relative sexual license prevailing in Europe during the Eighteenth Century, the relative absence of it during the Nineteenth Century and its return during the Twentieth Century.

Men court women with the hope of gaining sexual pleasure without marriage in societies where sexual license is liberal, and in societies in which sexual license is limited or absent, they may entertain marital aims as their main hope for sexual satisfaction. Their courting behavior is shaped accordingly. In societies in which sexual license is limited or absent, the young adult male may be subjected to strong superego prohibitions against fornication and adultery. He may approach a potential sex partner with the aim of marriage as the only sexual option permitted by his superego. In societies and in times in which sexual prohibitions are relaxed, he may experience a more accommodating superego and approach a potential sex partner with seduction as his principal aim. Normatively, the young adult male comes to accept marriage as his main hope for the regular reduction of sexual tension, and once that decision has been made he tends to accept also the whole marital relationship and the pleasures and responsibilities of family beyond sexual intercourse.

The courting techniques aimed at sexual seduction differ from those aimed at securing a marriage partner. The young adult male hoping to achieve a sexual seduction is compelled perforce to silence a recriminating superego by any or all of a variety of ego mechanisms such as suppression, denial and rationalization with respect to his seductive actions. In a society with relaxed sexual mores, the superego is more easily fended off than if the reverse were ascendant. The seducer will employ deception in his approach to the object of his seduction, allowing her to believe that a proposal of marriage may be in the offing. If he were direct, and stated his seductive aims forthrightly his chances of success would plummet. He knows that she wants marriage or would not favor him with sexual intercourse unless she considered him both suitable for marriage and a serious prospect for marriage. Otherwise, she may favor him with her company but without allowing herself to be seduced. However, often a woman comes to bond to her male who hopes to seduce her and allows herself to be seduced. Such behavior sometimes ends in marriage, but often enough the young adult male moves on to other females with the aim of seducing them.

Courting and the seeking after opportunities for sexual tension reduction by males gives rise to a complex of behaviors involving the contradictory sexual aims or men and women, which in turn gives rise also to a complex of societal organizations and institutions, mores and laws precipitated by the male-female courting interaction. These include the creation and maintenance of venues for courting such as formal dances, nightclubs, cocktail lounges, restaurants with romantic décor, automobiles with erotic ambiance, and the practice and rituals of dating. To appease the male craving for sexual arousal and satisfaction, erotic entertainments are created by their purveyors, and places of prostitution are established which make a profitable business of selling sexual services to men. Laws prohibiting prostitution and explicit erotic exhibitions are made and violated involving arrests and re-arrests. But courting and sexual predation and the purveying of sexual services to men goes on infinitely.

Where he has hope of doing so, the young adult male seeks to seduce the young adult woman, but the young adult woman he seeks to seduce seeks to entrap him into marriage if she deems him suitable. It is a testament to the success of women over men in this contest that far more marriages are brought about by the courting process than not.

Sex and Marriage in Young Adulthood

Sexual satisfaction and the mutual bestowal of narcissistic gratification and ego worth normatively are at the core of a durable marriage. These are the visible parts of marriage, and they are all but indispensable. The visible parts of marriage include what onlookers can see and hear—the residence in which the family lives, the possessions they have acquired in the marketplace, the family members including parents and children coming and going and laughing at play, their achievements and failures in career and school and the place they establish for themselves in society—but these are the periphery of the marriage and could not be sustained in the absence of a durable core. Without a durable core, the periphery will collapse. With a durable core, even if the periphery collapses creating great tension increase for the marital pair, the marriage itself will tend not to collapse despite the deprivations and assaults which a failed periphery imposes. Normatively, no marriage has an impervious core and many have a devastated periphery.

Sexual satisfaction is critical to the male, and if not available in sufficient measure, which will differ from one male to the next, the marriage will disintegrate. The disintegration may be slow in coming, but its effects will tend to be manifested in the erosion of the periphery. The male may fail at his career, the children may suffer from inadequate and conflicting parenting, the house and property may become shabby or be lost altogether. The diminution of sexual satisfaction for the male may come from unsatisfiable needs which he cannot or will not relinquish such as a homosexual male in a heterosexual marriage, or a heterosexual male craving multiple female sexual partners, or it may come from the young adult male perceiving his marriage partner as sexually unattractive. But the accumulation of unsatisfied sexual tension will precipitate for the male an unrequited craving for sexual tension reduction which will invade his attention and distract him from other critical aims.

The young adult female marriage partner may be unable or unwilling to afford her mate sexual satisfaction because the sexual expectations placed upon her are impossible of achievement. More often, however, her inability arises from inadequate narcissistic gratification and a concomitant diminution of ego worth. A marriage freely and heartily entered into by a young adult female will be characterized by a promise of the fulfillment of narcissistic gratification and ego worth. She expects a continuous demonstration of love in the most tender manner like that of the love bestowed upon her by her mother in her infancy. It was in infancy that the female extended narcissism to the parent which established a deficit of narcissism and a concomitant craving for a return of the narcissism in the form of a lavishing upon her of love from the depended-upon other.

If the young adult male marriage partner fails at the task of lavishing narcissistic affection upon the female marriage partner, she will become as deprived of narcissistic gratification as he is of sexual satisfaction. A paradox is established in which she does not give him sexual satisfaction because he does not give her narcissistic gratification, and he does not give her narcissistic gratification because he suffers from sexual dissatisfaction. Persistent non-sexually related conflict in the marriage may precipitate a withholding of narcissistic gratification from the female whose response leads to a withholding of sexual satisfaction from the male in a downward spiral of marital destruction which vitiates the durability of the marital core, undermining the periphery and destroying the family.

The young adult female's failure to afford her young adult male marriage partner the sexual satisfaction he craves deprives her of ego worth which must come from the value placed upon her by the husband upon whom she has transferred her filial relatedness. Ego worth is initially established by the approval and admiration of the parent and is later sustained by the approval and admiration of parental surrogates of which none is more important to the young adult female than the husband to whom she has transferred her filial relatedness.

Sexual dissatisfaction in the marriage for the male may result directly from his failure to satisfy the narcissistic cravings of his marriage partner which itself may arise from her failure to satisfy his sexual cravings. The satisfaction of sexual lust, narcissistic cravings and ego worth are at the core of a durable marriage, and in their absence no amount of achievement at the marriage periphery will enable the marriage to sustain itself and to spare the offspring of that marriage tension increase which is damaging to that offspring. The male of the marital pair also craves the return of narcissism and the bestowal of ego worth from his mate, but these are no substitute for sexual satisfaction which is more exigent. The degradation of ego worth by either of the marital pair will tend to undermine the core of the marriage and may fatally weaken it.

Much as sex is the principal instrument of the female to attract a suitable male marriage partner, it is often employed by the female to manipulate her marital partner. Tempting him with a promise of sex was used to attract and ensnare him before marriage and becomes a principal controlling instrument after marriage. To get her wants met, the female of the marital pair may extend or withhold sex to manipulate her mate to obtain and favor her with the satisfaction of her wants. This may be done with great subtlety or in an open and aggressive way. The male used his wealth before marriage in his effort to seduce the woman he ultimately married by bestowing gifts and luxuries upon her.

Thus in many marriages the wife uses sex in the effort to get her way, and the husband uses money to get his way. She favors him with sex or withholds sex from him until he favors her with presents or gratifies her narcissistic cravings, and he favors her with gifts and narcissistic gratification to get sexual satisfaction. These manipulations may work well in a marriage if they are not too heavily relied upon. The more durable marital core is based upon sexual satisfaction willingly given as it is needed, and narcissistic gratification and ego worth willingly bestowed as often as it is needed.

Marital Infidelity in Young Adulthood

Marital infidelity perpetrated by either against the other is perceived by either of the marital pair as treachery. She had provided him with sexual satisfaction as her part of the marital bargain, and he had provided her with the necessities of physical survival and with narcissistic gratification and ego worth as his part of the marital bargain. The cuckold male is outraged that another man has enjoyed what he has paid for, and the cuckold female is outraged that another woman has robbed her of the principal tool of control over her marriage partner which is her capacity to provide sexual satisfaction. The cuckolded man is outraged with the cuckolder because the cuckolder has stolen sexual property that he has bought and paid for, and he is angry with his wife because she has given away to another man the sex that he bought and paid for.

The cuckold female is angry with her husband for accepting the favor of sex from another woman which she had bestowed as a gift upon him in exchange for the benefits he owed her in reciprocation. The marital core may be sundered by cuckolding because cuckolding violates the vital male-female bargain that lies at the core of the marriage. Cuckolding attenuates the bond between the marital pair, and threatens decathexis with all of the tension increase resulting from the shattered filial-parental transference which each member of the marital pair has displaced upon the other.

Begetting and Rearing Children
In Young Adulthood Marriage

The begetting of offspring tends to be a nearly universal outcome of young adult marriage. Modern means of contraception available in technologically advanced societies are widely employed to postpone childbearing. Normatively, however, offspring sooner or later tend to come to the marital pair, and the tension producing burdens of childrearing are incurred. Fortunate are the few who are able to shift the childrearing burden in whole or in part to a nanny or to extended family members, for to avoid a measure of the tension increase which child rearing imposes is a blessing devoutly to be wished.

From the time of latency onward, the child knows the difference between his parent and other care-givers who tend to him. While surrogate care-givers are capable of giving a measure of cathexis gratification to the child during the administration of care-giving, it is essential from the child's perspective that demonstrations of child-parent cathexis nurturing be evident. Normatively, it is not the amount of time spent by the parent in nurturing the child-parent cathexis but the quality of the nurturing which reduces decathexis tension for the child. The amount of time and quality of the nurturing minimally necessary to sustain the child-parent cathexis adequately tends to vary from one child to another, but if it is insufficient the child-parent cathexis will attenuate, and the child will suffer increased decathexis tension which surrogate care-givers alone cannot satisfactorily reduce. An inadequate child-parent cathexis when continued too long will tend to lead to forms of waywardness in the child which the child assumes in an effort to reduce the ego tension arising from the attenuated child-parent cathexis.

Parental inattention to the child which causes child-parent cathexis attenuation may arise from any of many causes—chronic illness of the parent, the absence of the parent because of work or military service, or parental rejection of or indifference toward the child—but it is cathexis attenuation for whatever reason which disturbs the healthy ontogenesis of the child's ego, and leads to ego failure dealing with the sources of impinging stimuli to which the child ego is subjected. Bad parenting in the form of misguided parenting from following bad advice, from misunderstanding parenting advice, from over-zealousness, from administering too harsh punishment, or from failing to punish willful misdeeds—none of these and other forms of bad parenting is so likely to harm the child irreparably as is unremitting child-parent decathexis tension.

For the young adult parent, the tension increase resulting from the burdens of childcare can become so severe that the child is abused by the caregiver who has found no adequate way to reduce the ego tension produced by the demands of childcare. Few sources of impinging stimuli are as productive of tension increase as the incessant crying of one's child when the young adult parent is too stressed out or unable to discover and rectify the source of the child's discomfort.

Until the child has resolved the Oedipus conflict and established the superego, it is incapable of knowing right from wrong in the parent's terms and cannot be corrected by techniques of reward and punishment. The parent who applies reward and punishment techniques is engaged upon a futile aim during the primordial period of the child's experience. However, beginning with the latency period and onward the child not only can be taught by these techniques, they are the principal techniques employed by parents to teach right and wrong behavior. These are not only the principal techniques relied upon by the parent to instill correct behavior in the child, they are also the principal techniques employed by the criminal justice systems of major societies to correct unwanted behavior by members of society. Despite weak efforts at rehabilitation, prisons are primarily places of punishment justified by the theory that the punished person will upon release after serving his sentence lead a life of rectitude while enjoying the reward of freedom.

His child readily becomes a major object of both displacement and projection for the young adult parent. The young adult father will tend to identify with and introject his child and will strive to impose upon the child the obligation to achieve the aims in life which the parent held for himself. In other words, the father strives to re-live his life through his child, not only to achieve the goals of his life not yet attained, but also to correct the failings in his life to requite the urgings of his superego. To aid in the identification and introjection of his child, the father strives to imbue his child with his values and to manipulate the child by reward and punishment techniques—often in the form of the alternate extending and withholding of affection and approval—into manifesting those values in his behavior.

The child during latency tends to accommodate the father in the latter's value-instilling aims. As a consequence, the child becomes a target of the father's use of the mechanisms of projection and displacement, and the weight of the burden which the child is compelled to assume becomes a function of the intensity with which the father subjects him to projection and displacement. The father's superego guilt, his self-perceived shortcomings, his unfulfilled ambitions will tend to devolve upon his offspring. The father will also tend to relate to his child with displaced filial ambivalence, displacing upon the child selected experiences of hostility and affection, often tending not to recognize that he is doing this, which he had experienced in relation to his own parent. The child will tend not to understand these transferences of his father, but nevertheless will struggle to accommodate his father despite his perplexity.

The young adult father will relate to his son differently than to his daughter. The daughter will more likely be related as the father related to his mother than to his father, but the father may nevertheless relate to his daughter in some respects as he did to his father. When the latter occurs, the daughter may suffer significant confusion. For example, the father may impose upon his daughter an obligation to achieve masculine values which his father had imposed upon him. Thus, the daughter to win paternal approval and ego worth may be leveraged into awkward and defeminizing roles such as athlete or tomboy as she struggles to define her identity and establish her ego ideal. The father may also displace suppressed erotic relatednesses aimed at his mother during his Oedipal struggles on to his daughter which might lead to father-daughter incest on the one hand or to the subjecting of the daughter to erotic suppression to compensate the father for his superego guilt arising from his suppressed eroticism toward his daughter. Later, in striving for paternal approval in the pursuit of ego worth, the daughter may reject the approach of a suitable marriage partner because of fear of succumbing to seduction and losing paternal approval and the ego worth which it affords.

The son may be driven to take up his father's career, or a career at which the father had aimed in his own life but was unhappily diverted from, in order to win paternal approval to gain ego worth. At the onset of puberty when the child is impelled to rebel in some way in order to establish a separate and unique identity, he may reject the career imposed upon him by his father with severe filial-paternal conflict resulting with tension producing consequences.

The young adult mother will tend to impose her unfulfilled aims upon her daughter and to strive to correct her own self-perceived mistakes in life by training her daughter not to make these mistakes. She wants her daughter to marry well, even better than she married. Instilling in her daughter a predilection for cultivating sexual attractiveness in appearance and manner becomes a primary goal of the mother's maternal teachings. She strives to instill in her daughter a resolve not to give in sexually to a male pursuer for fear that doing so would vitiate her power to achieve an advantageous marriage. To attract a male suitor by sexual provocation without giving in to sexual advances requires skill and judgment which the mother is hopeful of bestowing upon her daughter. If the daughter appears to be making the same mistakes in life made by the mother, or to be in danger of making those mistakes even if the mother successfully avoided them, it produces great tension increase for the mother and a redoubling of the effort to guide her daughter with the aim of obviating them.

Normatively, the mother wants her daughter to be a "good" girl and to manifest in her behavior the rectitude which the mother would want to exemplify herself. Implanting such values in her daughter's superego becomes a primary child-rearing aim of the mother. In identifying with and introjecting her daughter, the mother strives to guide her daughter along a path that the mother would have followed if she had been capable of it, or did follow. To this end, she warns her daughter away from males of doubtful morals and precarious future prospects and from girls who might lead her astray. After the onset of adolescence when the daughter is struggling to establish her unique and separate identity in part by rejecting parent values, the mother may find herself in conflict with a daughter determined to set her own course by repudiating maternal advice and admonition.

The young adult mother relates to her son differently from her daughter in specific ways. Normatively the mother wants both her son and her daughter to display civil rectitude, to be good citizens and attract the admiration of others for their manifest rectitude. But her aims for her son differ in many ways from her aims for her daughter. She wants her son to marry well, and marrying well is different for the son from what it is for the daughter. While the daughter must strive to marry wealth and social position, the son must strive to marry a wife much like the mother would want to be herself if she could achieve her ideal.

The mother is confronted with the prospect of experiencing conflict with her son's wife as she relates to that wife with filial ambivalence transferred from the mother's relatedness to her own mother. Thus the mother may embrace her daughter-in-law, introject her and identify with her as she did her own mother when resolving her Electra conflict, or she may project filial hostility upon prospective daughters-in-law as she did upon her own mother when coping with her Electra conflict. The young adult parent tends in the majority of cases to cope with the tasks of child rearing less than optimally but nevertheless adequately so that his offspring have a chance at growing to maturity successfully, reproducing, rearing successful offspring and carrying on the species.

Normatively, filial rebellion of his offspring begins at the time of or near the end of young adulthood for the parent, and becomes a burden for the middle age parent. The young adult parent at the beginning of his or her fourth decade may find his child entering the early stages of adolescence. The young adult parent tends to remember his own adolescence because it is still fresh in his mind. He remembers his frustration with his parent who seemed so old fashioned, uninformed and restricting of the adolescent's freedom.

Now the young adult parent has himself or herself become the parent of an obstreperous adolescent and is confused as to whether he should approach the child as he had wanted his parent to approach him or to approach his child as his parent actually did approach him—to be the old fashioned, uninformed and restricting parent which his parent had been. Usually, after much angst, the latter approach is taken with the acknowledgement that his parent had been right when he was an adolescent, that his own adolescent child is too inexperienced and imprudent to be given the freedom which the child demands, and that he at the time of his adolescence had also been too inexperienced and imprudent to be given the freedom which he had then demanded. The tension crease of parental doubt tends to sweep over the young adult parent of an adolescent child, and he may turn to his own parent for advice which he tended to be unwilling to do during his child's primordial and latency years.

Parental Failure and Unhappy Child
Rearing Outcomes of Young Adulthood

Unhappy childrearing outcomes will occur for a variety of reasons, not all of them the result of inadequate childcare. Physical disease, crippling accident, inherited frailties and difficult child rearing circumstances are among factors which may lead to unhappy child rearing outcomes. But more often, unhappy child rearing outcomes arise from child rearing failures owing to the devolution of ego ontogenetic imperfections incurred by the parent during the parent's ego ontogenesis. In other words the harm done to the parent during his upbringing is passed on by the parent to his child. Because perfection is seldom attained in any human enterprise, harm done to a child by his parent during his upbringing is relatively commonplace but seldom so severe that a child is hopelessly impaired. Consequently, while most children suffer the consequences of imperfect upbringing which may precipitate their inflicting imperfect upbringing upon their own children, the capacity of society to surmount the ontogenetic imperfections of its members tends nevertheless to be preserved.

Some imperfections of upbringing have more serious consequences than most. The most serious parenting imperfection is that of the inadequately nourishing of the filial-parental cathexis which may lead to narcissistic inadequacy and unworth, and further lead to anti-social behavior in the child's attempt to reduce the ego tension produced by these imperfections. Efforts to reduce the ego tension of the narcissism and worth deficits resulting from the decathexis tension of inadequate upbringing may lead to criminal conduct or to financial fecklessness or to social inadequacy. Such individuals may spend much of their lives in orphanages, or foster care homes or correctional facilities.

The rearing of children suffering from Physical disease, crippling accident, inherited frailties and difficult child rearing circumstances demands from the parent a much greater effort than the rearing of unimpaired children. While many parents through great exertion and self-discipline are able to rise to such demands and rear children with outcomes similar or occasionally even superior to the norm, many more do less well and have childrearing outcomes which lead to waywardness and inadequacy.

5

MIDDLE ADULTHOOD

The Severation Trauma of Middle Adulthood

As with the transition from adolescence to young adulthood, which occurs over time, the transition from young adulthood to middle age also occurs over time and culminates in the individual's realization that he has fewer years remaining to live than the number of years already lived. The physical stamina he enjoyed before begins to wane, and he begins to experience a diminution in his capacity to perform activities requiring physical strength and coordination such as sports and heavy physical labor. As the ego resolves the issues of young adulthood and as the years pass, and as his children grow and move through their own ego ontogenesis from adolescence into young adulthood, and as the conditions of his life change, the sources of stimuli which impinge upon him are reordered so that newer ones supersede older ones in the intensity of their impingement, and the individual looks back and realizes that his life has changed and that he has become middle aged.

Never before has he worried much about the shortness of life and the inevitability of his own death. To the middle age individual life begins to seem more precious, and he becomes less prone to taking risks with his life. He becomes the prudent driver on the streets and highways. Auto insurance carriers may rate him as a better risk than they did a few years earlier. There are exceptions to this prudent posture which may be found in individuals who took up rebellious ways during adolescent individuation and made a career of it. Among these rebellious individuals may be found middle age soldiers of fortune, middle age racecar drivers, middle age mountain climbers and middle age motorcyclists. But normatively for the middle age individual, many of the concerns of young adulthood have lessened, and he now has new concerns with which he is compelled to cope. He becomes concerned for the success and welfare of his children and grandchildren and the welfare of his community and nation, and the durability of the civilization of which he is a part because if it falters, (like oszymandius), there may be no one to remember that he passed this way.

Normatively, no one leaves behind all of the tension sources of the stage of ego ontogenesis from which he has recently moved. Invariably some issues remain unresolved or only partly resolved and follow the individual into the next stage of ego ontogenesis which he must continue to deal with even as he must take up dealing with new tension sources produced by the new stage of ego ontogenesis which he has just entered. The baggage of unresolved tension-producing conflict tends to accumulate throughout the course of life so that at the end of life the individual, like the ghost of Jacob Morley, may find himself dragging the chains and locks of his life into the hereafter.

Narcissism in Middle Adulthood

The craving for narcissistic gratification suffuses almost every aspect of human experience. Certainly, the middle age adult craves narcissistic gratification as much as the young adult, but he looks to a different mix of parentified entities for that gratification. Normatively, the middle age adult has achieved a degree of success in power, status and mastery that he did not enjoy during young adulthood and comes to regard himself as an established and responsible citizen. He tends to be more likely to read the newspaper or to pay attention to news reported over the radio, television and the Internet about public affairs and to vote in public elections than when he was a young adult. He is more likely to take an interest in the welfare of his church, his *alma mater*, and his employing organization than he did during young adulthood. He may volunteer to work for charitable organizations or his church, or his political party in an election. He is more likely to become a political activist during election campaigns and even to run for public office himself. It must be recognized, however, that the young adult who chooses a career as a political activist will be as active politically as middle age adults. The same holds true for the young adult who launches a career as a political scientist, journalist or politician who will perforce be as concerned about politics as any middle age adult.

From all of the aforementioned entities, the middle age adult will expect the bestowal of narcissistic gratification. He will expect his church to recognize in some formal way his contributions of money and service. He will expect *alma mater* to recognize his money donations and any noteworthy achievement he has made in his life. He will expect political leaders of the political party he supports with his money and active participation to recognize his gifts and labor. He may hope to see his name in the news for his charitable work or civic activities. He especially hopes to be recognized by his employer for the special contributions he makes above and beyond what is normally expected from an employee. All of these acts giving of money, work or support are intended partly to solicit a return of narcissism from the parentified entities to which the boon is given. The employing organization that fails to recognize a gift of service from an employee above and beyond what is normally expected, the church or university which fails to recognize a gift of money from a communicant or an alumnus, the political leader who fails to acknowledge a campaign contribution or other service of a supporter—may find that the boon they failed to acknowledge is never repeated.

From the members of his family, the middle age individual expects a return of narcissism because of the affection, protection and care he has bestowed upon them. The middle age mother narcissistically expects fond recognition of her unstinting devotion to the rearing of her children, if not from the children at least from their father. She hears of women who receive "mother-of-the-year" recognition and would want this for herself even though she may modestly regard herself as unworthy of such recognition and holds out little hope that the finger of favor would ever likely point to her.

The middle age father who has looked after his family through all of the tribulations of his young adulthood struggles will quietly regard himself as worthy of some sort of recognition from his family but like his wife does not expect it from his children. He may look back upon his own childhood and remember that he never gave such recognition to his parents. As middle age parents did during the early years of their child rearing lives, they must gratify each other's narcissistic wants in middle age if they are to be gratified at all. For parents who have divorced, separated or merely drawn apart, the unfulfilled desire for narcissistic gratification in middle age because of their parenting achievement is particularly poignant.

To reduce the ego tension of middle age longings, middle age individuals are particularly drawn to works of fiction, motion pictures, television and internet drama which depicts middle age men and women struggling with unfulfilled lives and finding either the means to become fulfilled after all or to learn how to cope through the solace of a personal philosophy or religious faith. Particularly appealing is the couple depicted as coming together again to review their lives and to give each other the praise long overdue.

Power in Middle Age

Normatively, personal power is at its height during middle age, although many whose lives did not flower as they would have wanted may experience a middle age of deprivation. While the peak of his physical power will likely have passed, normatively, the middle age individual is at the apex of his financial power, wealth being for most the basis of personal power. If he is an employed man, he is likely to have advanced in his work as far as he will, although many may be forsaken by their employing organization or the industry in which they have passed their working lives. Capitalist democracies tend to be particularly cold hearted toward the plight of the laid off middle age worker or unsuccessful businessman or businesswoman.

The successful businessperson will tend to be at the zenith of his business career, and the personal income and assets he enjoys gives him the experience of power. He may feel competent to step into public life by joining a charitable organization as board member or as its chairperson, or to take up leadership in a fundraising drive for his church or *alma mater*. He may join the board of a civic organization, and he will tend to hold his own opinion upon public matters as superior to the opinions of others, and may not hesitate to make his views known at meetings or in letters to the editor of news publications.

If he is a publicist, he may write a monograph, a magazine or Internet article or go on radio or television talk shows to expound his opinions. He views the antics of politicians with whom he disagrees as silly, and he knows in his mind that he could do better, but if he is like most middle age individuals he will not run for elective office. However, if ever he is to run for elective office, it will likely be in middle age that he feels powerful enough to attempt it. If he has not pursued a political career, he may find such a task particularly formidable. Many fantasize that they would serve, but few are called, and even fewer are prepared to undertake the arduous and risky task of political campaigning. In his family, he is king even if the members of his family tend to be unenthusiastic subjects.

The professional person will likely be at the height of his professional life, although he may hope to go higher. He will tend to feel well established and be filled with confidence that his views are sound, and he will likely assert himself appropriately in whatever setting he finds himself. He may have published books or articles or he may have advanced his position in the hierarchy of his professional organization. His position and status will serve as the source of his personal power unless he coincidentally has acquired or inherited wealth which may increase his personal power more than his professional position does.

The social position and status of the individual will tend to be at its peak during middle adulthood, and the connections he has made with others in the community, in his profession or business will tend to serve as a source of power. To be able to trade favors with others of like status who are in a position to render a useful quid pro quo is an instrument of power in middle age. But his increased wealth relative to the lack of money he experienced in childhood, adolescence and young adulthood will tend to be his principal instrument of personal power. With his wealth he can enter the marketplace and purchase status assets such as a more impressive residence and automobile, the latest technology gadgets, leisure time opportunities and move in more prestigious social circles without having to give up, unless he chooses to do so, the lower status intimate friends he has acquired earlier in the course life. If he possesses inherited wealth, he may not feel socially generous to other middle age individuals who rose from lower social ranks.

Ego Worth in Middle Adulthood

Ego worth is ineluctably linked to narcissism. The pursuit of ego worth assets is not only a seeking after approval and admiration from parents and parentified others, but also a bid for the return of the narcissism which the ego extended to the depended-upon parents during primordial life. For an adult, being admired is an experience not unlike that of the child being doted upon by the introjecting parent. Ego worth assets in middle age differ from those of childhood. To earn the praise and approval which is the substance of ego worth, the infant need but coo, giggle and squeal to his parents' delight. But for the middle age adult, the nature of ego worth is different. It comes in the form, for example, of admiration by parentified others such as family members, friends, and through public recognition by means of the public communications media or being invited to speak at meetings or gatherings.

To gain ego worth, the individual tends to acquire status assets such as receiving the bestowal of plaudits in public forums, honorary academic degrees, laudatory plaques from civic organizations and particularly by entering the marketplace with his wealth and purchasing status assets available there which he can display to the envy or admiration of others. Expensive and stylish clothing bespeak the man or woman, an impressive residence and automobile or watercraft such as a yacht or cabin cruiser or personal airplane, expensive pleasure travel and being a known contributor to prestigious museums, universities and endowments—all accomplished through the wealth, modest or great, acquired by the time of middle age tends to attract the admiration of others.

For the modestly wealthy working class individual whose financial resources were derived from his manual labor, his forays into the marketplace will likely have garnered him more modest acquisitions such as a new row boat for fishing, a rifle for hunting, a better television or other entertainment device, or a somewhat better residence. The middle age individual, regardless of the degree of wealth he has acquired, may wish to point to the accomplishments of his children and grandchildren and vicariously reflect in the light of those accomplishments.

The middle age individual who has gained few tokens of esteem during the course of his life may suffer a degree of tension-producing unworth, but normatively the most deprived of middle age individuals can find something to point to, no matter how humble, to enable him to experience moments of worth. Even the homeless derelict may bring out of the pocket of his tattered clothing pictures of grandchildren in whom he takes pride and expect praise from onlookers. The respect of others is essential to the experience of worth, and it is a convention of most societies that tokens of respect be offered to others as a perfunctory courtesy regardless of the person's station in society.

Ego Surety in Middle Adulthood

The middle age individual tends to be surer of himself than at any other time during the course of life except during adolescence. However, the sureness of one's judgment in middle adulthood tends to be characterized by a degree of caution often lacking in the overweening brashness of adolescence. The adolescent, impelled by the need to individuate and exhilarated by the newly found confidence he enjoys about his knowledge and judgment, is unimpeded in asserting his astuteness. The middle age individual tends to be more prudent in his judgment, having been wrong many times in his life, he is less quick to declare the validity of his views.

Surety is the experience of being sure of the validity of one's knowledge, views and judgments. Surety is essential to the process by which the ego guides behavior to assess the nature of reality and the source of tension-producing and tension-reducing impinging stimuli in a given circumstance and to decide in that context how to reduce tension either by avoiding the sources of tension-producing impinging stimuli or by defeating the sources of tension-producing impinging stimuli. It is in the nature of the human ego that it be able to explain everything which comes to its attention. Not knowing is intolerable. The popularity of mystery fiction is in part explained by the human desire to reduce the tension of curiosity in a factitious way to appease the ego tension which the mysteries of human existence impels.

The human ego is compelled to know, and when it does not know, it tends to invent answers so that it thereby can reduce the ego tension produced by not knowing. Theories not proven by reality and religion not validated by reality are examples of the human ego's determination to create answers to questions for which it can find no answers in reality. The human ego does not know what it will experience after the individual has died, and therefore tends to create scenarios of after death experience in which it places belief in an effort to reduce the tension of its ignorance as well as of the fear of death. It is in middle adulthood that the individual begins to settle upon his religious beliefs if he has not already done so.

The middle age individual is more likely than at other stages of ego ontogenesis to support societal institutions whose purpose is to serve the aims of surety such as universities, research institutions and also the church which purports itself to be a source of answers to the great mysteries of human existence.

Mastery in Middle Adulthood

The middle age individual is likely to be at the peak of his mastery in many areas of human activity, although his mastery of tasks requiring physical strength and coordination will tend to be in the past for him. The faltering at life's tasks which he experienced during adolescence and young adulthood are likely to have been surmounted by middle age. He now thinks that he knows how to master the tasks of life, even if he has not actually mastered all of them in practice. How to derive a livelihood, how to live rewardingly with one's marital partner, how to rear children successfully to adulthood, how to be effective in one's line of work, how to obtain and enjoy leisure, how to be a citizen, how to understand the politics and economics of one's society—he or she is likely to be at his or her peak in all of these areas.

If he has not achieved perfection in these and similar venues of life—and virtually nobody does—the middle age individual will tend at least to have achieved a reasonably satisfying modicum of success. He will likely have come to terms with what he can accomplish, and find satisfaction in where he has arrived. If not, he will likely experience considerable ego tension from his mastery deficit, and struggle against a sense of failure. The severity of his deficits of narcissism, power and worth may have set him upon a lifelong course of tension-reduction whose likelihood of success far exceeded the reality of his reach. The overreach of ambition to still the ego tension of narcissism, power and worth deficits experienced during primordial existence is not an uncommon human state, and its palliation is virtually a universal task of middle adulthood life. As for the mastery of skills needed in his profession or employment and in his leisure activities, he will likely take at least a modicum of pleasure in what he can do.

Curiosity in Middle Adulthood

The ego is impelled by curiosity to know and to understand everything to which it attends in its surround. Indeed, curiosity is essential to the ego's guidance function of directing the individual's behavior with the aim of discovering and understanding the sources of tension-producing stimuli and tension-reducing stimuli without which the individual would perish. The wellspring of curiosity is innate and is found in many species of animals besides the human individual. Almost every higher animal must seek out and discover sources of impinging stimuli in its environment which may distress, harm or destroy it, and the human animal is no exception to this reality of living organisms.

Curiosity is the handmaiden of surety because curiosity provokes questions about reality which surety attempts to answer. Curiosity wonders about the mysteries of realty and asks why the grass is green, why the toast is brown and why the sky is blue, and surety answers these questions. If the middle age individual is educated he will know the answers to such questions which the enterprise of science has supplied, but the great questions of "where did we come from?" "why are we here?" and "where are we going?" continue to puzzle him as do entities about which he is informed by cosmologists such as supernovae, crab nebulae, black holes and the big bang. Sure of himself and circumspect, the middle age individual tends to assert his views whether based upon demonstrated knowledge or upon speculation with the confidence of one who has become wise.

Rectitude in Middle Adulthood

Rectitude in middle adulthood tends to be at its zenith and will continue at a high level into old age. Rectitude is conformity with reality. That which is right must be congruent with reality. Ethics, the science of right and wrong conduct, is dependent upon reality as its guide. To assess realty correctly and then to conduct oneself in conformity with reality is to act with moral correctness. Morality would be easy to achieve except for the disparity among different individuals' assessment of reality from which rectitude is determined and except for the difficulty of adhering to moral prescriptions and proscriptions because doing so is so often tension producing.

The maturity which the middle age individual has achieved through repeated adjustments to reality requiring the coping with tension-increase which the stimuli impinging from realty subject him to stands him in good stead as he nears the end of his course of life. The complexity of life due to the variety and inexorableness of impinging stimuli compel the ego to guide behavior towards settling for a net tension-increase or a net tension-decrease in most cases. While such simple sources of tension-producing stimuli as hunger and thirst can often be fully reduced by eating or drinking, most impinging stimuli require choices among possible tension-reducing solutions which increase ego tension before reducing it. For example, the adolescent must engage in tension-producing educational or training activity if he is to equip himself for citizenship and employment. Schoolwork and apprenticing tend to increase ego tension in the short run in order to reduce tension in the long run by gaining marketable skills and an understanding of the environment in which one abides.

The adolescent and young adult who tolerates tension-increase by limiting his tension-reducing sexual activity to partners allowed by the mores of society will likely enjoy greater tension-reduction in the future by conforming to the practices which prevail in the society upon which he depends. For example, he may wish to be promiscuous in a staid society to reduce immediate sexual tension, but doing so would produce a net tension-increase because of the penalties he would pay exacted by the institutions of the society whose mores he has violated. The mature ego learns to cope with short-term tension-increase to enjoy long-term tension-decrease. However, if the adolescent is homosexual, his adherence to the mores of a heterosexual society may give him tension-increase which conformance to societally defined rectitude cannot reduce.

Rectitude is the conducting of oneself in harmony with reality, and being in harmony with realty requires that the ego guide behavior to adhere to the morality prevailing in one's society. But there is a paradox in that social change tends to be engendered by rebellion against prevailing morality which perforce is change brought about by immorality. Adherence to the status quo tends to impede the change necessary to adapt to new conditions. Once the change has been established however, it becomes the new morality, and moral stability returns. There are many instances in human experience in which acts condemned as immoral later come to be regarded as moral, and contrariwise, there are many instances of behavior which was regarded as immoral which later came to regarded as moral. For example, women's bathing suits once covered their entire bodies except for their feet and arms. Less coverage was regarded as immoral. By the turn of the twenty-first century, women's bathing suits might be so skimpy as barely to cover their sexual parts, yet be regarded as morally acceptable. Taking the example of sexual morality during the eighteenth century, promiscuity was tolerated to a much greater extent than during the nineteenth century when condemnation of it as immoral was ascendant. By late in the twentieth century, promiscuity became much less condemned than in the nineteenth century. In the matter of sexual promiscuity, morality changed, and then changed back again.

Middle adulthood tends to be a time in the course of life when the individual's rectitude is strongest. He tends to be ready to condemn immoral behavior in himself as well as in others. While almost no individual is a paragon of moral rectitude, the middle age individual tends to want to think he is and will be particularly troubled when he thinks he has failed. He nevertheless strives to adhere to societal mores more than perhaps at any time in his adult life and to hold himself up as a paragon of virtue. If he is a judgmentalist, he will decry immoral acts of others and want to see them punished. If he is a rehabilitationist, he will be saddened by the moral failures of others and wish to urge them to find their way back onto the path of rectitude. This is not to deny that some middle age individuals commit moral wrongs and high crimes.

Individuation in Middle Age

Although in middle age, the individual still carries some individuation and identity baggage from adolescence and young adulthood, nevertheless individuation is less of an issue for the middle age individual than at any earlier time in his life. By middle age, the individual knows who he is if he is ever likely to know who he is. He is the parent of his children and the wife or husband of his spouse. He is identified by his vocation and his accomplishments in his vocation. He is the person who accomplished certain works that he can point to—one who worked on a certain construction project he can point to, one who wrote a book he can hold up, acted in a cinema or theater production he can name, one who held a certain public office in which he took pride, one who worked his farm for a lifetime, one who toiled in a certain factory, one who went to war and participated in a famous battle, one who was a teacher of children or a pastor of the church, one who reared his children to adulthood. Innumerable examples could be cited. But the middle age person is traversing a time in the course of his life when identity factors begin to diminish as his children become self-dependent and leave home to establish their own families, and as his career, whatever form it has taken, begins to ebb.

The middle age person sees his offspring struggling with individuation, striving to establish a role in life, a career, a family, and social status which gives him identity and worth, and vicariously the middle age person suffers with his children and strives to help them. But he cannot substitute himself and his capacities for their struggles. Like the parent of the toddler who helps his child to walk with hands ready to catch him if he falls, the middle age individual figuratively hovers to catch his adult child should he stumble on life's road. But he could not walk for his child when the child was a toddler, and he cannot negotiate life's travails for his child who is struggling to find his way along the course of life.

Middle Adulthood and the Ego Ideal, the
Persona, Ego Real and the Ego Actual

The persona is the public face of the individual's ego ideal in so far as the individual is able to achieve his ego ideal, but because the ego ideal is almost never achieved, the persona perceived by the observer falls short of being the ideal desired by the ego. The ego ideal is the idealized ego which is equipped to defeat every tension-producing stimulus which the ego can imagine that might assail the individual. Thus, the ego ideal is comprised, for example, of comeliness to defeat the tension of rejection; it is powerful so that it can defeat impinging stimuli which assault the ego power deficit; it is loved so that it can defeat the tension of the ego worth and narcissism deficits and the possibility of decathexes; it is knowledgeable so that it can defeat the tension of the surety deficit and the tension of curiosity; it possesses mastery so that it can defeat a variety of sources of tension-producing stimuli impinging from the individual's surround. The ego ideal comprises many other attributes and capacities imagined by the ego needed to defeat all manner of tension-producing stimuli which it can envision. The ego real is the ego perceived as falling short of the ideal. The ego figuratively swings between the ideal and the real, and when the ideal is ascendant the ego experiences tension-reduction and concomitant pleasure, and when the real is ascendant the ego experiences tension-increase and concomitant unpleasure. The ego actual is the ego as it actually is at a given moment and is an abstract concept not knowable by the ego because there is no way to measure accurately the status of the ego.

In middle adulthood, the ego ideal tends to be ascendant more than during adolescence and young adulthood. This owes to the many accomplishments of the individual which reduces the tension of ego deficits. Normatively the individual has achieved personal power through wealth or social position, mastery of the common tasks of life, has seen his offspring gain success and establish their own families, has also mastered the tasks immanent in his career choice and the tasks associated with his leisure pastimes. On the negative side, his physical strength and the comeliness of youth have likely deserted him, but on balance these factors do not negate his greater realization of his aims than earlier and the greater proximity to the ego ideal than the ego real.

The individual's struggle to achieve the ego ideal and persona never wanes. Even in middle age, he wants to be found comely by others, to be physically vigorous and fit, to have power, to display rectitude, to find answers to perplexing questions, to understand his surround, to display mastery and skill at whatever activity to which he turns his hand, and to enjoy status in society and in his profession or trade. Impinging stimuli which produces ego tension by no means ceases in middle age, and the ego ideal requires that the ego be able to guide behavior to deal with all tension-producing stimuli to which the individual is subject. His personal power and mastery will be brought to bear upon the task of achieving the ego ideal and the persona which it sustains.

Counter Manipulation Behavior During Middle Adulthood

Counter-manipulation behavior is self-injurious behavior resulting from resistance to manipulation by one who is dependent upon the manipulator. In ego ontogenesis, this practice takes a lasting form when the infant ego resists forced toilet training imposed by the parent. The counter manipulating child resists adopting bladder voiding and bowel evacuation practices imposed by the parent who seeks through toilet training to reduce the ego tension he experiences because of the child care burden of changing diapers and washing soiled clothing and because of fear of societal censure for failing to bring his child into line with societal standards of hygiene.

For the child, toilet training constitutes a severation from its cathexis to the parent of its absolute dependence, which is terrifying and tension producing of traumatic magnitude. The child clings to the old ways of voiding and evacuating and being cleaned afterward because these practices form the filial-parental cathexis which he desperately wishes to retain.

The disparity of the child's power to get his way by retaining the existing toileting practices relative to the parent's power to get his way by changing those practices places the child at great disadvantage which he desperately struggles to equalize by resisting toilet training to the point of self-injury. Self-injuriousness occurs when the child soils his diapers which leads to uncomfortable wetness and chaffing and varying degrees of withheld love by the frustrated parent.

The self-injuriousness of counter manipulation behavior becomes harmful as the child grows older and refuses to cooperate in learning to discharge the tasks of self-dependence imposed by the parent and upon which his survival in adulthood will depend. Refusing to accept toilet training may later be followed by refusal to clean oneself and to dress, and still later by failure to perform well in school, or failure to learn a trade or to form and take care of a family, or to function as a useful and law abiding citizen as a means of counter manipulating first the parent and later such parentified societal entities as school, employer and government.

By middle adulthood counter manipulation behavior adopted by the individual will have hardened into enduring practices as a member of society and tends to be self-defeating for the counter manipulator. For most individuals their counter manipulation behavior may be relatively mild, manifesting itself in innocuous conduct such as outlandish dress, offbeat career choices and counterculture life styles.

Or more extravagantly, it may be reflected in anti-social behavior such as marring public places with graffiti, participating in protest activities or simply being uncooperative with the practices established by society to facilitate the smooth operation of societal processes such as taking one's place at the end of a queue instead of butting in, not running stop signs and depositing refuse in waste receptacles rather than littering parks, walkways and floors. All such behavior tends to be harmful to the counter-manipulator by making him less welcome among the conforming members of society whose help might make his struggles in life easier and more rewarding.

In middle age, counter manipulation behavior may take the form of resisting certain impositions of government intended to promote the welfare of society. Avoiding the paying of taxes used by government to meet the costs of the amenities and infrastructure of society, not cooperating with traffic laws and regulations and with environmental protection rules, not cooperating in the smooth operation of societal practices by shoving ahead of others. Many additional examples could be offered, but each of these has a self-injurious element. Any behavior which defeats society's efforts to provide a wholesome, accommodating and pleasant environment for its members will redound to the disadvantage of a counter-manipulating citizen and therefore is self-injurious.

The Superego in Middle Age

The middle age individual tends to impose the dictates of his superego upon others with greater firmness than at any other time. He believes that his perception of rectitude is superior to that of others, particularly of younger individuals than himself. The moral failings of others, which come to his attention, elicit his critical eye and become the targets of his rebuke. The content of his superego tends to have become less flexible than earlier. He knows right from wrong and is impelled by the tension of a demanding superego to impose his morality upon others. Demonstrated failures of the self-dependence training which all parents impose upon their growing children tend to annoy the middle age adult, and he is likely to display his annoyance.

Those members of society who fail to support themselves financially, who misspend their income, who litter the streets with their discarded waste such as cigarette butts and candy wrappers, who do not maintain their property in good form, who rear wayward children—these annoy the rectitudinous middle age adult. If he has shortcomings of his own, he may project guilt upon others who display shortcomings to reduce the ego tension produced by his guilt. The decades of superego guilt, and the forms into which it devolved throughout the course of life, and which came to haunt the middle age individual have likely diminished in their intensity to allow him a modicum of peace which he did not experience earlier.

Filial Ambivalence in Middle Adulthood

By the time of middle adulthood, the individual has likely accumulated a great many filial ambivalent relatednesses to others of greater or lesser propinquity. In particular, his spouse will have been selected for this purpose, at times related to as a beneficent parentified entity and at other times as a maleficent parentified entity. The spouse in turn relates back as to a parentified entity. Consequently, between the spouses there tends to be a mutual parentification which may be confusing to each of the middle adulthood marital pair.

For example, if the husband relates to his wife as he did to his mother of childhood, he may reject her out of mistaken filial fear of provoking paternal retribution. The middle age wife then may mistake her husband's rejection as an absence of spousal affection. Because displaced relatedness tends to occur episodically, there will tend to be times when the husband relates to his wife in a way uncontaminated by his fearful rejecting childhood filial-maternal relatedness and other times when his spousal relatedness is contaminated. Say, each time his wife nags him for failing at some household chore, his childhood filial-maternal relatedness propensity tends to return, and he lashes out angrily at his wife, resulting in a marital squabble of intensity disproportionate to the issue at hand. If the middle age couple fails to analyze the childhood roots of the squabble, they will also tend not to understand the intensity of their squabble which may then escalate to more severe proportions and place their relationship in danger.

It is during middle age more than any other period in the course of life that the individual is likely to displace filial ambivalence upon bifurcated parentified pairs of societal institutions, organizations and their functionaries. Typical societal entities and their functionaries which are related to as parentified pairs include employers, governments, political parties, schools, churches, chief executive officers of business organizations, health organizations, law enforcement agencies and courts. This owes to the middle age individual's greater sense of power and belief that he has a say in what society does. A bifurcated parentified pair might include a government which the individual relates to as a beneficent parentified entity as one moiety of the parentified pair and the political party in power which he relates to as a maleficent parentified entity as the other moiety of the parentified pair.

Or he might relate to his church as a beneficent parentified entity but relate to a particular church official as a maleficent parentified entity, the two moieties together making up a bifurcated parentified pair. Such parentified pairs allow the individual to bifurcate his filial ambivalence when he displaces it upon parentified societal entities and thus to obviate the experience of filial fear and the risk of provoking filial decathexis by separating filial hostility from the target of filial affection and dependence.

As a more active participant in his society, the middle age individual tends to manifest in his behavior greater support for beneficent parentified entities and greater negativism toward maleficent parentified entities. He may support his government with greater zeal while condemning the political party in power with equal zeal and voting against its candidates during elections. Or he may support his church affectionately with financial donations but speak ill of an important church official whom he related to as a maleficent parental surrogate. The great concerns of the day are more likely to attract the attention and interest of the middle age adult, leading to his taking action with respect to parentified societal entities.

The middle age adult may also relate to his child with displaced filial ambivalence. The adult may parentify his child and expect to be treated by his child as he was treated by his parent. This absurdity is a paradox in which the parent treats his child as if his child were the parent's parent, and expect the child to treat him as he was treated by his parent. For example, an adult child of a parent may occasionally rebuke his parent for some failing such as failing to groom himself or to tidy up after himself. The adult child may offer such a rebuke to project his guilt for his own similar failings. The parent may then respond to his adult child in the way he had responded in childhood to such rebuke from his own parent. In such a situation, the parent and child have reversed roles.

More serious instances of parent-child role reversal might include such issues as an adult child rebuking his parent for failing to find gainful employment to support his family, or failing to attend to the maintenance of the family residence, or failing to treat his spouse—the adult child's mother or father, as the case may be—with proper devotion because of philandering. Such parent-child role reversals are often severely tension producing for both parent and child, and a bane of middle age life for the failed adult.

It is not uncommon for the middle age adult to find that his young adult child is burdened by unresolved issues which impede his journey through life. For example, the adult child may have lingering filial individuation failures and unresolved Oedipal issues which continue to abrade the filial-parental relationship between the adult child and the middle age parent. The middle age adult will likely feel that he has earned respite from the aggravation of filial-parental conflict and feel exasperated that at his stage in life his child continues to provoke unpleasantness in their relationship.

The middle age adult may have issues of his own with his adult child which give him unpleasure. These might include his child's having married someone the parent did not like, or having taken up a career which the parent could not take pleasure in, or his child's espousing religious or political preferences which oppose those of the parent. Or the middle age adult may dislike the way his child is rearing his grandchildren. There may be espousal issues subjecting the middle age individual to various forms of unpleasure including unsatisfying sexual relations, a degree of estrangement from his spouse and a lack of a pleasing social life.

6

OLD AGE AND DEATH[1]

The severation trauma of old age is the reality of approaching death. Death is the final severation from all external objects to which the ego is bonded; the recognition of death's approach is highly tension producing. To reduce the tension produced by the stimulus of approaching death, the ego inventories the armory of tension-reduction instruments it has accumulated over a lifetime and utilizes as many of these as appears helpful in reducing the tension of approaching death. But it will tend to resort largely to those instruments it has habitually come to rely upon in the past.

Ego mechanisms and fantasies are salient among these instruments. Ego mechanisms heavily relied upon tend to be those of denial, rationalization and sublimation—denying death by suppressing thoughts about it, rationalizing by self-exhortation that death is a "natural" part of life, and sublimating by identifying with deities and contemplating one's after death future in heaven. In more practical venues, the contemplator of death will establish a posterity which survives his demise and with which he introjects and identifies and in that way lives on vicariously, by providing for his progeny, by performing good works which continue after his death and keeps his memory alive in others after death, and by providing his grave with a stone marker guaranteed to last to eternity. Fantasies indulged in tend to center upon how he will be remembered by succeeding generations when they honor his memory because of his good works and virtuous life.

Narcissism, Old Age and Death

The narcissism deficit, which emerges when the infant ego extends a quantity of primary narcissism to the depended-upon parent following the trauma of weaning, leaves the ego forever in pursuit of a return of the self-love

---

[1] This chapter draws heavily upon material found in the author's volume entitled *The Ego and the Pursuit of Happiness* published in 2003.

which was extended. The infant ego seeks parental love and filial worth attested by the parent's concern for the infant. Being valued by the parent assures the love of the parent in the form of narcissism compensated. The child-ego parentifies external entities to which it looks for love and valuing. This propensity devolves through successive stages of ego ontogenesis with modifications necessitated by the succession of changed circumstances inevitable during the course of life so that in old age it must adapt anew to the imminence of death.

Narcissism as death approaches tends to take the form of seeking the love of and being honored by one's posterity and generations to come after one's death. The individual seeks the love of those who will live after by such acts as leaving wealth to descendants, by endowing institutions and foundations, by establishing prizes to be awarded annually in his name, by contributing to his university or church with assurance that an academic chair or pew will bear his name into the future. If the individual is financially unable to make such gestures or believes they will not achieve his aim if he is able to make them, his pursuit of happiness will be impeded.

Power and Old Age

For most, personal power is at its nadir in old age. Physical strength, and sometimes physical health, are at their lowest ebb since infancy during old age. And for the great majority of the population, wealth being an instrument of power, is also at its lowest ebb at any time in adult life. Having only their labor to sell in the marketplace, the vast majority of elderly find few buyers for their labor and low wages when a buyer is found.

Those who aren't impoverished survive financially on state administered social security pensions or modest pensions from their former employers. Some have both, but unless the old age person has set aside savings throughout the course of his life, or made successful investments, or enjoys inherited wealth—and these are but a small proportion of the world population—the financial power of old people tends to be weaker than at any other time in adulthood.

An exception to this state of affairs obtains for those elderly who live in a welfare society where virtually every critical need of life for services and support is furnished as in certain Scandinavian countries. An exception also obtains in certain traditional cultures where the elderly are honored, cared for and deferred to by younger age groups, and also in cultures in which the elderly continue to possess legal ownership of the income-producing assets of the extended family such as farm or business.

For the proportionately few elderly who possess substantial wealth in the form of invested capital or ownership of income-producing assets operated by paid managers, old age is not a time of reduced wealth and diminished financial power. They continue to wield financial power as before, so long as their health is sustained, right up to the gate of death. But these are the few—not the many. Lack of financial power like the lack of health assails the ego's equanimity in the final time before death. In examining the ego and power in old age, it is important to make a distinction between the wealthy elderly and the rest of the elderly population.

The Ego and Wealth in Old Age

For those who have power in old age, it principally takes the form of wealth. It is useful to examine the power given to the wealthy in old age by their wealth and contrast the experience of the wealthy elderly ego with the elderly ego of the non-wealthy. As in earlier stages of life, wealth affords its possessor with the power to enter the marketplace and purchase ego worth assets. It enables its possessor to purchase the services of others—literally to command those services when the provider of services is dependent upon selling his services for his livelihood. Wealth begets wealth, enabling its possessor to gain more wealth and therefore more power by investing wealth.

The ego employs power to compel the compliance of objects in the external world to yield to the ego's tension-reduction aims. Wealth as power is used to achieve tension-reduction aims which wealth is perceived especially capable of achieving. For the old age individual confronted by the prospect of death, the power of wealth may be used to reduce the ego tension produced by the approach of death. The following are among commonplace examples of this sort of ego-guided behavior aimed at reducing the tension of the deficits of narcissism, ego worth and the decathexis of death which produce disequanimity at the end of life.

With his wealth the old age individual may endow an academic chair or academic building, or scholarship or fellowship which will bear his name long after he becomes deceased. In making the endowment he will enjoy the tension-reducing experience of contemplating that succeeding generations will know of his existence, his status, his worth and generosity. He may achieve the same result by endowing a church or church organ or a' hospital wing which bears his name. He may bequeath a valuable art collection bearing his name to an art museum.

He may contribute his palatial residence to an historic trust and endow its maintenance so that it can be visited by the public into the indefinite future, drawing attention to his former existence. He may establish a trust in his name to do charitable work or to support scholarship and science. Or he may support scientific research aimed at solving great human and societal problems to protect the civilization to which he is bonded so that his bond to his civilization will not be severed.

He may build a library named after him and donate it to the community. More personally, he may build an imposing mausoleum to house his remains, or have a biography written about him, or leave a trust to educate his progeny for generations to come. All of these measures assist the old age individual in reducing the tension produced by the impinging stimuli of approaching death and tend to be resorted to in his pursuit of happiness. By contrast the vast majority of the non-wealthy elderly are left to content themselves with a modest gravestone in a tended cemetery and perhaps to leave such assets as their ordinary residence and a life insurance policy to their posterity.

Individuation and Old Age

Normally for the elderly, individuation occurred long ago, and the old age individual may be annoyed by the individuation behavior of adolescents and young adults. When the individuation behavior of the young is manifested in unusual dress, idiosyncratic argot, ear-splitting music, repulsive life style practices, rebellious behavior, rejection of established moral values about sex, work and drug and alcohol use and social and political radicalism, the elderly often feel offended and annoyed. In his struggle for cathexis with youthful members of his family such as grandchildren, this disparity in values between the old and the young will tend to impair the equanimity of the old age individual. But a few will join the young in their anti-status quo antics as if to defy the reality of their old age status, having never relinquished the rebellious spirit of their youth.

Filial Ambivalence in Old Age

Filial ambivalence continues into old age but with less force. Most people who are objects of parentification because they occupy positions of authority are younger than the old age individual and therefore more difficult to parentify. An individual in his seventh or eighth decade of life is less likely than he was earlier to parentify, say, a president of the United States in his fifth decade and young enough to be the older individual's child. Yet such entities as church and state can evoke parentification in the old age person and' become objects of displaced filial ambivalence.

The old age individual becomes ever more frequently aware that the world will go on without him, and he begins to fear that he is irrelevant. This fact of reality is highly tension producing, and he becomes equivocal about it. On the one hand he wants the world to go on, and civilization to survive to carry his memory into the future to preserve the cathexis he experiences toward his kind. But on the other hand, it will go on without him unless he can establish a place for himself in posterity.

Often the old age individual is himself or herself an object of filial ambivalence of younger individuals, particularly living descendants. To the extent these grandchildren and great grandchildren and their spouses displace filial hostility upon him, his happiness will be impaired. But to the extent they relate to him with displaced filial love, he will enjoy the happiness of realized cathexis critical to the contentment of the departing generation.

Ego Worth in Old Age

Normatively the old age individual has garnered most of the ego worth assets he is likely to gain from the purchase of ego worth assets in the marketplace. He is no longer likely to be a shopper for self-indulgences. He may purchase items for his children and grandchildren and vicariously enjoy their enhanced ego worth which his gifts to them may contribute, but for himself he already has accumulated most of the material possessions he craves, and he tends to look elsewhere for the means to buttress his ego worth.

The old age individual looks to his children and grandchildren, to his good works, his honorable life, the social status he has attained regardless of rank, the respect and admiration in which he is held, his achievements no matter how humble, his piety as the assets with which he wishes to measure his worth. To the extent he has failed to achieve these ego worth assets or has lost them his peace of mind will be impaired.

Rectitude in Old Age

Rectitudinous conduct tends to be at its Zenith in old age. The old age individual is concerned about the reckoning which the deity will make on his life, and whether he should be rewarded in the afterlife or suffer punishment. This propensity to shape conduct by a duality of good and bad arises from the experience in infancy of the extending and withholding of favor and approval of the infant by the parent upon whom the infant depends absolutely, combined with the infant's projected filial fear of parental retribution for the infant's own filial hostility.

If the old age individual has created lasting great works during his life, he may enjoy some comfort in contemplating his remembrance by generations to come if that was an important tension-reduction aim of creating the works. But many who are honored with immortality by later generations did not know in life that they would be so honored in death. Did Bach and Mozart know in life that they would be immortalized in death? Certainly Kafka did not. Other great achievers no doubt are motivated in part by the hope of immortality. Standing in the Central Cemetery in Vienna and surveying the graves of Beethoven, Schubert, Mozart[2], Cluck, Brahms, Strauss and Wolf clustered together, while looking about at other graves occupied by the relatively unknown, much more pretentious in the form of little temples and great

---

[2] The monument to Mozart does not mark his actual grave whose exact location is unknown.

obelisks with statues to themselves carved thereon, one can observe the contrast between those who aimed for immortality but not achieving it with those who achieved it without necessarily aiming for it.

It is the fear of approaching death that produces the ego tension which propels the individual to confess the wrongs he committed in life in the hope of reducing that tension. Deathbed confessions by criminals are not unknown. The individual approaching death may be prompted to write his memoir to leave behind his version of his life, "to set the record straight." If he is a public figure, his memoir will inform posterity of matters he could not speak about during his career.

Often the individual approaching death will want to make amends for behavior about which he experiences guilt. By doing "the right thing" before it is too late, he hopes to reduce the ego tension produced by fear of after death retribution. To this end he may seek forgiveness or distribute valuable possessions to those he believes he has wronged. Commonly deemed virtues of truthfulness, integrity, right conduct and charitableness often become ascendant in the behavior of the individual approaching death. Such behavior is aimed at reducing tension in the final struggle for equanimity.

Ego Surety in Old Age

The paradox of surety in old age is that the old age individual tends to believe that his knowledge of reality and how to deal with it is greater than ever before, but he also tends to believe that there is much he will never know. The great questions of human experience still remain unanswered. The expansion of knowledge through science pushes back the frontier of ignorance but discloses that a final understanding of reality is still nowhere in sight. Where the universe came from and what exists beyond it still puzzles the mind. The enduring questions of "why are we here?"; "where did we come from?"; "where are we going?" remain unanswered cliché's. The peace of sure knowledge remains elusive. The old age individual has the choice of dying in ignorance or surrendering himself to the doctrine of his religious faith and taking comfort therein.

Mastery in Old Age

Skills requiring physical prowess often fade in old age. It is the rare old age individual who will maintain a high level of mastery in physical skills requiring running, jumping, lifting, hurling and carrying heavy objects. But in mental skills, the old age individual may sustain a high level of mastery, although a facile memory and a quick wit may not be among them. Accumulated knowledge, a memory of the past as it relates to the present and analytical ability often permit the old age individual to retain mastery in intellectual functions requiring reflective thought and the working out of challenging intellectual problems. Certain areas of intellectual mastery tend to peak during young adulthood or early middle adulthood. Creativity in mathematics and physics are two areas in which this early peaking tends to occur. But in scientific research, scholarship, literature and the arts, old age is often not a barrier to mastery. In all things pertaining to mastery, continuing to be fit and active is a concomitant to achievement both physical and mental and tends to facilitate the pursuit of happiness.

Mastery over the skills of family life and social interaction and daily living, if it was attained during middle adulthood, will tend to continue into old age, barring severe physical and health impediments which may or may not have been conquered. Normatively, the old age individual, if he begot offspring, will preside over a family in which the children have left the residence of their upbringing, contributing to felicity in old age.

The old age individual craves or longs for family survival so that his descendants will remember him after he has departed, and the old age parent will tend to continue his nurturing ways to insure that his family survives him to morn and to remember him after he dies. This is a form of tension-reduction behavior of the old age individual contemplating the approach of his death for which a mastery of appropriate skills is requisite. These skills include patience and diplomacy in dealing with younger family members and with quarreling family members; the capacity to cultivate in others a knowledge of and respect for the extended family and to pass on the history of the family and its ancestors. Many impediments will make the tasks over which mastery is required exceedingly difficult. These include such impediments as poverty, divorce and distance, chronic illness and disability which separate and hamper the maintenance of interpersonal cathexes and thwarts the effort of the old age individual to achieve equanimity during the twilight of his life.

Curiosity in Old Age

Curiosity continues into old age but often with less urgency than during earlier stages of life. The old age individual tends to have acquired the knowledge appropriate for dealing with tension-producing stimuli of daily living, and to have come to terms with the great unanswered questions of human experience. The problems of daily living may become more difficult to solve, but the old age individual will likely have gained most of the knowledge he is capable of obtaining to deal with problems and may have to depend upon others to help him. As for the great questions of life, he will tend to yield to the teachings of religious authorities or content himself with dying in ignorance.

If he is not well educated he may continue to wonder about mundane things which attract his attention such as why toast is brown and the grass green and the sunset red, and regret not having gained the learning during his life which would supply him with answers to such questions. The educated person will recognize that all knowledge gained through study tends to beget additional questions which remain unanswered, that the frontier of knowledge no matter how far it is pushed forward still borders on a vast ocean of human ignorance about which human beings are left in awe and uncertainty.

Counter Manipulation Behavior in Old Age

Counter manipulation behavior continues into old age, usually in a more muted form than it was at earlier stages in the course of life. Counter-manipulation behavior tends to be self-injurious because it is designed to injure the parent who has identified with and introjected the child and thereby suffers tension increase any time the child is perceived to suffer. The counter manipulator's message to the parent is that by hurting himself he will hurt the parent whose manipulation of the child is resented by the child. Because counter manipulation behavior is self-injurious, it tends to take the form of self-inflicted harm.

The old age individual tends to seek strengthened cathexes to bonded-to others such as spouse, children and grandchildren and intimate friends. To the extent he has been unable to conquer the off-putting affects of counter-manipulation behavior vis-à-vis bonded-to others, his happiness will be impaired. But if in the wisdom and self-mastery of old age, he has overcome the negative impact of counter manipulation, he will be able to achieve pleasure in his relationship with significant persons in his life.

The Ego Ideal in Old Age

The ego ideal is a wished-for perception of the self which perfectly contains the means to deal with all tension producing stimuli which the ego perceives itself subject to in the present and in the future. The ego ideal is striven for but not attained. Reminders of its ego ideal short-fall functions as tension producing stimuli which the ego guides behavior to reduce. The ego will strive to reduce the tension by struggling to achieve the ego ideal, but will fall back upon ego mechanisms when it inevitably falls short. Fantasy is a frequently employed mechanism, as are denial and rationalization.

For the old age individual the requirements of the ego ideal include many of those which were present during earlier stages in the course of life but with new ones added which are singular to old age. As with middle age, the old age individual's ego ideal includes comeliness of person in face and stature: status among intimates, associates and in the community: achievement, power and resources, health and recognition; sexual prowess; success in life and pride in family; the good opinion of others and many other similar attributes.

But the old age individual is subject to impinging stimuli unique to his stage in life for which the ego ideal requires a capacity to deal with. This includes the means to deal with the tension-producing impingement of approaching death for which the ego ideal will contain a capacity to project oneself into the time after one's death. Good works to leave behind, grandchildren to keep one's memory alive, the capacity to erect monuments to oneself, wealth to leave behind charitable contributions in one's name, and other assets to negate the oblivion of death are tension reduction ego ideal wishes typical in old age.

Persona and Self-Image in Old Age

The persona reflects the ego ideal. It is the image the ego would present to the external world if it could achieve the ego ideal. The latter being unattainable, the persona is never achieved, but continually striven for. At moments when the ego believes that it has approximated the persona it strives for, the individual experiences a heady feeling. Examples would be the actor looking back upon a performance in which he believes he achieved excellence, or a scientist being honored for an acclaimed finding, or an author celebrated for a recently published work, or a craftsman being complemented for a product in which he believes that he achieved mastery; or an artist who has received a glowing critique for a work in which he believes he fully realized his aim. Many additional examples could be cited.

The persona that the old age individual strives to proffer is similar to that of the image projected by the individual throughout adolescence and adulthood, that he is still comely, admirable, accomplished, powerful, resourceful, socially popular, healthy, sexually appealing, celebrated and the like, but in addition he seeks to project the image of one who will be remembered after he is dead. For this he wants others to believe that his funeral, interment and his grave marker will be provided, or that he has provided for them, that he is capable of leaving assets behind which will be used to establish his presence after death in charitable works and endowments which will preserve his memory.

Ego Ontogenesis and the Course of Life

The human individual encounters many impediments placed in its way by the traumata of ego ontogenesis. To the extent and in the ways that the ego fails to traverse ego ontogenesis successfully, it will take on burdens which will weigh it down and impede the pursuit of its aims. Because each individual is unique and its passage through ego ontogenesis correspondingly unique, the burdens it takes on and their severity as impediments to its aims will be unique to that individual. But because the path of ego ontogenesis is composed of the same sorts of hurdles universally across the race of man, there will be displayed in the social context many similar sorts of impediments to an individual's aims which are manifested in societal structures aimed at defeating these impediments. Whether by formal or informal agreement, the members of a society will come together and organize themselves with the aim of promoting their common interest in the reduction of ego tension. Groups, organizations and institutions are formed and processes established aimed at dealing with tension producing impinging stimuli common to all flesh.

7

CAREERS

The career of the human individual is much more than an occupation from which a livelihood is gained but is a product of ego ontogenesis and the response of the ego to impinging stimuli from the surround in which the individual passes his life. Some careers are similar to each other, but for careers to be identical it would be necessary not only for egos to be identical but also for the surround of egos to be identical, which is unlikely and accounts for the unique nature of each human career. Identical twins come closest to having identical careers, but only if the array of impinging stimuli from their surround is identical are their careers likely to be identical.

The human career is the path through life which each human being takes, and the focus of this discussion is upon the role of ego ontogenesis upon the choice of and the unfolding of a career. The single most important element of ego ontogenesis in determining the path chosen by the ego to pursue during the course of life is the ego worth deficit and the ego's response to that deficit. The ego worth deficit begins with the trauma of weaning which subjects the ego to its first experience of absolute dependency upon an external agent.

Although prior to weaning the ego typically is exposed to various clues as to the state of dependency in which it exists such as the failure of tension produced by impinging stimuli to be extinguished at its command without delay, it is the onset of weaning which confirms its impotence. The infant ego reasons that if its dependence upon the external agent is so important, then the external agent is of supreme value to the infant ego. It reasons further that its cathexis to the external agent may be severed unexpectedly, and that it is in constant danger of being abandoned to a sea of tension producing impinging stimuli over which it is helpless.

It reasons further that if it were as valuable to the external agent as the external agent is to it, then the external agent would not sever the cathexis, and the infant ego would no longer experience the unpleasure produced by of fear of abandonment. From the moment at which this realization overspreads the infant ego, it thereafter aims to gain the admiration of the external agent as an indication of being valued by the external agent and therefore safe from the prospect of abandonment. The reasoning process for the infant is not like that in an adult but more an insight, often wrong, into the nature of its world and the way it works.

Every career in life is aimed at securing the approval and admiration of first the actual parent and later, after dependency has been transferred to parentified entities such as societal institutions and their functionaries in religion, education, employment and government, at securing the approval and admiration of parental surrogates. The ego of the infant and child learns what its parent approves and admires not only by being told specifically by the parent but also by assessing the parent's values and beliefs through observation. It then tends to adopt a great many of the parent's values and beliefs for itself, in part because it craves to know what to place value upon and what to believe about the bewildering surround in which it finds itself, and in part to curry favor with the parent upon whom its dependence at first is absolute. Later as it gains greater self-dependence capacity and learns itself to cope with the tension producing impinging stimuli which continually assails it, the ego of the infant and child comes to rely progressively less upon the parent and more upon itself and upon parentified entities.

The infant and child's perception of what the parent approves and admires expands and sharpens during the course of life from one stage of ego ontogenesis to the succeeding stage. During the primordial period, the infant and child learns that it is expected to feed itself and to control its bowel evacuations and bladder voiding, all accomplished with a degree of tidiness expected by the parent if the infant and child is to be rewarded with parental praise.

Ego Worth Deficit

Prior to experiencing the severation trauma of weaning, the infant ego had no sense of unworth. With the imposition of weaning, the infant discovers that the external agent upon which it relies absolutely is inconstant, that it may decathect the infant ego by depriving it of the breast or nursing bottle and concurrently the security of tension decrease which nursing brought. Rather suddenly the security is lost, and a tension producing deficit of worth is established based upon a parental decathexis which the infant ego reasons would not occur if the parent perceived the infant as having worth or value for the parent. Not possessing worth to the parent upon whom its dependence is absolute causes the infant ego to perceive itself as vulnerable to decathexis.

At first the infant ego struggles against the imposition of weaning in an effort to defeat the terror of decathexis but eventually yields to the requirement for sitting at the dining table and utilizing glass or cup, fork or spoon, bowl or plate and begins the journey toward eventually receiving praise for succeeding in using these utensils. With regard to toilet training, which follows hard upon weaning and imposes yet another unpleasurable experience of decathexis from the external agent of absolute dependence, it too is fought by the infant ego by means of sphincter control and untimely eliminations but is eventually yielded to and parental praise earned by acquiring and demonstrating the necessary toileting skills admired by the parent.[1]

It should be recognized that each infant and child's experience at being reared by its parent differs because parents differ and because a given parent tends to treat each of its children in some respects differently. Thus for each infant the weaning and toilet training experience is unique in ways which are singular to each child and are responded to differently by each child. These ways of responding tend to establish themselves in the child's unique reservoir of response practices to resurface anew during subsequent tension producing experiences to be utilized in the way they are deemed useful by the ego for reducing tension in the new context of impinging stimuli.

These response practices devolve through ego ontogenesis, being refashioned to suit later circumstances in the process of derivative relatedness transference devolution.[2] Each individual's response practices are unique and shape the individual's persona in a singular way, thereby helping to distinguish each individual from the next. As an example, consider the infant who responded to weaning by frequently spilling his food bowl in an angry tantrum and who continued this practice in a modified form during toilet training which consisted of "messing" his clothing by delaying bowel evacuation until he could no longer control his sphincter.

This practice later became refashioned into "messy" tantrums in response to parental demands for self dependence progress in putting away personal belonging such as toys in which he sometimes scattered his possessions about the room in angry protest or habitually left his possessions scattered about by consistently neglecting to put them away. By the time of the latency period a behavior pattern has become ingrained in the infant ego which this individual responds to the demands of authorities such as teachers by angry refusal with a disorderly treatment of the materials he is charged with looking after. He might scatter his clothes about rather than put them on, or messily mark the book he has been instructed by his teacher to read, or stuff his school materials into his locker rather than put them away in an orderly arrangement. This does not mean that he goes about his daily life in an angry

---

[1] Regarding toilet training following heard upon weaning, see **Ruth Monroe,** *Schools of Psychoanalytic Thought.* New York: The Dryden Press, Inc., 1955.

[2] See glossary for definition of derivative relatedness transference devolution.

tiff throwing things about, but that he responds to certain demands which he perceives as threatening, as the severation of weaning and toilet training appeared to him in infancy, by resorting again to the ancient response practices of angry frenzy.

During his latency period he begins to think about selecting a career for his future, which will take on sharper focus during adolescence. His proposed career choices may be fanciful, designed to deal with current forms of ego tension. He may think of becoming a cowboy, a fireman or an astronaught, rock star or circus performer, images which give him power and importance in fantasy. He will test these proposed careers by telling his parent and assess his parent's reaction and may find himself humored by the parent. Later in adolescence, the urgency to please his parent in his choice of career as the means to reduce his ego worth deficit as he tried to do during infancy and primordial childhood takes on more intensity. However, he must find a way to deal with the episodes of angry messiness that has become ingrained in his practices for dealing with threat from authorities, particularly decathexis threats which might deprive him of security as in cases of teachers or employers who might sanction him with academic expulsion or dismissal from employment for his angry behavior.

He will tend to search about among career options to select a career which will earn the admiration of his parent and avoid subjecting his parent and parentified entities to his disorderly wrath. For example, a female might select the career of homemaker because she has observed that her homemaking mother accords great respect to the career of homemaker and patently enjoys her own homemaking career. Taking up the career of homemaking, the female in this example gains maternal approval and admiration which unfortunately is compromised by her messy housekeeping practices which occur upon occasions when she experiences the threat of decathexis from her inconstant maternified husband who frequently indulges himself in philandering. The mother derives great satisfaction and accords great approval to her daughter for taking up the career of homemaking, but the mother is much displeased and disapproving when her daughter lapses into episodes of messy housekeeping. Messy housekeeping serves a dual purpose of enabling the ego to indulge in an infantile response pattern which also enables it to rebel against the parent in the service of individuating and establishing a separate and unique identity.

In a different example, the daughter might choose the career of lawyer because her parents intended that career for her brother with whom she experiences competitiveness and envy owing to the favoritism which she believes her parents bestow upon her male sibling. Knowing that her parents approve and admire the career of lawyer, she wants to arrogate that career for herself to attract the parental admiration which would go to her brother, as a means for her to reduce her ego worth deficit. But to her parents' dismay their daughter often allows her personal life to decline into a disorderly state, although she functions well in her legal practice. Marital problems, neglectful parenting, conflict with government over her income tax returns bring about a "messy" life which her mother disapproves. Her "messy" personal affairs allows her to continue to indulge herself in an infantile response pattern to filial decathexis fears and simultaneously to rebel as a means of sustaining her individuation against her parents' values of which one is the maintenance of an orderly life.

During the years of adolescence and young adulthood, the ego guides behavior to search for and establish a career in life that commonly includes founding a family of her own, obtaining a livelihood, begetting and rearing children, establishing a place in society and becoming a responsible citizen. To accomplish these aims, the individual must find and attract a mate, and for this purpose, being able to extract a livelihood from the economy is essential for the male adolescent and young adult. For the female, it is necessary that she either be able to earn her livelihood or attract a male mate who will provide a livelihood for her and for the children she will bear.

A critical aspect of a career is the choosing of it and preparing to carry it out. These steps tend to be taken up seriously first in adolescence in undertaking the education or training to perform the tasks of the career chosen. All careers require preparation in greater or less degree except perhaps that of indolent idler, and the adolescent finds himself under pressure to dedicate energy and purpose to the task of gaining the knowledge and skills required by the career he chooses.

The first requirement is the actual choosing of a career to pursue. The individual may passively await the tension producing demands which come his way and then respond to them with ego guided tension reducing strategies which in effect willy-nilly become his career, or he may anticipate and plan for a particular career path. Whether career choices are made largely in response to the demands of daily life or whether they are made through a planning process in which the ego looks to the future attempting to anticipate events which will affect him and to make career decisions in advance of their arrival, the career choices he will follow are in large measure the product of the ego's aim to reduce the tension of the ego worth deficit.

In choosing a career path, the adolescent will consider several sources of impinging stimuli with which he must deal regardless of the innate physical and intellectual capabilities which the adolescent ego perceives itself to possess. Achieving parental approval for the purpose of reducing the ego tension of the worth deficit is the chief determining concern of the ego. Regardless of what career path the adolescent chooses, whether in the forefront or in the periphery of his thinking the admiration or at least the approval of the parent is critical. Later, the young adult may place gaining the approval of parentified entities as equally or even more important than that of gaining the approval of the actual parent which was of principal importance earlier during adolescence.

The Career Choice Process

Rapidly for some, but more slowly for others, the adolescent comes to accept the importunity imposed upon him by the society in which he lives that he must choose a career, a path in life which commonly includes obtaining a livelihood, attracting a mate, begetting children and establishing a family for which he must provide and rear children to adulthood. The most urgent of these requirements as the adolescent looks to his future is finding the means to obtain a livelihood. In choosing a career, the adolescent has the example of the adults who have gone before him.

In primitive societies in which the period of adolescence may be extremely brief if it exists at all, the traditions of his culture may afford the adolescent little choice but to follow the dictates of the culture in which he lives. In traditional agrarian societies, career choices may be greater than in primitive societies, but not nearly so great as in modern industrialized societies. In the latter societies, the variety and range of career choices for obtaining a livelihood tend to be immense and may appear bewildering to the adolescent looking toward his future.

Early in adolescence, the ego tends to be concerned with the demands of reproductive urges which beset the individual as a concomitant of puberty. The social life now includes members of the opposite sex, and interest in members of the opposite sex tends to overwhelm so that attention given to career choice is minimal but when considered tends to be incorporated into social challenges of attracting members of the opposite sex to reduce the ego tension produced by the impinging stimuli of reproductive hormones.

To be attractive to females, the adolescent male perceives that he must present an image that he is someone who one day will earn a livelihood worthy of admiration. Consequently, he tends to consider and to indicate to his peers of both sexes a career choice, or a range of career choices, in which he is interested and that lend him a persona which he hopes will favorably impress females. As he becomes acquainted with the values of society, he will strive to incorporate those values into his career choice so that he will not only be attractive to females but also will be able to set himself upon the path to social status which he observes manifested in the careers and material possessions of adults. The female adolescent will look forward to a career in which she must attract a suitable male mate to provide for her and the children she will bear. In providing for her and her children and to reduce the tension of her ego worth deficit, she must attract a male mate who has the capacity to provide her with social status as well as a livelihood. The greater her attractiveness as a potential female mate, the greater her success is likely to be in attracting the male mate who will do best for her economically and socially. Consequently, a critical element in the career of the adolescent female is the development of attractiveness to the male peers from among whose numbers she will acquire a mate.

In the current milieu in Western industrialized societies, a portion of the female population strives toward careers in occupations formerly thought appropriate only for males. These female adolescents in their pursuit of careers must not only cultivate attractiveness to males but also learn skills and knowledge critical to succeeding in male careers. During early adolescence, both males and females tend to experience greater urgency in dealing with the tension generated by the reproductive hormones than they do in planning a career for their adult lives, which gradually assumes a greater proportion of their concerns as they move toward young adulthood.

Parental Influence upon Adolescent Career Choice

Strong Parental Influence

Parental influence upon adolescent career choice tends to range along a continuum between strong influence at one end to weak influence at the other. On balance, the stronger the parental influence the greater tends to be the effect of parental influence upon adolescent career choice, and conversely the weaker the parental influence the weaker tends to be the effect of parental influence upon adolescent career choice. While there are exceptions, these tendencies are generally likely to prevail in the adolescent career choice process.

Consider first the effect of strong parental influence upon adolescent career choice which may occur because the parent invests a great deal of dependence upon the child as a vicarious source of ego worth assets for the parent through identification with the child, enabling the parent to bask in the reflected light of the child. In such cases, the parent may exert pressure upon the child to adopt a career which the parent had longed to have for himself to reduce his own ego worth deficit. Parental pressure may take the form of the alternate extending and withholding of parental approval and admiration as the child considers other careers than the career choice proffered by the parent.

The parent may have reared an excessively dependent child who lacks sufficient self-dependence capabilities to individuate fully from the parent and to go his own way untrammeled by parental imperatives. The parent may be eager to have the child take up the parent's own career as a means to extend the parent's worth and presence into posterity, the child becoming a monument to the parent's sojourn upon earth. Or the parent may have cultivated in the child so strong a parental-filial bond that their shared values lead them to the same conclusion as to the career path most appropriate for the adolescent.

Or the child may simply follow the example of the parent by adopting the same career as the parent as in the case of the son who follows his father into the father's trade, business or profession or the daughter of a homemaker who follows her mother's example and chooses the career of homemaker. The parent may strive through his child to compensate for his own perceived shortcomings by pressuring his child by means of the alternate extending and withholding of admiration and approval into choosing a career which the parent would have chosen for himself had it not been for some obstacle in the parent's life.

The strength of the pressure placed upon the adolescent and young adult by the parent in choosing a career will vary depending upon the extent to which the parent chances to exploit his child for the purpose of reducing the tension of his own ego worth deficit. The parent may choose to reduce the tension of his own ego worth deficit in other ways than through his child, or the child may rebel against the parental pressure placed upon him to choose a career imposed by the parent, in which case the parent's influence becomes negative and tends to fail.

The Adolescent's Response
to Strong Parental Influence

In most cases, the adolescent responds to parental influence by accepting it in whole or in part as he makes his career choice, and is often powerfully shaped by it. But in cases in which the adolescent's individuation aims become entangled with career choice issues under pressure from strong parental influence, special results tend to occur which intermix individuation with filial rebellion. Although adolescent filial rebellion in the cause of individuation is commonplace, it tends to be less so in the matter of choosing a career which is an intimidating undertaking often causing the adolescent to seek parental counsel and support.

More often the adolescent tends instead to rebel in other areas of filial-parental interaction which are less formidable than career choice. Adolescent rebellion often occurs in such areas of life as choosing clothing fashions, leisure activities, music and entertainment which are offensive to the parent but otherwise less threatening to the parent's ability to continue to identify with and to introject his child and to maintain the filial-parental cathexis. The latter may be stressful for the parent but tends to be more annoying than critical to the filial-parental cathexis. Areas of filial rebellion which critically threaten the filial-parental cathexis involve such parental values as his offspring's choice of religion, choice of political party identification, choice of marital partner and particularly choice of career.

The parent experiences tension and unpleasure when his adolescent child takes up ways offensive to the parent and particularly when the child displays a liking for a career path the parent opposes. Adolescent individuation involves the establishment by the adolescent of an identity separate from that of the parent and unique in the world for which the adolescent is impelled to distinguish himself from the parent in some noticeable way, and the choice of a career different from the parent's wishes may be the way chosen.

Adolescent individuation also becomes enmeshed with a resurgence of the Oedipus conflict impelled by the onset of puberty as a consequence of which the child rather suddenly gains much greater size, physical strength and intellectual capability, greatly reducing filial inferiority and making filial competition with the parent much more realistic. Having drawn much closer to the parent in size and capacity, the adolescent becomes more competitive with the parent and less likely to accept out of hand the dictum of the parent as the child had done during latency. The suppression of filial competition and hostility with and toward the same sex parent lessens, and overt manifestations of filial competition and hostility become more evident.

Choosing a career inimical to the preferences of the parent as a principal means to individuate and to exercise Oedipal hostility tends to be adventitious. It might occur at a time when parental pressure upon the adolescent to choose a particular career important to the parent is juxtaposed with an episode of filial hostility and adolescent search for identity. To avoid precipitating parental decathexis from the child, which would happen if the parent could no longer identify with and introject his child, the child will tend to search for and find a means to compensate the parent for rejecting the parent's career preference for the child.

For example, the child may reject the career choice of lawyer imposed by the parent in order to choose a career in social work, but to compensate the parent and forestall parental decathexis of the child, the latter might take up the hobby of, say, bird watching intensely admired and indulged in by the parent. Consequently, the child in this example frequently goes upon bird watching expeditions with the father, which greatly pleases the father, but continues to rebuff all entreaties by the father to train for a career as a lawyer. By this stratagem, the adolescent preserves the parental cathexis and the continued ego tension reducing benefit of parental approval and admiration, even if it is attenuated by his rebellious career choice.

Ironically, the adolescent or young adult who becomes successful in a career opposed by the parent finds his success to be bitter sweet. In such cases, the ego worth tension reduction aimed for by the adolescent and young adult tends to be lacking because of the absence of or attenuation of parental admiration and approval. But the young adult may earn the praise and approval of parental surrogates such as companions, peers and his employer which affords him at least a modicum of ego worth gratification.

This phenomenon is commonplace in individuals who struggle against parental dominance, and who lead otherwise successful lives which never quite earn the approval of the parent and the self-esteem wished for by the individual. In the example above, the individual may become a superlative social worker but be denied the pleasure of enjoying the ego worth which is never accorded to him by the parent who wanted him to become a lawyer.

Numerous other issues in which the child rebels against parental preferences lead to the same loss of self-esteem. Selecting an academic institution to attend disapproved by the parent, choosing a marital partner opposed by the parent, rearing children in ways negatively criticized by one's parent, managing or mismanaging one's finances against parental advice are among the myriad examples which could be adduced to illustrate the phenomenon of the disesteem accorded the individual who takes up ways disapproved or not admired by his parent.

Strong parental influence may occur inadvertently and greatly affect the adolescent's career choice and ego worth. The parent may himself suffer low ego worth and consequently hold diminished ambition for the child with which he is identified. The parent who expects little of his child because he the parent expects little of himself may contaminate his child with the same low expectation to which the child responds by curtailing his ambition and choosing a career requiring only modest accomplishments. Or the parent may greatly favor one of his children, conveying a high expectation for that child, while conveying a low expectation for the child's sibling who is less favored by the parent. The impact of parental expectations communicated to the child extensively shapes the level of ambition adopted by the child and the degree of challenge presented by the career the child chooses for his path in life.

Weak Parental Influence

Consider the parent whose influence is weak which might be caused by the parent's preoccupation with other concerns of life such as earning a livelihood under severe economic disadvantage. The child of such a parent tends to move through adolescence acquiring a belief that earning a livelihood is extremely difficult and that one must take up any occupation which he can find which will reward him financially. The child may leave school before receiving a diploma, or graduate having attained little more than modest learning. He may take up with the girl or boy next door or down the street and eventually marry her or him or another girl or boy in similar circumstances after a series of liaisons.

The financially struggling parent, preoccupied with the challenge of economic survival, may take notice of his adolescent or young adult child only after the child has chose his future marital partner. The parent may approve or disapprove, but the parent's preferences will make little difference because the child's dependency upon the parent may be weak. Already in adolescence the child accepts the reality that he must make his own way with little help from his parent and is not disposed to attend very strongly to the parent's preferences.

The child may adopt the parent's political party identification without giving much thought to it because his circumstances in life are so similar to those of his parent that the parent's political party serves the interest of the child as well as it does the parent. The parent's religious views tend to have become known to the child and accepted by him during the latency period and will tend to be taken up unchallenged by the adolescent. The parent's path through life by example becomes willy-nilly the path followed by the adolescent and young adult child of the parent, in the course of time having similar employment, similar marital partner, similar leisure activities, the same political and religious preferences and the same social class identification.

*The Enduring Force of Parent-
ally Influenced Career Choice*

The power of the parent in influencing career choice is so great that the child is burdened with it throughout the remaining course of life and is virtually a prisoner of the choice he has made which he is all but unable to abandoned no matter how severely it is affecting his life in negative ways. Once the career is adopted it is almost impossible to change it or abandoned it no matter how painful it is. The degree of influence with which the parent's career choice determines the child's path in life is strongly dependent upon the degree of force which the parent exerts upon the child in the matter of career choice. If the pressure exerted by the parent through the alternate extending and withholding of admiration and approval was weak, the child as an adult may be able to escape a career which subjects him to great and persistent tension-increase. If the parental pressure was strong, the child may find escape all but impossible. Or if the child merely divined what pleases the parent without the parent actually voicing his view or pressuring the child, the child will tend nevertheless to adopt the divined parental view and submit to it with such profound acceptance that once upon that path in life, determined deviation from it is all but impossible. It often happens that the child is diverted from his career path by circumstances beyond his control, but the aim of gaining parental approval and admiration tends to be followed to the extent possible, nevertheless. It is commonplace for the adult to believe the illusion that the path in life he follows was freely chosen by him to serve his own purposes and not chosen to earn the admiration and approval of his parent.

It is not uncommon for an individual who strongly dislikes his occupation and the path in life he has chosen to appear unable to escape the circumstances of his life for lack of the will to walk away from the path he has been following. Such an individual may have chosen the path he has taken to please his parent in the search for ego worth and narcissistic gratification. The individual feels locked into his painful path. There are numerous barriers he finds impeding his wish to escape. He cannot "afford" to take a reduction in pay by changing jobs or by leaving a marginally profitable business. Or it would be too painful to uproot himself from the place he has made for himself in the community in order to pursue other opportunities or to give up the many friends he has acquired by moving away.

These impediments, being not without merit, help to keep him in place. Moving on is painful, producing more ego tension than staying in place and suffering less ego tension produced by the unhappy path in life which he has chosen. To abandon the path in life he has chosen in order to please his parent and earn the parent's admiration and approval would be to relinquish the ego worth he has acquired from following the path chosen. The longer one remains upon such a path, the greater tends to become the individual's investment in it and the potential loss which would occur if the path were abandoned. This condition in life tends to be widespread in mass societies and to range in severity from mild to overwhelming.

It is the rare individual in such circumstances who understands why he is there or remembers how she came to be there. He knows only that he feels awful, trapped and impeded at every turn in trying to escape. Typically, individuals do not analyze the ego ontogenic reasons for their behavior nor the history of their ego ontogenetic life, and thus do not know how they got to where they are except by projecting the causes of their failures upon others, or upon the unfair circumstances of their lives, while they tend to attribute those parts of their lives in which they enjoyed some success upon their acumen and superior capabilities.

Conflicting Career Choices

Particularly poignant is the individual who is trapped between two conflicting career choices, which may occur when he attempts to please both himself and his parent or when he attempts to please both parents who are not in agreement themselves as to the career the child should follow. Consider the example of the individual whose mother abandoned a career as a performer in order to marry, and whose father is bent upon his son eventually taking over management of the father's business organization. To please the mother, the son longs for a career in theater, but to please his father he must display the business capabilities he would need if he were one day to take over his father's business. Where does the career path lie which will facilitate the pursuit of the ego worth the son craves?

He finds himself caught between two antithetical career paths and is torn between becoming an actor or becoming a businessman. He cannot gain the full approval and admiration of his father by pursuing acting, and he cannot gain the full approval and admiration of his mother by abandoning acting and sticking to business. The tendency is for the individual caught in this sort of circumstance to pursue both careers simultaneously and to do well in neither of them. He may drift into a compromise posture by becoming, say, an arts manager, thus combining a career in theater with one which involves management. He may experience the pain of being neither an actor nor a businessman and frustrated in his attempt to reduce the tension of his ego worth deficit.

The two-career individual is a widely observed phenomenon in human experience. Many examples can be offered: the physician who plays in a community orchestra, having pleased his father rather than his mother by choosing the career of medicine over music; the business man who pursues a hobby of wood working in his hobby shop, having abandoned a career in crafts with which his mother occupies herself to pursue a career in business as his father wanted; or the lawyer who is a silent partner in an antiques shop who abandoned a career in art history admired by his mother to become the lawyer his father wanted. The list of examples of individuals divided between two careers, excelling in neither, which could be cited is extensive.

8

THE POWER OF PRAISE

Because the pursuit of ego worth to reduce the tension of the ongoing ego worth deficit is virtually universal in the race of man, the ubiquitous deficit of worth invites the exploiter of the deficit in others to employ the instrument of praise in order to control others. It is commonplace among human beings that they all crave to receive praise from others. The use of praise to control others is widespread in human society, and those who exploit others by lavishing praise upon them are themselves equally susceptible to being controlled by the power of praise exerted upon them by others.

The origin of the power of praise is found in ego ontogenesis at the creation of the ego worth deficit in which the child ego comes to seek parental approval and admiration as the means to be worthy of parental admiration and affection, which is the basis of infantile security. The human propensity to parentify others extends the desire for praise, which is verification of one's worth, to innumerable external objects. It is important to note, however, that praise from someone not parentified tends to have but little ego tension reduction effect for the recipient of the praise. For example, the concert violinist may not experience reduction of the ego worth deficit tension in response to praise from an individual whose musical predilections normally lie with popular music. Such an individual will likely not be parentified by the accomplished artist of esoteric music because he is viewed as lacking in musical authority. Lacking the authority necessary to elicit parentification, the praise offered is discounted and deemed nearly valueless as a reducer of ego worth deficit tension.

The pursuit of praise is the pursuit of ego worth deficit tension reduction and is a universal condition of human experience. No one can live comfortably in the absence of praise or being able to regard himself as praiseworthy. The longer the individual experiences a lack of praise from parentified others the greater becomes the tension of the ego worth deficit, which may be manifested in anxiety and depression. Such an individual tends to seek accomplishments and assets which he believes are valued in the society in which he lives as a substitute for the lack of the praise of others.

Such an individual is David Reisman's "inner directed man" who does not look to others for admiration and approval, having established himself as his own source of admiration because of his demonstrated competence and power.[1] He tends to eschew praise from others, asserting self-reliance and the absence of a need to receive encomium from others. However, this individual denies and suppresses his want of praise from others but nevertheless is susceptible to praise urged upon him, which he fears might vitiate his self-dependence if he should allow himself to descend into dependency upon the praise of others. Reisman's "other directed man" is dependent upon the approval of others for his validation and for the reduction of ego worth deficit tension.

Praise comes in many forms and often in subtle ways. Merely being recognized in a public place or at a large social gathering by someone not known to one constitutes a form of praise because it is experienced as an indication of one's importance to be recognized by name by someone of lesser status. But to be addressed respectfully by name by someone of greater status is even more gratifying. Politicians know this, and they rely upon it heavily in electioneering and campaign fundraising. To address a potential voter or campaign contributor by name is received by the voter or contributor as flattering and reduces the deficits of both ego worth and of narcissism. Addressing their clientele by name is a practice heavily indulged in by innkeepers, restaurant hosts, salespersons, consultants and a great many others who wish to ingratiate themselves with their customers and inveigle them into purchasing products or services in pursuit of more flattery and validation.

Ego Worth Assets

Praise tends to be bestowed upon those who possess ego worth assets, and those who seek praise tend to pursue the acquisition of ego worth assets, which is virtually a universal activity of human beings. The value of an ego worth asset is derived from its perceived capacity to reduce ego tension for anyone who possesses it. There is a hierarchy of ego worth assets and a hierarchy of ego tension producing stimuli. The greater the tension produced by a source of stimuli, the greater the value of the ego worth asset which can reduce tension produced by that source of tension producing stimuli. There is not only a hierarchy of sources of tension producing stimuli but also a correlative hierarchy of ego worth assets determined by the perceived capacity of the asset to defeat sources of tension producing stimuli.

---

[1] **Riessman, David; Glazer, Nathan; and Reuel, Denney.** *The Lonely Crowd: A Study of the Changing American Character.* Garden City, New York: Doubleday Anchor Books, 1953.

A hierarchy of sources of tension producing stimuli derived from the relative severity of the source will include from the severest to the least severe the deficits of narcissism, power, worth; the lack of basic capacities such as skills, abilities and knowledge; the lack of attractiveness assets such as comeliness of face and figure, lack of physical strength and intelligence; inadequate faculties of locomotion, manipulation and coordination, and inadequate senses of hearing, seeing and feeling; the lack of material possessions such as money, a residence, clothing and a conveyance; and the lack of social status, prestige and leisure time. The foregoing deficits and inadequacies are the major sources of impinging stimuli affecting ego worth and narcissistic gratification for human beings.

Instruments of power to defeat the sources of tension producing stimuli also fit into a hierarchy with the higher in the hierarchy of a source of a tension producing stimuli which the instrument of power can deal, the higher in the hierarchy of ego worth assets the instrument of power occupies, and the more important is the ego worth asset, the greater is the capacity of the ego worth asset to reduce the tension produced by the ego worth deficit.

To have a house or apartment to live in is a more powerful reducer of ego worth deficit tension than, say, having a new pair of shoes, although having a new pair of shoes is a reducer of ego worth deficit tension which would be provoked by having no shoes at all. To have a palatial house or apartment of great size and embellishment is normatively a greater reducer of ego worth deficit tension than having a small and unpretentious house or apartment. House and shoes are ego worth assets because possessing them reduces ego worth deficit tension, and possession of a house is higher in the hierarchy of ego worth assets than possessing a pair of shoes because not having a place to live is a much greater ego worth tension producer than not having a pair of new shoes, although not having a pair of shoes at all in a cold climate would produce substantial ego worth deficit tension.

At a given time, it is the ego worth asset which one lacks, even if he had all of the others, which is the most urgent producer of ego tension and commands the tension reducing effort of the ego. Having a large and embellished house but no source of narcissistic gratification will tend to elevate the lack of narcissistic gratification to a position of precedence over concerns about having a house because the lack of narcissistic gratification is a source of tension producing stimuli while having a house is not. But if the house were threatened or lost it would vie with lack of narcissistic gratification as a source of tension producing stimuli.

Possessing ego worth assets tends to elicit the admiration, and sometimes the envy of others, as well as earning the praise of others either tacit or expressed. The possession of ego worth assets tends to substitute for manifest praise expressed by others because their possessor knows that ego worth assets are universally recognized as praiseworthy. They are like badges of importance with which their owner establishes his worthiness as well as the level in the social hierarchy which he occupies. They are reducers of ego worth deficit tension, which always returns eventually after it has abated because of the acquisition or possession of an ego worth asset.

The ego worth deficit continues throughout the course of life, impelling the ego repeatedly to guide behavior to reduce ego worth deficit tension because the tension of the deficit always returns after it has been reduced. Tension reducers are mere palliatives giving temporary relief at best because the deficits of narcissism, power and worth are permanent and can only be relieved but never eliminated. Thus, the human ego continually guides behavior to seek narcissistic gratification, power, and worth assets. In a mass-market economy, this human propensity produces an unending struggle by populations to seek expressions of affection from others, to strive for power particularly through wealth, and to purchase and acquire in the marketplace ego worth assets, particularly in the form of impressive residences, fashionable clothing, automobiles, electronic products and a great host of consumer goods which accords status to their possessors. This propensity of human beings, engendered by ego ontogenesis, to acquire ego worth assets in the marketplace tends to be the principal impulse to economic activity in mass market economies, which drives these economies beyond merely supplying to potential consumers the necessities of shelter, nourishment, clothing, health, safety and the protection of their persons and property.

Fusion of the Deficits of Worth and Narcissism

The aim of much human behavior is to reduce the ego tension of both the ego worth deficit and the narcissism deficit by means of the same activity. For example, when the performer takes his curtain call and hears the applause of an appreciative audience, which he has parentified, he may believe that he has not only earned the praise of the audience, thereby reducing the ego worth deficit because of his acting achievement, but also has attracted the affection of the audience, thereby reducing the narcissism deficit as well.

The fusion of the deficits of worth and narcissism is a consequence of ego ontogenesis. The aim of the infant ego in extending primary narcissism to the parent is to bind the parent to the infant with bonds of affection so that the parent's love of self is extended to the parent's love of the infant. The infant ego's pursuit of worth shares the same aim as the infant ego's pursuit of narcissistic gratification. Behavior which elicits the admiration and approval of the parent may also elicit parental affection, reducing the tension of both the deficits of narcissism and worth by the same activity.

The seeking after praise and affection is a continuous activity in human behavior. The small child just entering latency looks to his parent for praise and affection when he pedals his tricycle with a burst of speed past his mother looking up at her as if to say "Look at me. See how good I am, riding my tricycle so fast!" Ironically, while he pleads for maternal praise and affection, his mother may become alarmed by his recklessness and fearful for his safety scold him, to his puzzlement.

The little girl at the kitchen range playing with a frying pan from which the flames of a grease fire are shooting upwards, turning toward her father just entering the room calling out expectantly, "Look, Daddy, I'm cooking your breakfast." Expecting praise and affection from her father, the little girl is startled by her father's alarm and anger. In the learning process required by maturation, the child learns what pleases the parent distinguished from what alarms the parent. Learning to perform toileting on his own, to dress himself without assistance and to put his play things away without prompting are among behaviors which the early latency child comes to recognize will often elicit affection and praise from his parent.

The older latency child learns that such behaviors as doing well in school, putting away his belongings and performing minor household chores will elicit parental praise and affection. But these self-dependence chores tend to yield only a net tension reduction because performing them is tension producing in itself. The child tends to seek other ways to please his parent which are entirely tension reducing such as displaying skill when playing at games, bragging about accomplishments at play and surpassing play peers at some skill in the presence of the parent. The child is interested in independence more than in self-dependence.

At each stage in the course of life during the ontogenesis of the ego, the individual learns which behaviors elicit praise and affection and which provoke ire and rebuke from the parent. The adolescent learns that displaying social skills, achieving high marks at school, looking after his belongings, appearing presentable in attire and grooming, evincing ambition at becoming self-dependent, at choosing a career and at being capable of attracting a suitable mate all evoke praise and manifest affection from the parent. But there are many behaviors which reduce ego tension for the adolescent which are not praised by the parent or by parental surrogates. These are behaviors which may earn the admiration and approval of the individual's peer society, which he parentifies, without necessarily earning the admiration and approval of the actual parent.

Each stage of ego ontogenesis presents new challenges to the individual which are tension producing, impelling the ego to guide behavior to reduce the tension. For the adolescent, individuating from the parent is such a challenge and requires the child to establish his own identity separate from that of the parent and unique in the world, to extricate himself from parental dominance impelled by his growing parity of power with the parent and to deal with old issues reactivated by the Oedipus conflict which surfaces anew at the onset of puberty.[2]

While the adolescent is seeking to establish a new identity and to move out of the shadow of the parent, he is also struggling with the Oedipus conflict, partly reemerging from its formerly fully suppressed state. While the Oedipus conflict tends not to become as open and flagrant as it was during primordial life, it nevertheless rises near enough to the surface of awareness that the adolescent must make great effort to sustain its suppression. Ego mechanisms are resorted to, particularly rationalization, projection and displacement. By identifying external objects to parentify, the adolescent is able to abate the intensity of the filial hostility prompted by the resurgent Oedipus conflict by displacing it upon parentified external objects. As a consequence, the adolescent may display great hostility toward, say, a teacher or public figure such as a government official disliked by the parent, and by this means direct filial hostility avoiding the risk of filial-parental decathexis to a parental surrogate and away from the parent. Filial hostility may still be visited upon the parent but its intensity kept sufficiently in check so as not to exceed tolerable proportions which would sever the filial-parental cathexis. The adolescent will tend to rationalize his filial hostility as justified when in actuality he has transferred hostility to his parent in reaction to some grievance in his life such as being treated unfairly by play peers.

The adolescent will seek and discover values held by the parent for the purpose of rejecting them as a means to establish his separate identity so that he is not simply the child of his parent but is a separate member of society in his own right. He will survey the array of values which he believes that his parent embraces, and select certain of them to reject and the rest to continue to retain. Salient values for this purpose include those of choice of religion, choice of political party identification, choice of social class identification, choice of social friends, career choice and myriad others. He tends to establish a balance of retained parental values over rejected parental values in order to promote his separate identity without provoking the parent to decathect a child he could no longer identify with and introject. It is a phenomenon of mass societies that a proportion of offspring become alienated or estranged from their parents and are disowned or forsaken by their procreators.

The adolescent's inescapable pursuit of a separate identity inevitably brings him into conflict with his parent, which places him at risk of undermining the parent's capacity to admire and approve the child. An adolescent child who strikes off in life in a direction disapproved by his parent may succeed spectacularly in his career but receive only perfunctory approval and admiration for his accomplishments by his parent. The mother who dreamed of her son becoming a minister as her father had been but who became a successful professional football player instead may never be able to

---

[2] See **Blos**, loc cit.

reward her son with more than perfunctory displays of approval and admiration for his achievement, leaving the son to experience a want of worth and narcissistic gratification. The son may look to parentified others such as his spouse and progeny[3] and his coterie of social acquaintances for the admiration and approval not coming from his parent to reduce the tension of the ego deficits of narcissism and worth.

Parentified Objects as Sources of Praise and Affection

While individuation tends to be most dramatic in adolescence, the drive of the child to seek independence of the parent begins when the child first perceives himself as dependent upon a controlling parent. This phenomenon occurs first during primordial life but can be detected in the behavior of latency age children who persist in ranging away from an area designated by the parent as circumscribing the limits to which the child is permitted to wander. In early latency, this area may extend to the boundaries of the family garden, but later may extend to the neighborhood and to the playground. As the child ranges farther and encounters a widening array of individuals such as other children, teachers, policemen, clergy and shopkeepers, the child begins to parentify persons external to the family. These figures are perceived to possess authority because they appear powerful and often instruct the child, and because they are in some degree related to as parental surrogates, the child often seeks praise, approval and a measure of affection from them or would like to be perceived by them as worthy of praise, approval and affection.

The parentification of others and relating to them as sources of praise, approval and affection expands exponentially as the individual journeys through the course of life. During latency, teachers and older siblings and play peers are commonly parentified, and the child seeks to earn their praise, approval and affection. During adolescence, the child expands his perception of parentified entities to include male and female friends and intimates, leaders in his peer society and prominent sports figures and to seek their approval, praise and affection. In young adulthood when the individual has found a mate and established a family, his spouse may become the primary parentified object in his life, rivaled only by his employer, or his customers if he is in business, and persons in authority such as public officials.

As a university student, as an apprentice or as a factory worker, the adolescent and young adult will tend to parentify his professor, his mentor or foreman and to look for praise and approval for his performance at school or work and for narcissistic gratification by pleasing his superiors. He will

---

[3] Strangely, perhaps, a parent may parentify his own child, having seen character traits in his child which remind him of his parent.

seek to earn their praise and affection by such behaviors as bestowing presents upon them, presenting compliments to them, seeking their company, conspicuously complying with their wishes, emulating their manner, displaying his acceptance of their values, all to earn their praise and affection. In manner and in dress, in leisure pursuits and social activities, the individual will seek to please his mentor in a variety of ways.

The same applies to his social peers and colleagues, whom he parentifies and looks to for praise and affection. He will tend to show his desire for acceptance and camaraderie in various ways including adopting their argot, their life style, their fashions and customs. These practices extend far beyond young adulthood and into old age. The need for praise and affection from parentified others continues throughout the course of life, and one submits himself in varying degree to the control of others to gain their praise and affection.

From the time of young adulthood through old age, the individual pursues praise and affection in myriad ways, from family members, employers, supervisors, colleagues, social friends, and innumerable others whose paths he crosses in the course of life. Ego worth assets, which he seeks to earn the praise and affection of others, include a prestigious occupation, items of conspicuous consumption purchased in the marketplace, achievements in education, the arts, sports and career. He looks after his appearance with the aim of presenting as comely a physical façade as possible, affects as charming a social posture as possible, acquires goods and chattels which are as impressive as he can afford and pursues as trendy a life style as he can aspire to. These ego-guided behaviors are aimed at achieving a fusion of ego worth and narcissistic gratification by commanding both praise and affection.

The Use of Praise to Control Others

Praise comes in many forms such as flattery, expressed compliments, admiring glances, smiles of warmth, obsequious deference, the bestowal of unsolicited gifts and awards—a complete list would be immense in length. The giving and receiving of formal praise is a societal function huge in its extent. The awarding of honorary academic degrees, ceremonial promotions in fraternal and social organizations, the awarding of merit badges, the awarding of plaques by civic organizations to worthy citizens, citations given to policemen and firefighters for conspicuous performance in the line of duty, admissions to honorary academic fraternities, presentations of keys to the city, parades honoring war heroes and life time achievement honors given to performers in the arts are among the many examples which can be cited. Human beings crave praise and are ever ready to bestow it upon others both to enjoy the experience vicariously as well as to use it as a technique for controlling others. Many seek praise with as much avidity as others seek wealth.

Persons charged with the care of children such as parents, teachers and scoutmasters heap praise upon those children who behave themselves, that is who accede to the control of supervising adults. Praise is one moiety of the praise and punishment duality which is the common means employed by human beings to control those who would behave aberrantly. The use of praise and punishment, approval and disapproval, reward and penalty, extending and withholding affection and approval is sometimes castigated by some child psychologists as a means to control children, but is commonly relied upon by parents in the rearing of children and by societal institutions for the control of society.

It is a reality of human experience that one uses praise to control others and that one is himself controlled by praise or by tokens of praise. Walks of life which require exemplary behavior by their very nature serve to reward their pursuer with the esteem which formal praise would bestow. The minister, the teacher of children, the judge in court are examples of walks of life whose pursuers experience ego worth merely because they occupy their walk of life. But their behavior must be exemplary, and if it fails to be exemplary such individuals may experience the wrath of a society which feels betrayed. The phenomenon of praise and approval and reward and punishment has its origins in the ontogenesis of the human ego and has a strong determining effect upon the behavior of individuals and the institutions of society.

9

MASTERY

The impulse to mastery is innate and is powered by the will, which drives toward ego tension reduction by whatever means are at hand. The capacities inherent in the human organism become known to the ego, and the impulse to mastery assures that they will be employed in the reduction of tension and be developed to serve the ego's aim of reducing tension. As the ego encounters impinging stimuli, it brings to bear whatever capacity it perceives itself to possess able to assist it in reducing tension in the given situation. This has the effect of expanding the use of capacities by mastering their potential, as they are perceived to be capable of contributing to the reduction of ego tension.

The perception by the ego that it possesses a capacity compels it when confronted by tension producing stimuli to guide behavior to maximize its mastery of that capacity with the aim of employing that capacity in reducing tension. When a source of tension producing stimuli is encountered which cannot be reduced in other ways, the ego tends to guide behavior to master the capacity perceived as helpful in defeating or avoiding the source of tension producing stimuli. Capacities which are not mastered are those which are perceived by the ego as not needed to deal with any source of tension producing stimuli encountered or anticipated. The less needed a particular capacity is perceived to be, the less well developed it tends to become.

The pursuit of mastery is impelled by encounters, or anticipated encounters, with sources of tension producing stimuli. Much as a muscle is strengthened in response to encountering greater resistance, the capacities of the human organism are strengthened by the impact of tension increase. But the ego also guides behavior to increase mastery of capacities even when the source of ego tension is not one which the increase of mastery would reduce. For example, the aim of a medical researcher in most cases is not to master his research capacities in order to find a cure for a disease because he is afflicted by it, but rather to deal with impinging stimuli from other sources than the disease whose cure he is aiming to find. More likely he is challenged by one or more of the deficits of narcissism, power, worth or surety or the impinging stimuli of curiosity. He may have found his way into the occupation of medical researcher because a member of his family was threatened by the disease, or because he was striving to please his parent or a parental surrogate such as a teacher who influenced his career choice, or because he perceived that the outcome of his discovery of a cure would be an ego worth asset which would relieve the tension of his ego worth deficit.

One of the earliest capacities which the ego guides behavior to master is crying. The infant discovers early on that crying brings relief. At first it seems as if crying causes relief to occur, but after the infant ego comes to associate the ministering external agent, usually the parent, as the reliever of tension and that the function of crying is to summon the parent's assistance, the infant begins to develop the capacity of crying as an instrument of power to assist it in achieving its tension reduction aims. This activity is among the very first behaviors in the pursuit of mastery.

During the course of ego ontogenesis, crying leads to the mastery of fashioning audible sound into language expressed in speech with which the parent can be more effectively controlled than by crying alone. The infant learns to modify crying in various ways so that it can communicate to the external agent what the source of the impinging stimuli is, whether it is hunger, thirst, excretory wetness, extremes of temperature, boredom or cathexis deprivation.

As greater mastery of crying is achieved, audible sounds become articulate, and the child is able to utter words to express his tension reduction wishes to the external agent upon which he is dependent. The capacity of crying is fused with the capacity for language. Utterances may have a plaintive sound like crying for relief from decathexis tension, or it may have an angry sound indicating frustration at inattention by the external agent, or it may have a poignant sound indicating sadness, or it may have a whimpering sound indicating narcissistic deprivation. The mastery of utterances for the ego grows and expands during the course of life to include a great and powerful variety of expressions including sarcasm, seductiveness, exhortation, obsequiousness, pomposity, authority and many other forms aimed at controlling others for the purpose of reducing one's ego tension. In other words crying becomes speech and speech is a capacity which is mastered with the aim of controlling others to serve one's tension reducing aims.

Consider sphincter control mastered by the infant who employs it to manipulate the external agent of absolute dependence. Toilet training severs the ego from its cathexis to the external agent of absolute dependence which produces ego tension of traumatic proportion. To reduce the tension of cathexis severation, the ego guides behavior to defeat the source of cathexis severation. It discovers and then acts to master the capacities which it finds at hand to defeat the toilet training severation. Sphincter control is the capacity it finds in its search for a tension reducing capacity after crying has failed. Crying fails in part because its potential for controlling the external agent has not been mastered and will not be mastered for many years to come.

The mastery of sphincter control requires the ability to clamp down with the sphincter against pressure to force it open by peristalsis or to defeat peristalsis itself so that constipation results. The mastery of sphincter control is a forerunner of other forms of seizing and manipulating and devolves as it is mastered into such capacities and skills as snatching and seizing. By the derivative relatedness transference devolution process, sphincter control may lead to collecting or hording against future deprivation.[1] Saving as self-deprivation becomes a capacity developed by the ego to protect against the tension producing fear of future want.

Expelling feces after the sphincter has released them produces ego tension reduction and concomitant pleasure. The child learns to manipulate sublimated fecal matter such as mud on the playground, modeling clay in kindergarten, and oil painting in art class. Later an affinity may be developed for materials reminiscent of bodily wastes such as cooking sauces, sausages, creamed vegetables and pureed potatoes. Other sublimations may include such diverse behaviors as delving in the garden, rearranging the furniture, even shopping for furniture, and in still more abstract forms, the "massaging" or repeated rewriting of materials such as reports, academic papers and monographs which may reduce ego tension as derivatives of the original toilet training continuations.

Mastery is an aim of the ego in all of these pursuits, and for each of them individuals may look for appreciation from parentified others for the mastery they achieve. However, each of these behaviors may instead come to serve as a reaction formation with the result that the ego rejects each of them as tension producing. In this case, the ego comes to guide behavior to reject foods that may remind the individual of body wastes, to reject delving in soil, and finds working with written materials as boring and tension producing.

As ego ontogenesis progresses into the Oedipus conflict stage, the ego perceives its possession of new capacities for dealing with the conflict, capacities which the ego strives to master during the remaining course of life. The capacity to traverse complex social situations in which one seeks to reduce ego tension by achieving tension-reducing aims or by defeating tension-producing sources of stimuli which the Oedipus conflict engenders is strengthened in response to the experience. Jealousy, competition, forbidden lust are experiences repeatedly encountered throughout the course of life, and the resolution of the Oedipus conflict is the earliest encounter with these

---

[1] See the glossary for a definition of the derivative relatedness transference devolution process.

tension producers and the first important training for gaining and mastering the skills to deal with them. Assertiveness, empathy, self-control, perseverance and courage, are among the tension reducing capacities which the ego strives to master during the struggle to resolve the Oedipus conflict which become capacities that the ego relies upon throughout the remaining course of life.

The pursuit of mastery of these capacities proceeds apace after the child enters the latency period of ego ontogenesis and becomes a "little man" or a "little woman" striving to achieve self-dependence requirements imposed by the parent and by societal institutions. Development of the capacities for locomotion, manipulation, acrobatics, memory, reason and understanding which were underway but limited during primordial life accelerate during the latency period. Running, jumping, climbing, playing with toys and tools, amusing oneself with complicated games, reading stories, comprehending drama on television and cinema tend to be performed by the latency child, but mastery of them awaits the greater competence of adolescence.

Normatively it is during adolescence that the individual begins to demonstrate a degree of mastery of the tasks required for fulfillment of human potential. The adolescent gains greater physical size and strength and a broader perspective regarding the nature of reality, especially social reality, and a more insightful grasp of the nature of social interaction and where the course of life may take him. Normatively, by the time he has progressed to young adulthood, he has mastered the tasks of finding a mate, begetting offspring, founding a family, embarking upon a remunerative occupation, finding a place in the community and establishing himself as a functioning citizen.

It is during the adolescent-young adult continuum that the ego must guide behavior to choose and master the tasks exigent to a gainful occupation. Even for those individuals who choose homemaking as their occupation, many special tasks must be mastered. Mastery of the many tasks of an occupation tends to involve an extensive range of human capabilities. Mastering the tasks of the occupation by which the individual provides for himself and his family reduces ego tension produced by multiple sources of stimuli including the deficits of narcissism, power, worth, surety as well as stimuli impinging from the superego, from unsatisfied curiosity, fear of decathexis and failures of ego ontogenesis such as achieving the ego ideal which include stimuli impinging from the ego real.

Mastering the Tasks of an Occupation

Commonplace thinking mistakenly tends to associate the pursuit of mastery not so much with succeeding in the tasks inherent in the course of life, but principally in mastering tasks encountered in one's occupation or leisure pursuits. Every occupation from which a livelihood can be derived requires the mastering of particular skills and knowledge. Even the most menial occupations involve tasks requiring mastery. The ordinary laborer, whether assembly line worker or construction worker, farm hand or roustabout, regularly encounters tasks requiring skills and knowledge normatively not present at the outset. There is no occupation so menial that the performance of related tasks is so lacking in required skills and knowledge that the worker who masters them does not take pride in that mastery, and which others who have mastered the tasks associated with even the most demanding of occupations can step in and perform them up to the standards which have been established by workers regularly in the occupation. Even a rocket scientist might find himself faltering at first if he took up the occupation of fry cook in a diner.

The pursuit of mastery is an innate human proclivity evident in virtually everything the human animal does. The intensity with which mastery is pursued varies depending upon the importance to the reduction of ego tension that is involved. The computer programmer may not invest as great an effort at a leisure pursuit such as a card game as he does in the gainful occupation with which he earns his livelihood where more is at stake for him than in a pastime amusement. Still, he may take some pride in his skill at the game, say, of bridge, but accept with equanimity the outcome of a game when he loses.

The degree of mastery of human capacities required by various occupations tends to form a hierarchy of difficulty and associated prestige, the more difficult occupations garnering greater social status than the less difficult ones. As a consequence, the mastery of occupational tasks contributes to achieving ego worth as well as gaining income to meet the expenses of survival in a marketplace economy. However, there is not necessarily a perfect correlation between the levels of financial reward reaped by the mastery of the tasks of one occupation over another. The chief executive officer of a large business corporation may garner millions of dollars in stock options and bonuses while an Albert Einstein or a Jonas Sauk, having mastered tasks of as great or even much greater difficulty and prestige than the CEO, realize substantially less financial reward for their effort than the CEO.

The competition between individuals among different occupations as well as within the same occupation attests the hold which the pursuit of mastery has upon human beings. Within an occupation, employers may hold ceremonies which award prizes recognizing the most effective worker, and associations of persons in the same occupation—say salesmen—may also reward outstanding achievers with a token of recognition. Few occupations which could be accorded the appellation of profession fail to form associations which ceremonially recognize those among their ranks who demonstrate the greatest mastery of the tasks of the profession. There are few experiences pleasanter than being recognized formally by one's peers as outstanding in the performance of the tasks of one's occupation.

The mastery of human capacities is admired by all who witness it. Each human capacity may deal with any of myriad tension producing sources of stimuli, and the individual who masters the capacity to reduce the tension produced by the stimuli tends to be admired by others who may be subject to the same stimuli. The many kinds of sports which emerge under tension producing circumstances illustrate this phenomenon. The ancient Greeks who developed the Olympic games created contests in which skills needed in war were featured. Examples include running, jumping, javelin throwing and hurling, all of them important in combat. The list of sports which involve skills necessary to defeat specific sources of ego tension is a long one.

Numerous occupations can be cited which inspire the pursuit of mastery of skills important to reducing ego tension arising from the occupation. Examples would include log rolling contests to demonstrate the mastery of loggers; corn husking contests to demonstrate the mastery of corn huskers; fire-fighting contests to demonstrate mastery of putting out fires and plowing contests to plow faster and straighter than anyone else.

In leisure pursuits, there are contests which simulate war to demonstrate mastery of combatants such as football, basketball and soccer which require skills useful in combat such as running, jumping, throwing accurately, catching and weaving, dodging and physically outmaneuvering adversaries. There are awards to reward the achievements of researchers, writers, and artists; such as science prizes, Kennedy Center lifetime achievement awards for entertainers, and there is the example of prizes awarded to Greek dramatists in classical times. The Nobel Prize is perhaps the pinnacle of awarding recognition for mastery of the tasks of an occupation in the present era.

Particularly frustrating are the conditions which produce the ego tension of conflict with one's employer concerning the content of the work. In the pursuit of mastery, the worker craves to do the tasks of his job well so that he can enjoy the tension reduction which results from mastery. But too often for workers, the employer places burdens upon him which frustrate his pursuit of mastery. The boss wants the tasks done "his way," which frustrates the employee who has his own ways to achieve the same or similar outcome. Of particular concern in modern times is the problems encountered by the assembly line worker whose work has been so broken down into discrete tasks of which he performs only one or a very few that his principal sense of mastery is in keeping up with a rapidly moving assembly line, which is a paltry reward for the pursuer of mastery. Gaining greater remuneration and benefits becomes for the assembly line worker the principal tension reducing rewards he is able to perceive. Also, for the office worker much stultifying work is assigned to him which frustrates him in his pursuit of mastery.

Hobbies

Another activity in which mastery is pursued for no gain except the pleasure of achievement is that of the hobby. Hobbies are distinguished from occupations in that they tend not to be pursued for financial gain. They are tension reducers with respect to general sources of tension producing stimuli. They provide relief from the stresses of gainful employment, of spousal relations, of parental stresses, of social intercourse, of failures in activities in which one does not succeed. They are self-indulgent and therefore appeasers of the narcissism deficit.

The hobbyist tends to become so ardently absorbed in his hobby that often he invests devotion to the tasks of the hobby as intense as in his gainful occupation. Often hobbyists achieve a mastery which equals or exceeds those performing similar tasks in their gainful occupation. The hobbyist, say, who rebuilds antique automobiles may become so skilled that he converts his hobby into a gainful occupation. In golf, the hobbyist may achieve the ability to earn his livelihood as a professional player, by teaching others and playing for financial prizes.

In taking up a hobby, the individual gives himself the opportunity to choose tasks for which he has a proclivity and therefore can master those tasks. The ego would not long guide behavior to pursue a hobby whose tasks were beyond the capability of the individual to master. A hobby is recreation, which by definition is an activity which restores the individual's élan by reducing ego tension produced by particular sources of stimuli such as one's gainful employment, family conflict and ego ideal failures or produced by the multifarious tensions of daily living.

Mastery and Ego Worth

Reducing ego worth deficit tension fuels the pursuit of mastery. Doing a task well or mastering a capacity often tends to be pursued to command the approval and admiration of others. This propensity is first manifested after the ego has suppressed the Oedipus conflict and wishes to palliate the sting of capitulating to the same sex parent. By showing off to the opposite sex parent, the little boy or girl is able to convey his or her wish to be admired and loved by the opposite sex parent and to gain a return of the narcissism which the ego had earlier extended to the parent. The pursuit of worth and love are often fused when the object from which admiration is sought is also an object of love. Often, to be found worthy is to be found lovable.

The pursuit of ego worth tends to take different forms at each stage of ego ontogenesis as the ego guides behavior to deal with the sources of tension producing stimuli which are peculiar to the different stages of ego ontogenesis. The latency age little boy reducing the tension produced by the residue of the recently suppressed Oedipus conflict may ride his scooter recklessly to display his mastery of the toy, or he may manipulate his skateboard with great skill for the same purpose. His mother may think that he is risking injury and be dismayed by these antics, but the little boy is saying figuratively that he is wonderful and worthy of her admiration and love.

To strengthen the filial-maternal cathexis, the little girl will tend "to be good." She will do her school lessons well and show up the boys, who tend not so much to be good in order to be admired but to be daring and masculine in the pursuit of approval and admiration. The little boy will climb high in the tree to display his mastery of climbing and his bravery. The little girl will help her mother bake cookies to display her pursuit of mastery of the tasks associated with her mother's role upon which she will model herself. Aberrantly, the little girl may take up the practices of little boys in the hope of earning her father's praise and approval but risk being called a tomboy. At every stage of life, the individual pursues mastery at tasks for which he will expect to be admired and garner affection.

The adolescent is confronted by a much greater and more severe array of challenges which he must master. He must master the tasks associated with individuation, which include establishing a separate and unique identity. He must master again the control of his filial hostility and competitiveness erupting anew as a consequence of a reemerging Oedipus conflict. To accomplish these tasks he may resort to the mechanisms of projection, displacement and denial. He must accomplish these tasks also to sustain and burnish his ego ideal which suffers retribution from an aggravated superego.

He must master the commonplace tools of his culture such as, in present day European and North American culture, hammer and saw for the little boy, and for the little girl the cooking range and food processor, and later in adolescence, driving an automobile and riding an escalator. The list of contrivances in common use in the present era is immense and includes such diverse items as televisions and computers, telephones and radios, power tools for carpentry and tractors for lawn care, electric can openers in the kitchen and thermostatically controlled furnaces in the basement. The little boy and little girl in their progress toward adulthood must master all of these devices and a great many others. They must master the ways of their culture, both social and physical, in order to avoid dangers which would lead them into failure or destruction.

They must gain the social skills which will enable them to attract a mate and to establish a place in society. They must gain the civic skills which will enable them to function as citizens. They must learn to cope with competition and to surmount failure. They must discover a career which affords them a path in life and master the knowledge and skills required for gainful employment so that they can provide for themselves and the families they beget in the marketplace. Failure to demonstrate mastery in any of these areas may diminish ego worth and deprive of the love which gratifies narcissism.

The adult must be the master of all of these capacities and of other capacities as well, which are necessary to deal with the sources of ego tension to which the individual is exposed in middle adulthood. If he has successfully traversed the challenges which confronted him earlier, he will find that middle age is less stressful than his earlier experience. This more pleasant state of affairs is due to his success in mastering the capacities required of him in earlier life. However, if he has been unsuccessful in his earlier life, he will find that the accumulated stresses from his earlier life added to the sources of tension impinging in middle adulthood may be so burdensome as to make middle adulthood worse than anytime earlier. Normatively each individual will traverse adulthood heartened by successes from earlier stages of ego ontogenesis admixed with failures from earlier stages, and the greater the balance of the former over the latter the greater pleasure he will experience in adulthood.

10

FANTASIES AND EGO ONTOGENESIS

The ego guides behavior to engage in fantasy with the aim of reducing tension. Fantasies are reveries involving mental images and sounds, often in narrative form, deliberately conjured up by the ego in response to tension producing stimuli provoked by a disturbing event or by general circumstances. Because the array of sources of ego tension differs at each stage of ego ontogenesis, fantasies tend to differ at each stage to reduce tension from stage-specific sources of tension. Consequently, in the overall array of tension producing stimuli, there are tension sources common to all stages of ego ontogenesis such as hunger, thirst and extremes of temperature as well as tension sources peculiar to each stage of ego ontogenesis. Fantasies often intermix tension from stage-specific sources with tension from sources common to all stages of ego ontogenesis.

Fantasies during primordial experience are inaccessible to investigators and therefore unknowable directly. Fantasies aimed at reducing ego tension produced by the weaning trauma may be inferred from post primordial experience. The infant may envision the maternal breast when wishing for it in its absence as being present and available in whatever form it may take in his limited distorted perception just as the adult male may fantasize about the female breast when he is experiencing sexual lust. For the infant, the breast he craves may take on unusual gratifying forms in his fantasies, and when he contemplates his bowel while constipated, it may be symbolized in fantasy for example by images of little men with shovels excavating the fecal matter or as a fairy tale beast beating against his insides, which would reflect a wish for relief from the tension of bowel pressure.

During the ascendancy of the Oedipus conflict, the infant may fantasize about heroics in which he runs, jumps or rides his scooter or skateboard with extravagant skill before an admiring mother, or the little girl might fantasize about her father or a paternified male figure bestowing affection upon her. During post primordial experience, which begins with the start of the latency period, the little boy may fantasize about conquering formidable paternified adversaries such as the dragons he learns about in fairy tales, or scary villains like those he sees on television. He may envision himself as an heroic figure in a narrative which he conjures up in his imagination. The little girl may fantasize about surpassing the wicked witch or a feared female teacher, who although not recognized as such represents her powerful mother.

Latency is a time in the course of life when fantasies tend to flourish. The latency ego is beset with tension producing stimuli from a broad spectrum of sources. Typical of these sources of tension producing stimuli are: being small in size and always having to look up to older children and adults; being physically weak compared with adults and being inferior to adults and to older children. Tension sources include having to wait to grow bigger, which seems far off, so as to have more power, status, worth, and privileges like older children and adults, and being limited in what one is permitted to do by adults and authorities. They also include being derogated as too small to be permitted to do certain desirable things that older children and adults are allowed to do such as being allowed to stay up late and to watch forbidden television programs, and being repeatedly reminded of one's small size by furniture and apparatus which is designed for adult sized persons. They include being constrained by adults everywhere such as in church, school, theaters, playgrounds and parks so that one always has energy and desire to be active beyond what is permitted.

Other sources of tension include frequently being afraid of older children and adults because they are bigger, and continually feeling fear of authority because it might act retributively. They include often feeling inferior to anyone bigger such as older children and adults and feeling limited in what one can do or accomplish because of one's small size and lack of strength, and of feeling powerless. For boys it may include being afraid of girls, and for girls it may include being shunned and deprecated by boys.

For boys it also includes fear of being labeled a sissy and for girls fear of being called a tomboy. For both boys and girls it includes being compelled to do chores which are boring and keep one away from play. It includes difficulty with school studies—being unable to understand them, being unable to remember them, being bored by them, being over-burdened by them and wanting to escape them. It includes hating to be in school because it takes one away from play and it includes being scolded by teachers. It also means being admonished by Dutch uncles and being punished by parents and teachers and other authorities.

Fantasies of latency age children tend to be aimed at reducing the ego tension produced by these impinging stimuli. The latency child may conjure up fantasies about being larger and more powerful, outrunning the older boys and besting them at games on the playground. Or he may fantasize about being older and expert at sport or in classroom recitation. He may fantasize about being the first one chosen to be on the better team in playground sports. He may picture himself as the center of attention on the playground, in the classroom or in the neighborhood. He may fantasize about thrashing the playground bully and sending him off ignominiously defeated. He may fantasize about winning academic prizes. such as being the best in class at spelling or arithmetic. He may fantasize about skipping school and escaping with playmates to their favorite haunts where his parents forbid him to go. He may fantasize about the future in which he has grown older and is permitted to enjoy privileges granted to older children and to venture to places where older children are allowed to go. He may fantasize about being a sports hero or participating in adventures along with heroes of fiction, cinema and television drama.

Adolescence

The Sturm and Drang of adolescence generates its own special sources of tension producing stimuli. The narcissism deficit fused with sexual tension may produce fantasies in the adolescent boy of being sought out by the prettiest girl around and regarded admiringly by her or seducing and copulating with her, and the adolescent girl may fantasize about being desired by the most admired boy at school and envied by her female schoolmates. Adolescent boys subjected simultaneously to sexual tension and sexual deprivation may repeatedly fantasize about sexually stimulating images and engage in masturbation to reduce sexual tension. Adolescent girls, subjected to the tension of reproductive hormones, may fantasize about attracting a lover, giving birth, holding and looking after her infant.

Tension produced by the ego power deficit may provoke fantasies in the adolescent boy about being strong physically with bulging muscles and defeating a bully in a schoolyard brawl, and the adolescent girl dealing with the *ego power deficit may fantasize about being the prettiest and most sought* after girl in the school. Ego worth deficit fantasies may conjure narratives in which the adolescent male is cheered by the school population in a football game in which he scores at a critical juncture and is carried from the field in triumph on the shoulders of his teammates.

The adolescent boy dealing with the tension of his ego ideal shortcomings may engender fantasies in which he is comely, stylish, heroic, accomplished, virtuous, admired by his schoolmates, pursued by the prettiest girls in school and famous beyond his customary precincts. He may imagine his persona to reflect the ego ideal which he conjures up in fantasy. If he perceives himself as socially awkward, he may fantasize about being urbane in manner, charming the prettiest girls and recognized by male classmates as their leader.

The adolescent may be tormented by the demands of his superego in the form of newly emergent filial hostility manifested in mordant criticism of his father and surliness toward his mother and guilt for sexual wishes, for seducing a girl and for acquiring pornographic materials and masturbating. Adolescent girls may experience guilt for wishing to surpass their mothers, and adolescent boys may experience guilt for wishing to surpass their fathers. Both adolescent boys and girls may salve their filial guilt by failing at endeavors which if they succeeded would lead to the surpassing of their same sex parent, and then doubly assailed, experience ego tension because of their failure of achievement. They may engender fantasies in which they achieve their goals in spite of failure, and fantasies in which they earn and receive the respect and admiration of the same sex parent despite their rivalry with the same sex parent.

Both the adolescent boy and the adolescent girl will experience individuation tension, tension produced by the impulse to individuate, and by failures to master tasks required by individuation. Salient among these tasks is the problem of establishing a separate and unique identity. The adolescent ego guides behavior toward discovering values to adopt which are different from parental values but to do so without alienating the parent. Fantasies aimed at reducing the tension produced by these tasks may take the form of mental images envisioned by the adolescent in which he or she is manifesting differences from the parent toward which the parent manifests displeasure short of disowning the child. In fantasy there may be scenes of child and parent disagreeing, and the child holding his own triumphantly.

Because behavior often tends to be over determined, these mental images may reflect not only identity differences but also filial hostility provoked by the re-emergent Oedipus conflict as well as mental images in which the adolescent in some way surpasses the same sex parent or a parental surrogate. An example might be an image in the adolescent's mind of him or her attired in the outlandish fashions often worn by adolescents which are offensive to the parent. This fantasy simultaneously exercises hostility toward the parent, differentiates the adolescent from the parent, and in the adolescent's view surpasses the parent in fashion because the adolescent sees himself or herself as more trendy than the old fashioned, behind-the-times parent. It also may contribute to the reduction of ego tension produced by the ego worth deficit by enabling the adolescent to experience in fantasy elevated social status among peers whose attire may be in his or her view less trendy.

The adolescent will experience tension produced from challenges to his or her mastery. The competitiveness of the re-emergent Oedipus conflict will confront the adolescent with an invidious comparison between himself and the same sex parent. The capabilities of the parent so obviously superior to the latency age child now in adolescence emphasizes the adolescent's filial inferiority which he craves to reduce. He or she is eager to demonstrate that he or she can do what the parent does as well if not better.

*For example, the adolescent boy wants to drive the family car with greater skill than his father, to use power tools with superior efficacy, to lift burdens more powerfully than his father and to be more up-to-date in his awareness of public concerns than his father. The adolescent girl wants to select her own fashions and be more avant-guard than her mother, be able to dress her hair with more panache than her mother, use household appliances with greater proficiency than her mother and display greater knowledge than her mother about how to do things but not necessarily want to perform household chores.

If the adolescent girl was brought up in a high-income household, she may wish to order servants about as her mother does. The adolescent is impelled to demonstrate greater mastery of the capacities and means for dealing with the everyday concerns of life than the parent. Ironically, while the adolescent is eager to "show up" his parent in the mastery of knowledge and capacity, he is not necessarily eager to take on the responsibilities of the adult and share the burdens borne by the family. The adolescent will tend to fantasize about his filial superiority, envisioning himself or herself in settings in which he or she is publicly recognized and admired for his or her mastery of adult prerequisites. The adolescent may fantasize himself or herself in circumstances in which he or she accomplishes these aims.

The adolescent faces many demands imposed upon teenagers which require him or her to master prerequisites of adulthood which appear formidable. The adolescent must master social skills so that he or she can make a place in society, find and marry a mate, form a family, provide for and rear children, decide upon and establish a career in life and obtain a gainful occupation necessary to secure a livelihood. These are capacities the parent has mastered which the adolescent is faced with mastering but has not yet mastered.

Fantasies, which relieve ego tension produced by these challenges, may reflect the accomplishing of these tasks, or may engage in general escapist fantasies of traveling to and having adventures in far off places or engaging in adventurous space travel. The adolescent may envision himself in the future home he expects to established for himself with his own adulthood family, or at work securing the livelihood needed to provide for his family, or in a public setting being honored by adult citizens for his contribution to society.

He may fantasize himself at the head of a parade in which he is the leader or grand marshal. He may fantasize about being in public office presiding at a meeting of public officials about urgent public business. He may fantasize himself at the helm of a great industrial enterprise giving orders to division heads seated around a great table. The adolescent may have chosen an occupation and fantasized about being a successful practitioner of that occupation—as a surgeon in the midst of a challenging operation, as fire fighter climbing a high ladder to the roof of a burning building, as a general in command of a great army or an admiral on the bridge of his flagship surveying his fleet, or a scientist being awarded a Nobel prize. Because adolescence merges gradually into young adulthood, the young adult may also engage in these same sorts of fantasies.

The adolescent and young adult may choose an occupation which he believes will earn the approval and admiration of his parent or of parentified others and gain for him ego worth and narcissistic gratification, but to which his natural endowment is unsuited. Examples might be the young man who is of no more than normal height who is bent upon becoming a professional basketball player, the young woman who feels driven to become an actress but who has limited acting ability and who is extremely shy in public gatherings, the young man who dreams of becoming an opera singer but is not gifted with a pleasing singing voice, the young man or woman who wants to be a novelist but has no gift for writing, the young man or woman who wants to be a concert pianist but lacks coordination and dexterity beyond normal, the young man who wants to enter the ministry but who is dull and inarticulate when speaking in public—the list of potential examples of persons who wish to enter an occupation to obtain the approval and narcissistic gratification of parents or parentified entities whose natural gifts lie in other fields than the one they have injudiciously chosen is a long one.

They are destined for persistent disappointment until they finally find their way into a more appropriate career venue in which they are competent but finish out their lives with regret that their original choice was ill-fated because it had been chosen at a point in ego ontogenesis when it mistakenly appeared as ideal to reduce the ego tension of the ego worth deficit and the threat of decathexis. The persistence with which it is pursued throughout life is a function of the persistence of ego tension produced by the deficits of narcissism, ego worth and the fear of decathexis and a function of the filial relatedness transference devolution process springing from the moment the occupation was chosen fortuitously to reduce the tension of the deficits of narcissism, ego worth and decathexis fears.

The adolescent may choose a field of endeavor for which he has an aptitude but fail at it because of unrecognized Oedipal fears of surpassing the same sex parent which he or she mistakenly fears would bring down the wrath of the same sex parent. This condition results from the filial relatedness transference devolution process in which Oedipal conflict resolution stratagems are carried forward in ego ontogenesis in a suppressed state until adolescence where they resurface anew to impinge painfully upon the ego. In the effort to keep them suppressed, the ego maintains them in a penumbra of awareness disguised as a different source of tension from that of Oedipal conflict. For example, the adolescent girl thinks of herself as not being as comely as her mother even though her own appearance is fresh and blooming while her mother's appearance is that of a fading middle age woman. She may conjure up fantasies of herself as a celebrated fashion model to reduce the ego tension of her misperceived lack of comeliness. The adolescent boy may fail at his studies because he finds them too formidable, and therefore not surpass his intellectual father even though intelligence tests rate the boy very high. To reduce the tension of his intellectual failure, he may fantasize himself as a renowned author.

Young Adulthood

The young adult may experience ego tension impinging from the tasks of providing for the family he creates and fantasize about effectively discharging these tasks. The young adult, struggling with the challenges of his chosen occupation, may fantasize himself masterfully surmounting these challenges to the admiration of colleagues, friends and family. He may fantasize himself as greatly advanced in his chosen occupation, surpassing his peers and receiving plaudits from his superiors. He may experience the constraint of marriage and a duty to provide for offspring, and reduce the tension produced by the limitations of his new state by fantasizing himself as, say, a boulevardier flirting with stylish women in nightclubs and at fashionable gatherings.

Still burdened by the challenges of individuation, the young man may fantasize himself surpassing the status of his father in an occupation which his father objected to, such as receiving acclaim as an actor when his tradesman father had wanted him to be a carpenter. The young woman may fantasize herself surpassing her mother in marriage to a man her mother objected to but a man who nevertheless is doing well as a provider.

The young adult will be in the process of consolidating his or her ego ideal and persona and will likely still be indulging in fantasies in which comeliness, social skills and intellectual accomplishment are featured but added to by achievements in providing for his family and homemaking accomplishment which are also featured. In cases in which the young adult has deferred or shunned marriage and the establishing of family to pursue a demanding career, fantasies about career accomplishments will tend to be experienced.

The young adult will also still be striving to strengthen his separate and unique identity the main structure of which normatively will be established by young adulthood. Those aspects of it dependent upon his gainful occupation will tend to be the most urgent producers of ego tension. He will likely be in the earliest phases of his career, striving to establish himself as a credible practitioner of its requirements. Whether it be a profession, a trade, a managerial position, an entrepreneurial undertaking or merely a laboring job, its challenges will tend to assault the ego with impinging stimuli which will likely engender fantasies of achievement which buttress the identity of the ego.

The mastery of the tasks of his gainful occupation will likely continue to challenge him, the greater the technical knowledge required, the greater the tension producing challenge. Fantasies of achievement will help to reduce the ego tension to which he is subjected. If he is employed in a large organization, fantasies of achievement will tend to incorporate scenes of recognition by higher authorities in the bureaucracy and admiration by peers for his job skills.

To appease the tension of the narcissism deficit, the young adult man or woman may fantasize about being praised by employers, or admired and sought after by members of the opposite sex in flirtatious situations. They may fantasize about bygone times when in adolescence and still unmarried they were popular with opposite sex age mates. They may fantasize about being in an entirely different life course than the one they are actually in, perhaps a life course of adventure, accomplishment, sexual escapades and flirtatious banter with members of the opposite sex.

The young adult may acutely experience the ego power deficit. While the young adult has traversed adolescence and gained intellectual power equal to his parent and physical power which may surpass that of his parent, because he has become independent of his parent, having formed his own family and launched himself upon an income earning occupation, he nevertheless will tend to be less powerful than his parent vis-à-vis society generally.

He will also likely begin to be aware of his power inferiority vis-à-vis parentified entities in society—great organizations and institutions and the functionaries who are in charge of them. He may have surmounted his filial inferiority in relation to his parent, but now must deal with his filial inferiority to more powerful parentified entities. Fantasies of success within the context of his society in which he is praised and envied by others and has mastered his relationship with parentified societal entities will tend to be resorted to as a means of reducing the tension of inferior power. He may fantasize himself in charge of great organizations such as corporations, governmental agencies, criminal justice institutions, medical centers, schools and churches or having defeated them in a contest of power.

The young adult will continue to experience ego tension because of the ego worth deficit, but now in adulthood his sense of worth will depend a great deal more upon earning the approval and admiration of parentified entities in the larger society and in the family he has formed, particularly from his spouse or significant other, which begin to displace his actual parents as bestowers of worth. If he was unable to gain worth from his actual parents, he may encounter difficulty in obtaining it from parentified others.

The young adult tends to find himself or herself in between the status of adolescent, who is not viewed by conventional society as yet having social status or social place other than that of being the offspring of his or her parents, and having the status of a middle age adult who normatively has established a social place and social status. Fantasies of the young adult will tend to reflect this uncertain status and place by envisioning circumstances in which he or she is far ahead in surmounting the challenges of life's demands than middle age adults, but often without appearing older so as to retain in fantasy the physical advantages of youth in order not to lose the strength and comeliness normatively no longer experienced by those in middle age.

Middle Adulthood

Middle adulthood fantasies deal with many of the same issues as young adult fantasies but add to them fantasies aimed at reducing ego tension to which the middle age person is particularly exposed. The most profound source of ego tension to which the middle age individual is exposed is the reality that his allotted number of years on earth are half gone and more, that his offspring are grown and on their own, that the life cycle has been completed and that he has no further biological function to discharge except to die. To reduce the ego tension produced by this state of affairs he searches for and launches himself into activities which he hopes will give significance to his remaining years. He fantasizes about worthy projects he will undertake, and he also fantasizes about the success of those worthy projects he has already undertaken and the plaudits due him. He fantasizes about overcoming obstacles impeding the success of his various projects.

He also is left with much that he failed to accomplish during the years which went before, and he fantasizes about rectifying those failures. Projects he started which were beyond his capabilities he now resolves to complete despite their difficulty by redoubling his effort. Difficulties in his marriage and with his children he resolves to correct. He may have to come to the rescue of his children who may be stumbling in their lives and need help, particularly if they suffered the misfortune of becoming disabled or ineffective in their gainful occupations. He will likely be at the apex of his career and will wish to enjoy the rewards of his success and to suppress thoughts of his various failures. Fantasies from earlier stages of ego ontogenesis aimed at reducing tension arising in those stages but which fail may continue into middle age because the residue of failed tension resolution tends to continue into later life. For example, the youth ambitious to become an acclaimed athlete who never succeeded beyond the ordinary nevertheless continues his interest in athletics into middle age and afterward into old age, fantasizing the glory which is never afforded him in reality.

The middle age individual tends to seek to enjoy the special benefits of middle age such as experiencing the greatest status he is likely ever to attain in society, and the greatest he is likely to attain in power, narcissistic reward, recognition of worth and success in accomplishing the aims of life. While for many, complete success tends to remain elusive, nevertheless typically the middle age individual can find things to take satisfaction in such as the love of his family, if his marriage has remained intact or been replaced by a successful marriage; the power of financial assets if he has risen in his job or career or succeeded at least moderately at business or in his profession; the respect of family, friends and society if he can point to a life responsibly spent with accomplishments he can proclaim, even if modest; and a sense of mastery over the challenges of life if his family, his career, his social status are flourishing with at least normative success. To the extent he perceives himself to have fallen short in any of these areas, he is likely at times to fantasize greater success to reduce the tension of these deficiencies.

In realizing his place in society and the community, he may seek greater status and importance than he has actually attained and fantasize about achieving greater significance. He may envision himself chairing a meeting of a civic organization, or lodge or charitable fundraising drive of which he is at the head. If he is a union member, he may fantasize himself as an officer of the organization leading an important project. He may fantasize himself as a lay person presiding over a meeting of his religious organization in which he is directing laity and clergy alike in some important project. He may picture himself in fantasy being reported upon or interviewed in the news media about a newsworthy event in which he is involved.

He may fantasize about his job, occupation or profession in which in fantasy he is far more successful than in reality and in this way reduce ego tension arising from failure to achieve his most extravagant aims. Whether married or not, he may fantasize about his sexual prowess, envisioning himself at the center of attention among women at his place of work, or if a woman she may imagine herself the object of male attention. He or she may fantasize about his or her children and their successes and his or her place in their lives, and particularly in the lives of his or her grandchildren. He or she may fantasize about an impending visit from grandchildren and their visit to the museum, zoo or amusement park.

Old Age

The old age individual continues many of the fantasies from earlier stages because memories of the past assume ever more importance as the future grows shorter. But there are special sources of tension producing stimuli in old age which the ego may guide behaving to reduce through fantasy. The old age individual tends to fantasize about how he will be remembered by his posterity and those who knew him or her. He or she may fantasize about his or her grave marker, legacies left and how they are received, one's life work and the impact it may have, one's adult children and one's grandchildren and how well they will do in their lives and one's heirs and posterity and the inheritors of the benefits of one's having been here.

Debility, which afflicts many in old age, tends to produce fantasies of recovery or the ease of pain. Fantasies may be indulged to reduce the tension of the oblivion toward which one is headed by afterlife images and narratives in which one is a participant or the good will of those who later remember and remark favorably about one's sojourn on this earth.

The Abnormal

Pathology produces its own special fantasies, but it is not the aim of this presentation to comment upon fantasies produced by abnormal sources of ego tension. However, it is not abnormal for normal individuals to sustain sources of ego tension which produce fantasies about non-normative states, or states would appear non-normative if they were exposed to public scrutiny. Fantasies tend to remain private partly because they would appear to be extravagant and embarrassing to their authors.

Fantasies of rapists, murderers, suicides, perverts, sadists, masochists and other aberrant persons will be aimed at reducing tension produced by the circumstances of their aberration which might be found in the processes of their ego ontogenesis. Pathology and aberrancy is caused by unhealthy tension reduction strategies during ego ontogenesis which persist through the derivative relatedness transference devolution process without being resolved sufficiently to enable the ego to guide behavior in normative modes. Many factors might cause aberrancies such as biological damage through physical trauma, or malformation of brain functioning, child abuse or unhealthful psychological environment impacting maturation. Fantasies of persons subjected to such calamities to the ego will tend to reflect the wish to reduce the tension produced by them. Fantasies, like ego mechanisms, can never be more than temporary palliatives in dealing with tension producing stimuli because they can do no more than fend off reality in the short term. Reality always returns to challenge anew the ego's capability for reducing tension.

11

PLAY DURING
EGO ONTOGENESIS

Play is a form of recreation. Recreation is intended to "refresh" the ego by cleansing it of stress. Play is ego-guided behavior aimed at reducing ego tension by engaging in activity designed principally to draw upon tension reducing stimuli to distract the ego from experiencing impinging tension producing stimuli. As in the case of fantasy, many forms of play are stage-specific during ego ontogenesis to reduce tension from sources specific to the stage of ego ontogenesis which the individual is experiencing, but much play and recreation is general in form, aimed at reducing accumulated unreduced tension from multiple sources.

Stage-Specific Play

Much tension reducing behavior is aimed at defeating impinging stimuli from a specific source identified by the ego. Play reduces ego tension by supplanting the experience of tension producing stimuli with tension reducing stimuli. Play has to be sufficiently intense to displace the tension it is intended to reduce. Circumstances may be such that the tension which it is intended to reduce is so intense that no activity of play can supplant it. The condemned prisoner may be unable to find any diversion which can take his mind off his execution scheduled for the morning. In other words play, like fantasy, substitutes the experience of tension increase by deceiving the ego into setting it aside and suppressing it and instead turning the ego's attention to stimuli which reduce tension. For example, playing or watching a game of football turns the ego's attention from tension producing stimuli such as earning a livelihood, performing chores, doing homework or contemplating one's guilt about some misdeed to the joy of the game. If the ego's interest in the game is sufficiently intense, the sources of tension producing stimuli may be temporarily supplanted and not re-experienced until the intrusion of reality compels the ego once again to pay attention to the tension producing stimuli and suffer the tension increase and concomitant unpleasure they bring.

Primordial Play

Normatively play begins in the very earliest days of the postpartum period usually induced by the parent or nurse who smiles and talks to the infant with the aim of exciting pleasure in the infant. This activity tends to be tension reducing for the infant who is experiencing a degree of de-cathexis as a consequence of having been ejected from the womb. This activity is the first awareness of play experienced by the infant and consti-tutes teaching the infant the pleasures of play.

The infant is soon introduced to toys designed by his caregivers to amuse him. To the extent the infant can be amused in self-conducted play, he produces less tension increase for the caregiver, which encourages the caregiver to ply him with toys and to teach him how to play with them. Almost any object of amusement may be supplied to the infant as a toy so long as the caregiver deems it not to be dangerous for the infant to have it in its possession.

Eventually the infant learns to reach out for objects supplied to him as toys in a thrust for mastery over his tension producing environment. The mobile dangling over his crib may attract the infant's outstretched hands, usually in vain. By this time the infant has experienced the tension increase of boredom or physical discomfort or physical pain, which he can do noth-ing to stop except to cry, which summons the caregiver who normatively will provide relief. Boredom produces tension which can only be reduced by the excitement of competing stimuli. By this time the infant has learned that play reduces tension, and he seeks it to deal with the unpleasure which he has come to perceive as a frequent experience.

Prior to weaning, the most severe impinging stimuli which the infant experiences normatively is boredom or the unpleasure of tension produc-ing stimuli of hunger, thirst, excesses of temperature, excretory wetness, chafing and the like which tend to be rather promptly reduced by the ad-ministrations of the caregiver. Frequently the caregiver is able to shush the infant who is crying in response to the tension producing stimuli of bore-dom, or other cause of discomfort, by attracting his attention to a proffered toy, which affords the caregiver a modicum of respite from the tension increase of the crying infant, but typically the reality of whatever is assail-ing the infant reemerges into the infant's awareness, and the crying resumes.

Gradually the human ego learns to amuse itself with self-provided play which is the beginning of a lifelong practice pursued throughout ego onto-genesis right up to death's door. The ego tends to guide behavior so that the individual occupies his time with play as often as necessary to reduce the tension produced by the circumstances of ego ontogenesis or produced by stimuli from multiple sources.

During the primordial period of ego ontogenesis the impingements of weaning, toilet training, and the Oedipus conflict are the major ontogenetic stage-specific tension producers which are added to the general sources of tension producing stimuli such as boredom, hunger, thirst, excessive tem-perature, chaffing, physical pain and the like. The infant often responds to the ego tension produced by the severation of weaning by playing with his mother's breast, or with the nursing bottle, eating utensils and food to dis-tract him from the unpleasure of the decathexis as well as to defeat wean-ing. Playing with the maternal breast may become sublimated in adult-hood and fused with erotic propensities of playing with a lover's breast.

In response to toilet training, the infant may dawdle on his way to the potty as he dawdled with his food in his failed attempt to defeat weaning. Also to defeat the severation tension of weaning, he may have played with the bottle or the breast rather than suckled to obtain the nourishment as he was encouraged to do. In toilet training he may wish to play with his feces or to dip his finger into the urine to divert his attention from the decathexis tension imposed by toilet training. Such play may later be sublimated by playing with reminders of urine and fecal matter such as puddles, bath wa-ter, finger paints, mud and modeling clay. In adulthood, such hobbies as cooking as a pastime may constitute play involving the reduction of a resi-due of decathexis tension produced by toilet training in infancy carried by ego ontogenesis into adulthood via the derivative relatedness transference devolution process.

Play during the Latency Period

In response to the severation tension imposed by the Oedipus conflict, more play activities become possible. To reduce the tension of filial com-petition, the little boy may pretend that his toy wagon is a truck which he pretends to drive to emulate his truck driver father. The little girl may pre-tend to bake cookies emulating and rivaling her mother. The toy manufac-turing industry has capitalized upon this Oedipal propensity by designing and marketing many toys which attract the oedipal child by facilitating his wish to emulate the parent with whom he both identifies and experiences competitive feelings.

This child-play phenomenon continues into the latency period as the Oedipus conflict is resolved, but toward the end of latency diminishes as the child looks to the approach of adolescence and the different interests which that period of ego ontogenesis stirs. The child propitiates the narcissism deficit by playing with a favorite personified toy such as a teddy bear or doll upon which he lavishes love and pretends that the love is reciprocated. He will admire the teddy bear or doll, telling it how good it is and how well behaved, thus by identification with the teddy bear or doll reducing tension of the ego worth deficit. He may examine the teddy bear or doll to find their genitalia in an attempt to reduce the tension of curiosity.

Throughout the whole of the latency period, the fact of the child's small size will tend to be a source of tension producing stimuli and provoke the seeking of toys and the playing of games which reduce the tension produced by his smallness. These include climbing high into a tree to be able to look down upon objects which the child ordinarily must look up to; playing at games and with toys which enable the child to pretend to be an adult such as toy automobiles and doll houses; dressing up in the parent's clothing and pretending to be an adult; and playing with the parent's implements and utensils such as father's tools and mother's kitchen equipment. Rummaging through chests and closets is a form of play aimed at appeasing curiosity.

The latency age child becomes aware of his greater size and capacities than earlier which overcome the limitations he had earlier known. To reduce the tension which besets him because new size and capacities, he seeks to play in active ways which utilize his energy and his capacities of locomotion, acrobatics and manipulation. Climbing in trees, running about the garden, turning summersaults and cartwheels, rolling down a grassy incline are among the tension reducing play activities favored by the latency child. Proprietors of amusement parks have exploited these proclivities of the latency child by providing him with rides which whip him about at great speed, roll him upside down and revolve him vertiginously. For this, the amusement park proprietor has devised the merry-go-round, the Ferris wheel, the roller coaster and the octopus.

In dealing with tension produced by the superego and ego ideal, the latency child may look to imaginative activity in which he exemplifies rectitude and righteousness. In this vein, he may engage in play activity in which he emulates heroic figures who invariably do the right thing. He may imagine himself as an heroic firemen saving victims from a burning building, or a policeman capturing a dastardly criminal or as a comic book hero foiling an evil villain.

Play during Adolescence

At the onset of adolescence, play abruptly changes. Toys in the sandbox, sand pails at the beach, cap guns and cowboy and Indian games in the back garden, the seesaw and the swing, turning cartwheels and somersaults—lose their pull upon the ego of the young person. As he experiences sudden growth in size and strength, he looks to more challenging forms of play to reduce the ego tension specific to adolescence. The desire to demonstrate in many ways his new and exhilarating gains in size, strength and intellectual prowess, he looks to amusements more like those of adults. He wants to ride a bicycle so that he can travel farther and faster than on his tricycle or scooter, and soon after wants to drive the family car or to own an automobile himself which he treats as much as a toy as he does as an essential means of transportation in a geographically dispersed infrastructure.

During latency, the tricycle affords him a sense of speed of motion, and later in adolescence the automobile provides him with a sense of power as well as speed. In less affluent societies, a motor scooter or motorcycle will suffice instead of an automobile. The adolescent driving an automobile is as powerful as an adult driving an automobile, enabling the adolescent to reduce the ego tension produced by the power deficit and by his wish for the status and privileges of adulthood, which are still largely withheld from him. Most middle age adults have experienced occasions when an adolescent or young adult driver has recklessly sped around him and cut in front of him on the streets and roads of his community, or as a pedestrian in, say, Rome or Florence has been nearly knocked down by a speeding motor scooter weaving through narrow streets.

The adolescent tends to continue his enjoyment of amusement park rides, but now in the company of a member of the opposite sex, the young male can sooth and protect the screaming girl terrified by the roller coaster and enjoy a measure of stolen erotic pleasure. As for games of sport, the adolescent wants to become a competitor rather than merely a player to demonstrate his greater capacities. He may join a league in which teams compete with each other in pursuit of a trophy. Perhaps unwisely, many parents of latency age children insist that their offspring play in competitive leagues while their child to the contrary merely wishes to enjoy playing the game to experience his increasing capacities of locomotion, coordination, manipulation and acrobatics. Adults often like to play with childhood toys with their young children or grandchildren hoping to experience again vicariously the joy they relished in their own childhood.

To enhance his sense of strength, the adolescent likes play which distinguishes him from the latency age children he left behind. He wants to engage in play at which latency age children cannot do well because of their smaller size, strength and intellect. Thus, rough and tumble contact sports such as football and ice hockey are favored. In baseball, the bases are moved to greater distances and the ball itself becomes a hardball rather than softball. He may take up more complicated card games than "Old Maid" and "Go Fish." He wants to play the same games and by the same rules and with the same equipment as adults to attenuate the ego tension he experiences at not yet being accepted as an adult and because of the competition he experiences with peers in their headlong pursuit of adult status. The adolescent, impelled by sexual urges, may choose games which titillate sexual lust and excite reproductive drives to reduce the ego tension which these propensities arouse. "Spin the Bottle" and "Post Office" are such games and are indulged in by adolescents, often with as much social trepidation as erotic delight.

Among male adolescents, physical hostility fuses with competition to impel "roughhouse" play in which informally males physically push and shove each other playfully in the locker room, the back garden, while walking along in groups or sitting together in automobiles, fast food restaurants and watching sports events together. Young boys new to adolescence may play by pushing girls on the playground as a means of social interaction, however clumsy, with the opposite sex. The increase in testosterone and the absence of an appropriate outlet for the urges it produces drives the adolescent male into physical "horseplay" while he is still learning how the mores of adult society expect him to behave in response to the impulses of puberty.

Narcissism deficit tension in adolescence may be appeased by play such as family card games, family picnics and any games and play activity participated in by the family in which the adolescent is able to exhibit his physical and intellectual capacities to make himself worthy of admiration and affection by his parents. Also, socializing with adolescent friends in playing at games, both physical in form as well as parlor games, may have the same result of eliciting admiration and affection from others, which appeases the narcissism deficit. Such activity tends to reduce narcissism tension and also ego worth tension because whatever activities commends the adolescent to those who would bestow affection will also tend to elicit admiration and worth.

Play behavior aimed at reducing the tension of individuation may find the adolescent and his peers engaging in rebellious activity such as graffiti defacing, overturning trash receptacles, soaping automobile windows and engaging is boisterous noisy behavior in late night hours to the discomfort of sleeping neighbors. By breaking free of parental restraints, the adolescent can demonstrate his separateness from his parent and his individuality. He may gain status among the adolescent population of his community with such daring rebellious and defiant behavior, thus reducing tension produced by the ego worth need for social status among peers.

The pursuit of the ego ideal will impel the adolescent to choose play in which expressions of his ideal may be exhibited. Building model airplanes may appease his ideal of becoming an aviator; reading fiction will assist him in sustaining his dream of becoming a novelist; exploring places forbidden by his parent will reduce tension of his desire to become an adventurer; repairing his bicycle or the toys of neighborhood children will assist him in his fantasy of becoming a mechanic or engineer. The play of the adolescent will tend to incorporate many of the attributes of the ego ideal he is constructing for his future as an adult.

Play during Young Adulthood

Young adult play tends to leave behind the practices of latency and adolescence. The young adult would not often want to be seen amusing himself with activities associated with latency age children and adolescents. The young adult is in the process of establishing himself in the walk of life he intended as an adolescent to achieve on his path to adulthood. Nevertheless, the young adult tends not to part easily with the joys he experienced during adolescence. If a part of his play during adolescence was riding his motorcycle, he may continue to ride it, but suffer some rebuke from his wife or girlfriend for his juvenile ways, urging that the motorcycle be given up for an automobile. If he played baseball or football with his adolescent chums, he and his friends may be looked at askance by more mature contemporaries if he continues to play these games. Such play is likely to be limited to backyard picnics privately indulged in with childhood friends. The young adult woman will likely have given up play such as spin the bottle, pizza parties and pajama parties for leisure activity such as looking after her small children in the park or in the back garden with other young matrons and attending gown up dinner parties with young adult friends.

Such pleasures as visiting nightclubs with friends, holding dance parties, vacationing at beaches or mountain cabins, taking sight-seeing trips with friends, going on hunting or fishing expeditions with intimate companions are typical of those engaged in by young adults who tend to be limited by modest financial resources. These activities allow them to reduce the tension of affiliation and gregariousness desires in ways which provide tension reducing support from other young adults similarly constrained financially. Young adults of wealthier families tend to indulge in more expensive play activities such as horseback riding, yachting, skiing, snorkeling and sojourning at costly resorts.

Narcissism deficit tension reduction is partly achieved through play in which husband and wife, or members of mutually committed pairs, amuse themselves with romantic activities such as in courting or in repeating courting activity enjoyed in the past. For example, the couple may revisit sites of former romantic interludes such as parks, historic sites, camp grounds, nightclubs, restaurants and hotels, or if they are new in their relationship, they may visit such places for the first time, showering each other with acts of affection which appeases each other's narcissistic cravings.

There are many ways in which young adults may attempt to reduce ego power deficit tension through play. Games requiring physical strength such as football allow them to demonstrate physical power. Card games such as contract bridge enable them to simulate the exercise of interpersonal power by defeating opponents. Hunting enables the young adult male to demonstrate his power by shooting game which try to escape him. Coy flirting is a diversion in which young adult females are able to demonstrate their power over males.

Play in which young adults are able to attract the admiration of others helps them to appease ego worth deficit tension. Any sort of show off play serves this purpose. The winner at card games, the accomplished dancer at the ball, the home run batter in the pickup baseball game, the prize winning marksman at the carnival shooting gallery, the Frisbee tosser who achieves the longest throw in a game of catch—are among the innumerable activities in which young adults can earn the admiration and affection of their peers.

Such play also may appease the drive for mastery for those young adults who stand out. Curiosity may be gratified by play involving mystery or puzzle solving. Crossword and jigsaw puzzles provoke curiosity when they are undertaken and reduce the tension it produces when they are successively completed. The scavenger hunt is a game that challenges both curiosity and mastery and appeases both when they are successfully concluded.

Play during Middle Adulthood

For the middle age adult, play involving physical activity progressively diminishes until he becomes more likely to content himself with merely attending sports events participated in by others or watching them on television. Unless he has made a special effort to sustain his physical prowess, he tends to be past his physical prime and to choose more sedentary forms of play to amuse himself. Sagging muscles, increasing avoirdupois and the probability of becoming winded when physically active tend to keep him on the couch or in the bleachers. Vicarious enjoyment of physical activities of younger people gradually takes over his interest in diversions requiring strenuous physical effort. He may engage in hunting or fishing outings, which are likely to be slow paced and furnished with creature comforts, or he may play golf strolling the fairways or traversing them while riding a motorized vehicle.

Sponsoring sports teams with financial support derived from his successful business may serve as a form of vicarious play for the middle age entrepreneur. The fortunes of his team in league competition may garner him a return of narcissism from friends by the expressions of admiration showered on him. To be able to own a professional sports teams because of one's affluence demonstrates power in the form of wealth which reduces ego tension, albeit temporarily because the power deficit always returns to require reducing again.

Power for the middle age adult most often manifests itself in the form of wealth gained from business, career achievement or the higher salary of the journeyman worker. While great disparities of wealth among the middle age population exist, at each level of wealth, whether great or modest, the middle age individual is likely to be wealthier than those younger and less advanced in their careers in the same walk of life. Play often tends to take the form of expensive activities requiring costly equipment, expensive travel or pricey accommodations which demonstrates the power of wealth of those middle age individuals able to indulge themselves in such activities.

The admiration and social status which the middle age individual is better able to demonstrate than younger individuals in the same walk of life also attracts respect, often mingled with envy, reducing his ego worth deficit. From staying at expensive resorts to play on their golf courses and tennis courts for the wealthy to owning or renting a more sturdy fishing camp or traveling in a more sumptuous recreation vehicle than neighboring less affluent fishermen and travelers demonstrates the greater power of the middle age individual over younger individuals even for those whose middle age prosperity is relatively modest.

For the middle age individual, play becomes less physical and more social in terms of socializing with age and social peers. Visiting friends, entertaining at home or dining out, socializing at one's club or lodge and watching televised sports events together at home, club, lodge or bar tend to be common play activity for the middle age individual.

Play during Old Age

Play during old age tends to reflect an extension of middle age play into even more sedentary ways. There are many exceptions in which old age people who have retained their vigor extend their physical life into their later years, but for most the body weakens and the sedentary way of life takes over. Play which would require vigorous moving about tends to be abandoned for card games or dominoes or other static parlor games and nattering with other elderly contemporaries on the park bench, in the tavern or in the retirement home.

The Commercialization of Play

The wide acceptance of play as a desirable and approved human activity early on spawned an industry aimed at supplying players with paraphernalia, physical accommodations and personal assistance for a price. The number of businesses in the play industry is extensive. They include among myriad others horseback riding stables, amusement parks, swimming pools, cruise ships, golf courses, vacation resorts, skating rinks—a complete list would be immense. These play activities are aimed at reducing general ego tension from a variety of sources rather than tension primarily from a particular stage of ego ontogenesis. The play industry companies tend to be among the first businesses which suffer reduced revenues or bankruptcy following a downturn in the business cycle. Individuals in the less affluent circumstances tend to forego indulging themselves in expensive play activity and revert to forms of play which require no or little expenditure of money.

Games

Games are a special form of play because they tend to simulate conditions found in real life, and playing games draws upon the capacities needed in real life. For example, the game of patty cake and peek-a-boo played with the infant simulates real life situations which the child will one day encounter in interacting with people. Patty cake teaches the pleasure which may come from working together cooperatively with another individual. Pick-a-boo teaches that when mother disappears, she may be relied upon to return, but only after the child achieves object constancy.

Games played by the latency child such as musical chairs and hide and seek teach competition and the experience of winning and losing on one's own. Team games such as baseball and football teach the power of cooperation in a group effort and the experience of winning or losing collectively. The members of a group which loses console each other, and the latency child is taught the tension reducing benefit of comradeship when competing against others. Such games as playing house enables the latency child to practice in simulated fashion the tasks of an occupation she may undertake later in adulthood. The game of cops and robbers teaches the latency child to become law abiding as well as the consequences of failing to become upright. The latency child may play numerous games which permit him to practice various occupations in a simulated way as he looks ahead to choosing a career path in life. Besides cops and robbers there is fireman, soldier or sailor, teacher, doctor or nurse, truck driver and countless other occupations which the latency child can play at.

The adolescent tends to avoid pretend games because they do not satisfy his drive toward acquiring a practical occupation on his way to adulthood. The games he plays must have consequences which bring the experience of real pleasure or real pain. He may plan to become a policeman, fireman of aviator and is not satisfied merely to play at any of these occupations.

The adolescent also comes to prefer games which have real consequences such as card games in which the loser may suffer tension producing embarrassment when losing or earn tension reducing admiration when winning. In the football games of adolescents and young adults, the physical contact with another player may be physically painful. In baseball, the adolescent or young adult player may be accidentally and painfully hit by the ball.

Parlor board games such as "Monopoly" teach about money and investing, and give the adolescent the incentive to save in order to attain reward for deferred spending. Chess teaches strategy and it teaches the adolescent to analyze the present to anticipate future events so that one can prepare for them. Card games of chance such as poker teach the adolescent and young adult that risk can lead to loss, and that luck—bad and good—are concomitants of risk. All games more or less simulate reality and afford the individual an opportunity to practice dealing with reality and learning to endure the tension increase of bad outcomes resulting from one's decisions and from different degrees of risk.

In middle adulthood, games which simulate reality tend more to be enjoyed for the tension reduction which playing them affords as a means of relaxing from the demands of the real world in which the individual actually lives. A game of chess or contract bridge lost can quickly be forgotten by the player who engaged in it to enjoy the social interaction with other players, and the act of playing the game merely enable the individual to gain temporary relief from escaping the stress of coping with reality.

Entertainment, which closely borders on play and serves the same purpose as play, will be discussed next.

12

ENTERTAINMENT DURING
EGO ONTOGENESIS

Play is distinguished from entertainment principally because play requires active participation by the experiencer while entertainment is generally a passive experience. In places, the two merge into each other because reality is presumably a continuum which human beings attempt to understand by conceptually dividing it into parts for the purpose of analysis. For example, a game such as football requires strenuous activity to play but becomes mere entertainment for observers who only watch the play from the bleachers or on a television screen from the comfort of their lounge chair. Play and entertainment have in common their capacity to reduce ego tension for those who experience them, and both tend to reduce ego tension specific to different stages of ego ontogenesis. Because the sources of ego tension differ at different stages of ego ontogenesis, the form of entertainment sought by the ego varies in order to respond to the tension in ways specific to each stage.

Entertainment During Primordial Life

During primordial life, physical and intellectual limitations of the infant make it largely dependent upon its caregivers for amusement. Entertainment must be selected for it and brought to it by caregivers whose aim includes diverting the infant's attention from various needs and discomforts which are tension producing and cause it to cry. Talking baby talk to it, playing patty-cake with it, dangling toys in front of it and shaking a rattle before it are forms of entertainment typically proffered by caregivers.

As the child becomes older, it may be entertained by simple stories and by watching entertainment on television designed to amuse small children. Stories of personified animals simulating experiences of small children are typical. For somewhat older children upon the threshold of the latency period, these stories often involve subjects of rectitude such as characters trying harder to perform self-care tasks, settling disputes without crying or hurting the other child, being helpful to parents and other children, particularly children with disadvantages such as being small or disabled. Often the figures in these narratives are personified animals. The success of these characters at accomplishing tasks like those imposed by the parent is tension reducing for the young child because the child experiences the character's tension reduction vicariously by identifying with the story's characters. The caregiver may entertain the child with music by singing to him simple songs intended by their creators to amuse children such as "Pop Goes the Weasel", or "Rock a by Baby" to help him fall asleep.

Entertainment During Latency

Stories of family life in which family members are reunited after an intervening separation afford the small child an opportunity to reduce the residue of decathexis tension remaining after experiencing the oral, anal, and Oedipal severation traumata of primordial life. The classical tale of Hansel and Gretal serves as an example of children angry with their controlling parents who go off into the woods on the their own only to be captured by the evil witch from which they make their escape and are reunited with their parents. Red Riding Hood is a similar narrative, only it is a terrifying wolf who is the villain rather than a witch. Many children's stories presented on television replicate this theme with variations.

During infancy, the child learns to wait for entertainment to be brought to it by the caregiver, but upon entering latency, the child begins to seek entertainment on its own. The suppression of primordial severation traumata does not fully extinguish the tension produced by these sources which is ever present in a subliminal state. Oedipal fears and wishes become displaced upon entities of which the child ego is consciously aware. Witches and goblins, mean nannies and teachers and other miscreants either in their own form or presented as personified animal characters are found in the entertainments favored by the latency age ego.

It is for the entertainment of latency age children that adults, remembering their own latency experience, whether as parents, teachers or workers and entrepreneurs in the entertainment industry, that narratives and characters are created in which deeds first put the characters in the way of harm, after which they manage to escape or are rescued by other characters who are protective. Involved in these narratives are malevolent parentified entities and benevolent parentified entities, the first in the form of evil doers and the second in the form of good characters, which assist the latency child to reduce the ego tension produced by the suppressed but subliminal Oedipus conflict. The action of the narrative first produces increased tension in the form of fear of the suppressed malevolent same sex parent represented as, say, an ogre or witch and then achieves tension reduction by means of the rescuing benevolent same sex parent represented as a hero or fairy godmother, these pairs of good and evil being the product of bifurcated suppressed filial ambivalence.

As the child progresses into the latency period, tension sources particularly salient during latency grow stronger. Filial ambivalence, small physical size and strength, limited capacities of locomotion, acrobatics, coordination and manipulation and general ignorance, puzzlement and curiosity about the world around it are strong tension producers for the latency child who tends to seek entertainment which has the capacity to alleviate this ego tension. Thus, preferred narrative entertainment, often of an adventurous format, tends to involve totally evil villains and entirely good heroes such as the cowboy hero who wears a white hat and the "bad guy" who wears a black hat, or the heroic cop versus the dastardly criminal, or the comic book superhero versus the arch villain. The defeat of the villain serves to reduce ego tension subliminally attributed to the malevolent parental surrogate, and the victory of the hero serves to reduce ego tension vicariously by means of the child's introjection of and identification with the hero.

Through identification with and introjection of the hero, the latency age child can also reduce the tension assailing him because of his small size and limited capacities. The entertainment industry tends to feed these predilections of the latency age child to its great profit, not only by purveying entertainment to the children but also by selling it to advertisers who in turn strive to sell their products to the children who are attracted to these entertainments.

It is during latency that the child tends to introject with greatest enthusiasm and in the greatest volume the values of his parent and of parentified mentoring adults. These values tend to be virtuous and ideal and often beyond the reach of ordinary mortals to achieve. The parent and mentoring adults such as nannies and teachers are wont to teach latency age children reality as ideal—that one should behave with absolute moral rectitude, which leaves little room for the foibles of mere human beings. Religion is taught, and the child during latency comes to perceive god for the first time as some form of being more powerful than the parent and upon whom the child can depend in circumstances when the parent's protective efforts fail to prevail. Like the parent, the god demands rectitude and may exact retribution upon those who fail his commandments. But god is more powerful even than the parent and must be obeyed by the parent as well as by the child.

Characters in entertainment narratives indulged in by latency age children often are depicted as overcoming some failure of rectitude after having learned anew the lessons taught to latency age children by adults. These entertainments tend to be homilies aimed at teaching children rectitude and apprising them of the consequences of unrectitudinous behavior. These narratives tend first to increase ego tension for the latency age child by depicting a character with whom the child identifies as behaving in conflict with rectitude and being sanctioned for it, then reduce ego tension by depicting an outcome in which the character repents and is forgiven. Such homilies teach children rectitudinous behavior and are used by religious teachers to inculcate the doctrine of the church as it governs behavior.

Fear of the consequences of behaving badly plague the latency age child, whose small size and dependence constitute powerlessness, raising ego tension in the form of fear of decathexis by parents and societal institutions. Entertainment in which narrative characters are saved from the error of their ways and returned to the fold are tension reducing for the latency age child and tends to permeate much of the entertainment proffered to the latency child and is eagerly obsorbed by the child. The ego ideal begins to form as a consequence of the establishment of the superego and tends to be comprised of these rectitudinous concepts taught to the child during latency. The ego ideal intensifies during the individuation process in adolescence.

Adolescence and Entertainment

The turbulence experienced by the ego during the Oedipus conflict returns during adolescence brought on by the child's sudden growth in size and capacity which begins to rival that of the parent, reducing the child's fear of the parent and attenuating the suppression of the Oedipus conflict. The child begins to experience rivalry with the same sex parent as he did during the experience of the original Oedipus conflict, an upsurge in self-assertiveness, and a wish to individuate from the parent by establishing an identity separate from the parent and unique in the world. The adolescent strives to become known no longer as merely the child of his parent but as someone in his own right.

Many of the issues which were suppressed with the suppression of the Oedipus conflict resurface after the onset of puberty and must be dealt with anew usually by the employment of ego mechanisms which displace pleasurable filial affect upon parentified entities targeted by the ego for that purpose and project filial hostility and fear upon other parentified entities targeted for' that purpose. Entertainment selected by the adolescent tends to provide tension reduction experience vicariously through identification with narrative characters who are subjected to and surmount the travails of adolescence.

In fiction and drama, the white hat cowboys and black hat villains of latency tend gradually to morph into more realistic representations of characters which populate the world of the more mature adolescent. In cowboy and Indian battles, characters who are shot appear actually to die in pain and bleeding to the dismay and grief of their fictional friends and relatives and are given formal burial rather than simply left where they lie to the unconcern of the fictional characters around them as the narrative of the entertainment blithely moves on to the next scene. Arch villains of the comic books are gradually abandoned in favor of more complicated characters whose journey through life has shaped them into the villains they became. The adolescent may not immediately give up comic book quality literature, which may continue to interest him while he learns to enjoy more mature literature preferred by the adults whom he wishes to emulate in his aspiration to become an adult.

The adolescent becomes interested in narratives depicting romance between males and females (in the case of heterosexuals). Often, female adolescents become infatuated with male characters, and male adolescents become infatuated with female characters. The phenomenon of infatuation extends beyond fictional characters to the actual actors who perform the roles of the fictional characters in the theater, cinema or television drama. "Stars" among performers are often idolized and related to as if deified like the parent of the Oedipal child. Such entertainment helps the adolescent to reduce ego tension, if only temporarily, produced by erotic stimuli through vicarious enjoyment of the trials and triumphs of romantic characters.

For the prurient adolescent, pornography accompanied by masturbation is often resorted to as a means of relieving sexual tension, which tends to be intense during adolescence. Much tension producing fear and guilt may accompany masturbation for the adolescent who has been inculcated with or adopted a belief that masturbation is sinful and may lead to damage or damnation. If he has been abstinent, he may enjoy fiction in which those who fail to abstain are punished, which temporarily reduces ego tension produced by superego prohibitions. For those adolescents who are not abstemious and are not plagued by guilt, masturbation may serve as a practical reducer of sexual tension.

Entertainment in the form of music which the adolescent tends to favor because it is different from that favored by the parent's generation, tends to serve the adolescent's individuation propensity. Adolescent music is often rebellious in its aim and offensive to the parent. Too loud, too ridiculous and outlandish for the parent, it is fun for the adolescent and helps him to celebrate his difference from his parent and from the parent's generation and thus is tension reducing. Adolescent music is also tension reducing because it accompanies adolescent social dancing, which is a form of erotic socialization between the sexes and a facilitator of courting and seduction, and becomes play rather than entertainment when the music is no longer simply listened to.

Entertainment in the form of drama and fiction which depicts idealized characters in the context of a narrative in which they conduct themselves with great rectitude against malefactors or great adversity and overcome danger and hardship triumphantly tends especially to attract adolescent and young adult consumers of such entertainment. Such entertainment tends to appease ego tension for the adolescent and young adult which is produced by his struggle for individuation, for establishing a separate and unique identity and the ego ideal. The adolescent and young adult particularly enjoy adventure in which characters sojourn to far away places with strange ways and circumstances, which appeases the ego's curiosity about other places and other lands.

The adolescent and young adult also enjoy dramatic entertainment in which the protagonists struggle to build careers, court and marry an idealized member of the opposite sex, found a family and establish a place in society. Such entertainment gratifies the ego's desire to attain these same goals in life. Drama depicting patriotism, the triumph of rectitude in a social context and the reward of hard work and honest living also tends to be gratifying to the ego of the adolescent and young adult. Such entertainment helps to reduce ego tension produced by the difficulty in adhering to the imperatives of the superego during the establishment of the adolescent ego ideal.

Entertainment During Young Adulthood

The young adult gradually becomes attracted to entertainment which appeases the ego tension from sources particular to young adulthood. Nevertheless, much of the entertainment that captivated adolescents continues to attract the young adult. For example, spectator sports, adventure drama and romance continue to attract him as it did the adolescent. Much of the music preferred by the adolescent continues to appeal to the young adult, but the members of these two stages of ego ontogenesis begin to part their ways as the young adult moves toward middle adulthood. The young adult seeks the privileges of young adulthood—marriage, his own family, a remunerative career, an adult status in society, a degree of wealth with which he can enter the marketplace and purchase ego worth assets of his own choosing, and of particular importance he seeks to finalize his own separate and unique identity and to leave childhood behind. Many of the entertainments enjoyed during adolescence continue to satisfy, but new ones are needed to satisfy the tension reduction aims of young adulthood.

Dramatic narratives which depict the young adult overcoming obstacles to achieving young adult status are sought by the young adult to assist in the reduction of ego tension produced by these obstacles. The young man in conflict with the older man over issues of rectitude, judgment and resolve may be found in various formats. The young army or naval officer in conflict with the general or admiral, the young corporate executive impeded in his progress toward higher rank in the corporation by a stubborn chief executive officer, the innovative young priest blocked by the old fashioned rector of his church, the young assistant professor whose pursuit of tenure is thwarted by the old tenured professor who is chairman of the academic department—endless examples of such dramatic presentations in motion pictures, in the theater, in novels and on television appeal to the young adult in his struggle to establish himself against impediments imposed by malevolent parentified fictional entities. Such presentations may also appeal to the adolescent looking ahead toward his future, and to the middle age man thinking back upon his own climb to middle adulthood status. As circumstances change in the twenty-first century for woman in North American and European societies in the direction of greater career opportunity for women, young women also become interested in such narratives, especially with young women characters as the successful protagonists, because of the tension reduction effects of this theme.

Slow to give up the music of adolescence, the young adult continues to derive pleasure from the music of his adolescent years, but he gradually moves on to music preferred by the middle age adults whose status and privileges he seeks to achieve for himself. The young adult wishes to put away the playthings of his adolescent years including the music which gave him tension reduction pleasure. Normatively the young adult is no longer courting or seeking to seduce members of the opposite sex because he has become married or is cohabitating with a "significant other" so that he has the heterosexual relationship which he had sought during adolescence and no longer needs to seek it. He will listen to the old music but more to reminisce than to utilize it for adolescent purposes of seduction and courting.

Entertainment During Middle Adulthood

As the young adult moves toward middle adulthood, seeking the privileges and advantages of middle adulthood but clinging to the joys of adolescence, he eventually completes the transition into the province of middle adulthood. For the middle age adult, the music of the new adolescent generation becomes annoying when indulged in by the new crop of adolescents and is perceived as too loud, too ridiculous, confrontational and undesirable. He tends to forget how outrageous the music of his own adolescent days was regarded by the older generation and instead remembers it as worthy, while the music of the new generation of adolescents often appears unworthy and to be avoided.

The middle age adult tends to remember the music of his own adolescent and young adult years wistfully and pleasurably because it still reduces ego tension but for different reasons than originally. Now, it helps to reduce the tension of decathexis from lost youth. As time moves on toward his ultimate demise, he remembers the time gone by and contemplates nostalgically, in the words of Longfellow's poem, "My Lost Youth."

Middle adulthood is the age of maturity, the time of the individual's acme in all things cultural, in judgment, in wealth, in social status, and the sort of entertainment which tends to appeal to him bears few of the elements which amused him in young adulthood, in adolescence, and in his latency period. The simplistic characters of fiction such as white hat and black hat cowboys and the super heroes and arch villains of comic books appear ludicrous to him, and even the more complex characters admired during adolescence and early young adulthood no longer hold his attention. Villains must be characters produced by difficulty in accommodating to the vicissitudes of life, a fatal self destructive flaw in character development like that of Shylock in *The Merchant of Venice* or Miss Havisham in *Great Expectations* so that disaster of his own making envelops the villainous character.

The middle age individual tends to have acquired a concern for civic affairs. He is worried about the success of society and its organizations and institutions. He tends to have more interest in government and public policy than at any earlier time in his life, unless he had been a politically rebellious adolescent, and is more likely to vote in elections, to be a political activist, to contribute to civic organizations and non-profit organizations and to serve on civic committees such as the school board and the governing board of his church. Hence, entertainment which attracts his interest tends to be drama about societal concerns, politics and government, and historical themes and non-fiction television programs about science, nature, sociology and anthropology. He tends to follow the news on radio, television, the Internet and in the newspapers which, because of his intense interest in it, virtually becomes a form of entertainment. He tends to be particularly interested in the observations of news commentators who interpret events.

He is more likely to read learned periodicals and professional journals than any time earlier. Having become aware of the passage of time, the brevity of life, and the fragility of civilization, ego tension elevates as he contemplates the ultimate demise not only of himself but also of his civilization and the planet itself without which memory of his having been here will be extinguished forever. Conservatism about human affairs assumes greater importance than the promotion of change toward the untried and unproven. If he has not traveled much during his life, middle age will be his last chance to travel while still fit enough to tolerate its vicissitudes. Travel tends to overlap the distinction between play and entertainment because while traveling in play, seeing new places and places heard of and longed to see is a form of entertainment.

Old Age and Entertainment

For the old age individual, the entertainment which appeals to the middle age individual continues to attract his attention. The entertainment designed for the adolescent and young adult population tends to be rejected out of hand by the old age individual who takes no interest in it except for looking back upon his own life when as a young person he himself enjoyed such entertainment. However, the old age individual might enjoy latency age entertainment vicariously while holding his grandchild on his lap. There tends to be much less entertainment aimed specifically at the old age individual because old people tend to be retired or failing physically and unable to produce entertainment for their own time in ego ontogenesis.

The old age individual tends to enjoy entertainment which dwells upon the continuity of life and the enduring nature of nature. Themes such as that exemplified in such presentations as Samuel Butler's novel, *The Way of All Flesh,* may attract him. In particular, he enjoys narratives about older individuals because he is more likely to identify with them than with characters of adolescence and young adulthood who may seem to him to be shallow, unwise and cocky.

The Commerce of Entertainment

Entertainment can be sold in the marketplace, and the entertainment preferences of persons at different stages of ego ontogenesis affects the marketplace for the entertainment industry. In a word, the population which is offered the greatest variety and availability of entertainment in the mass marketplace is the one in the stage of ego ontogenesis which is most populous and therefore comprises the greatest remunerative market for entertainment products and services. When the middle age population was not overshadowed in numbers by the adolescent and young adult population, it was catered to by an entertainment industry which regarded middle age people as having the most money.

In the present era, one can observe the affinity of the entertainment industry for submitting to the marketplace entertainments which are believed to appeal to the largest ontogenetic population. This affinity is disclosed by the effect of the so-called "baby boom" generation born to the returning veterans of the Second World War. The ranks of this generation bourgeoned through the second half of the twentieth century and beyond and formed the largest market niche in the commercial marketplace. Toys for children in the marketplace abounded during the fifth and sixth decades of the century, and during the seventh decade when adolescents were affluent commercially produced "rock" music deluged the marketplace and continued to the end of the century as the baby boomers moved through young adulthood and middle adulthood.

The dramatic themes of baby boomer adolescence and young adulthood' prevailed as well as themes of romance and revolution against the ways of their parents dominated the entertainment industry, leaving little of interest to the old age generation available in the mass entertainment market. When the baby boomers became the producers of commercial entertainment, the self-importance of the baby boomers ballooned into evidence when television situation comedies and motion pictures began to emphasize the self-proclaimed great significance of the baby boomers' "social revolution" against war and middle class values. The unkempt long hair, the ragged and dirty working class clothing, the street drugs, the casual sex and the "Wood Stock" phenomenon symbolized the entertainment and life style predilections of the baby boomers.

The ontogenetic specificity of commercial entertainment should be noted in the capacity, or lack of it, of individuals in different stages of ego ontogenesis to favor or tolerate entertainment specific to a different stage of ontogenesis than their own. This phenomenon tends to be attested by the lack of appeal which middle age and old age entertainment has for latency, adolescent and young adult populations. The classical novels of Thackery, Butler and Dickens, among others, often fail to hold the attention of younger generations. By contrast, stories preferred by adolescents and young adults may in some cases hold the attention of middle age and old age individuals who recall their own youth.

13

PATTERNS OF SOCIALIZING
DURING EGO ONTOGENESIS

The human ego evolves into what it becomes in the context of social interaction. The question of what the human ego would become in the absence of social interaction cannot readily be answered because the infant and child invariably interacts with others, particularly its caregivers. Infants who are deprived of normal care giving often do not do well.[1] Upon rare occasions, infants have been known to survive in the care of animals, which presumably they would not have done well without. But because normatively the infant ego evolves through its ontogenesis in interaction with human caregivers, this reality will be the focus of the affect of socializing upon the ontogenesis of the ego.

During primordial life the infant ego comes to perceive the external agent of parent or other caregiver and to cathect to the external agent upon which it relies absolutely for the reduction of tension produced by impinging stimuli. The interaction between the infant ego and the individuals to which it cathects assumes a form configured to the shape given to it by that interaction, determining the way in which the ego relates to other objects with which it interacts. Each response by the infant ego to the impinging stimuli of another individual which impacts it becomes a response technique to impinging stimuli which the ego retains and may utilize in responding to subsequent sources of tension producing impinging stimuli which it encounters. In other words, the ego learns by experience and applies what it learns to new circumstances.

External agents upon which the ego comes to depend to reduce the tension of impinging stimuli tend to form a succession of objects of dependence in which the ego's relatedness to any of them shapes its relatedness to the

---

[1] See **Berelson, Bernard, and Steiner, Gary A.** *Human Behavior: An Inventory of Scientific Findings.* New York: Harcourt, Brace and World, Inc., 1964. pp. 64-71.

immediate successor agent of dependence. The process by which this succession of relatednesses occurs is called derivative relatedness transference devolution. The way in which the infant ego related to the parent of weaning will be relied upon to deal with and relate to the parent of toilet training, who because of the absence of object constancy in the infant ego's repertoire of response techniques is related to by the infant ego as if it were a different object of relatedness than the parent of weaning.

The tension reducing techniques employed in responding to the parent of weaning are utilized, after being modified, to respond to the parent of toilet training and modified again to respond to the parent of the Oedipus conflict. The parental entity of the Oedipus conflict trifurcates and becomes in the perception of the infant ego three different parental entities of relatedness consisting of the generalized parent, the maternal parent and the paternal parent. The capacity of the infant ego to perceive these three entities is an outcome of the increased brain development which occurs during primordial life.

After the primordial period comes to a close with the resolution of the Oedipus conflict and the creation of the superego, thenceforce the human ego tends to relate to others upon whom the ego perceives any degree of dependence as it did to the primordial parent. Objects of dependence become parentified, meaning that they are related to as the infant related to the parent. During the latency period, the ego's filial relatedness greatly expands in size and complexity as it comes to relate to greater numbers of individuals with whom it comes into contact within and without the family, in the neighborhood and in the community.

Each additional object of relatedness tends to be parentified. Siblings become parentified, and then objects outside the family may not only become parentified but also become siblified—that is, related to as if they were one's brother or sister who had been parentified. Relatedness complexities become extensive. For example, an older play peer may be fraternified, that is related to as one's brother who was himself parentified so that, say, the protectiveness which was found in the father was extended to the brother and thence to the play peer. As a consequence, socializing becomes suffused with parentification and siblification.

The human ego craves social interaction because it is in the context of social interaction that the human being seeks narcissistic gratification, power and worth. By relating to others as to the parent, the affection bestowed by the others provides the ego with the experience of a return of the narcissism earlier extended to the parent, and facilitates the reduction of narcissism deficit tension. In the absence of others to interact with, the ego could not achieve narcissism deficit tension reduction.

The human ego craves the experience of worth, which is initially bestowed by the value accorded to the infant ego by the parent. To strengthen the filial cathexis, the infant ego seeks worth in the perception of the external agent of dependence. The infant ego places great value upon the external agent because of the infant's absolute dependence upon that agent and thus seeks to have the external agent value it by perceiving it as worthy. When the infant ego perceives the parent bestowing worth upon it, it experiences a reduction of decathexis tension, tension produced by the fear of being abandoned by the parent of absolute dependence.

The craving for narcissistic gratification and worth in relation to the parent tends to be transferred to older siblings and thence to persons and to groups of persons external to the family according the degree of dependence the ego perceives itself to have in relation to the sibling, individual or group of persons. As the individual transfers his reliance upon the parent in the context of the family to others external to the family, to groups and to societal institutions and their functionaries, he seeks their affection and admiration in order to experience the reduction of decathexis tension and to attain the security of being protected and looked after by depended-upon others. Elected public officials know this from their own experience and tend to beam in friendly approval upon their adult constituents whose reelection vote they seek.

For the primordial infant, it is with the members of the family that social interaction is experienced. As the individual enters the latency period and moves beyond the ménage and garden into the neighborhood and the school, his social interaction expands as does the array of external objects of dependence he encounters. He senses dependence upon the school and the church and the functionaries of these institutions, namely teachers and clergy persons. These functionaries are perceived to have power equivalent to that of the parent and often will be perceived as having more power than the parent upon occasions when the parent is seen by the child to pay deference to these functionaries.

By the time the child arrives at adolescence, he has come to experience dependence upon authorities external to the family with greater frequency and intensity than to the family and to transfer filial relatedness to them. In the matter of dependence, the parent begins progressively to diminish in importance as external agents increase in importance. Societal authorities are viewed as higher authorities than the parent in the social hierarchy. The individual will one day stand upon his own two feet as the equal of his parent in the eyes of the community and relate to the authorities in society as he once did to his parent as critical objects of dependence. He will then crave the affection and admiration of these objects to assure the cathexis to them which he greatly valued vis-à-vis his parent.

The patterns of socialization established during latency and adolescence tend to shape the individual's patterns of socializing for the remaining course of life. The way that he relates to others, his expectations about how he will be treated by others, what others will expect of him, his way of analyzing the behavior of others, which others he will parentify and which will be siblified, the degree of risk he exposes himself to with regard to the narcissistic and ego worth deficit tension which he hopes will be reduced by interacting with others are all affected by the patterns established during latency and adolescence.

Man is a gregarious animal and tends to seek others with whom to interact. And in his interaction, the individual will seek to satisfy a range of ego needs. Because all human behavior is aimed at reducing ego tension or obviating ego tension increase, the individual socializes with others to achieve these purposes. One can list the sources of ego tension perceived by the ego and analyze the individual's effort to deal with them through socializing activity.

Consider first the elements as a source of impinging stimuli. Excessive temperatures, physical impact, hunger, thirst and threat of violence are all perceived by many as better dealt with within the context of the group and the community. Although a relatively few individuals may achieve and sustain self-dependence outside the community, the overwhelming majority of human beings seek safety in numbers. The group and the community offer division of labor and specialization of function so that the group's members and members of the community have the benefit of a much greater array of skills, services and products than any one could achieve alone.

But individuals seek the society of others for many reasons which are not motivated so much by practical concerns as by concerns of the ego alone. To achieve narcissistic gratification, to exercise power, to sustain one's vision of surety and to facilitate rectitude, to establish social status, to validate the ego ideal, to project guilt, to parentifiy and to siblify, to identify with and to introject—these are some of the ego's tension reduction needs which impel the ego to seek the society of others.

The Stages of Ego Ontogenesis
And Patterns of Socialization

Primordial Life

During primordial life, socializing patterns of the infant ego are limited almost entirely to interaction with family members and caregivers. The infant ego's interaction with others is primarily one of demanding that his tension reduction needs be met. He gives little to others, whose willingness to interact with him arises from a combination of parental bonding and the prospect of societal sanction if they fail in the parental obligations imposed by society.

The parent and other caregivers introject and identify with the infant as a means of reducing the ego tension produced by the childcare burden imposed upon them. By identifying with and introjecting the infant, the parent and caregivers vicariously bestow care-giving services upon themselves and thus experience less of a burden by means of these mechanisms. Often these mechanisms fail to dispel the ego tension produced by care giving burdens, which then return with great tension and concomitant unpleasure for the caregiver. The caregiver tends repeatedly to struggle to reduce the tension of care giving by applying these mechanisms and reapplying them each time the tension returns to beleaguer him anew.

The social experience of the primordial infant is one of neediness. When later in adulthood, the ego occasionally experiences a deficit of narcissism and worth and consequently a great need for the care and concern of others, he is experiencing what he experienced during his primordial infancy in relation to his caregivers. The social interaction with others of the primordial infant is one of seeking to placate his neediness. He tends to be highly ego centric in relationship to others including play peers. His capacity for empathy, which is only just developing, tends to be more concerned with manipulating others to serve him than to extend consideration to them for their ego needs.

Patterns of Socializing During Latency

The latency child brings to social interaction capacities shaped by his responses to weaning, toilet training and the Oedipus conflict. He begins to play with other children in ways which he hopes will facilitate his dealing with the tension produced by the imperatives of the superego which compel him to accept eating and drinking practices required by weaning and to accept toileting practices required by toilet training. His continued resistance to behaving in support of these requirements often finds him projecting his own residue of resistance to weaning and toilet training upon his latency play peers, or conspiring with them to tweak the parental nose.

For example, the latency play peers may play together in the mud, which they know will annoy the parent, although it helps to reduce by sublimation the residue of tension remaining after the acceptance of toilet training has been fully established. At times, he may sublimate toilet training tension by playing in the mud with the protection of the group, mud by displacement serving as surrogate feces. When the parent appears and scolds the' latency child for playing in the mud, the child may project his guilt on to his play peers by accusing them of leading him astray. "They made me do it," is an oft-heard defense of the latency child when his parent has caught him engaged in disapproved behavior.

Latency children socialize together to escape the limitations placed upon them by the parent who is concerned for their safety. Unafraid of the danger perceived by their parents, they seek protection in numbers to evade parental proscriptions. They often go on adventures which their parents would forbid, such as roaming through shopping malls, exploring abandoned buildings and investigating parks, river banks and rail yards. Curiosity is the facilitator of individuation—to follow where wonderment beckons. Latency age children are drawn into social intercourse with each other also because children crave the society of their own kind just as adults crave the society of adults as a means to reduce decathexis tension, which is experienced as loneliness, and to unite against shared sources of tension producing stimuli. Children band together to escape the tension of excessive solitude, and they band together to gain the security of numbers. Latency age children continue the individuation process which began during primordial life and which accelerates as the course of life lengthens from childhood toward adulthood. Individuation by its nature is tension producing and is less painful if pursued in the company of others who are undertaking the same process. Children tend to want to individuate in step with each other to mitigate the ego tension which separation from the parent of dependence produces.

As children individuate they tend to explore the world of adults and wish to become adults. They come to envy the greater power, privileges and status enjoyed by adults, which are denied to children. They wish to model themselves upon adults in order to enjoy vicariously the advantages which they believe that adults enjoy. Latency children tend to play at games which simulate the adult world which children want to imitate because it is more prestigious than their own, which confers more status and bestows more worth, and because they want to occupy that world one day. The heroes and heroines of latency children tend to be the more powerful and higher status adults, which they emulate in play to enjoy that power and status vicariously. The latency child who lacks latency age play peers misses its advantages, and in adulthood he may tend to evince a degree of ineptness which might have been avoided.

The "best friend" syndrome tends to emerge during latency in which two youngsters bind together socially as veritable "partners" in the task of dealing with the tension producing challenges of latency. Best friends are confidents who commiserate with each other over their separate and similar troubles in coping with life. They often have secrets together which they keep from other play peers and which constitute personal admissions that would be harmful to the ego ideal if known to others, or they may share their extravagant hopes with each other such as vaunting future dreams or unrealistic romantic aims toward a member of the opposite sex. Best friend alliances tend to continue into adolescence and may be fondly remembered in adulthood. Sometimes best friend pairs are transitory, but the best friend syndrome continues permuted to a different pair often but not always from the same group of latency age peers.

Socializing Patterns during Adolescence

While adolescence tends to burst upon the ego abruptly at the onset of puberty, the socializing patterns which develop may evolve more slowly out of the socializing patterns which were established during latency. In the absence of imposed separation, the latency age best friend pair will continue into adolescence with permutations among friendship groups if a best friend falling out occurs or a new best friend may be found. However, the venues of the adolescent tends to expand beyond that of the latency child, moving up from the neighborhood school to a more centralized school serving a larger school district. As a consequence, he may be thrown into contact with age peers he has not seen before, and making new acquaintances may lead to the making of new friends.

As the impulse to individuate greatly intensifies during adolescence, the ego guides behavior to seek with greater intensity the society of other adolescents. As a function of individuation, adolescents tend to develop social patterns apart from and in opposition to their parents. This phenomenon is manifested in dress and argot, and in clothing and life style fashions not fathomed by parents and often offensive to parents. Cryptic slang the parent never heard before and cannot translate, outrageous clothing styles, awful sounding music and leisure pursuits of which the parent may disapprove are suddenly thrust into the parent's notice as the adolescent and his peer society strive to be different and rebellious in order for each to establish separation from his parent and an identity different from the parent and unique in the world.

It is ironic that in the adolescent's efforts to establish a separate and unique identity he often adopts clothing styles and ways which are virtually identical to the other adolescents in order to reduce the tension of decathexis produced by individuation by fitting in so as to be accepted in their adolescent society. These patterns of adolescent socializing tend to put the parent at arms length, but the adolescent is still dependent upon the parent for the basic supports of life—shelter, food, clothing, healthcare, education, and the accouterments of adolescent amusement and leisure activity. It is a mark of his transition into young adulthood when the individual begins to furnish his own needs without exacting tribute from his parent to meet the costs of his support.

The adolescent struggles to establish his ego ideal which includes the persona he wishes to present to others and hopes will be reflected in the way' others relate to him. He seeks a way about him which distinguishes him from his adolescent peers and which he hopes will elevate him in their eyes. He may decide to become an athlete, or a musician, or a scholar or display the accouterments of an adult career toward which he is heading. Such practices give him an identifiable image by which he hopes to be known and admired by his peers. In establishing his separate and unique identity, he relies heavily upon his persona, which reflects his ego ideal.

The adolescent must give evidence that he is in the process of becoming able one day to provide his own livelihood. This involves a demonstrated devotion to his studies which will qualify him for a remunerative occupation, or he must exhibit progress toward learning a remunerative trade or give evidence that he is prepared to work at any untrained occupation which will reward him with a livelihood. Adolescents begin to sort themselves out as to whether they are headed in adulthood to a professional or managerial occupation, or to an occupation as a trades person or merely to work at any paying job he can find no matter how menial.

Patterns of socializing which arose in latency begin in adolescence to sever along lines determined by the likely future occupation and social status which play peers are expected to take up in adulthood. In deciding upon a future occupation, the adolescent will test his predilections upon his play peers to observe their response as to whether his choice is realistic and how it will affect his social status in adulthood. In such testing, adolescents begin to see whether they are heading along pathways which will lead to socializing patterns which will separate them from each other or sustain them in their camaraderie.

The resurgent Oedipus conflict will tend to redefine the adolescent's relatedness to his parent. The competition and rivalry with the same sex parent for preferment with the opposite sex parent tends to return from its place of suppression during latency almost to the point of fully resurfacing. The effort to continue to suppress the Oedipus conflict intensifies as the Oedipus conflict disrupts the evenness of the adolescent's filial-parental interaction. The adolescent rebellion, which emerges in part to facilitate individuation and the establishment of a separate and unique identity, tends to suffuse with the renewed Oedipus conflict to lend a hostile tinge to filial competition and rivalry with the same sex parent. Thus, filial rebellion tends in one way or another to evince filial hostility as well as divergence from the parent.

Filial hostility may become so severe as to threaten severation from the parent and lead to filial-parental estrangement. Adolescents experiencing filial-parental estrangement will tend to be drawn to other adolescents undergoing similar experiences. A pattern of socializing is then formed in which rebellious spirits hostile to the parent and to the parent's generation of adults band together to sublimate their filial hostility sometimes by undertaking a noble purpose in conflict with the parents' generation. Protesting public policy or prevailing mores about sex or religion or social discrimination are examples of such sublimated filial hostility suffused with adolescent rebellion. Becoming wayward in opposition to established public mores is another form of adolescent rebellion. Other adolescents may remain in mainstream society while manifesting their filial rebellion and filial hostility in less disruptive ways such as rejecting the clothing and life style fashions of their parents' generation and carrying on a romantic relationship with someone anathema to the parents.

The adolescent's ambivalence toward the same sex parent impels him to entertain thoughts of surpassing his parent in his accomplishments, but he may experience guilt at these thoughts which diminishes the parent whom he once sought to emulate, identify with and introject as the means to elevate his own worth. His parent may give evidence of hoping his child will surpass him, which would elevate the parent through identification with and introjection of his child. But the child may continue to experience guilt at his aim of surpassing his parent and do poorly because of his guilt and irrational fear of parental retribution.

The son may aspire to a greater career than that of his father, and the daughter may seek to be more attractive to men than her mother and to marry a more prestigious man than her mother married, which is upsetting to her because such an aim demeans the father she competed with her mother to attract and also risks inviting the retribution of her mother. The daughter who entertains such fears may in practice seek out less desirable men and fail to evince the charm and sexual attractiveness which would surpass or even equal her mother. Adolescents who cope with the renewed Oedipus conflict often seek each other's companionship for commiseration and fortitude, which promotes a socializing pattern characterized by intimacy and mutual encouragement in which losers band together in each other's society for protection and commiseration.

The reproductive drives tend to propel adolescents into socializing patterns shaped by sexual desire and mating. The wish to find a mate and to seduce the opposite sex leads to particular courting patterns and venues facilitatory for such purposes. Formal dances and nightclub dancing, social get togethers, the search for stylish and sexually attractive clothing styles and sexually attractive ways are practices adolescents may follow. Adolescents as they advance closer to young adulthood find their wish to mate intensifying. To attract and secure a mate with which a family will be formed and children begot and reared cause adolescents to find venues for male and female socializing. The female wishes to hone her skills at attracting and securing a male mate, and males hope to find a female which they can seduce and perhaps marry. Marriage tends always to seem a possibility for the male, but to secure an idealized female to marry is less certain. These ambitions are exercised in social circumstances intended to mix the sexes together in an environment in which expectations of participants entertain the possibility of mating and seduction. While adolescents continued to value relationships' with same sex best friends, they are nevertheless impelled to seek social situations which bring them into contact with members of the opposite sex.

Young Adult Patterns of Socializing

A transition in patterns of socializing tends to occur between adolescence and young adulthood. While best friend pairs and same sex peer groups continue, they give way in importance to socializing patterns characterized by a mixing of the sexes. Homosexual young adults may seek same sex venues in which homosexuals socialize. The pursuit of sexual partners and marital partners tend to "break up that old gang of mine." The desire to marry and establish a family supersedes previous socializing patterns in importance. Marital families tend to socialize more with each other, and much less with unmarried peers. To socialize outside the family, marital pairs wish to find solace in the company of other marital pairs. Marital pairs not yet endowed with children tend to seek other marital pairs not yet burdened in that way. Unmarried pairs are seen as not knowing about life characterized by a state of sexual intimacy. They tend to view unmarried people as lacking knowledge about life, as behind hand in their passage through life and unable to share the critically important experience of being married and burdened with the care of children.

Social status problems intensify for the young adult. When he was still an adolescent, the possibility of social mobility remained. But in young adulthood, social mobility tends to bog down. The career chosen has the effect of determining income, social friends and social status and is difficult to change. In social democracies, the possibility of social mobility always remains, but the practicality of social mobility rapidly diminishes. Consequently, during young adulthood social status and socializing patterns tend to freeze in place, and the individual's social interactions tend to stratify along planes of social status. However, individuals united by special interests such as a hobby, or a political advocacy group, or a volunteer organization may have memberships which cross social stratification lines so that members are sometimes drawn from a variety of backgrounds and socioeconomic classes.

During young adulthood, socializing often occurs across socioeconomic class lines to serve special interests. Well-to-do merchants may socialize with less well off customers to promote business. The boss may socialize across socioeconomic class lines to enable his employee to entertain him socially. But an employee is more likely to socialize with other employees at the same hierarchical level than with his boss, and well-to-do individuals are more likely to socialize with other well-to-do individuals than with their lessers.

Socializing Patterns in Middle Adulthood

The ego experiences greater absence of tension increase in the company of others who are in similar circumstances rather than in the company of those with whom they perceive themselves as in various ways inferior. Thus, members of a social class prefer the company of their own kind, members of racial groups tend to be more comfortable in the company of others belonging to the same race, women are more comfortable in the company of other women and men tend to be more comfortable in the company of other men, and the rich often prefer to mingle with other rich people than with poor people or less affluent people.

It is not surprising that middle age people prefer the company of other middle age people to that of the company of mixed ages. Persons in similar occupations like to socialize together, hence the conferences of professional associations and the meeting halls where union members gather. This does not imply that grandparents do not like the company of grandchildren or that young adults do not seek the company of middle age individuals who might serve as their patrons, but when left to their own devices individuals of different age groups tend to seek the company of their own kind with whom to relax and safely be able to lower their social defenses.

Middle age individuals often see young adults as not having arrived yet, of not having established themselves and of not having proved that they can succeed. Middle age adults tend to see adolescents as callow and unproved, as over-dependent upon their parents and upon social institutions, and as pushy and disrespectful of the middle age adults who have succeeded when the adolescents may not succeed. When socializing in venues in which young adults and adolescents are present, the middle age adult expects to be regarded with deference by younger persons in the company and are miffed when they are not. Middle age adults are more likely to serve in civic organizations and in their churches, which constitute socializing patterns more characteristic of middle age individuals than of other age categories.

Socializing Patterns in Old Age

Old age individuals are often segregated against their wishes into old age ghettoes in the form of retirement communities and senior citizen centers. They tend to become survivors as their spouse and peers pass away ahead of them. More often they are left alone by families whose members have moved away or established life styles which exclude the elderly. Such old age individuals may experience great decathexis ego tension. Old age individuals tend to fare much better in traditional societies in which the family group stays together and in-law children move into the home of the parent of their spouse. Old age individuals who are the legal owners of the family's financial and property assets enjoy the power of wealth with which they can compel the bestowal of attention upon them by family members who might otherwise ignore them. Those who can afford it and still have sufficient health and spirit to embrace life may band together to seek joy in whatever venue they can find it. While their health remains intact, they cannot know when death will find them and can live their lives without deference to their inevitable fate. If they suffer from a disease or other impairment which limits their freedom, they will be challenged in their effort to wring pleasure out of their existence. If they suffer a fatal illness, they crave the comfort of pain-relieving treatments. The decathexis tension of loneliness is a common condition of those elderly who have failed, or tried and failed, to maintain cathexes with significant other persons.

14

EGO ONTOGENESIS AND
THE MARKETPLACE

The human ego interacts with the marketplace to guide behavior to reduce ego tension by defeating sources of tension producing stimuli which products and services available in the marketplace are perceived by the ego as helpful. Each stage of ego ontogenesis generates an array of tension producing stimuli singular to that stage, which has a determining affect upon the purchase choices of the individual. Patterns of purchasing determine the array of products and services available in the marketplace as new items are introduced to replace those which are ignored or too little valued by, or beyond the financial reach of, too many consumers. Sellers bring to the marketplace items created by them in the belief that they will find purchasers.

Of necessity sellers gamble that their judgment about what purchasers will buy is accurate, and they sustain financial losses when their judgment is mistaken. Thus, the marketplace is populated by sellers gambling that their assessment of what purchasers will buy and by purchasers looking for items which will assist them to reduce or obviate tension producing stimuli. An effective empathic capacity in the egos of sellers is essential to their success because they must put themselves into the place of purchasers to divine what purchasers will want.

Successful sellers are those whose assessment of the desires of purchases is on balance accurate more often than inaccurate. The seller tends to test his vision of what purchasers will buy by asking himself if he would want to purchase the item if he were in the place of the purchaser. But he goes beyond that criterion by performing market research to discover what purchasers might buy that he the seller might not himself want to purchase. Market research tends to take the form of asking samples of the marketplace population what they want to buy which the seller hopes to purvey, or whether they want to buy a particular item being offered, or to introduce the item in a sample market area. The seller also advertises to the population of purchasers not only to make that population aware of what he wishes to sell to it, but also to create a desire in members of that population to want to buy the items he seeks to sell. To create desire in the marketplace population, the seller appeals to ego tension reduction needs of potential purchasers. This activity involves appeals to the purchasers' deficits of narcissism, power, worth, surety, curiosity and mastery, and to the tension of superego guilt, to the vanity of the ego ideal and often to the sexual tension being experienced by potential purchasers. The seller also appeals to the purchasers' wish to reduce the tension produced by the stimuli impinging from the elements and from physiological functioning in the form of shelter, clothing, nourishment and health maintenance and restoration, but even these appeals are ensconced in the guise of appeals to reduce the tension of the deficits of narcissism, power, worth, surety, curiosity, mastery, superego guilt and ego ideal vanity.

Stages of Ego Ontogenesis and Marketplace Behavior

The Primordial Ego

During the oral, anal and Oedipus conflict stages of ego ontogenesis, the infant ego knows little of the marketplace because all good things appear to be furnished by his parent and other caregivers. He cries when he wants something which is not readily forthcoming. Crying is his primary instrument of power and his principal means to deal with the external world and the tension and unpleasure with which it assails him. Toward the end of primordial life and at the threshold of latency, the infant ego may observe acts of marketplace purchasing carried out by his parent or caregiver when he is given, say, an ice cream cone obtained from a vendor. He learns to recognize vendors of delightful items and to beg and cry for his parent or caregiver to purchase them for him.

Latency Age Marketplace Behavior

As the infant ego moves into the latency period, which is as long in duration as all his previous life, he becomes ever more aware of the marketplace, and in money economy societies he also becomes aware of the role of money in obtaining his wants from the marketplace. His parent may give him small amounts of money and teach him to save it as well as to apportion the spending of it over the period which elapses until he will be presented with another bestowal of money. The ego comes to grips with the necessity for self-limitation, which is tension producing. For some latency age children, severe poverty may prevent even this modest introduction to a money economy. If the child is reared in a family of substantial wealth, he may not become acquainted with money until much later if his wants are supplied by his parent or caregivers merely because he expresses a wish for some item. However, there are wealthy parents who purposely withhold money from their children with the aim of making those children aware of the marketplace and the importance of money to access it. Normatively, the latency age child learns that his wants exceed what he can obtain from the marketplace, and that he must deal with the ego tension produced by limitations upon the satisfaction of his wants and the unrequited tension which he cannot quickly reduce because of limited access to the marketplace.

As the child is repeatedly taken to the marketplace in the company of his parent or caregiver, he becomes evermore aware of its bounty and the array of products and services which are attractive to him and which he wants but can have only some of and sometimes none of. He comes to value money and to want money, which at first he perceives as in the possession of his parent who gives him too little of it, and then learns that he must earn money which in most cases is the way his parent obtains it. He becomes a candidate for marketplace participation and looks for ways to obtain money, particularly to earn money, so that he can go to the marketplace to purchase items which satisfy the ego tension he craves to reduce. His parent tends to serve as the model for the way one obtains money, whether by earning it from employment or from investment or by inheriting it. He learns to associate particular sources of tension producing stimuli with products and services in the marketplace which he perceives as being able to deal with the sources of tension and to want those products and services. But this is only the beginning of the individual's training to participate in the marketplace. He will learn a great deal more during adolescence and young adulthood.

In modern mass-market economies the array of products and services is enormous and expanding. The latency age child is bombarded by advertising about products and services especially aimed at arousing wants and desires by appealing not always to his practical requirements but also to his ego tension deficits of narcissism, power and worth. For the latency child, products which appeal to him or her because of their capacity to reduce narcissism deficit tension include toys such as dolls which the little girl can love and then fantasize that the doll loves her in return. An animal from a pet store will fulfill the same wish in the little boy who will love the pet and fantasize that the pet loves him in return. Much advertising aimed at children intermingle drama consisting of animated animal characters as well as characters consisting of children in the same age range with the products being advertised so that the child's identification with the characters increases the ego tension of his wants and focuses it upon the products being advertised. Very often, the products being advertised are breakfast cereals, sweet drinks, and fast food meals not recommended by nutritionists.

Toys which assist the child to fantasize about the family group in which family members love each other will help reduce the tension of the Oedipus conflict in which the child fears he is hated and threatened by the opposite sex parent with whom he rivals for preferment as the residue of the Oedipus conflict continues to defy the child ego's effort to suppress it totally. Such toys might include dolls which represent the family as in the case of the three bears in the Goldilocks story. Such toys are sometimes used by child psychologists to set up play activity in therapy sessions to uncover the child's conflict with parents and parentified siblings and extended family members

Older latency age children may be attracted to toys which facilitate "playing house" so that the·dynamics of family life can be played out. Miniature table service consisting of little cups, saucers and dinner plates enable the child to replicate in simulation a family at dinner with expressions of affection for the child by the parent that reduce narcissism deficit tension. Doll houses equipped with miniature furniture also serve this purpose. Little girls may also be attracted to toys in the form of kitchen appliances and utensils with which they can practice preparing dinner in simulation of their mother's role in the family. Little boys may play with toy guns in games which replicate the hero coming to save the child from the villain in an expression of displaced paternal affection. The advertising of products and services to reduce ego tension produced by the practical needs of the child for shelter, food, clothing and healthcare tend not to be aimed at the child but at the parents of the child. Products aimed at serving practical needs such as clothing, school books and nutritious food are often not appreciated by children, who tend to display little appreciation for them when they are given to them as presents.

As an aside it may be noted that an entire industry has evolved whose task is to devise ways to appeal to the ego tension reduction requirements of the human ego at the several stages of ego ontogenesis. Manipulative advertising on the television screen whose stated aim is to sell practical products and services tends to be suffused with the unstated aim of eliciting a desire in the viewer for the product or service by appealing to an ego need such as the desire to reduce the tension produced by the narcissism deficit. Products intended for women purchasers may be purveyed in an advertisement which features an idealized affectionate male character, and an advertisement aimed at men may feature an idealized affectionate and sexually alluring and potentially accommodating female character. It is through their powers of empathy that advertisers learn these techniques.

The same is true for products and services which would reduce ego tension produced by the deficit of power. The latency age boy is lured by toys in the form of cowboy, policeman or soldier outfits and accouterments which would enable him to act out fantasies of power over others such as over rustlers, criminals and enemy soldiers. The latency age girl is tempted by toy dolls which are given the form of glamorous adult women of the sort girls hope to become some day so that males will pursue them and be subject to their wiles. Both boys and girls are tempted by scooters, tricycles and bicycles which they can ride and conquer distance gratifyingly with a speed beyond their capabilities without such conveyances.

There are toys in the marketplace aimed at luring latency age children by promising to reduce their ego worth deficits. Such toys include games of skill and chance played on colorful boards, or the games of chess or checkers, or playing card games which allow children to win in triumph over other children and even over their parents when they are able to inveigle the parent to play with them, which gives them the allusion not only of power, but success for which their parents might reward them with narcissistically gratifying praise. Model-building kits, sewing kits and science toys help the latency child to earn the praise of his parent and thereby enjoy a sense of worth. They also appeal to his desire for mastery which working effectively with such toys promotes.

Science toys also assist the latency age child to appreciate the nature of reality by showing him how the world and its contents work and of what they are made. The latency child tends to be less concerned about reality than about satisfying his narcissism, power and worth deficits. He tends to ask his parent and parental surrogates about matters he does not understand, and is almost invariably satisfied with the answers he is given. He tends to associate science toys with school study which keeps him from his play and requires tension producing intellectual effort to utilize.

By the time that latency comes to an end, the child has learned what is involved in acquiring money to enter the marketplace, and the importance of having the means to obtain money in the future to make his way in life. He will likely have thought about how he will obtain money when he becomes an adult, and will have considered various careers he might follow which include the capacity to acquire money. He will have become practiced at utilizing the marketplace to gain products and services with which he hopes to reduce ego tension, especially ego tension produced by the deficits of narcissism, power and worth. But because these deficits are permanent and can never be eradicated, the ego tension they produce always returns to reawaken the craving experienced by the ego to re-enter the marketplace in yet another attempt to find the means to reduce ego tension. This proclivity of the human' ego is a major facilitator of a consumer driven economy.

The Adolescent in the Marketplace

The adolescent tends readily to leave behind the toys of latency, which he may bequeath to his younger sibling. A different order of toys is required to gratify his narcissism. He is eager to display his new status which a growth spurt has produced for him. If he is a male, he soon will have a beard and bulging muscles. If a girl, she will sprout breasts and a more shapely figure all around. The male adolescent will come to rival his father in size and physical strength, and the girl adolescent will come to rival—perhaps exceed—her mother in pulchritude. But dependency upon the parent for the practical necessities of life continues, and the adolescent child craves the independence which the drive for individuation impels. Consequently, he is easily attracted to goods in the marketplace which would help him experience a sense of filial independence, success in attracting the opposite sex and achieving parity with his parent in a range of capacities.

The toys of childhood made available in the marketplace become the necessities of adulthood available in the marketplace. For example, toy automobiles, tricycles, bicycles and scooters are abandoned in adulthood for actual automobiles which are no longer viewed as toys by their purchasers, but nevertheless are purveyed by their sellers with advertising appeals not dissimilar in their aim from those used in selling to children. When pressed, the sophisticated adult will acknowledge that the shiny new automobile he has purchased is in many ways like a toy to him as well as a mode of transportation and a testament of his social status.

Narcissism deficit tension reducing products include those which would seem to make the adolescent more attractive to members of the opposite sex. Female adolescents become preoccupied with clothing fashions which are trendy and aimed at piquing the sexual interest of male adolescents. Males seek to be viewed as physically strong and highly capable, which they believe will attract females. Males too seek in the marketplace trendy clothes which they hope will make them attractive to females.

Products which appeal to the adolescent's propensity for self-indulgence tend to attract him with great intensity. Electronic equipment such as radios and televisions and devices which play recorded music, personal computers, cameras videographic and digital and whatever the latest innovative device may be tend to be found highly attractive by adolescents wanting to reduce the tension of their narcissism deficit by means of self indulgence.

The male adolescent craves personal power, which he believes will make him attractive to females and also enable him to become less dependent upon his parent to reduce individuation tension. He is attracted by products in the marketplace which will make him strong, physical strength being equated with power for the adolescent more than is money. It will be when he approaches young adulthood that the transition will occur in which money is seen as a form of power preferred to that of physical strength. The adolescent male is attracted by all sorts of athletic equipment which could facilitate his physical strength and his capacity to bend to his will objects including other individuals. Athletic strength and ability suffuses with the desire for mastery. Heroics in sports are seen by the male as attracting the affection not only of female adolescents but also of his parents and parental surrogates whose manifest love his athletic performance may earn.

Mastery may also be expressed in the maintenance of and in the driving of an automobile. The automobile offers the adolescent a form of power in which he is as potent on the streets and roads as his parent and any other adult as well. While adult drivers tend to move more cautiously, the adolescent driver can wheel his car in and out of and through traffic with great skill and fearlessness because in comparison to middle age adults he has much less concern that he might die. The driving skill and the power of the automobile enable the adolescent to unite power and mastery into the same behavior. Those adolescents who develop the skill to repair automobiles add that form of mastery to their driving skill. The marketplace which purveys automobiles and parts and services, attracts the adolescent customer with great intensity. In advertisements, the seller of automobiles, replacement parts and services tends to appeal to the sex drive of the adolescent male, to his wish for power which the automobile engine affords and to his sense of mastery which wheeling an automobile along the road at great speed is aimed at satisfying.

The products which appeal to the adolescent's sense of worth are those which would help him commend himself to his parents and to those in his life whom he has parentified such as teachers, employers, older siblings and admired adults. He believes that his parent wants him to choose and work toward a career in life which includes finding a mate, preparing himself for gainful employment and responsible citizenship. Any product connected with academic studies or training for a profession or a trade would likely appeal to the adolescent on this account. School books and supplies, conservative dress (which ironically conflicts with the rebellious clothes the adolescent wears to fit in with his rebellious peers), tools necessary for a trade, sensible furniture for his or her room to facilitate academic study are among the products purveyed to adolescents. Obtaining such products may earn the adolescent the praise and approval of his parent and thus a reduction of his ego worth deficit tension. Yet such items tend to be net tension producing because their use requires tension producing effort.

The ego ideal is constructed of everything perceived as needed to deal with all existing and potential sources of tension producing stimuli, and as the adolescent struggles to establish and sustain his ego ideal, he may seek help from products and services purveyed in the marketplace. All of the aforementioned products are desired for this purpose, but the adolescent is' particularly beset by superego guilt because of the return of Oedipus conflict filial hostility. He both craves the praise of the same sex parent, but simultaneously wishes to best and to punish him or her to triumph in filial competition and to vent the hostility arising from the primordial reaction formation to filial fear which lingers throughout the remaining course of life requiring repeated acts of suppression to forestall its return to conscious awareness. Any products in the marketplace which would help him to experience a sense of superiority in capacity and power will tend to find whatever money he has available for such purchases gracing the merchants cash register. The adolescent about to become a young adult begins to crave social status vis-à-vis society in general, and seeks products and services in the marketplace which will help him achieve such status.

The Young Adult in the Marketplace

The transition into young adulthood tends to be a slower and longer-lived process than the transition from latency into adolescence. To appease narcissism deficit tension, the young adult tends to seek a member of the opposite sex with whom to bond. The manifest affection which emanates from the lover facilitates the reduction of narcissism deficit tension. All products and services available in the marketplace which the young adult can purchase and bestow upon his lover may potentially elicit the affection which he craves. The lover tends to be parentified, and affection from the parentified lover facilitates the return of narcissism by displacement of filially extended narcissism.

The young adult male may maternify the automobile he purchases in the marketplace, refer to it as "her," stroke it affectionately as a concomitant of waxing and polishing the vehicle and fantasize that it returns his love. The automobile also facilitates the craving for power which the toy vehicles of latency and the bicycles of adolescence no longer suffice. In modern American society, obtaining an automobile from the marketplace has become a major aim of the young adult who is not given a vehicle by his family. While this situation may occur less often in urban centers where population densities are too great to permit widespread ownership of vehicles, it is common in suburbs which often lack public transportation and in smaller population centers whose sparser population density allows nearly universal ownership of automobiles.

While the automobile serves in the marketplace as a product which facilitates the reduction of the ego power deficit, other products also may fill this need. Tools for use in repairing automobiles as well as tools to perform other work serve as reducers of the power deficit. Hammers purchased in the marketplace are powerful tools, and so are electrically powered tools such as saws and drills because they afford the young adult using them a capacity to' bend materials to his will. Even personal computers and other electronic devices available in the marketplace are perceived as instruments of power because of the work they can do and are desired partly for this reason by the young adult.

The young adult's ego worth deficit is no longer appeased by products and services which serve the adolescent for this purpose. While the adolescent experienced a necessity for displaying progress toward gaining a livelihood with which he can support himself and the family he is expected to form, the young adult is expected already to have established himself in a gainful occupation and to have established a family which he supports. The products and services in the marketplace intended to attract the adolescent may center on helping him to evince progress toward attaining what he will require in adulthood, the young adult tends to look for products and services which assist him with his obligations as an established adult with family and gainful occupation.

The young adult tends to look for products and services required to maintain a house and to support a young family. These might include home repair items, inexpensive furniture and appliances and an inexpensive automobile. They might also include paraphernalia for the care of infants such as crib, playpen and a child-sized bed. Success in obtaining all of these items in sufficient quantity and quality will likely commend the young adult to his parents and parentified others and consequently earn him praise and concomitant worth. Establishing his place in society is also a major element in the young adult's ego ideal.

The Middle Age Adult in the Marketplace

The middle age individual tends to be at the apogee of his capacities in the course of life except for physical strength which is well along toward waning. In modern industrialized societies he will be at the acme of his financial power if he is a worker or professional person, but if in business or an investor he may yet become wealthier. By and large the middle age individual tends to be more affluent and in a better position to indulge his narcissistic wishes in the marketplace than at any time in his life. He tends to be the principal target of venders in the marketplace who beguile him with blandishment in their effort to sell him expensive automobiles, water and aircraft, electronic devices and a more upscale residence and more expensive furnishings than they target to other age groups.

The middle age individual tends to experience greater power through wealth than at earlier times in his life. Whether his wealth is modest, substantial or enormous, it will tend to be greater than at any time previously, and he will indulge himself in goods and services whose cost reflects his financial capacity. His ability to enter the marketplace and satisfy his practical needs as well as to indulge his narcissistic whims reflects his power and his capacity to reduce the tension of the ego power deficit.

In modern mass-market societies, social status is largely based upon the capacity to purchase status assets and display them for all to see. The marketplace is the principal source of ego worth assets, and the middle age individual will tend to take advantage of his wealth to satisfy his ego worth cravings in the marketplace. Other factors enter into social status determination such as family pedigree, level of education attained and the prestige of occupation, but none is so great a determiner in a mass society as the degree of wealth and its display. The individual tends to be at his acme during middle age, and most middle age individuals enjoy the greatest sense of ego worth and ego ideal achievement than at any time in their lives. For those with little wealth who live in poverty, the capacity to appease the deficits of narcissism, power and worth in the marketplace is lacking.

Old Age and the Marketplace

Normatively, it is in old age that individual wealth is at its lowest since young adulthood. Those in old age who lack substantial invested wealth or other income-producing assets will find access to the marketplace to be limited. The vast majority of the population of old persons has only their labor to sell as a means to acquire a degree of wealth. But the labor of the old age individual tends not to be prized by those who pay money for the toil of workers. Thus, if the old age worker is thrown back upon a pension paid by his former employer or by government, his income is likely to be modest or even meager. He will be able to satisfy very little of his wish in the marketplace for narcissistic gratification, power and worth. He must look elsewhere for the means to satisfy these wishes, perhaps vicariously through his children and grandchildren.

The population of elderly persons does not appear to be a lucrative source of purchasers for marketplace vendors. These persons because of their financial limitations are limited largely to purchasing only the basic necessities of survival—food, medicine, shelter and clothing.

15

EGO ONTOGENESIS
AND CITIZENSHIP

Citizenship, which is shaped by ego ontogenesis, is the individual's cooperative participation in the governance of his society. In this volume, citizenship refers to the activity of rank and file citizens rather than to elected officials and those they appoint to government posts or to the merit service bureaucracy. The rank and file inhabitant of a nation-state does not attain citizenship in the absence of forces which shape his behavior as a citizen. As a citizen of a state, the individual is subject to the sovereign power of the state as it is imposed upon him through the organizations and institutions of government with which he must interact responsibly to display good citizenship. Citizenship in a popular democracy differs from that of autocracies and monarchies in that the citizen in a popular democracy, through his vote, possesses a share of the sovereign power of the state which imposes the will of the state upon him. He therefore has a say, albeit small, in how the sovereign power of the state is used to limit his activities.

The Primordial Experience
in Forming the Citizen

The epigenesis of citizenship evolves through the processes of ego ontogenesis. The human ego first experiences the exertion of power upon it in the individual's interaction with his parent facilitated by the trauma of weaning which conveys to him the reality that he is dependent upon an external entity for the reduction of tension produced by the impinging stimuli which envelops him, and that this external entity can withhold tension reducing support from him. A sense of impotence not experienced earlier impacts him, and the individual ego forever after seeks to utilize that external agent—the parent or other caregivers—to defeat tension producing stimuli.

The primordial individual's sense of dependence upon the external entity and fear of severation from that entity is profound and later tends to be transferred to government itself and to the organizations and institutions of government and to their functionaries. The infant ego's experiences of the traumata of the anal and oedipal cathexis serveration distress further shapes the future citizen's subservience to formal power. It is the resolution of the Oedipus conflict through the establishment of the superego that the human propensity for subservience to formal authority is formed. Because of the superego, the adult tends to parentify government and to accept and subordinate himself to the authority of government.

The Latency Period in
Forming the Citizen

It is during latency that the effect upon the infant ego of the traumata occurring during the primordial period is revealed. Profoundly fearful of the parent and totally subordinating itself to the parent, the latency ego is easily molded by the family into the citizen that the individual will become in adulthood by the way it adapts to the imposition of power upon it in the context of the family. It is subjected to the power of authority in a hierarchy formed by the seniority of family members as normatively determined by the order in which members enter the family, usually birth order, and the functions and exercise of authority distributed among family members, including extended family members when they are present in the family group.

This experience along with the inculcation of parental and familial values together with the family's perception of the nature of reality becomes inculcated into the latency ego and is carried into adulthood by means of the derivative relatedness transference devolution process, albeit with important modifications during adolescence, largely determining the form of citizenship which the adult will manifest. It is normatively during latency that the child ego absorbs the idealized values of the parent together with its perception of the parent's sense of rectitude. During adolescence the child will invest this perception of rectitude and the parental values into its concept of citizenship, modified by whatever form adolescent filial rebellion chances to take.

Adolescence and Citizenship Formation

Adolescence is a time of active idealism for the ego. The adolescent ego perceives itself as at last on the way to achieving parity in power and other capacities with the parent and is eager to put into effect the ideals formed during the latency period into the act of individuating. Three vectors of ego ontogenesis intersect at this point: the propensities to individuate and to establish a separate and unique identity and a struggle to resolve anew a resurgent Oedipus conflict fueled in part by renewed primordial filial hostility which is a reaction formation to projected fear. In struggling with these impulses, the adolescent ego chooses selected parental values to disdain while adopting other values at odds with those of the parent to embrace. These choices may be integrated with ideas of citizenship so that the adolescent's concept of a good citizen may include predilections which collide in some ways with concepts of citizenship held by the parent as well as by peers and other adults.

The citizenship values inculcated during latency, the adolescent now tends to advocate enthusiastically. Energized by his renewed filial competitiveness, the adolescent discovers that the idealism inculcated by his parent during the latency period now appears to him or to her to be indifferently honored by the parent. The adolescent experiences little difficulty in respecting the citizenship precepts taught to him by the parent during latency, but the parent often finds these precepts difficult for him to practice because they may conflict with his effort to provide for his family and himself, a burden not born by the adolescent. The adolescent tends repeatedly to remind his parent of the parent's failure to exemplify in his actions the obligations of ideal citizenship.

Typical among parental failings is opposition to taxation for purposes which the adolescent (who bears very little or no tax burden himself) regards as laudable, but which the parent views as onerous, unaffordable and unessential. Failure to journey to the polls on Election Day to cast the responsible citizen's vote is another commonplace failing among parents. Also, the unwillingness of the parent to support the election of, say, a reform candidate pledged to overturn the status quo in a good cause in the form of a proposed policy which may appear to the parent as rash, but to the adolescent as important and necessary. The parent's reluctance may appear to his adolescent child as less than honorable.

The unwillingness of the parent at times to volunteer to serve on any of various citizens groups in support of good causes aimed at benefiting the community is also an example of citizenship failure of the parent in the eyes of his adolescent child. Failure to comport himself in an upstanding and cooperative manner at all times is yet another example of the way a parent may fall short of good citizenship behavior in the view of his adolescent child. The child tends to hold the parent to an idealized standard which may be beyond human ability, and the parent under the burden of his own ego ideal tends to experience a painful sense of hypocrisy in himself as he struggles to justify his less than ideal behavior to his eager adolescent child. The adolescent may vow to become a good citizen when he reaches adulthood and compensate for what he perceives as his parent's citizenship failings.

Those adolescents concerned with citizenship issues to the point of employing them in the act of individuating tend to be in the minority of the adolescent population. The majority of adolescents look elsewhere in the array of parental values to find ways to individuate, and by and large they come to accept the parent's citizenship values with little objection to them. Other areas of filial rebellion include lifestyle choices, choices of clothing fashions, choice of career, choice of sweetheart, preferences in music and in pastime activities. Most adolescents choose among such values as these to rebel against the parent, and give little more than perfunctory thought to their own future citizenship role. Nevertheless, the ascendancy of the ego ideal during adolescence disposes most adolescents to regard good citizenship as a laudable value even though they give little thought to it.

Young Adulthood and Citizenship

The young adult is of voting age, voting being the most profound obligation of citizenship in a popular democracy. However, the non-voter may conduct himself as a responsible citizen in other ways such as by obeying the law, by willingly and correctly paying his taxes, by following and commenting upon issues of public policy and by looking after his property responsibly and by cooperating with prevailing practices in his public behavior. If the non-voter has thoughtfully considered the issues and candidates at election time and chooses not to vote (rather than simply being remiss), then it may be said that such an individual performed his obligation as a citizen because a non vote may effect the outcome of an election as well as a vote.

The thoughtful non-voter may have reached the conclusion after diligent consideration that no substantive difference for the commonweal will result from the election of one of the candidates over the other. But since failure to vote will tend to help one candidate at the expense of the other, a rational non-voter would have to assert that the candidates are identical, which is unlikely, or that the affect upon public policy would be the same or equally favorable or unfavorable regardless of which candidate were elected, which also is unlikely. Most non-voters fail to vote because of the inaccessibility of the polling place, lack of opportunity because of urgent conflicting commitments or out of indifference or laziness. Widespread non-voting in a popular democracy may be a symptom of the absence of any great public policy issue, or it may reflect the failure of leaders to bring to the attention of voters a public policy issue destined to affect them in an important way.

The young adult may still be animated by citizenship ideals formed in adolescence and take himself to the polling place out of a sense of duty and obligation. But the young adult who finds himself in circumstances typical for his sector of the population will tend to be overwhelmed by issues less concerned with citizenship than with mere survival in a matrix of obligations having to do with establishing a career and deriving a livelihood from an un-sympathetic economy to support a young family heavily dependent upon him.

Young adults among the rank and file who were active during adolescence in advocating upon behalf of idealistic causes such as those who joined demonstrations in front of government buildings, factory gates or in public plazas may continue such behavior for a time during young adulthood with progressively diminishing fervor. The rank and file tend to be unlike those young adults who launch a career in political advocacy, politics or journalism whose concern about political issues becomes a part of their careers. In the United States, the rank and file young adult forms a part of the general population of voting age least likely to vote.

The Middle Age Adult and Citizenship

The rank and file middle age adult, unlike the young adult, occupies a place in the general population of persons most likely to vote in public elections. The middle age adult enjoys the acme of his power and influence in his society. Whether he is extremely wealthy or moderately so, or poor, what he has by way of wealth, which is a major element of his power, is likely to be greatest at this time in the course of his life. Even if he is poor, he may command more respect than earlier because he will likely be seen as a journeyman citizen, experienced in the ways of society and government and possessing strongly held opinions born of years of experience in dealing with the imposition of the sovereign power of the state upon him by politicians and the functionaries of governmental agencies.

The middle age adult is in that time of life when the individual begins to recognize that his longevity is limited, that his life is half over and perhaps more, and that if he is to survive death in the memory of his posterity, then civilization and his society must continue after he has gone. He tends to become more conservative in his respect for society, and, even if he had been a social rebel in his youth, more circumspect and protective toward society in middle age, and less willing to support radical changes pursued by anti-status quo youths like those of which he had been one in his own adolescence. Typically, his anti-status quo propensity will not likely have left him entirely, but he will tend to be much more circumspect than the youthful rebels clamoring before government buildings during his own middle age years. He will have seen many attempts to change society come to nothing and others which succeeded produce nothing better than what they replaced. Nevertheless, he may still be offended by what he sees as great injustices sustained by the conservatism of those who have thrived amid the structure of power prevalent in the social order.

The politically conservative middle age adult who has prospered will enjoy the privileges which his advantages have afforded him and tends to believe that he deserves them, that he has acquired them because of his own superiority vis-à-vis those who have not done so well, and he tends to be loath to see changes made in society which would threaten his advantages. He tends to cast his objections not in terms of the damage anti-status quo changes would inflict upon him but the damage he perceives it would wreak upon the general welfare enjoyed in the present. He tends to perceive advocates of change to the status quo as self-serving, misguided troublemakers seeking publicity and acclaim for their own selfish purposes. If they happen to be among the disadvantaged of society, he tends to view them as motivated by jealousy of those who have succeeded and desirous of taking their honest gains from them. He also tends to see them as stirring up restiveness among a population otherwise at peace, thus placing the social order in jeopardy.

Narcissism

The middle age adult's narcissistic gratification wishes may imbue his citizenship with predilections which distort the purposes of good citizenship. For example, a citizen may confuse his objection to the creation of a proposed civic park or playground with his concern for the preservation of his own wealth. If he is in a high tax bracket, he knows that the financial burden would fall more heavily upon him than upon many who would use the park or playground. However, he may object to the project citing a lack of need for it or because its location would be unsound.

Or he may own a parcel of land different from the proposed location of the park or playground which he would like to sell to the community. He may genuinely believe that his parcel is better suited, and that the community would be better served to purchase it for the park or playground. Blind to his conflict of interest, and desirous of being rewarded by his community, he may assert himself forcefully in his attempt to persuade the community to buy his land. Such a purchase would gratify his narcissism because it would be received as a gift, or return of narcissism, from the community which he' parentifies in recompense for his civic devotion.

In many instances, narcissism suffuses behavior aimed at reducing the tension of the ego worth deficit. For example, the middle age individual may devote considerable time and energy taken from his business or employment to participate in civic activities for which he regards himself as exhibiting good citizenship. While he applauds himself for his good citizenship he may be unaware of his aim to earn the appreciation of his community because of his worthy behavior to reduce the ego tension of his narcissism deficit. His worthy behavior may simultaneously earn him ego worth and well as appease his wish for narcissistic gratification. What he may not be aware of because he has not analyzed his behavior is that his conduct as a good citizen has been in one way or another compromised by his desire for narcissistic gratification and the reduction of his ego worth deficit.

Worth

It is during middle age that the post primordial period individual typically experiences his greatest sense of worth. At the acme of his intellectual and financial powers, he is able more than at any earlier time to enter the marketplace and purchase ego worth assets which both enhance his personal prestige as well as elevate him in social status. It is ironic that the middle age individual in a progressive income tax society may derive worth out of his increased wealth but be required to pay greater taxes than earlier which diminishes his wealth and may threaten his capacity to purchase ego worth assets and sustain the higher status which his wealth has given him.

While paying taxes at greater rates indicates greater affluence and therefore may be viewed as a status asset, it also diminishes wealth with which the individual might purchase in the marketplace social status assets such as a luxury automobile or a more palatial residence which he could display to the admiration or envy of fellow citizens. Such a circumstance may challenge the individual's devotion to good citizenship by eliciting reluctance to pay the taxes, leading to various means to avoid some of the taxes.

The middle age individual of substantial means and public stature may search for ways to reduce his tax liability by a variety of methods such as lobbying government to enact laws or regulations which reduces taxes for the category of payers in which he is included, or he may seek skilled tax lawyers who can utilize various deductions and depreciations which reduces his tax burden, or apply special advantages inserted into the tax law and regulations by others in circumstances similar to his which allow him to escape taxation for a portion of his income or property. Such an individual may regard himself as an exemplar of good citizenship by arguing to himself that he is unfairly taken advantage of by the majority of citizens who are less well off because of their acquisitive inferiority who use government to deprive him of his gain for their own self-serving purpose.

Surety

Surety may play a strong role in citizenship behavior. Belief that one's perception of reality is accurate and that that of others which differs from one's own is ipso facto inaccurate will tend to affect one's behavior in the support of the community. Surety is often suffused with narcissism and the pursuit of ego worth. In his perception of reality, the middle age individual may confuse reality with the promotion of his special interest. For example, he may be bent upon building for himself a new residence of splendid proportions on land proposed for a new school building. In his justification that the school not be built upon the site, he may view the land as unsuited for a school building for various reasons which conflict with reality. He may see the site as too far removed from the population it is intended to serve, or requiring multiple story construction not optimum for young children, or that the site will be too expensive to build upon because the costly removal of a rocky outcrop will be required.

Others who urge that the school be built upon the site may have supporting arguments which this middle age individual rejects. For example they may see the site as not too remote because children are bussed to school anyway, that multiple story construction can be overcome by the installation of elevators and that the rocky outcrop will provide a strong foundation for school construction. The surety of the middle age individual in this example conflicts with the surety of the supporters of the school construction, the latter's perception of reality less shaped by self-interest.

Yet another example might be that of the middle age woman who serves on numerous civic and volunteer committees resenting the appointment to a chairmanship of a prestigious civic committee of a person more qualified but less deserving than she. In her perception of reality, she is unable to view her rival as actually better qualified because she is blinded by her own self-interest. The reality she perceives is the established practice that such a reward goes to the most deserving person among civic activists. Her perception of realty aims to reduce ego tension of both her narcissism deficit as will as her ego worth deficit.

Ego Ideal

Sustaining the ego ideal may come into play in the citizenship behavior of the middle age individual. The middle age man who is actively involved in many civic activities may not recognize the importance to his ego ideal of his conspicuous service to the community. His insistence upon placing himself in the forefront of civic activity may at times work to the disadvantage of the community. For example, he may use his prestige to get his way in the choice of an architect to design and construct a new civic center for his ' community. The architect he urges upon the building committee is from a prominent family in the community and his long time friend of whom he is proud and uncompromising in his high praise. He may not perceive his conflict of interest in sustaining his ego ideal by buttressing his relationship with the family of the architect to boost his social standing in the community.

Superego Guilt

The citizenship of the middle age individual might be distorted by his aim of reducing the ego tension of superego guilt. For example, a middle age individual's primordial filial guilt suppressed during the resolution of the

Oedipus conflict and the formation of the superego may have been so severe that its continual suppression throughout ego ontogenesis requires repeated use of ego mechanisms into middle age. In dealing with his superego guilt, which occupies a place in his awareness near to the surface, he may resort to the mechanism of projection in which the chastisement of his superego is appeased by projecting guilt onto others. By blaming others for their misdeeds, he repeatedly gains temporary relief from the reproach of his own superego.

In the act of projection, he may undermine the effectiveness of a fellow committee member who is pressing his colleagues to initiate a fundraising drive to generate funds for building a new wing on the county hospital. His projection may be taking the form of criticizing the committee member as self-serving, as striving to elevate his reputation in the community by a show of leadership in heading a fundraising committee. This behavior weakens the effectiveness of the committeeman to the detriment of the community and negatively affects the quality of the middle age individual's citizenship.

Old Age and Citizenship

The old age individual is compelled by infirmity, waning energy and sometimes poor health to yield much of the activity of citizenship to others who are still fit for it. While he may have to give up active civic committee work, he may still go to the polls on election day unless he is bedridden. Most of the aims of his life which he has not achieved he will now likely go to his grave having not achieved them. Yet he will likely continue to try. His failing energy may coincide with his preoccupation with the welfare of the family he will leave behind. His role as citizen will be dissolving bit by bit as he relinquishes that role or as it is taken from him.

Narcissism, Power and Citizenship in Old Age

The old age individual tends to look to his family for the affection of which the narcissism deficit has left him bereft throughout the course of his life. Normatively, he will have given his love to others, or believes that he has, and not received enough in return. If he is religious, he may look to God's love for a return of the narcissism he extended to others. If he has property, he may bequeath it with the aim of rewarding those he believes relate to him with affection.

In old age, power tends to take the form of financial assets or property. If the old age individual has accumulated substantial wealth, he may wish to extend his presence beyond the grave by leaving in his name a structure for the community such as a library or hospital or if he is less affluent leave money to pay for a new wing on the library or hospital. His bequests will likely be chosen with an eye to projecting his existence into the future in the form of something which will remind those he leaves behind that he was once here. If he were a citizen of modest means, such munificence would not be possible, and would have to be content with leaving behind a reputation as a good citizen for others to emulate.

The old age individual who was keen about his citizenship during his life is likely to feel protective about his community. He will tend to be saddened or appalled by criminal activity in the community and the defacing of public places with irreverent graffiti. If he is judgmental, his vote in elections will likely support law and order candidates, and if he is rehabilitative toward wayward persons he will likely hope that his community take a more helpful corrective action toward the offenders. If he is inclined toward literary pursuits, he may write a history of his community or some aspect of it to leave a record aimed at inspiring those who come after to greater appreciation of his community.

16

PARENTING AND
EGO ONTOGENESIS

Although normatively parenting does not begin before puberty and until after the development of reproductive organs, the disposition toward parenting and many of the skills which will be required for parenting are normatively gained before adolescence. The child learns about parenting from being parented by the parent who parents him. The parenting techniques employed by the child's parent in his own rearing and in the rearing of his siblings are introjected by the child during the latency years to be put to use later when the latency child has become a parent himself normatively during adolescence or young adulthood.

Parenting is one of the most difficult endeavors undertaken by human beings. The infant's dependence upon the parent at first is nearly absolute, but as the infant begins to do more upon its own behalf, the parent gains progressive relief from the total care it is compelled to provide for the child. The parent wants the child to gain self-dependence skills both to relieve the parent of the childcare burden and also to reduce the parent's ego worth deficit tension. Because the parent is expected by others to be the primary caregiver of his child, failure at care giving would tend to undermine the parent's ego worth by exposing his care-giving incompetence and subjecting him to the judgmentalism of society.

All parents are subject more or less to the same childcare burdens, except for those parents who are financially capable of paying others or are able to rely upon family members to do portions of the childcare labor. But even if the childcare labor is performed by hirelings or other family members, the fact of one's parenthood creates an interaction between parent and child which is unique and not a burden of which the parent can fundamentally divest himself. The parent will be forever identified with his child and suffer the disesteem of other parents if his child does poorly in the struggle toward self-dependence.

But his child can be a facilitator of ego worth gains for the parent. Achievements of the child, which are viewed as precocious earn admiration from others which redounds to the parent's good repute, thereby reducing ego worth deficit tension for the parent. Parenting has both favorable and unfavorable components for the parent's ego worth. The burden of the care, the shortcomings of the child, and the child's failure at self-dependence progress are tension producers for the parent, but the child's successes, natural gifts and precocity bestow worth upon the parent who is given credit by others for the child's attainments and natural gifts.

The demands placed upon the child by the parent are great. The parent tends to utilize the child as an instrument by which the parent reduces ego tension produced particularly by the deficits of narcissism, power, and worth. In particular, the parent demands that the child demonstrate self-dependence progress at a rate which is at least customary, and second that the child act in such a way as to bring praise to the parent. At the outset, the child is seen as an ego worth asset, as an object which can bring credit to the parent and reduce the tension of the parent's ego worth deficit. The parent looks for praise from his own parents and from grandparents and other family members, and from neighbors and sometimes even from strangers on the street. For the remainder of the parent's course of life, he will expect his child to achieve successes for which the parent takes credit. Needless to say, these parental expectations produce great ego tension for the child.

Normatively, the ego tension producing deficits suffered by the parent at the hands of his own parent tend to be passed along to the child as the parent identifies with and introjects his child and transfers to his child the relatedness which he experienced in the child-rearing interaction with his own parent. As a consequence, various elements of child rearing singular to a particular hereditary line tend to be passed down from generation to generation.

Narcissism and Parenting

The parent simultaneously returns to his child the narcissism which the child extends to him while seeking a return from his own parent of the narcissism which he extended to his parent. The return of narcissism takes the form of affection bestowed upon the child by the parent. Normatively, the parent loves his child and the child is loved by his parent. The child extends self-love to his parent, and in receiving the love of his parent appeases the narcissism deficit he creates by loving his parent as a concomitant of the cathexis with which he attaches himself to his parent composed of extended narcissism, identification and introjection. By identifying with, introjecting and extending narcissism to the parent, the infant strives to solidify the filial-parental cathexis which is the principal means by which the infant reduces the ego tension produced by the envelop of stimuli which continually impinges upon him from every direction. The narcissism deficit thus created sets the ego upon a lifelong quest for a return of narcissism which the love of the parent and later the love of parentified others helps to appease.

The parent introjects and identifies with the child he is compelled by superego demands and the mores of society to take care of. The parent extends self-love to the child with which he identifies and introjects, which appeases the infant's incipient narcissism deficit. Parenting is born of this compulsion, and takes the form of an urge to love and care for the child as the parent would want to be loved and cared for. The principal characteristics of parenting include identification with and introjection of the child, love for the child with the force of the parent's self-love, striving to shield the child from tension producing impinging stimuli, and taking action to reduce ego tension which the child experiences because of impinging stimuli. The parent's parenting actions tend to be confounded by the residue of parenting techniques which were created in the parent's interaction with his own parent during his upbringing.

Power and Parenting

A power struggle arises between the parent and the child with the child wanting to follow his own tension reducing whim, and the parent wanting to prevent the child from acting in a self-injurious way as well as wanting the child to act in ways which facilitates the reduction of the parent's own worth deficit. For example, the child behind in his schoolwork may wish to play with his neighborhood friends, which reduces decathexis tension, while the parent may want him to do his school work for the purpose of making progress toward self dependence. The child's aim is to reduce current ego tension without concern for future ego tension resulting from inadequate education, while the parent's aim is to guide the child toward a successful future. The parent has little difficulty in perceiving behavior which might bring his child to grief, but the parent may encounter great difficulty in discerning the distortion in his own parenting judgment by the demands of his ego worth deficit reduction wishes to which he expects his child to contribute. In the present example, the parent's aim is to urge to the child to achievement which will reflect favorably upon the parent. Both parent and child aim to reduce ego worth deficit tension in their mutual interaction as well as in their general behavior, which intensifies the power struggle between parent and offspring

The child may behave in many ways dangerous to his survival by the dictate of his own immature judgment, bringing him into conflict with his parent who tends to be ever alert to his child's bad judgment behavior. But in the contest for power, the child's ultimate weapon is self-injury by which the child places himself in danger or inflicts some sort of injury upon himself as a means of counter manipulating the parent in their struggle over particular issues contested between them. For example, the parent may physically struggle to get the child to evacuate the content of his bowel into the toilet facility, but the child, fearing decathexis from toilet training severation, refuses by clinching his anal sphincter shut. While the child defeats the parent in the short run, eventually an impacted colon will bring him great discomfort. The child wins the contest with the parent, at least in the short run, through the technique of self-injury.

Until the child experiences the increased physical growth and strength, which follows the onset of puberty, he assesses his power as greatly inferior to that of the parent, and adopts a posture of capitulation vis-à-vis his parent. The latency age child may resist self-dependence imperatives imposed by his more powerful parent, but he tends not to take issue with his parent over which of them is in charge of the parent-child relationship and whose judgment is supreme. As the latency child's superego becomes loaded with information, strategies for living and parental imperatives, he assumes that the parenting techniques worked upon him by his parent are standard and to be accepted and one day applied by him when he becomes a parent. This reality can sometimes be viewed in the way the latency child plays with dolls, handling the doll in the manner of his parent as if the child were a parent. The doll may be upbraided, spanked, "punished" or lavished with love as the latency child applies the reward and punishment based rearing employed in most civilized societies.

Reward and punishment, alternately extending or withholding affection and approval—these are the techniques of child rearing most widely used in modern cultures. They are not publicly approved methods, and they often are criticized negatively by childcare authorities many of whom recommend love and tender correction of waywardness in children, but in reality they are the most widely used techniques and even form of the basis of the criminal justice systems in most modern societies.

The law-abiding citizen is rewarded by the approval of the state, and the criminal is punished variously by financial fines, imprisonment and ultimately, when certain laws are violated, by execution—the supreme punishment. The child will apply these techniques to the parenting of his own child when he becomes a parent, having learned them at the hands of his parent and partly in projection of his own guilt for miss deeds during his childhood and because he introjected them as unimpeachable during his latency years. During adolescence, the rebelling child may resolve that when he becomes a parent he will not subject his child to the "oppression" he believes his parent subjected him. But as matters turn out, the child tends to parent his child with much of the same "oppression" with which he was parented.

Worth and Parenting

The gaining of ego worth by the child occurs when the child experiences approval and admiration by the parent. The infant ego reasons that because the parent is critically important to him, the filial-parental cathexis, which is indispensable to the child's capacity to defeat tension producing stimuli, must be preserved and depends upon the parent placing value upon the child in the manner that the child places value upon the parent. The child holds his parent in the greatest esteem which the child is capable of conceiving, and he wants his parent to reciprocate this esteem. To the child, the approval and admiration bestowed upon him by the parent is evidence of the worth which the parent places upon the child and attests the strength of the parent's cathexis to the child and the degree of reliance the child can place upon the parent upon whom he depends absolutely. To be admired and valued by the parent is tension reducing for the child because it gives the child a sense of security, that he is valuable to the parent, that he will be protected by the parent as a valuable possession and that the narcissism which the child extended to the parent will in part be returned.

The experience of being valued by the parent during the latency years and adolescence, when the child is forming his concept of appropriate parenting, creates a model of parenting which the child will tend to apply one day to the parenting of his own offspring. Parental approval, admiration and praise are highly desired by the child and supportive of his sense of security. It is a boost to his morale and is often used by persons in positions in which they might be parentified. For example, an employer or a military commander might lavish praise upon the underlings who parentify them such as an employer parentified by employees or a commander parentified by soldiers. The employer and commander hope that their praise will induce their charges to perform better in the hope of continuing to earn his praise.

Having been praised by his parent, the child-become-a-parent will tend to praise his offspring, having introjected this model of child rearing. Often the child who was not much praised by his parent will tend to replicate that practice in the rearing of his own child. Most parents tend to praise their offspring to some degree, but the parent who was short of praise in child rearing may parent children who become parsimonious with parental praise in the rearing of their own children.

Surety and Parenting

The primordial child grasps very little of his parent's values and indeed lacks the object constancy to perceive the parent of weaning as the same parent as the parent of toilet training and the latter as the same parent as the parent of the Oedipus conflict severation experience.[1] But during latency, which follows upon the creation and establishment of the superego, the child tends to absorb his parent's values, judgments and beliefs with great celerity as indisputable explanations of reality. The latency child absorbs many particulars about reality at the knee of his parent and entities to which the parent delegates his parenting authority including the nanny, extended family mem-

---

[1] For a discussion of object constancy, see **Mahler**, loc cit.

bers, the school, the church and functionaries of government. Mention of several categories of knowledge will illustrate the pervasiveness of latency age inculcation.

For example, the concept of the deity had little meaning for the primordial child, but usually as the child progresses through the latency period the god concept becomes highly important for the child. The child comes to recognize that there are circumstances against which the powerful parent cannot prevail, that the parent prays to a god for help much as the child beseeched the parent for help in difficult moments, that this god is more powerful than the parent so that the child must appeal to this higher entity just as his parent does.

The child then learns what he must know about this god and how to deal with it, which is much like the way he deals with his parent but with a greater experience and show of submissiveness and veneration. The whole lesson of religion is then absorbed by the child after being taught by those to whom the parent delegates his authority to teach his child, principally functionaries of the church. The concepts and information thus acquired by the latency child tend not to be contested by the child and will be conveyed by him to his children after he becomes a parent, unless he chances to rebel against his parent's religion as a concomitant of individuation.

Preferences in government and politics are also taught to the latency child by his parent, if not explicitly then by example. The latency child observes and absorbs his parents' political values as he understands them to be, and they form the basis of the political beliefs upon which he will act in adulthood and which he will teach the children he parents. The type of constitution which is preferable, the political party which is best, the candidates which are most worthy, the extent to which and the ways in which government should intervene in the lives of people—these are learned by the child from his parent and normatively will be taught by him to the children he one day parents unless he chances to rebel against these parental teachings during individuation.

Social distinctions among various classes, groups and races will be taught to the latency child or learned by him by observing his parent and will later' be part of the lore with which he will parent his children. Economic systems, or the way people earn their livelihoods, will be taught to the latency child or learned by him from observing his parent. He will be taught which is the preferred economic system, the preferred system typically being the one by means of which the parent derives his livelihood. Or he may be taught that the current system is unacceptable because the parent cannot derive a satisfactory livelihood from it. He will be taught what he must do to gain the ability to obtain his own livelihood when he becomes an adult, and he will be exhorted to take up these ways to become self-dependent. These beliefs will be imparted to his own children in the parenting process unless he rejects any of them as he struggles to individuate from his parent.

He will be taught history—where his family came from, the antecedents of his society, how his family came to be where it is and who are its members, what his community is about and the particulars of his state, or province and nation. These he will pass along to his children as a part of their parenting. He will be taught rectitude by his parent, the way in which persons should treat each other and should be treated by the functionaries of societal institutions and what should be expected of him in return.

The child will be taught the technology of his society, whether that society is primitive, traditional or modern. He will be taught how to use implements commonly in use in his society from kitchen appliances to farm equipment, or from machinery to "high tech" apparatus. He may be sent to school to learn to use special equipment not commonly mastered by everyone in the population such as a trade school or he may be apprenticed to a tradesman to learn how to apply a particular trade in a way with which he can earn a livelihood.

Or he may be sent to an institution of higher education to learn more complicated technology and to be brought abreast of the knowledge acquired by his society through research and scholarship, and he will usually be expected to gain expertise in a particular field. His parent will urge his child in these endeavors and employ whatever parenting techniques he has acquired to guide and compel his child to be an effective learner because he fears that his child will not succeed in his culture if he fails at these exigencies, and the parent would suffer ego worth deficit tension as a consequence as well as vicariously the pain experienced by the failing child whom he introjects and identifies with.

The Task of Parenting

The parent realizes that he has a great stake in the parenting of his offspring. He tends to arrive at this conclusion unawares rather than by thoughtful analysis. Parenting is so formidable that the parent often experiences a sense of incompetence and may turn to experts for advice. Books, magazine articles, web page commentaries and television programs are heavy purveyors of parenting advice, attesting to the great interest in the subject to be found among the general public. However, Parenting advice from "experts" tends to exhort the parent to do things beyond the capacity of the parent to do for much of the time, and the parent is subject to continual guilt for his parenting failings implied by his failure to perform as the experts recommend.

The parent tends to be able to do well at parenting some of the time and in certain situations, but fatigue and the obstreperousness of the child may at times overwhelm the parent with great tension increase in response to which the parent may break down and lose his composure. As a result, the parent may act toward the child with the anger of ordinary frustration and subject the child to various sorts of abuse, verbal or physical, mild or extreme, or out of fatigue or self-preoccupation may neglect the child, or the parent may project his own shortcomings on to his child. The resiliency of the child to surmount parenting failures of his parent and learn what he needs to know and to acquire livelihood skills tends to be adequate in the great majority of cases.

However, in some cases the child becomes wayward or feckless and evinces a poor degree of success in fending for himself in ways consistent with law and social mores. Some children become disabled because of biological abnormalities beyond the skills of the parent to overcome or society to correct optimally. In modern societies, great effort is generally made to develop the means to improve the capacities of these biologically disabled persons. However, in some societies the likelihood of euthanasia is seldom far from possibility for the biologically disabled, Nazi Germany being an example.

PROBLEMS OF PARENTING

There is much lore attached to the task of parenting children handed down from eons past and added to from generation to generation. Every parent has been apprised of such teaching from his own parent and from other family members and from well-meaning friends. This lore tends to consist of both wisdom and foolishness with no incontrovertible way for the parent to discern the difference. The parenting advice given by well-meaning persons tends to be contaminated by distortions arising from the outcome of the advisor's own derivative relatedness transference devolution process. It is through this process that the advisor confronted and dealt with tension producing impinging stimuli from stage-to-stage of ego ontogenesis in his own course of life. The adjustments and adaptations to the traumata of ego ontogenesis shapes the ego and its predilections for responding to impinging stimuli which in various degrees and in various ways are not opti-' mum and tend to have a self-injurious element in them.

Projection

Projection is a common contaminant which distorts the parenting judgment of parents and their well-intended advisors. The advisor's own childhood experience of being parented contains numerous episodes in which he rejected the parenting imposed by his own parent for which he experienced the guilt of disobedience. The superego tension increase resulting form this guilt tends to seek a means of relief. It is commonplace for individuals to chastise others for their failings as a means to reduce the superego tension of their own guilt. The advisor may project his own guilt for parenting failures on to the parent he advises. The parent then takes up this advice and applies it to the rearing of his child to the detriment of the child. Such advice may contain subtle punitive measures in the guise of doing the child good but which undermine the child's experience of worth and filial security.

Displacement

Displacement is another contaminant often distorting parenting advice. The advisor may displace upon the child of the parent he is advising his own childhood propensity for, say, risky behavior. Thus the parent is advised to give his child room to experiment in areas in which the child is not mature enough to avoid injudicious behavior. As a consequence, the parent may permit his child to socialize with unsavory play peers, venture into physically dangerous environments or neglect the obligations of self-dependence progress.

Overprotection

Overprotection is another misstep into which the parent might be misled by advisors who experienced neglect in their own upbringing. Identifying with the child of the parent he is advising, the over-protector may exhort the parent to keep a close eye and short leash upon his offspring so that they do not venture into the dangers which pervade modern life. As a consequence, the child fails to gain social skills which are likely to come from interactions with peers in other ethnicities and income classes. Such a child may be harmed by limitation upon his capacity to interact optimally with others in work or business.

Sublimation

The advisor, having suffered from frustration in his own life because of a fear of pursuing desired aims, advises the parent to encourage his child to' pursue leisure pleasures to the neglect of self-dependence progress. The child becomes a wastrel incapable of fending for himself as a result of excessive parental indulgence.

The Task Master

The parent reared in fear of failure and loss of worth by a parent who experienced these tension producing states during his own upbringing may infect his own child with these maladies as well as push his child toward achievement with the drive of a taskmaster. Just as the parent drove himself to achieve, he later drives his own child to achieve with uncompromising relentlessness. The child becomes a merciless self-driving adult bereft of the pleasure in life enjoyed by those capable of a degree of tension reducing self-indulgence.

Excessive Parenting

The parent who makes the task of childrearing central to his own tension reduction behavior tends to involve himself in his child's life to a smothering excess, inhibiting the child's own initiative in coping with the challenges of living. Out of fear of failure the parent may focus too must attention upon his child's rearing. Armed with books of advice about parenting and filled with advise from friends and relatives, this parent over-involves himself with his child to the detriment of the child's development of self-dependence skills.

A parent may engage in excessive parenting as a result of vicariously living his own life through that of his child. Having failed for whatever reason to achieve in life what he had hoped to achieve, the parent seeks vicariously to live his child's life as he would have lived his own by imposing his own objectives and aims upon his child. The child is then caught between pursuing his own tension reduction aims on the one hand and on the other hand pursuing those of his parent which conflict with his own. The child in this bind must sacrifice his own pursuit of narcissistic gratification, power and ego worth in order to gain that which his parent would bestow, which tends to stifle his own growth in self-dependence.

Excessive Parental Praise

The parent may praise his child to excess, giving the child a false sense of superiority which leads the child to adopt an exaggerated sense of his own capacity and importance. This state of mind tends to lead the individual to interact with others in a manner which offends and alienates them, in consequence of which the child fails to gain the support of others which would assist him in dealing with impinging stimuli which are greater than one person can cope with.

Child Abuse

Child abuse is the failure of the parent at the task of parenting. Child abuse is widespread if defined liberally but relatively rare if defined in strict terms. Child abuse can range from simply neglecting the child at one extreme to actually physically assaulting the child at the other extreme. Child abuse can be inflicted as a result of the ignorance and self-deception of the parent who rationalizes his misdeeds or fails to recognize his misdeeds as child abuse. Physically assaulting the child may be rationalized as necessary corrective action to prompt the child along the road to self-dependence for his own good.

Projection and judgmentalism and the emergence of suppressed hostility may be major ingredients of the abusing parent's behavior. The sexual abuser may be looking for a convenient tension-reducing outlet for sexual tension. Sexual abuse of one's child may involve projections or displacement of any of various suppressed tension reduction aims arising from failures of ego ontogenesis such as failure to resolve the Oedipus conflict adequately. The affect upon the child may be devastating and arouse the experience of filial guilt as well as the experience of filial worthlessness. The child may introject the model of parenting characterized by the abuse he experienced and apply it to the rearing of his own child, projecting the worthlessness and guilt he experienced in his upbringing on to his own offspring.

The Parenting of Siblings

Siblings reared in the same household tend to become rivals for the affection and favor of their parent. The Oedipus conflict rivalry first experienced during each sibling's primordial life tends to be transferred to his sibling. Consequently, he tends to relate to his sibling as he did to his parent. Competition with the same sex parent for preferment with the opposite sex parent is transferred by the sibling to his brother or sister.

During latency, after the formation of the superego and the suppression of the Oedipus conflict, the sibling experiences a great reduction of ego tension which formerly accompanied his oedipal experience because he transfers that oedipal relatedness to his sibling. The latency sibling experiences filial warmth in his interaction with his parent but antagonism with his brother or sister. The parent of siblings is put to the task of trying to appease the rivalry and jealousy of each of the siblings for their brothers and sisters. The parent will unlikely be able to eradicate the hostility between and among the siblings he is parenting, but he may be able to mitigate it. Parents tend to grasp this reality, and strive to apply fairness and evenhandedness to the treatment of their children, but with limited success.

The parent of multiple children also must deal with sibling alliances and conspiracies. Two or more siblings may form alliances against another or others of their brothers and sisters. These alliances may conspire against other siblings, and the children as a group or as members of an alliance may conspire against the parents. Firmness, diplomacy and skill at balance of power politics may assist the parents in dealing with these inevitable problems of rearing a family, but no means to eradicate them are available. Parenting remains the most difficult and intractable undertaking with which human beings are confronted.

The Lifelong Duration of the Parenting Obligation

The parent's job is never finished. His child may come to him for care as long as the parent continues to live, and even after the parent's death he is expected to provide for his child in his will. Conflicts established among his children often tend to extend into adulthood and even to the end of the parent's life, challenging the parent's capacity to deal with them indefinitely. Even after the parent's death, his will must bestow benefits upon his offspring in a pattern of distribution which is perceived by his offspring as evenhanded and fair, lest the parent be treated to execration by the child who believes he was unfairly treated and inadequately loved. Perceived unfairness among surviving siblings may cause a sundering of the family and the undermining of the parent's posterity needed to prolong his existence in the memory of his children. The filial-parental cathexis binds the parent to the care of and concern for his offspring forever. There is no escape for the parent from the burdens of parenthood. Even if he becomes estranged from his child, the filial-parental cathexis will continue to haunt him to his dying day.

17

THE PROBLEM OF SELF-DISCIPLINE

Self-discipline or self-control is a human preoccupation which tests the patience of every human being and stretches the imagination of philosophers. Why are human beings concerned about self-control, and how do they hope it would benefit them? No one has self-control except intermittently, but everyone seeks to obtain it. Those who are perceived to possess it are admired or envied by almost all others.

Self-control is exercised when the ego seeks to effect a net tension increase or a net tension decrease by guiding behavior to tolerate a degree of tension increase for the purpose of achieving a greater tension decrease as a consequence of tolerating tension increase. The ego is repeatedly confronted by circumstances in which the exercise of tension producing self-control may lead to tension reduction or to less tension increase. The following commonplace examples may illuminate this phenomenon.

As an example of net tension decrease, consider the reluctant college student who chooses to pursue an education from which pursuit he derives no pleasure. His academic studies are tension producing, and he wishes to reduce the tension by abandoning his studies. But he believes that if he completes his studies and obtains an academic degree he will be rewarded financially and socially with greater wealth and status than if he abandoned his studies. The behavior of pursuing education is tension producing, but the reward from completing the education will tend to be tension reducing so that the net of tension reduction from completing the studies exceeds the tension increase from performing the studies.

In an example of net tension increase, a soldier participating in a tension producing forced march wishes to bolt into the woods to escape the pain of fatigue and boredom, but he exercises self-control and remains in rank. His ego has evaluated the relative difference in tension increase from remaining in the march to the tension of military punishment which might befall him if he bolted and were caught. The ego reasons that the tension increase from military punishment would be greater than the tension increase from remaining in ranks.

Many commonplace examples of this phenomenon from daily life can be cited. The husband goes to work each day to toil at a tension producing job which he does not like. But the income he obtains from his employment enables him to provide for his family, which is tension reducing. The housewife toils at cleaning her ménage which is tension producing, but having a tidy house in which she takes pride is tension reducing. The children in the household put their clothes away in the closet, as they are required to do by their parents, which is tension producing. But suffering punishment from their parents for failure to put their clothes away would produce a net tension increase because punishment is a greater tension producer than putting away clothes.

The daily life of almost any individual is replete with incidents in which he must tolerate a lesser tension increase to avoid a greater tension increase. The husband is angry with his wife because dinner is not ready, but he holds his tongue for fear of reprisal later in the bedroom if he vents his anger upon his wife. The institutions of society recognize the human propensity for self-control and buttress the individual's propensity for self-discipline with tension producing sanctions which would be imposed upon him if he failed at self-discipline. In most modern societies, fines, imprisonment or execution may await the individual who fails at self-control.

The desire for self-control arises during ego ontogenesis with the formation of the superego in which it resides. The superego is formed by the process of resolving the Oedipus conflict, which the infant ego must accomplish to rid itself of the terror of fear of parental retribution. The Oedipal child wishes to annihilate the same sex parent with whom he competes and reasons (mistakenly) that the powerful same sex parent is aware of this wish and in return wishes to annihilate the child. The anger, fear and hostility with which the ego relates to the same sex parent with whom it competes for preferment with the opposite sex parent confronts the infant ego with a dread of annihilation at the hands of the same sex parent. The dread of annihilation produces an intolerable tension in the infant ego which forms the superego to rid itself of the tension which overwhelms it. By capitulating totally to the powerful parent, the infant hopes that it will not be attacked. This mechanism enables the infant ego to reduce the tension produced by filial fear. But it must sustain the practice of filial capitulation in order to continue to reduce the tension of filial fear. The construct of the superego is the principal means by which it sustains its posture of filial capitulation.

During the latency period, the ego consolidates its practice of filial capitulation and transfers that filial relatedness to other authorities in its perception which are viewed as more powerful than the parent, such as societal institutions. The deity and the church, the school and the teacher, the policemen and the courts are salient among the numerous authorities to which the latency child transfers his filial capitulation. To avoid a return of the terror experienced in relation to the primordial parent, the latency child sustains his capitulation to authority for which self-control is essential. The potential failure of self-control elicits the experience of dread which tends to prompt the ego to restore self-control.

Self-Control in Daily Living

Self-control is a struggle within the ego between the desire to achieve tension reduction by means of forbidden behavior and the stemming of this desire by tension producing inhibition. The range of behavior which is incorporated into the superego and forbidden by the mores and laws of society is immense and reaches into almost every area of life. In daily life, the ego nevertheless guides behavior to breech the restraint upon forbidden behavior in numerous ways which invokes the tension producing reprimand of the superego. These behaviors tend to range from breaches of minor mores to heinous crimes universally condemned. Many in society may forgive breeches of minor mores but become outraged by those who commit major crimes.

Various social mores and societal laws are violated at times by rank and file citizens. Running a traffic light at an inactive intersection, pilfering a few office supplies from the workplace, pocketing a piece of fruit from the green grocer, fudging the amount of a deduction on one's income tax, jumping the queue at the checkout counter, rattling the collection plate at church without putting in a donation, not carrying out onerous minor duties for which one is obligated and many other such negligible transgressions are all done upon occasion by the otherwise responsible citizens and would be done more often without the chastisement of the superego and the exhortation of the ego ideal, which provide the self-control which makes an orderly society possible.

Heinous crimes such as murder are prevented by the superego buttressed by prohibitive law and its enforcement and by the condemnation of the society of which the individual is a member. Premeditated murder, that is, murder carefully thought through before being committed, is much less' frequent than a killing done in moment of anger and the loss of self-control. The prospect of the death penalty is much less of a deterrent to murder than the constraint imposed by the superego. The ego guides behavior to suppress murderous intent because of the ignominy and loss of ego worth which the murderer would suffer should he commit the crime. The relative peacefulness of sparsely populated societies lacking abundant law enforcement personnel attests this reality.

However, the ego which regards itself as a member of a criminal subculture may commit murder without the chastisement of the superego. Also an ego which is capable of rationalizing that guiding behavior to commit murder in a noble cause is acceptable to the superego may commit murder with impunity so far as the mores to which it beholds itself are concerned. Thus, soldiers kill in war and terrorists kill innocent civilians and avengers kill those they accuse of a wrong. Persuading such egos that they have committed a moral wrong is an uphill struggle.

The prospect of losing self-control is frightening to the ego and produces ego tension which impels the ego to seek self-control when confronted with the prospect of losing it. It is the chastisement of the superego which frightens the ego, but the condemnation of others and the prospect of criminal sanction adds to the fear. An important tension reducer for rank and file members of society is the mechanism of projection. Paradoxically, the failures at self-control of some members of society furnish the opportunity to other members of society to apply the mechanism of projection which enables the other rank and file members of society to reduce the tension of their own failures and fear of failure at self-control by projecting them onto others who are guilty of breeches of mores and law.

The beginnings of projection occur at the time of the creation of the id which the ego establishes to serve as the target of its blame for thoughts and wishes which are dangerous such as those produced by the rivalry with the same sex parent for preferment with the opposite sex parent. These wishes for the annihilation of the same sex parent impinge upon the infant ego with great fear of parental retaliation which the ego wishes to reduce by attributing them to the id. "It made me do it" is the ego's claim to establish its innocence and reduce the tension of filial fear, "it" being the id.

Projection is suggested to the ego by the infant's practice of spitting out the unwanted food being forced into his mouth by the parent struggling to complete the infant's transition from breast or bottle-feeding to the taking of nourishment from eating utensils. The spitting out of unwanted food serves as a model for spitting out or projecting unwanted objects from within.[1] Unwanted thoughts, attitudes and practices whose possession is tension producing may be removed by attributing them to others. Thus tension producing attributes one perceives in himself are ejected by perceiving them as belonging to someone or something else outside the self. Such perception reduces ego tension produced by perceiving the thing as external.

Free Will

The concept of self-control inevitably encounters the concept of free will. If the ego is to have the capacity for self-control, the will must be free to decide between or among courses of action. The ego experiences free will almost all of the time whether it actually possesses free will or not. There are times, however, when the ego experiences paralysis of action, unable to

---

[1] See **Ruth Monroe**, loc cit.

decide which action to take. In the absence of a belief that it possesses free will, the ego would be unable to establish the superego. The superego assumes that the ego can make choices between what it should do and what it should not do.

The concept of free will is embraced by religion which teaches its adherents that they have the intellect to know right from wrong and the capacity to discipline themselves to do right and refrain from doing wrong. Religion also teaches its adherents what is right and what is wrong. Any adherent in doubt can go to his clergyman and be informed of what is right and what is wrong in a specific case that may perplex him.

The concept of morality—right or wrong conduct, how to distinguish between them and how to remain upon the path of rectitude—has throughout human history attracted the interest of ethicists. They have puzzled over the problem and devised various "systems" of ethics, but no universally agreed upon system has been found. The lack of agreement arises from the disparity among egos of first principles from which to reason. Each ego perceives reality in a way which is unique to that ego arising from a unique superego. Because the perception of reality is in some respect different for each ego, the superego of each ego is in some respect different from all other egos. The preoccupation of ethicists over questions of right and wrong behavior is impelled by their experience of superego tension which they hope to reduce by discovering the one true principle which distinguishes right from wrong. Like teachers of religious doctrine, many secular ethicists believe that the will is free to choose between right and wrong conduct.

Is Free Will a Bogus Issue?

Human behavior is impelled by the will and guided by the ego to seek tension reduction or to avoid tension increase alternatives among those perceived available to it by the ego.[2] The alternatives chosen abide by the principle of choosing the least tension increase or greatest tension reduction among the alternative courses of action perceived by the ego. The ego is an observer of its own experience of tension increase and choice of tension reduction alternatives. The ego has no choice except to choose the least tension increase or the greatest tension reduction which it perceives, but it experiences these choices as if it could choose otherwise, which it cannot.

Many impinging stimuli intrude upon the equanimity of the ego to channel its decision making into the direction it by necessity chooses. The ego

---

[2] No one knows the locus of free will. Brain research has yet to identify definitively a part of the brain in which it can be said that free will resides, if it exists at all. For a discussion of brain research and free will, see *The Brain in the News,* September 15, 2001, Vol. 8, No. 15, Randy Talley, Ed. The Dana Press, 1001 G. Street, NW. Suite 1025, Washington, D.C. 20001.

must guide behavior to reduce tension by the most efficient path it perceives. While the ego is choosing among perceived alternatives, its awareness of its decision making gives it the illusion of free choice. It must choose the path it chooses, but because it selects among competing alternatives, it believes it has free choice. A river flowing down hill must follow the channel which constricts it, but it can also alter its path by eroding the channel. It can only erode the channel in the way the channel is susceptible to erosion. Softer parts of the riverbed will erode before harder parts of the riverbed erode. But the channel can be changed by external forces such as a flood or a landslide.

The ego choosing the path of tension reduction acts in a similar way by choosing the path which confronts it with the least tension producing impinging stimuli which it perceives as being in its way. But the paths open to it may be changed by external forces such as trauma or changed circumstances. If the river had a consciousness so it could witness its own experience and a will determined to follow the channel least obstructive it would be like the human ego witnessing its own behavior in the belief that it could make choices other than the choices it actually makes.

Freedom

When the ego is compelled by others to choose a path which would cause a net tension increase, it tends to perceive an impediment placed in the way of its free will, which corroborates its belief in the existence of free will. If the ego would choose one path but is prevented by someone, it tends to believe that its free will is artificially frustrated. The ego first experiences significant frustration against its exercise of free will when weaning is imposed during the oral stage of ego ontogenesis. When the breast and nipple, which is the mode of filial cathexis which the infant ego craves, is withheld, it is profoundly frightening, frustrating and tension producing.

Perforce, the infant ego must guide behavior to accept the cup, the spoon and the bowl to reduce the tension of hunger, after which it eventually adjusts to the new conditions of filial cathexis which exclude the breast and the nipple. Thenceforth, the cravings for the breast and the nipple are sublimated and manifested in other ways. Over-eating, smoking cigarettes, kissing, talking volubly and engaging in oral sex are among the numerous behaviors in which the ego guides behavior to appease the craving for the nipple and the breast forever forbidden to the ego after weaning.

As the ego evolves through the course of ego ontogenesis, subjected to the series of severation traumata entailed, it modifies the sublimations resorted to for appeasement of the oral cravings to deal with the unique conditions of each ontogenetic stage. Suckling at the breast may be replaced by sucking on a drinking straw or by sucking the thumb. Thumb sucking may be replaced by sucking on candy. Sucking on candy may be replaced by smoking cigarettes, a pipe or cigar. Smoking may be replaced or expanded upon by oral speech aimed at seeking affection or the cathexis of others to which filial relatedness occurs. Oral speech may expand into written communication in the form of poetry or fiction aimed at eliciting admiration from readers.

The anal stage succeeding the oral stage may lead to coprophilia practices involving the eating of one's feces or fantasies about eating ones feces. The prohibition against eating one's feces may lead to indulging in toilet humor. The prohibition against toilet humor may lead to the eating of sublimated feces in the form of foods which are reminders of feces such as pureed vegetables, link sausages, and gravy. As the ego guides behavior to obtain these items, it believes that it is exercising choice in its path aimed at reducing ego tension. But too much eating of rich foods may produce ego tension from fear of ill health and compel the ego to guide behavior to desist from such eating practices. The giving up of the eating of unhealthful tension reducing foods is a tension-producing act of self-discipline aimed at preserving or enhancing health.

It is ironic that when the ego is impeded from its aims by natural phenomenon such as great distances, the force of gravity and natural obstructions, it does not perceive a loss of freedom. If it cannot travel over a great distance, erect a structure which will not topple or cross a wide body of water, it does not experience a lack of freedom. But if human beings who are functionaries of organizations and institutions block it from its journey, forbid it to erect a structure or prohibit it from crossing a body of water, the ego perceives itself as being denied its freedom.

This perception of the ego derives from impediments placed in the ego's way by the parent who weans it. What the parent does is viewed as a restriction, but what nature does is viewed as an inanimate obstruction. The latter can be overcome by effort, but the former can be overcome only by defeating an adversary. All institutions, organizations and their functionaries to which the individual ego relates as it did to its parent of infancy, it perceives as deprivers of its freedom. But natural obstacles tend not to be seen so much as deprivers of freedom as they do barriers to be overcome.

Freedom is seen as a function of human interaction, while natural obstacles are seen as innocent impediments. Frequently, natural obstacles are personified and bombarded with blame as if they were human beings or human institutions. The farmer may personify the drought or deify the weather as an angry god and blame it for the lack of rain and the ruin of his crops. The aborigine may blame the volcano god for the disaster which befalls his village. But geologists will perceive the weather and the volcano as natural phenomena and be unable to hold them morally accountable for the disasters they cause.

Freedom, then, is a human concept dependent upon human beings and their institutions for its reality. Freedom requires a belief in the ability of the ego to make choices in the absence of restrictions imposed by others. When one is unimpeded by others, he tends to view himself as responsible for his choices because he believes he is free to choose one way or another. Open societies depend upon a belief in unimpeded and fair freedom of choice because with that belief present in the ego's of the rank and file members of society they will blame themselves for their individual misfortunes and not societal institutions or those who are more successful.

Impediments to Self-Control

The chief impediment to self-control is immaturity. It is during infancy that the ego emerges to experience its own existence, and the passions animated by the will to reduce tension by whatever means is perceived regardless of the possibility of such means producing a net tension increase. The infant ego lacks the intellectual power and the empathy to recognize actions it might guide the infant to take which would redound to produce more tension than it would reduce. As the infant ego gains intellectual powers of reason and memory it comes to recognize the possibility that some of its tension reducing actions would produce a net tension increase, and it perceives the need to inhibit impulses which would produce these outcomes. Inhibition is a difficult practice to establish because it directly contravenes the impulse to reduce tension by the most direct means perceived. Learning to assess the prospect for producing a net tension increase resulting from one's actions and to abnegate oneself to avoid a net tension increase is a step in the acquisition of maturity not easily learned and put into practice.

Failure to acquire a self-abnegating capability becomes a barrier to self-control and tends to lead to indulgences which appease ego tension in the immediate circumstances and in the short run, but leads to greater tension in other circumstances and in the long run. The propensity toward self-indulgence is common in mankind, but the maturity to avoid self-indulgence is also common among human beings. Self-indulgence may occur at times in the behavior of everyone for which later a price is paid. Commonly, eating or imbibing to excess, enjoyed at the time it is indulged in, produces tension increase later in the form of pain or illness which counterbalances the pleasure of the indulgence. But the mature ego will keep these behaviors to a minimum.

The acquisition of maturity is an uneven phenomenon in human behavior. Some individuals acquire maturity to a greater extent than others, and some display maturity at some times but not at others. An individual may descend into self-indulgence in the pursuit of tension reduction to alleviate the stress in daily life. He may over indulge in forbidden behavior or eat and drink to excess. He may gamble away the rent money or spend it on a prostitute. He may allow himself to express anger openly against an enemy or public figure to whom he has projected hostility. He may commit an outrage against someone or something he relates to with anger and resentment. But most individuals most of the time restore themselves to maturity after a period of excessive indulgence and resume a mature life. For some, the consequences of their indulgence cannot be repaired. The acquisition of maturity is one of the most important gains which the ego can make in the interest of human survival.

18

RELIGIOUS FAITH

Religious faith is an omnibus ego mechanism to deal with the fears and frustrated aspirations of the human ego in all matters not handled effectively by other mechanisms, and it is the last resort of the ego when all else fails. It arises as a result of a combination of the resolution of the Oedipus conflict, the establishment of the superego, the creation of ego mechanisms, and the will's demand that all tension producing stimuli be explained and dealt with. As the Oedipus conflict is resolved the infant ego subordinates itself totally to the parent in order to reduce the tension produced by a naïve but profound filial fear of parental retribution. The infant ego reasons that if it subordinates itself totally to the parent, then the parent will have no reason to exact retribution from the child.

To the child ego, the parent becomes all-powerful, all knowing and ubiquitous so that the child cannot escape parental power or subordination to it. These attributes of the primordial child's parent are transferred by the ego during the latency period to the deity who comes to the child's attention as the latter discovers that his parent is actually not omnipotent, omniscient, and omnipresent, but that it is the deity who possesses these attributes. Thenceforth, the reliance of the primordial ego upon the parent of infancy for its protection and reward is transferred to the deity who thereafter is prayed to for the same sorts of benefits and protections as the primordial child beseeched his parent to bestow during his toddler days.

The child continues to seek tension reduction benefits from the parent, but at times when the parent fails to provide these benefits, it is to the deity that the child turns. The majesty in which the primordial child held his parent, the latency child also holds his parent. The great house in which the parent of the primordial child lived, the latency child now discovers that an even greater and more impressive house has been erected by adults for the deity. The awe and veneration in which the primordial child held his parent, the latency child discovers his parent holds the deity. The latency child begins to look to the deity for everything which the parent appears unable to provide that he once looked to his parent to provide during primordial life. Typically, the latency child wants to grow strong and big and smart, the boy to have large size and muscle strength and the girl to have charm and physical attractiveness.

But the latency child poses the question that if he could not have looked to his parent for everything he formerly believed he could, can he now look to the deity for everything he had looked to his parent for? The child is told that the answer is faith and piety. While faith in the parent it turns out had not been fully justifiable, faith in the deity is justifiable if one can establish and sustain the faith. The key to religion is faith and piety, and failure of faith and piety is the fault of the believer and not the fault of the deity. Whatever happens is attributed to the deity's will which the faithful and the pious will not question just as the latency child would not doubt the wisdom of his parent.

The latency period child tends to be subjected to religious indoctrination by adult society which varies in intensity from one culture to the next and in varying degrees at different times and in different parts of the same culture. Fear or lack of it tends to have a strong affect upon the intensity with which religious faith is embraced and piety practiced. Religious faith and piety tend to be most intensely held by individuals living in fear such as those in poverty, those in circumstances of constant danger and those suffering anxiety because of stressful situations or from mental illness, severe disability or life-threatening illness. Those living in relatively peaceful and protected circumstances in places and times of affluence and in good health tend to evince weaker intensity of religious belief.

What the Ego Expects of Faith

In some cultures, religious faith requires the subordination and allegiance of the believer exclusively to the deity. For example, both the Christian and the Jewish God demand that their adherents "have no other god before them." Allah demands that his followers acknowledge that he is the only god. These requirements buttress the adherent's faith in the deity. Religious leaders expect adherents to acknowledge that their god is the only god and that they are the only ones who can convey what the deity expects of them and would do for them. Instructions from other sources tend to lack authority and are suspect.

Martin Luther challenged this concept in the Christian religion by advising individuals to interpret the Bible for themselves. A consequence of Luther's teaching was the ego emergence of many denominations of Christians with different religious leaders interpreting the Bible differently, but rank and file adherents continued to seek religious advise from religious leaders whom they believed could understand and explain God's word more accurately than they themselves could.

This form of allegiance to the deity and recognition of who speaks for the deity is similar to the latency child's relation to his parent. The parent tends to serve as the model for the way the individual relates to his god, and the

concept of god tends to be modeled upon the child's perception of and relation to the parent during the child's latency years. The child's perceived dependence upon the parent is transferred to dependence upon the deity for
what the parent appears unable to provide. This model of filial relatedness continues into adolescence where the adolescent ego may rebel against it in his
struggle to individuate from the parent or instead be more profoundly accepted if the child's filial rebellion takes another form, which it does in the
great majority of cases. The religious rebel, while he forms a part of the pool
from which leaders of religious rebellion may rise, is much less common
than adolescents who accept the religious beliefs of their parents and look to
the god of their fathers for the tension reduction benefits that their parents
are no longer seen as able to provide.

The onset of adolescence confronts the ego with a requirement for resolving the Oedipus conflict anew. The resolution of the adolescent Oedipus conflict involves the displacement upon the deity of the filial relatedness to the
parent. In searching for identity and to establish an ego ideal, the adolescent
ego tends to accept the parent's religious values wholesale while rebelling
against other parental values as a means to be different from the parent. Because of a requirement for a lengthy education or apprenticeship in modern
technological societies, adolescence tends to continue to be a time of dependence for the child ego for the wherewithal of survival such as shelter,
food and clothing. The overwhelming majority of adolescents continue to reflect their parent's religious values, their parent's vision of the deity and what
one's relation to the deity is and should be. They tend to relate during adolescence to the deity of their parent as they had related to the parent of latency.

Thus, the adolescent ego may displace upon the deity the filial ambivalence transferred to the deity from the parent. This transference of filial relatedness tends to bifurcate so as to relate to some external objects as beneficent and others as maleficent. In religion this tends to manifest itself in the
establishment of beneficent objects of displaced filial relatedness such as the
deity and maleficent objects of displaced filial relatedness such as the devil.
Dependence upon the validity of these beliefs tends to sustain religious faith.
Accordingly, those who believe in the existence of the deity also tend to believe in the existence of the devil.

The ego tends to look to religious faith to satisfy the various wants
which the individual cannot provide for himself and which are created by
tension reduction needs produced by each stage of ego ontogenesis. The adolescent boy wants to obtain attributes which will elicit the admiration of and
provide him with status among his peers and attractiveness to members of
the opposite sex or in the case of homosexuals to the same sex. Attributes and
assets desired by the adolescent, by the adult and by the old age individual
tend to differ from one culture to the next and from one era to the next.

Religious Fanaticism

Religious fanaticism derives from ego tension produced by an inadequately resolved Oedipus conflict. The religious fanatic tends to want to believe that everyone to whom his fanaticism is intended to appeal holds the same religious beliefs and aims as he does. The ego of the religious fanatic tends to relate to the deity as it did to the same sex parent. The religious fanatic held the parent in awe and fear, and in his effort to resolve the Oedipus conflict established a superego intensely severe in its demands. The superego continually bombards the fanatic's ego with tension producing demands difficult to achieve so that the fanatic's ego struggles in vain to satisfy the superego, and consequently, it tends to be unable to reduce the tension of superego impingement. The religious fanatic needs to have others believe in the same deity as much as he does and in the teachings of the deity as he the fanatic interprets them. What the fanatic believes the deity wants him to do, the fanatic also insists that others believe the same to reduce the tension of doubt.

The fanatic's incomplete resolution of the Oedipus conflict is displaced upon the deity during adolescence when he again must resolve the Oedipus conflict, and he suffers great fear of the deity and a great desire to please the deity as a means to reduce the ego tension produced by the demanding superego. The religious fanatic lacks ego worth, perceiving himself as having failed to earn the admiration and approval of his parent so that his fanaticism is aimed not only at alleviating his fear of the parent but also at earning the admiration of the parent and of the deity to which he transfers his filial relatedness as a means to reduce his severe ego worth deficit tension as well as the tension produced by his unfounded filial fear.

The strength of the fanaticism is a function of the intensity of the filial fear and the lack of worth experienced by the fanatic. The fanatic's devotion to a religious doctrine which supports his perception of reality virtually deprives him of the capacity to analyze the thinking he experienced during the ego ontogenetic process which brought him to the posture of religious fanatic. His fanaticism helps reduce the tension of his filial fear and lack of worth, and he becomes so filled with the determination to put into effect the declared aims of his fanaticism that he is able to give attention to little else.

The fanatic tends to become extremist because the logic of his aims does not accept doubt. Doubt would vitiate the effectiveness of the fanatic's beliefs and undermine the capacity of his beliefs to reduce the ego tension of displaced filial fear and the ego worth deficit. The intensity of the filial fear and ego worth deficit tension demands that the beliefs upon which tension reduction is relied upon to achieve drives the intensity of the fanatical aims. Any attempt to dissuade the fanatic from his beliefs or his aims would threaten the entire structure of his tension reduction apparatus and would tend to be resisted with the full force of the fanatic's tension reduction aims. Religious adherents who are not fanatics tend to suffer less intense superego tension and are able to rationalize any religious doubt they may experience. Fanatics who are terrorists inflict terror in part because they experience terror themselves in the form of misguided and unrecognized filial fear and know the power of terror and project it upon others in an effort to rid themselves of it.

Religious Conversion

Religious conversion tends to come at a time when the ego feels lost, gone astray and confused about the individual's identity. This may occur when the ego senses that it has taken the wrong path or followed a course with which it is uncomfortable and feels confused about its identity. This may occur at any point along the path of ego ontogenesis during a transition from one stage to the next when the ego experiences severation or decathexis from connection to a major object of dependence. It may happen at any point in the course of life when a realization has come to the ego that it is on the wrong course and may have been on the wrong course for a considerable length of time.

Although religious conversion may come at any age, it is most likely to come during adolescence when the individual's belief system normatively tends to be most labile. Religious conversion may be from one religion to another or from non-belief to belief in a particular religion. During adolescent individuation, which arises from the ego's re-experiencing of the Oedipus conflict, which precipitates a search for a separate identity from that of the parent, the adolescent ego may choose the parent's religious values as entities against which to rebel. Or the child may seek a new identity by becoming even more devoted to the parent's religion than the parent, which retains the parent's religious values and thus avoids offending the parent and risking parental retribution.

The adolescent may simply exceed the piety of the parent by some measure which is less than extravagant, or the adolescent may go to extravagant lengths in embracing the parent's religious views to the point of fanaticism. Or the adolescent ego may reject the parent's religious views and convert to another religion or become a disbeliever. Or he may reject his parent's atheism or agnosticism and become religious. The degree of extravagance of the religious views which the adolescent comes to hold—whether fanatical or not—depends upon the intensity of superego tension which the adolescent ego experiences and his response to that tension.

Religious conversion from a weakly held religion to a strongly held religion may occur when the adolescent ego of a child whose parent's religious views are weakly held is seeking a separate identity by surpassing the intensity of the parent's religious values. The child thus distinguishes himself from the parent with the aim of establishing a separate identity without risking retribution from the parent and perhaps earning the admiration of the parent, which reduces the ego worth deficit. As the adolescent becomes converted, he tends to experience a reduction of severation tension, which fear of parental retribution produces.

Religious conversion also tends to occur at other times of transition from one stage of ego ontogenesis to the succeeding stage. Times of decathexis tension, when the ego is in transition from one stage of ego ontogenesis to the succeeding stage, the ego is particularly vulnerable to fear and insecurity and tends to search for a means of security because security is no longer adequately experienced and produces great ego tension which the ego is impelled to reduce. Thus, as the individual transitions from adolescence to young adulthood and from young adulthood into middle age, and as he approaches the end of life he tends to experience great increase of decathexis tension. For a large proportion of human beings these decathexis experiences prompt a turn to religious faith as the means to reduce the tension of decathexis and the fear of future uncertainties.

Religious conversion may occur for other reasons than reducing the tension of filial severation. For example, an individual may convert to the religion of the person he marries as a requirement of his spouse or his spouse's religious institution. Or a religious conversion may occur because of the successful efforts of a missionary in dealing with a credulous prospect who is vulnerable to persuasion by a determined and able proselytizer.

Religious Faith and Rectitude

Religion is used by societal institutions and their functionaries to uphold rectitude, which is essential to social stability. Social stability does not mean social ossification. Social stability allows orderly change which replaces the old with the new without demolishing social equilibrium. Pervasive rectitude in human behavior is necessary for orderly change, and religious belief tends to buttress behavioral rectitude. Religious institutions and organizations depend, as do all established social institutions and organizations, upon social stability for their preservation. Social upheaval threatens social institutions and their organizations with displacement by new institutions and organizations which may emerge from the chaos of social disruption. The church uses the fear of god to compel populations to respect law which supports the status quo and preserves their continuance.

During times of societal stability, religious institutions tend to inculcate in their adherents a reverence for rectitude in the form of devotion to accepted modes of behavior and opposition to disruptive behavior whether in oneself or in others. Church approved mores are applauded, and those who adhere to them enjoy the approval of the church. Thus, the individual ego of the child and the adult which tends to seek the reduction of ego worth deficit tension strives to adhere to church approved mores in order to enjoy tension reduction from the approval of the parentified church. Devotion to and the demonstration of religious faith serve as a reducer of ego worth deficit tension. If rectitude has been instilled in the child by the parent, the child may display a conspicuous rectitude impelled by his need to earn parental approval to reduce the tension of ego worth deficit. Individuals who attain a deserved reputation for honesty, uprightness, dependability, loyalty and piety may have come to their rectitude by this route.

Religious faith tends to preserve social order mainly in societies with a monolithic church, which tends to curb expansionist aspirations of minority religions. Where religions compete in a multi-religion society such as in twentieth century Northern Ireland or sixteenth century Germany or fifteenth century Spain, social disorder may arise as competing religions seek access to the sovereign power of the state to enhance their own religious institutions and to suppress rival religious institutions.

Religious Faith and Guilt

The church serves as a societal extension of the aggregate superego writ large. The church functions as a societal Dutch uncle which takes everyone to task who violates the prevailing mores of society. The presence of the religious institution stands as a constant reminder of what the superego expects of the individual ego. Guilt is the experience of unrequited superego tension, which persists continually. Meeting the expectations of the superego may produce an intolerable tension increase. For example, sexual lust in the celibate may painfully persist causing the ego to guide behavior toward performing a sexual act to reduce the tension of lust but come into conflict with the superego, which orders the ego to desist from sexual intercourse because of a prohibition against fornication. If he carries out the prohibited act, then the superego may persist in punishing him by continually reminding him of his transgression.

Any act performed which violates the imperatives of the superego will beget ego tension which inflicts unpleasure upon the ego. The church, which is the societal authority for conveying the deity's imperatives to rank and file adherents, may permit the penitent to request forgiveness for his misdeed and be granted absolution, which relieves him of the guilt he earned by his indiscretion. Religious faith can be a palliative for a tormented soul. The church and its functionaries being parentified enables the supplicant to obtain parental forgiveness for indiscretions inculcated as such by the parent and displaced upon the religious institution which removes the filial fear of retribution for an act which offends parental teachings.

Rectitude requires obedience to the imperatives of the superego, and religious faith provides an avenue of escape from the tension of guilt for violations of superego proscriptions and prescriptions. Great guilt can bring the penitent back to his faith from the wayward state to which he has wandered in his errant tension reduction aims carried out in the form of prohibited sexual intercourse.

Embracing Religious Faith

Religious faith tends to be embraced first during ego ontogenesis by the latency age ego because it is in latency that the child first discovers that his parent cannot provide all of the tension reduction wants and needs which he experiences, and it is also in latency that the ego first begins to accept the inculcation of religious faith by the parent. The child ego learns to pray to the deity to allay those of his fears which the parent appears unable to alleviate. The experience of religious faith enables the latency child to put his fears to rest so long as he is able to continue to experience the faith. If his faith waivers, he must avow anew the depth and constancy of his faith. He must believe in the reality of his faith if he is to believe in the validity of his faith. If he is surrounded by believers, he tends be helped in sustaining his faith and in the tension reduction benefits for which he prays.

The benefits for which the latency ego prays tend to center upon the aims which the child has adopted to reduce the tension of the Oedipus conflict which he continues to suppress in the face of its repeated threat to reemerge. He wishes to continue to attract the constancy of the same sex parent and the affection of the opposite sex parent. The little girl tends to want to be pretty and appealing to her father, and she may pray for the clothes and the physical appearance which she believes will accomplish this aim. She may pray that she be given a doll which she can play with and identify with which if she were like it, she would more strongly attract her father. She may also wish for a doll to play with in simulation of the way her mother takes care of her in order to earn the respect of her mother for having childcare skills, more firmly to identify with her mother and strengthen the filial-maternal cathexis. Both the little boy and the little girl may pray for academic success to meet their parents' expectations.

The little boy may pray for the fulfillment of tension reduction wants his parent cannot or refuses to supply. He may want toys which will help him simulate his father's role such as toy tools reflecting those his father may use in his employment or in maintaining the family ménage. These might be toy carpenter tools if the father is a carpenter, or a toy truck if his father is a truck driver. He may pray to become great in size and strong in body, which would enable him to surpass his father. Whatever his parents admire in persons, the little boy may pray to attain when he is unable to gain it through his own power.

The adolescent girl, finding herself in competition with her peers, may pray to become attractive so as to elicit the approval of her parents to reduce ego worth deficit tension, to elevate her status among her peers and to attract members of the opposite sex to assure her capacity eventually to find a worthy marriage partner. She may hope eventually to surpass her mother in attractiveness assets and in the quality of the husband she will acquire. The adolescent boy may pray for superiority in, say, athletics or perhaps academics, depending upon which of these is important for gaining parental approval so as to reduce the tension of the ego worth deficit. The adolescent boy may pray for more mundane assets such as a bicycle or when older an automobile when his parent fails to provide these for him. Both the adolescent boy and the adolescent girl may pray for wishes which their parents cannot supply such as blemish free skin, luxuriant hair, social popularity or academic success.

The young adult will tend to pray for satisfaction of the various needs left unfulfilled from adolescence and for success in establishing himself in the occupation he has settled upon to make his or her way in the course of life. For the man, this may be a desired job, profession, trade or business. For the girl, it may be any of these but it may also be the acquisition of a desirable husband, social status and attractive children. The young adult may pray for greater affluence to enable him or her to enter the marketplace and purchase the various needs he or she has established both for basic necessities and for wants which would afford social status and the luxuries of a satisfying material life. If the young adult has failed during adolescence to achieve its requirements, the young adult may pray for the rectification of these shortcomings. The young adult may pray for the ability to get along with others or to have others treat him kindly and with respect and esteem, and he or she may pray for the acquisition of status in society in order to command the esteem he or she craves. If they pursue studies in higher education, both the young adult boy and the young adult girl may pray for success in their academic undertaking.

The middle age adult is likely to pray that all that he has gained during the course of life be protected and preserved, knowing that to replace any of his gains should he lose them might not be possible given the limited time remaining for him to achieve his aims in life. He may pray variously for the preservation of his family and the health of his family. He may pray for the preservation of the material possessions of his family, its residence and its various properties and chattels. He may pray for the success of his offspring and for his own success in sustaining his social status and his achievements. If he is particularly pious, he may pray for the salvation of his soul, but he is more likely to become intense about salvation after he has entered old age' and is approaching death. At any age, the ego may pray for a solution to any of myriad special problems related to income, health, the success of one's children and any of a thousand other special problems which human beings are heir to.

In old age, fear of damnation and the hope of escaping it may enter the old person's prayers. Atheists, agnostics and the faithful alike experience profound fear at the inevitability of their own deaths. The former may stoically accept the prospect of their own deaths, but the faithful tend to erect in their imaginations a better life to which their death serves as a transition.

Sustaining Religious Faith

Because religious faith contradicts common sense reality, the human ego experiences difficulty in sustaining it. Numerous devices are created by the ego to reduce the tension of religious doubt. A behavior widely resorted to is the surrounding of oneself with persons believing in the same faith and avoiding those who do not share one's faith. Consequently, the faithful attend church in part to be in the company of large numbers of like-minded believers, to pursue a social life among the faithful and to avoid those who hold different beliefs from their own. Belittling the beliefs of those of other faiths also is often resorted to as a means of bolstering the alleged validity of one's own faith. Denial that religious faith is a form of superstition is vehemently proclaimed by the faithful to ease the disquiet of doubt.

Believers may seek converts through missionary work and by proselytizing heathen in order to enlarge the ranks of likeminded believers. Growing numbers of likeminded cohorts is comforting. Believers through publicity may attempt to increase the awareness of members of the larger society to the alleged importance and size of their church. Believers may seek to diminish non-believers and believers of faiths which conflict with one's own through argument, adverse publicity and restricting legislation. By the use of the mass media, they may strive to spread the word of their own faith and invite others to join.

They often erect huge structures such as cathedrals, temples, tabernacles and shrines which will impress others with the importance of their religious institution in order to dominate adherents of other faiths. They may seek to conquer foreign lands where other religions abide in order to dominate those with rival faiths. The Crusades of the Middle Ages may serve as an example of this strategy. They may seek to inform the public about the teachings of their religion in order to influence social policy so that their religion gains ascendancy in accepted mores and laws of society. For this, the faithful may resort to television and radio broadcasts and to door-to-door proselytizing. It has not been uncommon through the ages for one religion to go to war to conquer territories of other religions to spread their faith. Salient examples in history include the spread of Islam across North Africa, the Middle East and southern Europe; the Crusades aimed at "freeing" the Holy Land from Muslims and the Thirty Years War aimed in part at establishing Protestantism in Central Europe.

Man's Image and Likeness

That man is created in God's image and likeness is a deeply held belief for many of the faithful. But it may be argued with equal conviction that God is created in man's image and likeness. In Christianity, God tends to have the principal features of the beneficent parental surrogate and the devil the principal features of the maleficent parental surrogate. God tends to be perceived as being like the beneficent parentified entity, perceived as exalted, benevolent, all powerful, all knowing, prescient and incapable of evil, wrong doing and unfairness much like the beneficent parent of early latency. Likenesses of God rendered by artists tend to be given the appearance of a human being represented as awesome and majestic or as supernatural represented as a burning bush with voice over commentary.

The devil tends to be perceived as a mirror opposite of God and as being perceived like the maleficent parentified entity tends to be perceived as evil, threatening, punitive and powerful, omniscient and prescient. While God is created in the likeness of the benevolent parental surrogate, the devil is created in the likeness of the maleficent parental surrogate. While the individual looks to the benevolent God for forgiveness of his bad behavior and to be saved from hell, he looks to the devil in fear of punishment for the same bad behavior. These forms of relatedness reflect the good and evil of filial ambivalence, of displaced filial hostility and its feared repercussions and displaced filial affection and the glorification of the benevolent parent.

The parentifying adult creates for his God a great house reflecting the great house the latency child's parent lives in. The church or temple erected for the deity tends to be much larger than the house of an ordinary mortal so that the adult standing in God's house is relatively small as he was during his latency years standing in his parent's house. His inferiority to God is emphasized by his small size relative to God's house as his inferiority during latency was emphasized relative to his parent's house. He is welcome in God's great house so long as he does not profane it just as he was welcome in the great house of his parent during the latency years of his diminutiveness and powerlessness. That God is like the parent of childhood is a profound reality for the human ego. The human ego exalts God, then asserts that he is made in the image and likeness of the God he exalts. By this means—identifying himself with the God he exalts—man exalts himself just as the latency child exalts himself by identifying with the parent he exalts.

Good and Evil

Good and evil are concepts created by the ego to explain the phenomenon of beneficence and maleficence. They reflect the continuing experience of the ego characterized by tension increase and tension decrease, between stimuli which increase tension which are related to as being bad and stimuli which decrease ego tension which are related to as being good. Tension increase and concomitant unpleasure is bad, and tension decrease and concomitant pleasure is good. The duality of good and evil arises as a consequence of resolving the Oedipus conflict. Good and evil are the two moieties of the ego—the bad which is kept suppressed and the good which is encouraged to flourish.

Before the Oedipus conflict is suppressed, the infant ego has no awareness of the concept of good and evil. But upon suppressing the Oedipus conflict, erecting the superego and entering the latency period of ego ontogenesis, the child ego becomes aware of good and evil when it is alerted to it by adults. Good comes to be understood by the child as a characteristic he is expected by his parent to achieve, and evil is a characteristic he is expected by his parent to eschew at all costs. Evil is bad and is perceived as a controlling force to which one may succumb if he is unable to ward it off. Evil is something one may do himself if he fails to suppress his propensity for it. The child may be aware of evil thoughts and wishes which tempt him, but under the reign of the superego he strives to suppress both the thought and the wish. Upon occasions when he fails to suppress the thought, which is tension producing, he may project it onto external entities such as another person or to groups or institutions with respect to which he experiences fear and anger.

Religion recognizes good and evil and warns adherents to embrace the first and to avoid the second. Good means to follow the authorized teachings of the religion, which tend to correspond to the content of the superego. But evil tends to consist of all of the wishes which the ego strives to suppress but which occasionally surface in the thoughts of the individual which frighten him because they are dangerous and may overwhelm him with desire to do what is bad which will bring retribution. These bad thoughts and desires are the content of the suppressed Oedipal wishes which were suppressed precisely because they were profoundly frightening.

Evil resides in every ego but occasionally surfaces, or threatens to surface, and at times is seen to break out into the activity of others whose evil proclivities have failed to remain in check. When evil is seen in others to break out unchecked, those others are related to with fear and dread and are to be banished if the power necessary to banish them can be found. These nemeses appear in many forms such as characters in fiction, as malevolent gods or devils, as villains and evildoers, but the credence given to them springs from the suppressed Oedipus conflict and is formed of projected ego wishes which might provoke ultimate retribution.

The presence of religious faith, or other form of superstition, is nearly universal in the human ego. Even those who reject all forms of superstition may upon occasion experience profound fear whose source they cannot attribute to natural causes. The hair stands up on the back of the neck, and a shiver spreads through the body. The superstitious individual may attribute the cause to a supernatural phenomenon, but the rejecter of superstition can do little more than wonder at it and conclude that not all experience can be explained.

19

REALITY

For the human ego, reality is a paradox. On the one hand the ego must discover reality and behave in harmony with it if it is to find and defeat sources of tension producing stimuli as well as to find and access sources of tension reducing stimuli. However, try as it might, the ego cannot define reality nor verify absolutely that it has found it in its searches. The human ego is a prisoner of its own intellectual limitations. Gaining an awareness of reality and verifying the validity of that awareness has occupied metaphysicians throughout written history, but all of man's study of reality has yet to satisfy him that what he believes to be reality can be proved to be reality.[1] He may do his best, but his best is not definitive.

In the human race, one man's reality is not always another man's reality, and the search for a reality that is universally accepted continues without end. That fire burns the flesh, that water quenches thirst and that ingesting food satisfies hunger almost all men tend to agree, but that the god of one religion is the true god while the god of another religion is not the true god, or that there is a god, men cannot agree upon. The human ego has discovered no absolute criterion which can assure it without error that it can define and know reality absolutely and universally. Yet, man is animated to live his life seeking to avoid tension producing stimuli or defeating it and seeking and accessing tension reducing stimuli. He engages in this behavior not knowing absolutely what reality is or whether he has acted in accord with it. There are those among the human species who ponder reality, but the rank and file denizens of the Earth go about their daily lives little concerned about definitions of reality.

---

[1] See the **Thomas Nagel** review in the *London Review of Books,* volume 23, Number 18, 20 September 2001 of *The Quest for Reality: Subjectivism and the Metaphysics of Colour* by **Barry Stroud**, Oxford, January 2000.

If the ego cannot define reality or know definitively when it is in the presence of reality, then how can it guide behavior to behave in accordance with reality? By and large, the ego detects what it believes to be reality by trial and error. In its encounters with the external world it discovers that some of what it encounters is repeatedly encountered and repeatedly responds and interacts in a predictable way. From the many encounters which are similar, the ego draws principles from which to act. However, from time to time, the ego acts upon principles that respond in unexpected ways, and the ego then tends to modify existing principles to conform them to the new reality or to search for new principles. But its knowledge of reality continues to be unproved absolutely by the common sense means the ego has at its disposal. The ego nevertheless tends to come to rely upon principles drawn from experience with the perception that some principles are more reliable than others because they less often fail in unexpected ways to predict reality. The ego cannot choose to relinquish its guidance function, so that it must continue to rely upon the principles which it draws from experience and to modify and adapt those principles when they are not validated by experience.

The search for reality begins during the earliest stage of infancy when the ego engages in reality testing as a consequence of perceived experience.[2] The infant ego experiences the impingement of tension producing stimuli and becomes aware of an inexorable driving force from within impelling it to act to reduce the tension. Each tension producing interaction with its surround impels the ego to guide behavior to avoid or defeat the source of tension producing stimuli as the means to reduce the tension and concomitant unpleasure which it experiences. It tends to cry and to fuss and to wish that the tension cease.

The experience of repeated encounters with the external world teaches the ego to act synergistically with what it believes to be reality because to act otherwise is to fail to defeat sources of tension producing stimuli or to access sources of tension reducing stimuli. The ego learns to harness the power of reality to aid it to defeat tension producing stimuli. An example would be the use of gravity to enable the ego to guide behavior to move a heavy object or to divert a stream to irrigate a field or to conform an aircraft wing in a way' which gives lift to the aircraft.

Nevertheless, when it acts in accordance with what it perceives as reality, the ego does not always succeed in defeating tension producing stimuli or accessing tension reducing stimuli. The ego then often resorts to mechanisms which defy reality but which the ego treats as if they were in harmony with reality such as, for example, superstition and denial in their various forms which tend to be resorted to vainly by the ego to accomplish its tension reduction aims. Through each stage of ego ontogenesis, the ego learns more about reality in terms of principles it discovers through analysis of the con-

---

[2] Reality testing is a fundamental concept in Freud's psychoanalytic theory.

tent of its experience. Each time these principles are upheld by the predictability of experience, which enables the ego to guide behavior to reduce tension, the ego becomes more confident that it understands reality. But when it addresses specifically the question of how to define reality or how to verify absolutely the presence of reality, its effort breaks down and it becomes lost in a labyrinth of speculation, which tends to leave it dissatisfied and perplexed.

The ego's earliest dealings with reality occur during infancy when impinging stimuli distress it, and it wants those stimuli to cease, which they tend to do apparently in response to the infant ego's wish. But accompanying the infant ego's wish are crying and fussing which attracts the attending parent (or other caregiver) who normatively rectifies the circumstances which produce the tension producing impinging stimuli, and the unpleasure ceases seemingly in response to the infant ego's wish. In the course of time and repeated experience, the ego learns to associate crying and fussing with the cessation of unpleasure and establishes the principle that crying and fussing brings about the cessation of unpleasure. This is the beginning of the ego's contact with perceived reality and the development of principles to deal with reality. But it does not understand at first that crying and fussing do not defeat the source of tension producing stimuli but only summon the caregiver who does defeat those sources.

As the ego traverses the successive severation traumata of ego ontogenesis, it gathers experience of perceived reality and acquires principles and concomitant tools and techniques with which it can interact with perceived reality to reduce tension and concomitant unpleasure. But acting upon these principles is not always successful in reducing tension, and the ego struggles to modify or replace them so that its guidance of behavior will be more effective in reducing tension. Eventually the tension producing impingement of curiosity comes into the ego's perception, and the ego begins to contemplate the nature of reality as an abstract concept to identify it with absolute validity to reduce the tension produced by the impingement of curiosity.

Much about reality which puzzles the infant ego is appeased by instruction from such entities as parents and age mates, and later from teachers, books, television, radio and the home computer. Often, the infant does not need to ask questions because he is so bombarded by information, which he does not actively solicit, that his mind is filled with information. When he does wonder about his surround and wishes to ask questions about it, there tends to be no lack of persons and other sources of information which will supply him with answers to the questions he may ask.

As the individual traverses the stages of ego ontogenesis, he is confronted progressively by more complex sources of impinging stimuli and develops greater skills and capacities for enquiring and analyzing these sources of impinging stimuli. Reality testing occurs at every point in the course of life because the ego's need to employ the contents of reality to reduce or access tension producing and tension reducing stimuli is unending.

Reality Testing

Infancy

The first reality testing for the infant ego is the relief it experiences from tension producing impinging stimuli resulting from crying and fussing. As a consequence of the experience of weaning, the reality of reducing tension by crying and fussing is replaced by the reality of dependence upon an external agent to respond to the crying and fussing which intervenes to defeat the source of tension producing stimuli—say, hunger—and replaces it with tension reducing stimuli in the form of nourishment. The reality discovered here is dependence, and the principle learned here is the critical importance of retaining the cathexis to the depended upon external object and inducing the depended upon external object to intervene to reduce tension.

Weaning deprives the infant ego of its cathexis to the external agent of dependence, which is the next major experience of reality. The principle learned earlier of crying and fussing largely fails the ego in its aim to retain the cathexis, impelling it to devise another principle with which to deal with reality, the principle of accepting defeat and making the best of it. This principle may be observed in the behavior of every individual who failed in his aim whether, say, to complete his education, or to obtain the career or job he wanted, or to secure the mate of his choice, or, say, the failure of a nation to repel an invader. Having failed, the individual takes up a career not requiring the education he sought, accepts a career or job less desired than the one he wanted, makes a life with a less desired mate than the one he wanted, and the people of a defeated nation settle into a life under the heel of the invader.

The infant ego adjusts to a state in which the breast or bottle are gone, and to reduce the tension of hunger he must accept the cup and the spoon to ingest the nourishment which will relieve the unpleasure of hunger. The infant ego searches for another mode of cathexis to the external agent of absolute dependence and adopts the parental attention given during the elimination of body wastes as the new principle of cathexis retention. The infant ego discovers from experience that elimination periodically occurs and is followed by the attention of the external agent to clean it and remove the unpleasure of chafe and dampness, a process which becomes the new filial cathexis to the external agent of absolute dependence.

During toddlerhood, the infant ego becomes aware of the reality of other children and other places. By toddling away from his caregiver, he can explore sounds from another room and perhaps from other children playing there. Eventually he experiences tension arising from his separation from the external agent of absolute dependence and toddles back to his parent as the means to reduce the tension and associated unpleasure. This experience verifies the reality of his dependence upon the external agent for tension reduction and the necessity of retaining the filial-parental cathexis.

The advent of toilet training reaffirms the fragility of the infant ego's cathexis to the external agent of absolute dependence and its helplessness to retain that cathexis when the external agent himself is determined to sever it. Having acquired object constancy,[3] the new reality is the cathexis to a trifurcated external agent and the requirement of individualizing father and mother and the generalized parent. The generalized parent becomes a mother and a father, and the infant ego must choose with which one he will identify with, normatively the same sex parent.

Competition with the same sex parent for preferment with the opposite sex parent becomes an imperative of sexual identity and a frightening reality with which the child ego must deal. Dangerous hostility toward the same sex parent and fear of retribution for his competition with the latter must be resolved to remove the tension producing fear and dread. This aim is accomplished by establishing the superego and suppressing all awareness of filial fear and competition.

Latency

This done, the child ego fully enters the latency period of ego ontogenesis, and the child's world opens up broadly as he travels farther than before—from the family ménage to the family garden and from the family garden to neighboring gardens and to the neighborhood and the near environs of the community. The content of reality expands to include school and schoolmates, books and teachers, the Sunday school and the church, police and firemen and the things which such persons employ in their activities.

The child's wonder at the content of reality tends to be appeased by explanations of it furnished by informants everywhere at hand, particularly by teachers at school, entertainers on the television and adults in the neighborhood and older, more experienced play peers. With respect to the content of its experience the child ego continually ponders about it and experiments with it in testing reality, and comes to understand its nature, what it is and what to expect when interacting with it. This growing fund of knowledge enables the ego to guide behavior with a greater measure of effectiveness in dealing with sources of tension producing stimuli and defeating those sources to enjoy the pleasure of tension reduction. The latency period ego tends to accept as reality virtually everything its parent presents to it as being reality as well as everything those whom the parent empowers to act for it as reality including teachers, other adults in the family, newspapers, the radio and television. Of course any of these whose pronouncements the parent denounces, the child will also tend to denounce and not accept as an accurate representation of reality.

---

[3] See **Mahler** loc cit.

Adolescence

With the onset of adolescence, the ego confronts a new reality. The adolescent discovers that the freedom to play and amuse himself with leisure activities will be less tolerated by adults. While he may have experienced a requirement for performing chores before, he is now put upon to take much more seriously an imposed obligation to assist his family with contributions of his own labor and to demonstrate progress toward achieving the requisites of adulthood. Normatively, he is expected to display progress toward gaining the skills, capacities and attitude of one who provides his own livelihood. Succeeding in school or in an apprenticeship or displaying the acceptance of a future as an unskilled, willing laborer are among the dispositions he will be expected to adopt.

He will be expected to demonstrate a capacity for social intercourse necessary to search for employment and to find a mate. He will be expected to exhibit evidence that he will one day be able to mate, form his own family and beget and rear children. Reality is the importunity of these expectations and the tension producing stimuli they occasion and the imperative that he must achieve these aims to reduce the tension and concomitant unpleasure they produce, and that achieving these aims appears difficult, and that he may not be capable of achieving them.

Meanwhile, the adolescent may wonder why the sky is blue, why the grass is green and the toast brown and how all of the technology he encounters in his daily life is accomplished, how automobiles are made and how they operate, how airplanes fly and rockets traverse space and how he can establish a career from which he may extract a livelihood and satisfy his craving for worth and status among his peers and in the world. He will devise a methodology for accomplishing his aims and repeatedly test its effectiveness. He will also repeatedly modify his concept of reality as he strives and succeeds and sometimes fails in mastering his grasp of reality and his capacity to deal with it. Can he attract a mate, gain the knowledge and skill which will enable him to make a livelihood, find friends with whom to socialize who validate the persona he strives to present, establish a place in society that appeases his ego worth deficit, master the capacities necessary to succeed and achieve a state of being which he can only describe as happiness, although not being sure what happiness is?

Beginning in adolescence, the ego may start to wonder more intensely about the nature of reality in a general sense such as the extent of the universe, the nature of natural processes, the nature of logic itself, of what the universe is made and its origins, where human beings and animals came from and their nature. Men launch themselves upon a course in life in which they study and wonder systematically about such phenomena. For some, it will become their life's work. For others, it will become a scientific enquiry and for still others it will become a religious or philosophic enquiry. But far and away most will not be detained by it but rather will devote their daily lives to obtaining their daily bread and otherwise dealing with the envelope of tension producing impinging stimuli which it is the lot of all human beings to experience.

The adolescent is confronted by the reality that he must separate from his parent and establish his independence from and an identity different from merely being the child of his parent, an identity which is unique in the world. But his continued dependence upon his parent for sustenance and protection means that he must not sever the cathexis to the parent while undertaking to establish his unique identity. He continues to need his parent as the main appeaser of his narcissism, ego worth and power deficits. He is in a transition mode between childhood and adulthood, and to one degree or another almost every adolescent grasps this reality.

Conflict with reality, particularly an undesired reality, becomes a tension producing interaction for the ego during latency, becoming more complicated during adolescence and prompting the creation of techniques to deal with it. The numerous demands placed upon the adolescent ego tend to overwhelm it, and the means available to deal with the tension produced by these demands tend to be perceived by the adolescent ego as inadequate.

The adolescent ego tends to relate to objects in the adolescent environment with displaced filial relatedness, misperceiving sources of tension producing impinging stimuli as if they were the parent of childhood or other entities to which filial relatedness had been displaced such as other family members including siblings, aunts and uncles and play peers and societal authorities. Thus a member of the opposite sex to which he or she relates with lust or affection may be interacted with as to the opposite sex parent which precipitates tension increase as it did when earlier relating to the actual opposite sex parent.

Teachers, employers and law enforcement authorities may be related to as to the parent of latency and be perceived as threatening and responded to as to an object of threat. Or they may be related to as to the beneficent parental surrogate. These misperceptions of reality are as significant as correct perceptions of reality because the ego guides behavior based upon what it believes is reality whether correct or incorrect. Reality testing becomes very confused when the reality perceived is misperceived, and the interaction with the misperceived reality is perforce faulty.

The student who resents his teacher, the workman who resents his supervisor or the merchant who resents his customer because he wrongly relates to him as a maleficent parental surrogate will surely risk offending the individual he relates to and perhaps eliciting a negative reaction which may be harmful to the relating individual. The individual who relates to any of these entities with displaced filial affection tinctured with Oedipal desire may invite rebuke or subject himself to tension producing disappointment at the lack of reciprocated affection and desire.

The adolescent may attempt to pursue a career for which he is not naturally suited and confront tension producing disappointment. He or she may pursue a member of the opposite sex with the aim of seducing or mating with him or her and find himself or herself rejected, giving rise to a tension producing reappraisal of his or her own attractiveness to the opposite sex. The reality of his or her capacities to deal with the tension producing impinging stimuli of the external world will continue to be tested after the individual enters young adulthood.

Young Adulthood

Normatively by young adulthood the phenomena of the human environment, which includes human beings other than oneself, the works which human beings have brought into existence, the natural environment with its processes and matter, have been encompassed by the human ego. The young adult confronts the new reality that he is expected by this time in his life to have gained the means to provide himself with a livelihood, to have acquired a mate, begot offspring, formed a family, established himself in society and have acquired social companions to validate his persona and with whom to engage in tension reducing leisure activities. If he has not accomplished these imperatives, reality impinges upon the young adult ego with great tension and concomitant unpleasure.

The reality of natural phenomena, of technology, of the social and political processes in which the young adult makes his way, all occupy his thoughts to one degree or another, and he continues to test his understanding of them as he encounters them on a day-to-day basis. The reality of his environment, about which he continually informs himself so that he can deal with tension producing stimuli, is a subject about which he builds a structure of knowledge and understanding which tends to grow' with experience. Being a prisoner of his environment, he looks ahead and strives in the moment to improve his lot, which differs for different individuals from one culture, time and place to another. Normatively, he lacks the degree of wealth and status of older members of society in his walk of life who have had more time to establish themselves. There are exceptions in the form of young individuals upon whom fortune has smiled more broadly such as inheritors of wealth, celebrated entertainers, famous sports figures and the like who have advanced far at a relatively young age but may slip back as a result of imprudence or misfortune.

Normatively, the young adult tests the reality of his circumstance which may include inferiority to older adults who have established their place in society and enjoy status, wealth, ego worth assets and amenities which continue to allude the young adult. The reality for the young adult is that he must advance himself if he is likely ever to savor the benefits in which the older adult is able to immerse himself.

The young adult struggles to find the way to acquire the advantages possessed by older adults. He becomes interested in the career paths which were followed by successful older adults and seeks to map out a path of his own by emulating older adults. He may seek out a mentor or patron to help him on his way. He tends repeatedly to test the reality of his plans if not through interaction with his environment, then by imagining such interactions in his thoughts. His perceived inferiority to older adults is a tension producing reality with which he tends to deal by fantasizing about a future in which he is more successful in acquiring amenities and status assets. He tells himself or herself that his or her time will come if he can stay on course. But if he has fallen away from the path toward success, he may experience discouragement, disillusionment and depression and become angry with himself for conducting his life imprudently.

Middle Adulthood

Reality for the middle age adults is that their lives are half over, and that they have not achieved their aims, that their achievements do not exceed those of young adulthood and may even have diminished as their strength and health begin to subside and the energy and fortitude necessary to accomplish the tasks called for by their aims also subside. They may test the reality of their capacities and find them lacking. Others more fortunate will forge ahead and exceed the accomplishments of their youth and add to their status and ego worth assets. They may look back upon their young adulthood with the satisfaction that they have done much better they did in their youth and have been rewarded for their diligence and perseverance. They have confronted the reality of their existence and have· prevailed.

Reality for the middle age adult often includes the possession of personal power vis-à-vis others among his friends and in the community, and recognizing his increased power he may choose to exercise it for good or ill and to confirm its presence by the results he obtains through use of it. The degree and nature of middle age personal power varies from income level, education level, from cultural subgroup and within society in general, but every walk of life into which the middle age adult may fall tends to have its social circle with its values and mores and criteria for what counts as success or failure. Being awarded a prize by one's peers can be enormously gratifying even if the trophy has no financial value in the marketplace.

The middle age individual may arrogate to himself an obligation to contribute to his community as well as to participate in its governing either formally by obtaining public office or informally by becoming active among other middle age citizens who take it upon themselves to become involved in the decision making process of the community. The reality is that he can do this, and that he can affect policy and outcomes of socio-political processes, if only to a limited extent. The middle age individual tends to regard himself as more important, more capable and more prudent than younger members of the community and justified in wielding his modicum of power to steer the course of community life in the direction which he thinks it should go.

Nevertheless, many things go wrong or not as planned in the life of the middle age individual. His child may have met with accident or sickness and died or become feckless and unable to provide his livelihood, or he or his spouse may have suffered a disabling illness or lost his employment or career because of a reversal of fortune. Because the deficits of narcissism, power and worth are never satisfied for long and always come back to produce tension and unpleasure, the middle age individual is ever confronted by tension producing stimuli with which he must deal. Challenges to his sense of surety and prods to his curiosity are never absent for long. The middle age ego is never free for long from its task of guiding behavior to reduce the tension produced by the envelope of tension producing stimuli ever present in the human environment.

Misfortune of any of his family, especially adult children and their offspring, may challenge his capacity to assist them in their difficulties; the threat of financial difficulties may assault him as well as his children; his own health and that of his spouse may fail and require a strenuous effort on his part to compensate or assist; his church or *alma mater* may be threatened financially or spiritually and require his help and protection; his community may be threatened by changes in the circumstances of its existence such as, drought or flooding or loss of industry; any of these may prompt him to undertake to attempt to correct them or moderate their affects.

Old Age and Death

Reality for the old age individual is that he will soon die, a perception which is highly tension producing and tends to be responded to with a combination of denial and acceptance, fear and preparation. He does not know exactly how long he has left to live, unless a medical practitioner has pronounced the time of his impending demise, but he knows that it is not long, and that he must make the best use of the time he has left. To complete his aims in life now appear overwhelming because the shortness of time means that he cannot accomplish them, but he can make certain preparations to deal with high priority needs.

He may arrange his funeral and grave marker, prepare his will and provide for his heirs, complete his memoirs, endow his church or alma mater or take care of other matters which will tie up the strands of his life. The old age individual may be a survivor of his family whose other members have predeceased him. He may find himself alone because all of his contemporaries have gone to their graves. He may experience dismay because public figures of his generation have died. He may have no friends left with whom to reminisce about the times they shared. The decathexis experiences of early childhood when the ego is severed from the external agent of absolute dependence tends to return with the terror of abandonment. The brink of death can be a lonely and forlorn place to occupy for those who have survived everyone else. He confronts the reality of his impending demise with the hope that his God will rescue him and reward him with life everlasting, but he is not certain that he has earned that reward or that it will be provided to him or he may doubt the reality of an after life. He cannot test the reality of an after life but must accept it on faith.

20

DETERMINISM IN THE PATTERNS OF EGO TENSION REDUCTION

The course of life is shaped by the ontogenesis of the ego interacting with the external world. The shape thus given to the course of life by ego ontogenesis is so conforming that departure from it tends to be infrequent, and when it occurs tends to be precipitated by impinging stimuli from the world external to the ego. Each major severation trauma of ego ontogenesis is responded to by the ego in ways aimed at reducing the tension produced by the trauma, and the ways created by the ego tend to reduce tension imperfectly so that a residue of tension is left behind which requires repeated attempts by the ego to reduce it. These residues become the tension producing baggage of ego ontogenesis with which the ego struggles interminably, ceasing only at death.

Patterns of Stress Reduction Behavior

Stress is defined here as the experience of inadequately relieved ego tension produced by persistent impinging stimuli. For example, the persistent toothache, a continuing period of unemployment, relentless poverty, a severe and lasting disability, an intolerable marriage, working under a harsh employer, serving a long period of incarceration or suffering a terminal illness all tend to be stressful experiences produced by unrelenting impinging stimuli. But patterns of stress experienced because of ego ontogenesis grow out of failures of adjustment to impinging stimuli produced by severation traumata during ego ontogenesis. These failures create patterns of tension reducing behavior which tend not to be extinguished during the entire remaining life of the individual from the time of the pattern's inception and defines the character of the individual. They are the compulsions created by ego ontogenesis, the chains which Charles Dickens' "old Morley" forged while in life. These patterns of behavior are the fixations cited by Freud which produced neurosis in his patients. The failures of ego ontogenesis create ineffective patterns of behavior aimed at reducing the tension of the stress, which are repeated throughout the remaining course of life after they are formed. They are the fixation behavior produced by the major severation traumata of ego ontogenesis. They tend to be reshaped by subsequent ego responses to successive severation traumata which emerge during ego ontogenesis, but the modifications given to them do not remove them nor change the purpose for which they were established.

The Oral Stage

In struggling with the patterns of stress created by the severation trauma of weaning, the ego establishes tension reduction behavior patterns which do not fully succeed in reducing the ego tension produced by the trauma. For example, the tension producing severation trauma caused by deprivation of the breast or nursing bottle can engender any of a number of tension reducing responses of which some are effective while others are not. Effective responses would include learning to take nourishment by means of the cup, bowl and spoon, which reduces the ego tension of hunger and mitigates the severity of the weaning trauma. But the ego's struggle with the imposition of weaning to defeat the tension it produces tends to involve the rejection of weaning and the use of manipulative techniques which once established tend to remain as vestiges of the trauma's impact throughout the remaining course of life. Crying in anger and pleading for restoration of the breast or nursing bottle may be the beginning of a pattern of ineffective tension reduction behavior which may extend throughout the remaining course of life, although modified in various ways but always failing to extinguish permanently all tension it is aimed at reducing.

The techniques established by the ego to reduce the tension of weaning tend not to be abandoned even when they are ineffective because they constitute the only means the ego could find at its disposal at the time they were first called upon. By the process of derivative relatedness transference devolution they are applied again at subsequent decathexis impingements with the same failure to succeed in their aim. In their later applications they may undergo modification, but the aim remains the same—to reduce ego tension produced by decathexis. Whereas during weaning the form that decathexis took was that of severing the cathexis to the external agent of absolute dependence—the parent—while the later decathexis may be that, say, of dismissal by a parentified employer from one's employment. In the latter case, the guidance given to behavior by the ego may be in part practical such as beginning a job search or launching an income producing business, but it will also tend to resort to crying and fussing although now modified into articulate speech in the form of complaining and remonstrating in the face of insuperable opposition. Because crying and fussing were perceived by the ego as the only means it could find at the beginning of the severation trauma of weaning, the application of the later version of crying and remonstrating at being fired is also perceived by the ego as the only means at its disposal beyond the practical steps of searching for employment when prospects are not encouraging.

The individual tends to resort at first to the same failing techniques in adulthood as he did in infancy. He tends to apply the old techniques which fail again to reduce the tension, but then normatively he goes on to the newer more effective modified techniques which do reduce tension, although less than fully. Thus the weaned infant when confronted by toilet training attempts first to defeat the decathexis tension by using the old techniques of crying and fussing which were used to resist weaning. Then hard upon the experience that accepting the imposition of weaning and learning to use the cup, bowl and spoon had reduced the tension of hunger and restored a modicum of the filial cathexis, he applies these modified techniques to dealing with toilet training by accepting sphincter control and evacuating the content of his bowel and voiding his bladder into the potty.

It is a commonplace behavior of the human individual when encountering tension producing stimuli to attempt to reduce the tension by the archaic means of crying and fussing, then when these means fail, to go on to more mature means established as modifications of the archaic means. As the ego gains maturity, it learns at times to pass quickly beyond the archaic means, even to consider them silently before rapidly bypassing them, to employ the modified mature means to deal with the source of tension producing stimuli. This mode of behavior is accounted as mature by observers, even when it does not fully reduce the tension.

As an example, consider the mature adult who is dismissed from his employment because of the contraction of his employer's business. He may at first experience anger which he directs at his employer but suppress his wish to express it in vocal whining as he did when he was an infant deprived of the breast or bottle during weaning and move quickly on to more mature behavior such as beginning a job search. As time passes without his finding suitable employment, his ability to resist resorting to the whining and complaining behavior displayed at the time of his weaning weakens, and he becomes more vocal, perhaps complaining to his spouse or friends about his ill treatment and hoping for sympathy from them. But as his maturity reasserts itself, he returns to his job search effort, re-evaluating his job search strategies and techniques and modifying them in the hope of their becoming more effective.

The response to weaning or crying and fussing leaves behind a residual behavior pattern which tends to reassert itself each time the individual is confronted by a source of tension producing stimuli to which he relates as he did to the parent of the weaning trauma. Thus at each succeeding severation trauma of ego ontogenesis, the ego may guide behavior to cry and fuss at first, often silently, before moving on to deal with the tension producing trauma with more mature behavior. The crying and fussing pattern remains, but it is suppressed as "hurt feelings" rather than expressed as a display of immaturity.

The patterns of behavior which may be left behind by the oral stage trauma are numerous, and different egos will choose different responses with different patterns of behavior. A given individual may react to weaning by more vigorous suckling at the breast or bottle to which the parent may respond by lengthening the time suckling is allowed to continue, or a different parent may abruptly withdraw the nipple when the infant begins to suckle more vigorously as the nipple is being withdrawn. Residues of these two different responses will tend to establish different patterns of tension reduction behavior.

The more vigorous suckling response may establish a tension reduction behavior pattern which is repeated in reaction to subsequent experiences of tension producing impinging stimuli resulting from rejection or neglect by a parentified entity such as a teacher, employer or lover. Such behavior patterns may take the form of such oral behaviors as, say, overeating, or heavy cigarette smoking, or garrulousness. These behaviors may not only fail ultimately to reduce ego tension, but also may instead produce greater tension increase by eliciting negative responses from others.

The abrupt withdrawal of the nipple may lead to a hostile response such as biting the nipple during withdrawal of the breast or bottle. The biting response may establish a tension reducing behavior pattern of angry hostility as a response to severation or rejection by a parentified other such as a teacher, employer or lover. Such patterns may take the form of protesting, scolding, denouncing or bitter negative criticism. Both the suckling response and the biting response tend to be ineffective at dealing with the source of tension producing stimuli, but in a later stage of life precede the more mature behavior of dealing with rejection or neglect by more effective means devolved from modifying the immature response techniques into practical techniques. For example, crying and fussing may devolve into articulate and persuasive speech, and angry biting may devolve into aggressive vocal advocacy. The precise form any of these tension reduction techniques take will be singular for each individual and form a part of the character by which observers will identify him.

The Anal Stage

The anal stage involves the infant's voiding and evacuating his bladder and bowel and the ritual of cleaning up afterward. The imposition of toilet training deprives the infant of these desired tension reduction experiences and by so doing severs the infant's cathexis from the parent, which is profoundly tension producing. To deal with this severation trauma, the ego guides behavior to defeat toilet training, for which the ego first calls upon the techniques initially resorted to during weaning, namely, crying and fussing and biting the nipple and squeezing or pummeling the breast. But in applying these techniques to resist toilet training, the ego modifies them to fit the different circumstances. Crying and fussing may remain much the same, but biting tends to be modified into constricting the anal or urethral sphincter, which enables the infant to withhold the elimination of waste products, at least for a time, as a means of resisting toilet training.

Anal stage patterns of stress reduction behavior through derivative relatedness transference devolution may become such behavior patterns as withholding one's cooperation by serving one's employer with only the minimum acceptable performance, or withholding expressions of love to a spouse or child, or delaying the completion of a project by procrastinating, or clinging to money rather than spending it for reasonable purposes, or taking up a profession which deals with the accumulation and sorting of details such as accounting.

These withholding techniques devolved during ego ontogenesis into the modified forms they took later in the course of life in response to decathexis tension produced, for example, by fear of the disfavor of the parentified employer, or by fear of rejection by the spouse and displacing this fear upon one's child, or by anger with others for lack of their support in completing a project, or miserliness as a derivative of withholding the release of the bowels during toilet training or taking up a profession which enables one to massage and manipulate data derived from frustration at not being allowed to play with feces and the practice of withholding feces during toilet training

The expulsive phase of the anal stage is formed by the uncontrolled release of feces and urine prior to achieving sphincter control. The untrammeled release of body waste is a pleasurable tension reducer, and the requirement that the ego control this activity as a requirement of toilet training is a tension producer. The frustrated expulsive phase leaves in its wake numerous tension reduction behavior patterns. Messiness about one's belongings; taking up occupations which involve materials which serve as reminders of body wastes such as cooking, oil painting or modeling with clay; and spendthrift behavior may serve to reduce the tension produced in infancy by the deprivation of anal expulsive pleasures and passed along by the derivative relatedness transference devolution process to later stages in the course of life.

The retentive phase of the anal stage made possible by the physiological development of sphincter control tends to call upon tension reduction behaviors employed during the biting phase of the oral stage. The clamping down of the sphincter to withhold the elimination of body wastes may have been suggested by the biting of the nipple during the oral stage. Anal tension through the process of derivative relatedness transference devolution may become such patterns of tension reducing behavior as miserliness, collecting objects such as books, figurines or art, or pursuing a career ranging from bookkeeper to lepidopterologist.

Once a tension reducing technique is established, the economy of reducing tension by the least net tension increase or greatest net tension decrease insures that the pattern established will be resorted to at least at first each time similar tension producing stimuli are encountered. Thus, the individual who laughs nervously when confronted by guilt will tend always to do so; the individual who lies when confronted by a question which would expose his ignorance or reveal his guilt will tend always to do so in similar circumstances; the individual who flees timidly when someone in authority approaches will tend each time to do so; the individual who becomes hostile in the face of danger will invariably tend to do so; the individual who begins to boast when his capacities are challenged will consistently tend to do so.

The individual who redoubles his effort after he has failed in an endeavor will time and again tend to do so as the individual who gives up once he has failed at an endeavor will tend always to do so; the individual who laughs at himself when he has made a mistake will usually do so; the sarcastic individual will tend always to resort to sarcasm when disappointed or when entertaining hopeful but uncertain expectations; the individual who invariably expresses optimism when confronting difficulty will always tend to do so just as the individual who expresses pessimism when confronted by difficulty will always tend to do so. Examples of tension reduction behavior consistently applied in similar circumstances are infinite, and they almost always have their beginning in ego ontogenesis.

The Oedipus Conflict

The ego's response to the Oedipus conflict has a more far-reaching affect upon tension reduction behavior than other severation traumata. Resolving the Oedipus conflict establishes the ego's social patterns in interacting with others. For the first time, the ego parentifies individuals and then guides behavior to relate to them in ways it relates to the actual parent. Thus, an older sibling may be paternified, meaning that the sibling will be related to in some ways as the actual father is related to. Filial ambivalence may be displaced upon the older sibling so that the individual behaves toward the older sibling as if he expected to be treated by the older sibling as he expects to be treated by the father. Thus the older sibling may be related to as a maleficent parental surrogate or as a beneficent parental surrogate depending upon the tension reduction needs of the younger sibling at the moment he perceives the older sibling as a target of either affection or hostility.

Competitiveness with the father may be transferred to competitiveness with the older sibling. And fear of the father because of filial competitiveness may be transferred to competitiveness with the older sibling. Tension reduction because of competitiveness and fear of the father takes on a form which is repeated in tension reduction behavior because of competitiveness and fear of the older sibling. For example, tension reduction behavior in dealing with the father, which takes the form of passive hostility such as stealing personal belongings of the father, may be transferred to stealing personal belongings of the older sibling.

While the child might take a forbidden tool from the father's tool chest, the child may take a favorite toy from among the older sibling's belongings. Or the child may resist the temptation to take a forbidden tool from his father's tool chest and instead take a toy from his paternified older sibling, which may be perceived as less risky. What brother or sister has not taken without consent a toy or personal article belonging to the other? Such purloining may be a tension reducing behavior caused by filial jealousy with respect to the father and sibling rivalry with respect to the brother or sister.

The tension reducing behavior of stealing may have begun in response to toilet training manifested in, say, stealing pennies from the parent's change purse to reduce the tension of severation from the parent. The tension reducing tactic of stealing may have been transferred to the Oedipus stage as fear of severation carried out by the parent because of resentment of filial rivalry. The latter tension reducing pattern is then transferred to the rivalry with the older sibling.

These tension reduction behavior patterns may be transferred to still later situations in ego ontogenesis. Any circumstance in which the individual relates to another as he did to the parent or to the older sibling, such as to a supervisor, teacher or lover will tend to elicit the same response pattern to tension increase produced by conflict with the object of relatedness. Each case of tension reduction will tend to be unique in its detail for each ego. For example a given ego may guide behavior to steal only personal items such as tools or pocket change, while another may guide behavior to steal jewelry and still another to steal credit cards and checkbooks. Such individuals without wanting to may in this way inadvertently induce others to relate to them with distrust and coldness.

An important outcome of resolving the Oedipus conflict is the creation of the superego, whose establishment makes the resolution of the Oedipus conflict possible. The creation of the superego enables the ego to suppress almost all competitiveness with the same sex parent and the wish to banish the same sex parent. This event enables the latency child to live largely in peace with the same sex parent and to elevate himself or herself by glorifying and identifying with the same sex parent. The more the latency child ennobles the same sex parent, the more he or she by identification with and introjection of the same sex parent ennobles himself or herself. Glorifying the parent by extension glorifies the self.

The superego shapes the tension reduction behavior patterns of the latency child and of the adult which the latency child later becomes. The effort to avoid guilt tends to steer the ego away from tension reducing behavior which violates parental proscriptions and to steer the ego toward adhering to parental prescriptions. Thus, tension reduction behavior shaped by the superego is kept on a track which steers between parentally approved behavior and parentally disproved behavior. The ego must find tension reduction behavior within the context of the prescriptions and proscriptions inculcated by the parent or which the child believes the parent holds. Needless to say, failures at times occur, and the individual goes off the track and often pays a price for so doing. Wayward children and criminal adults are examples of individuals who go astray.

As the ego searches for the means to reduce tension in ways which do not conflict with the prescriptions and proscriptions of the superego inculcated by the parent, it is confronted by a narrow range of possibilities shaped by the constraints of the derivative relatedness transference devolution process acting upon infantile techniques of tension reduction. These constraints insure that the tension reduction techniques chosen will be repetitious and similar to other techniques of tension reduction from earlier tension producing circumstances and therefore of a pattern repetitive of tension reduction styles established by the ego during previous tension reduction episodes.

For example, the infant ego's tactic of aggressively biting the nipple during weaning may have devolved because of the advent of sphincter control into the technique of untimely bowel or bladder elimination during toilet training and from there devolved into the withholding of cooperation from the same sex parent during the Oedipus conflict struggle; and from there devolved into an obstreperousness during the latency years when self dependence imperatives are imposed such as putting away belongings; and from there during adolescence devolved into a rebellious practice of refusing to perform household chores demanded by the parent; and from there to failing to perform homework required by teachers; and from there to withholding cooperation from an employer when asked to work overtime or to help with a project which had been assigned to a co-worker; or in middle age to withholding the contribution of service to volunteer projects of the community; and thence to the refusal in old age to bequeath financial gifts to one's church, community or alma mater. This pattern of tension reduction behavior tends to be repeated each time a decathexis threat is encountered, although modified each time to suit the new source of threat.

Latency

Latency is a time of consolidation of tension reduction techniques created during primordial life. The techniques form behavior patterns which persist throughout the remaining course of life but are subject to modification each time they are resorted to as a means to deal with new circumstances which are perceived as similar to those in response to which the patterns were originally formed or last modified. For example, the ego may have resorted to messiness when commanded by the Oedipal stage parent to put away his toys after playing with them. The tension reduction technique of messiness may originally have been established in response to toilet training and modified to become a behavior pattern of untidy practices with respect to one's belongings during the Oedipus conflict struggle and from there modified into a behavior pattern of disorderliness in latency. ·

Adolescence

The tension reduction behavior patterns consolidated during latency tend to be confirmed in adolescence but also subject to further modification to deal with new circumstances. During adolescence, the disorderly practices reinforced in latency may be transferred into adolescence and modified as obstreperous rebellion during the ego's struggle to establish a separate and unique identity vis-à-vis the parent. The messy practices may be selective in the patterns they establish. The adolescent whose filial rebellion is manifested in messiness about his sleeping quarters may in contrast be extremely tidy with respect to his academic work. The sleeping quarters are identified with the parent who always hounded him to clean his room, while the academic work was chosen by him to become the basis of his new and unique identity, which he treats with great commitment and perseverance.

The practice of projection as a convenient means of reducing ego tension comes into regular use during the Oedipus conflict struggle. Projection, which was suggested to the ego by the experience of spitting out the unwanted nourishment during weaning and put to use in blaming the id for dangerous incestuous wishes during the resolution of the Oedipus conflict, becomes a convenient mechanism for the latency child to rid himself of the tension produced by his own guilt at times of failure to adhere to the imperatives of the superego. When displacing filial hostility onto siblings and playmates in the form of physical aggression, the latency age ego may handle the tension of fear and guilt for such transgressions by projecting it onto others. It is not uncommon to observe children at play who blame one another for the squabbles they get into. Projection is a widely employed mechanism in ordinary life by rank and file members of society to slough off their guilt for great and small transgressions alike.

Young Adulthood

In young adulthood, the tension reduction behavior pattern of care and devotion to academic work may be transferred to the venue of employment, and the ego may guide behavior to handle the tasks of the job with meticulous care and exactitude as a tension reduction tactic to sustain the new and separate identity, while continuing the practice of untidiness about one's person by keeping a messy desk or work bench. There are numerous tension reduction behavior patterns transferred into adolescence where they are modified to reduce the ego tension produced by severation traumata, by individuating from the parent, by establishing a separate and unique identity and by undertaking to gain the capacity to establish a career, obtain a livelihood, acquire a marriage partner, form a family and rear children. Messiness as a means of adolescent rebellion may manifest itself in messiness about one's grooming which continues into young adulthood and spoils the young adult's chances of attracting a mate, although he or she may do well in his or her employment where excellence is a tension reducer both for sustaining a separate identity and for reducing the tension of the ego worth deficit.

Patterns of anal expulsive behavior modified during latency into a pattern of improvidence manifested in, say, inattention to school work, may during adolescence be expressed in improvident spending which continues into young adulthood as spendthrift behavior financially destructive of the family which the young adult has formed. Patterns of oral biting behavior modified during toilet training into refusal to eliminate body waste in a timely manner and expressed as stubbornness during the Oedipus conflict struggle may be observed during latency as refusal to attend to self-dependence requirements such as generosity in social circumstances which would attract the social acquaintances and friends necessary to a fulfilling social life. In young adulthood such a behavior pattern might stifle the working career by failing to attract the support of others in the workplace necessary to effective work performance.

Middle Adulthood

In middle adulthood, the ego normatively achieves its acme in maturity and its capacity to achieve its aims. While its physical skills and abilities may have waned, they nevertheless remain in evidence, and intellectual achievement tends to be at its most productive. Later, in old age, physical capacities have waned dramatically but the individual may yet evince greater achievement in his aims even than during middle adulthood. During middle adulthood, the physical and mental capacities as a totality tend to be at their acme. Neither before nor after middle age are the physical and mental capacities likely to coalesce as powerfully. Patterns of tension reduction behavior which require combined mental and physical capacities tend to be at their most mature during middle adulthood.

An ego, which guided tension reduction behavior during latency to consolidate tactics and techniques and confirm them during adolescence and to further solidify them during young adulthood, transfers them into middle age affirmed anew. For example, the anal expulsive behavior consolidated during latency as messiness about one's quarters and belongings and transferred to adolescence where it was reaffirmed as rebellious tension reducing behavior aimed at establishing a separate and unique identity and contrasted with academic persistence which served as the basis of the new identity, and which was thence transferred to young adulthood as dedication to the tasks of one's gainful employment becomes in middle adulthood a behavior pattern exemplifying highly responsible behavior committed to excellence in the performance of one's job, of keenness in the performance of good works for the community, in conscientiousness in the care of one's family and offspring and husbandry in ones personal affairs but by contrast untidiness about one's person and residence.

Old Age

In old age, physical powers tend to have diminished substantially, but intellectual powers may still be in place, although the flexibility and quickness of the intellect may have declined. Patterns of tension reduction behavior change accordingly. Reducing tension through the use of physical capacities will tend to have given way to obtaining the services of younger persons to perform physically what the old age individual can no longer do well or do at all. But the intellect, if it has not succumbed to senile dementia, may continue to display patterns of tension reduction behavior requiring intellectual prowess.

The Persistence of Tension Reduction Patterns

Altering established patterns of tension reduction behavior in response to similar tension producing circumstances is unlikely because the drive for economy in tension reduction is an imperative of the ego. Behavior aimed at tension reduction itself produces tension so that the least tension producing reducer of tension is invariably chosen. The least tension producing tactic will tend to be one already practiced rather than one that is new and untried. In far and away most cases of tension reduction behavior, tension is produced by the very action intended to reduce tension. Consequently, it is invariably a case of achieving the least net tension increase or the greatest net tension decrease in any behavior aimed at tension reduction. A hungry man must grow a crop to obtain food to reduce the tension of hunger, but the activity of growing food produces tension. The ego tension produced by hunger is greater' than the ego tension produced by the activity of growing food. The latter produces a lesser tension increase than the former. Even the choice of career is a tension reduction behavior pattern. When the choice of career is freely made and not compelled by overwhelming financial need, the choice made is guided by the ego's need to reduce tension and is a part of the ego's tension reduction pattern.

Consider the simple circumstance of having to work at an unpleasant job to earn a livelihood. The unpleasant job produces ego tension, but not performing the job would lead to a circumstance of even greater ego tension produced by being unable to meet the expenses of maintaining one's house and family. Thus, working at the unpleasant job leads to a lesser net tension increase than forgoing the job and being unable to meet the expenses of one's family and household.

An important determiner of patterns of tension reduction behavior is the concept of purpose entertained by the ego which is driven by purpose in everything it guides the individual to do. The overall purpose of the ego is to avoid or defeat sources of tension producing stimuli and to reduce tension when it is experienced. Thus purpose becomes a primary concern of the ego.

21

PURPOSE IN
HUMAN BEHAVIOR

The human ego is preoccupied with the idea of purpose. The ego perceives itself always as having a purpose. The human ego asks, "What is my purpose, and what is the purpose of human life"? The ego muses that there surely must be a purpose to everything but questions whether there may be no purpose to anything, which is an appalling tension producing thought that the human ego is quick to deny and to devise concepts and practices aimed at defeating that source of tension producing stimuli.

Man is preoccupied by the concept of purpose, and it guides his life. The idea of purpose is central to the ego's guidance of human behavior. It is by attributing aims to human behavior that an observer comes to know the individual he is observing. It is by understanding the purpose of objects or attributing a purpose to them that the human ego comes to relate to the objects.

The ego guides behavior to fulfill identified purposes, which invariably are aimed at defeating or obviating sources of tension producing stimuli. In interacting with others, the ego guides behavior with the aim of discovering the purposes of others. The ego knows other individuals by their deeds because their deeds reveal their aims. Regardless of what an individual may state that his aims are, which may be misleading to others as well as to himself, it is by his deeds that his aims become known even to him. The individual's aims are established in the course of ego ontogenesis. His deeds reveal his' aims, and his aims grow out of his experience of ego ontogenesis.

The Oral Stage

During the oral stage experience, the ego establishes aims which it pursues throughout the remaining course of life. The initial aim of the oral stage infant is to reduce the tension of hunger, and the secondary aim is to retain the cathexis to the parent who nurses him to reduce the tension of hunger. It is the process of nursing which reduces the tension of hunger and also testifies to the reality of the cathexis. It is weaning which alerts the infant ego to the reality of the filial-parental cathexis, his absolute dependence upon the filial-parental cathexis and the profound source of tension to which a severation from the cathexis would subject him.

Thus, during the oral stage period of his experience, the child ego becomes aware, however dimly, of his aims of reducing tension by taking in nourishment and by retaining the filial-parental cathexis. This experience of cathecting to and retaining the cathexis to an agent of primary dependence is an early aim of the ego, which continues throughout the course of life. Later in the course of life, the ego will parentify external objects to which the individual relates as to the parent of childhood and will experience decathexis tension if he perceives the cathexis to parentified objects as threatened or attenuating in strength. The ego will guide behavior to strive for the retention of the parentified cathexis by applying selected techniques devolved from those employed in the struggle to retain the oral cathexis during infancy.

The Anal Stage

The experience of toilet training, which follows traumatically upon the experience of weaning,[1] subjects the infant ego to the reality that threats to the filial-parental cathexis continue, and the purpose of retaining the cathexis and of acquiring means to retain the cathexis becomes central to his aims. The secondary aim of reducing tension produced by bowel and bladder pressure is subordinate to the primary aim of retaining the filial-parental cathexis and the tension reducing pleasure which evidence of the cathexis brings in producing the waste products to the approval of the parent and experiencing the sensory pleasures of the diaper change and cleanup all of which attest the persistence of the filial-parental cathexis.

Anal stage experience establishes and sets into motion the aim of sustaining the anal stage cathexis, which through the derivative relatedness transference devolution process successively takes on new forms during ego ontogenesis creating ego aims intended to exploit those new forms. For example, the aim of the infant of playing with his feces and urine, which the infant is prevented from doing by the parent, may be sublimated into playing with objects which by transference are related to as substitutes for the body wastes such as food in the form, for example, of sausages, pureed vegetables which are cooked and eaten (played with) and imbibing flavored drinks. Cooking and eating these foods and imbibing flavored drinks in part substitutes for playing with feces and urine during the experience of toilet training.

The Oedipus Conflict

In its aim of reducing the tension of the Oedipus conflict while continuing to retain the filial-parental cathexis, the ego resorts to many of the tech-

---

[1] **Munroe** loc cit.

niques it employed in its struggle to retain the oral and anal stage cathexes. Purposes of the ego are revealed in the behavior it guides the individual to perform. Primary purposes are those aimed at applying the old techniques but modifying them to suit the new decathexis threat. Thus the oral stage technique of biting the nipple when the parent withholds the breast or bottle tends to devolve into a new form such as clamping down on the sphincter to withhold the release of urine and feces. Clamping down the sphincter during toilet training was suggested by clamping down with the teeth to defeat weaning.

Withholding the release of urine and feces becomes the aim or purpose of the ego, which the ego recognizes. Its purpose of retaining the filial-parental cathexis tends to be unknown to the ego because it is preoccupied with its immediate purpose of preventing the release of body wastes to frustrate toilet training. Later in the course of life when the ego experiences decathexis tension, it resorts to techniques suggested by the techniques employed in infancy to retain the cathexis but reshaped to suit new circumstances. The delay in the release of body wastes in infancy becomes in adulthood, by the process of derivative relatedness transference devolution, the new technique of collecting things such as money or works of art, or withholding assistance requested by others such as workplace supervisors or withholding compliance required by teachers. As the ego passes through the successive stages of ego ontogenesis, the central concept or purpose is progressively driven into the ego's awareness of its aims. It identifies a source of tension producing stimuli, then looks for ways of defeating it. This is the purpose which repeatedly weighs upon the ego. The ego is goal driven, and the goal is to defeat the source of whatever tension producing stimuli is currently assailing it.

Latency

The latency period is that phase of ego ontogenesis which is precipitated by the resolution of the Oedipus conflict and characterized by the establishment of the superego and the suppression of filial competitiveness with the same sex parent for the preferment of the opposite sex parent. The aims of the latency age ego are to defeat the sources of tension producing stimuli which are produced by the circumstances of the latency period experience. These sources arise from parental imperatives imposed upon the latency ego to succeed at self-dependence tasks insisted upon by societal organizations, institutions and their functionaries as well as by the parent. Developing practices of taking care of himself in the form of cleaning, grooming and dressing himself, tidying his personal quarters, performing household chores and attending school and religious training which tend to be required of him by parent and society.

All of these tasks are tension producing, and the latency ego must deal with these sources of tension. Ego mechanisms come into intensive use. Rationalization, denial, suppression, reaction formation, undoing, projection, displacement, introjection, identification, parentification, regression and sublimation are among ego mechanisms employed and refined by the ego during this period to palliate the tension experienced by the impinging stimuli produced by these tasks. The ego becomes accomplished at tension reduction through the use of mechanisms, which by their nature can provide only temporary relief because reality always returns. But the use of mechanisms eases the way for the latency ego, which must guide behavior to accomplish the tasks of the latency period regardless of the tension and unpleasure they occasion. To reduce tension by refusing to accomplish these tasks would only encumber the ego with accumulated burdens which would in the course of time overwhelm it, which in the cases of some latency age individuals actually happens, leaving them in a state of disability in which they fail to move on in the course of life.

The principal aim of the latency age ego is to accomplish the tasks imposed by parents and society with as little unpleasure as possible. When the child enters adolescence, many of the aims of the latency period are achieved for him simply by the physiological fact of becoming an adolescent. His powerlessness vis-à-vis the parent and adult society, the restrictions upon his comings and goings by parents and adult society, the limitations of his diminutive stature, the lack of esteem he suffers from the general derogation of importance placed upon children by society, his limited ability to enter the marketplace and purchase ego worth assets—all of these sources of impinging stimuli greatly diminish for the adolescent simply by his growth in size, in strength, in intellectual capacity and sexual attractiveness resulting from the physiology of adolescence. He adopts purposes of enjoying the benefits of these new capacities. As a consequence, the adolescent often becomes unruly, brash, rebellious and pursues aims which his parents regard as imprudent.

Adolescence

The latency period lasts until the onset of adolescence when the Oedipus conflict arises anew but in a form reshaped by the necessity of retaining the filial-parental cathexis. The adolescent's sudden growth in physical size, intellect and power and his wish to individuate from his parent by having his own separate and unique identity and independence precipitates a resurgence of filial-parental competition, which in part is displaced upon parental surrogates such as teachers, law enforcement functionaries, employers and rival age-mates, brings an end to latency.

For the adolescent, the sources of tension producing stimuli include the resurgent Oedipus conflict in which the adolescent ego must deal with renewed filial rivalry with the same sex parent, which is dealt with in part by displacing the rivalry and the filial hostility, which tends to accompany it, onto parentified external objects. Thus, the adolescent boy, unaware of his motive, may select disliked age-mates as well as villains of literature and entertainment, opponents of sports teams with which he identifies and foreign leaders who are perceived as enemies of his own nation or culture and displace his filial fear and hostility upon these entities, which permits a venting of filial hostility toward his actual parent without provoking retribution from the same sex parent.

Impelled by the impact of sex hormones, he may also romanticize females to whom he is attracted such as female age-mates, female stars of the entertainment industry and heroines of fiction and drama. By displacing his lust and possessive proclivities upon females not his mother, he avoids antagonizing his father. These are important aims of the adolescent to deal with the tension producing stimuli emanating from his renewed filial rivalry with the same sex parent and desire for the favor of the opposite sex parent. The female adolescent experiences a resurgent Electra conflict and traverses much of the same territory as the male adolescent but in competition with the mother for preferment with the father and displacing romanticizing relatedness upon males rather than upon females.[2]

The resurgent Oedipus conflict is so quickly suppressed and placated with the strategies of displacement and denial that the adolescent male virtually succeeds in avoiding the conscious experience of fancying his mother and challenging his father. But his experience of craving the maternified entities such as girl friend and female entertainment star and hostility towards maleficent parentified entities often become intense. Schoolboy and schoolgirl crushes aimed at idealized adults and schoolboy and schoolgirl infatuations with opposite sex age mates are widely observed among adolescents.

Other salient aims of the adolescent male include the goal of gaining a livelihood so that he will one day be able to establish and care for a family. Depending upon the accepted practices of his culture and the realities of the economy of his culture, he must begin to develop the skills and knowledge which will enable him to obtain a livelihood. In modern industrialized technological societies, this means adopting a goal of acquiring an education, or a trade, or the skills and knowledge of a profession. Many years of education' and apprenticeship will confront him to comply with these requirements which are highly tension producing. To succeed in these endeavors becomes a major purpose of the adolescent's life.

The adolescent must also advance toward citizenship in order to take his place in adult society by acquiring the knowledge and skills required of adult citizens of the community. How to participate in society without becoming

---

[2] Freud eschewed the term Electra complex preferring the term female Oedipus complex. See **Freud, Sigmund.** *The Standard Edition of the Complete Psychological Works of Sigmund Freud.* Edited by James Strachey. London: The Hogarth Press, 1971. Vol. 18 p. 255n, Vol. 21 p229, Vol. 23 p. 194.

enmeshed in conflict with laws and established mores and by contributing to the community in ways expected of adults becomes a developmental aim of the adolescent. Looking after his property, volunteering his services to the community, participating in the political life of the community perhaps by running for elective office or campaigning on behalf of other elective office seekers, or at the very least by voting in elections are behaviors which will be expected of the adult into which the adolescent will grow and for which he must prepare himself during adolescence. These are purposes which the adolescent recognizes as aims he must pursue.

Young Adulthood

Many of the purposes of the adolescent follow the individual into young adulthood where the principal aims of adolescence are to achieve their realization. The aim of the young adult is to realize the ambitions of adolescence. During young adulthood, the ego is confronted with such exigencies as deciding upon a career, actually establishing the means to gain a livelihood, satisfying sexual and reproductive urges, finding a mate and forming a family, providing for his children and adapting to the laws and mores of the community. These exigencies become major purposes which the young adult strives to achieve. They act as sources of tension producing impinging stimuli which, although they may be palliated by employing ego mechanisms, eventually must be resolved in the only way possible for the ego which is to succeed at achieving these purposes.

The young adult continues to struggle with sources of ego tension arising from the deficits of narcissism, power, and worth and impinging stimuli from curiosity, from the uncertainties of surety, from rectitude as well as from superego importunities. The goals he pursues to reduce ego tension from these sources tend to be to gain knowledge through education and from mentors among older adults, from established authorities, from books and from the communications media and to develop and enhance capacities and abilities to equip him to attain these goals.

Once the young adult has found a mate and established a family, he' is confronted by the requirement to support and care for them. This means extracting a livelihood from the economy which for most is no easy undertaking, and becomes a major, preoccupying goal for all but the few blessed by inherited wealth or a place in society on the path of preferment. Other goals sought by the young adult include establishing a social place, obtaining ego worth assets, rearing his child successfully and solving the inevitable problems of matrimony.

Middle Adulthood

Normatively, the middle age individual will have achieved the purposes of young adulthood. He will likely have acquired a spouse, established a family, borne and reared children to adulthood or near to it, made a place for himself in society, obtained at least a modicum of wealth and have settled down to enjoy the rewards of success. However, many adults may achieve only limited success by middle age, having suffered misfortune or been impeded by circumstances of poverty, disability, calamity, or by having lived in a society visited by the destruction of war, famine or drought. But in industrialized technological societies, most will enjoy circumstances which are better than those they experienced earlier in their lives.

Although the goals of young adulthood may have been met, the middle age individual will also have purposes singular to middle age. The middle age adult typically will experience tension producing stimuli from a variety of sources characteristic of middle adulthood including problems arising from the difficulties his adult children may have in establishing themselves, or he may lack the ability to purchase ego worth assets sufficient to keep at bay the tension produced by the deficits of narcissism, power and worth. Thus, he may crave a more impressive residence in a higher status neighborhood, or a more impressive automobile to reduce the tension of his ego worth deficit. To the same end, he may want a summer home, a trip abroad or money to pay for an expensive wedding for his daughter. All of these wants are tension producing and induce the middle age individual to form goals aimed at reducing the tension which they cause.

Consequently, the middle age adult establishes purposes aimed at reducing the ego tension produced by these sources of tension. For example, he may strive to gain wealth sufficient to purchase the embellished or fashionable residence which he desires, purchase a more impressive automobile, purchase a summer home, a trip abroad and a more elaborate wedding for his daughter. Whether he is employed by a large corporation, operates his own business or works at a profession or a trade, he may be motivated to strive for greater income. In a large corporation, this may mean competing more ruthlessly with fellow employees; in business it may mean competing more fiercely with rival businesses and exploiting customers; and in a profession or trade it may mean charging higher fees or rendering less service for the same fee.

The middle age adult tends to set other purposes to pursue in his time of life such as treating himself to various self-indulgences such as working fewer hours (if he can manage to do so), or buying the fishing boat he has longed for, or traveling extensively abroad, or taking a leading role in the community in politics or in community organizations. Regarding himself as successful may tempt him to speak out about his opinions upon a range of matters affecting the community in public meetings and in letters to the editor of periodicals.

Or taking more drastic measures, the middle age individual may decide to end a marriage or long term relationship which has declined and no longer renders pleasure, or he may quite his job, business or profession and strike out to fulfill a fantasy he has nurtured for many years such as taking up a hobby or entering upon a business which allows him to escape the bureaucracy of the corporation or government agency. The key element of middle age is the realization that one's life is more than half over, and that if one is going to pursue important aims he has been deferring, he had better do so before time runs out.

The middle age individual tends to be surer of himself than at any time since the onset of adolescence, or at least he tends to believe in the superiority of his own judgments and opinions. He becomes more judgmental and less tolerant about the failings of others in conduct and rectitude. He tends to be intolerant of the attitudes and values of the younger generation, particularly their choice of fashion in dress, preferences in leisure activities, in music and entertainment. He may be irked particularly by their condemnation of the older generation for the "mess they have made of things." Among the purposes of the middle age individual is to have his opinions and judgments prevail over those of others with whom he disagrees.

Old Age and Death

Purposes of the old age individual are to preserve his posterity, which in most cases will be his children, grandchildren and great grandchildren. He will want to see to their education, health and survival. They will carry his memory into the time after his death and give him what temporal immortality he can expect. The great achiever in old age will have the purpose of preserving his achievements in whatever field of endeavor that he toiled. If he has wealth, he will tend to apply it to the task of preserving his achievements into the future as a means to extend his life beyond death. He will want to see to his grave plot and grave stone, and perhaps establish a university chair or a building in his name, or pay for the church organ or have a hospital wing named after him. He will strive to avoid going to his death having left behind no trace of his having been here.

The Displacement of Purpose Upon External Objects:
Animate and Inanimate, Physical and Metaphysical

Because the human ego has purpose in its behavior, it tends to displace purposefulness onto external objects as well as to attribute purposefulness to every object it can recognize, in some cases even to inanimate objects such as stone idols and mosaic figures of saints on cathedral walls. The universe is seen as having a purpose, and God is seen as having a purpose, and man is seen as being on Earth for a purpose. The ego may ask, "What is my purpose? Why are we here? Where are we going?" The assumption is that there has to be a purpose if only it can be discovered. The human ego is a teleologist and sets out to discover the answer to these questions.

Those things that man perceives beyond the reach of his senses and that he cannot prove by common sense means, he tends to explain their being and activity as serving a purpose. Thus, he speaks of God's purpose. He does not ask the question of whether God has no purpose or whether man has no purpose except to reduce or defeat tension producing stimuli or for the purpose he invents for himself to reduce the tension produced by of fear of purposelessness. Consequently, the human ego is forever looking for purpose in the universe and assuming that there is a purpose but not asking the question whether man's only purpose is to avoid or reduce ego tension, or whether the universe has no purpose but simply exists.

To reduce the tension of the ego worth deficit, the ego must find a purpose that gives it worth. The ego must justify man's existence to achieve worth that it may reduce the tension of the ego worth deficit. The ego guides behavior to gain worth in the eyes of the parentified God, which it invents to supplant the actual parent as its protector when the child ego comes to recognize, typically during latency, that the parent is neither omnipotent nor omniscient.

The ego does not recognize that its behavior is aimed at defeating sources of tension producing stimuli and reducing tension but perceives the secondary aim as its purpose. For example, the ego guides behavior to grow food because it experiences a desire to eat. The secondary aim of eating has assumed such great importance that providing tempting meals has become an intensive industry operating all over the industrialized world and not with the aim in mind of reducing ego tension produced by the impinging stimuli of hunger. Restaurateurs do not advertise their service by inviting the potential customer to come in and reduce ego tension produced by hunger but rather promises him that the food is delicious and will delight him.

The human ego attributes purposefulness to reality rather than attributing purposelessness to reality because the ego displaces its own purposefulness onto reality. It does not occur to the human ego that reality has no purpose, that reality is indifferent, that all things which are not human beings may have no purpose but simply exist without a purpose. The human ego displaces its own aims onto objects in the external world and onto the external world itself. The human ego relates to objects and to the external world as if they and it have needs for narcissistic satisfaction, for power, for worth, that they too have a conscience, an ideal, a sense of surety and a desire for cathexis. The human ego displaces these attributes onto objects in the external world and onto the external world itself.

To the extent that it can identify with objects, the human ego finds them more like itself and displaces with greater intensity its own attributes to those objects. The tendency is to personify non-human objects. Unseen objects such as Gods which tend to be fashioned in man's image and likeness are seen as having attributes of human beings but greatly superior to human beings. For example, certain Hindu gods are depicted as having many arms while man has but two arms. The anthropomorphic gods of classical Greece were given the form of human beings of idealized beauty and proportion. It may be argued that religious beliefs exist only in the minds of human beings, and in the absence of human beings to believe in their existence, beliefs would not exist at all and cannot exist except in the minds of human beings. If so, God exists only in the minds of human beings.

22

CLOSING COMMENT

Ego Ontogenesis

There is the concept that a human being has two parallel minds operating separately from each other, one of which is conscious and the other unconscious, and that the unconscious mind governs the conscious mind without the conscious mind's awareness. In other words the unconscious mind tells the conscious mind what to think and what to do without the conscious mind knowing this, and further that the conscious mind guides human behavior unaware that it is doing the bidding of the unconscious mind of which it is oblivious, and that often the unconscious mind guides behavior in ways which are harmful. The author of this volume finds this concept to be unpersuasive. It offers no explanation of how the unconscious mind transmits its orders to the conscious mind nor why the conscious mind would perceive itself as compelled to implement those orders.

The explanation presented in this volume holds that there is no independently operating unconscious mind. The author does, however, believe that there are mental processes operating in the mind set into motion by insensate stimuli produced by chemicals crossing the blood-brain barrier and impacting the ego without the ego's awareness of the stimuli. Moreover, there are other mental processes of which the mind is not aware until it is made aware of them by impinging stimuli which call attention to them. This may occur when a thought is provoked by stimuli which awaken conscious awareness of them so that they are retrieved from memory and thought about again.

Think of conscious awareness as a spotlight which roams about the mind from one thought to the next as the spotlight illuminates awareness of a thought or memory and then moves on to another thought or memory stimulated by the thought or memory just illuminated or by impinging stimuli from sources external to the mind. Stimuli external to the mind awaken the mind to memories of which the mind then becomes aware and which then may point to other memories which are in turn awakened anew by the stimuli.

Thus the mind, which is the seat of the ego and can be aware of only a limited amount of thought at a given time, ranges over the reservoir of memory from thought-to-thought uncovering thoughts it would otherwise not be aware of. Thoughts that it does not think of are thoughts of which it is unconscious, but they are thoughts which can be made conscious when attention is brought to them when stimulated by associated thoughts and external stimuli. A successful analysis of the content of the mind by uncovering thoughts which are in the reservoir of memory or excited by stimuli both internal and external in origin will explain the current aims of the ego.

There are certain thoughts which cannot be uncovered because they were first thought during primordial life, prior to the resolution of the Oedipus conflict and the start of the latency period, which tends to be the point at which autobiographical memory begins.[1] The content of the primordial mind is known only by inference made from the content of the post primordial mind or from observable behavior. What the latency child thinks and does points to the thoughts contained in the primordial mind and uncovers those thoughts not by conscious memory of them but by inferring what they were in primordial life.

For example, consider the root pattern of a tree, which is not visible to the eye, but may be inferred from the pattern of the tree's trunk and branches, which is visible. The primordial thoughts of the individual cannot be directly perceived but can be inferred from the origins to which post-primordial behavior and thoughts point. To achieve this outcome, much difficult analysis often is necessary whose accuracy is less than fully reliable and therefore will be relied upon cautiously by the prudent person until they are corroborated by behavior which validate them. Reliance upon primordial thought tends to be risky and should be resorted to and relied upon only when the risk is warranted by exigent necessity.

Current behavior can be analyzed by following the chain of thoughts which preceded it to their origins. This chain of thought inevitably leads back to its point of origin, which may be in the primordial mind from which it originally sprang. Because the thought content of the primordial mind is accessible only through inference, it should be relied upon only if the need is urgent enough to be worth the risk. For example, to rid someone of debilitating anxiety might be worth the risk of relying upon an analysis of primordial memory which leads by concatenation to an analysis of the current thought

---

[1] For comment about autobiographical memory, see **Larry R. Squire** and **Stuart Zola-Morgan** in Science, September, 1991, cited in *The New York Times*, September 24, 1991, Science Section

which is disabling. Disabling anxiety may also be caused by biochemical dysfunction in the brain, which in treating such a disorder should be determined before analysis of primordial thought processes is undertaken. In circumstances less urgent than disability, analysis of the primordial mind can be made but with less reliability than it can in a psychotherapeutic situation and should therefore be relied upon with a great deal more caution. Nevertheless, what has become known about human behavior generally from the analysis of a great many individuals supports theories of behavior whose validity is reaffirmed by innumerable examples in the practical world. They can be relied upon to explain human behavior in specific circumstances but not relied upon absolutely if their origins are in the primordial mind, which cannot be known directly.

It is in the nature of human beings to guess about the motives of others who are not themselves aware of their motives. For example, someone may ask a friend to accompany him to the theater to enjoy a drama. The friend may agree to attend but guess accurately that the trip to the theater is not so much to watch a play as it is to meet a particular someone of the opposite sex in a factitious chance encounter who is scheduled to be there. The individual may not be fully aware that he hopes to meet the person of the opposite sex, but the invited friend may accurately guess as much because of his familiarity with the behavior of the individual who is invariably bashful and indecisive toward persons of the opposite sex.

Countless such examples could be presented to validate the human propensity to analyze and attribute motives to others who may be unaware of their motives before they are charged with holding them. Current thoughts and actions impelled by the ego's guidance of behavior to reduce the tension produced by impinging stimuli and techniques to deal with that tension inherited from the distant past come to the present by the process of derivative relatedness transference devolution. Both the tension experienced in primordial life and the response to that tension devolve through ego ontogenesis to the present after being successively reshaped by a succession of later circumstances to which the ego responds.

There is no parallel unconscious mind telling the conscious mind unbeknown what to think and do. There are tension producing thoughts from the past which have taken on new forms through successive rethinking, new forms whose progenitors originated in primordial experience. As an example, consider the case of a factitious present day accountant who, because he is struggling unsuccessfully to reconcile his client's account books, experiences tension increase just as he did during toilet training in primordial life when he feared severation from the parent of absolute dependence. Now, he fears that his client, whom he parentifies, may dismiss him (sever him) from employment for failing to reconcile the client's account books as he was hired to do.

The concatenation of responses to tension producing stimuli might have led in succession from toilet training to, say, the sedulous tidying in his room to please the parent from whom he feared decathexis, and from there to great devotion to school work also to please his parent which was like tidying his room because it required figuring out how to sort and organize things, and from there to the careful looking after of his residence and belongings, having parentified acquaintances as well as members of the public who observe his property from whom he fears reproach, and from there to studiousness in his academic work to become an accountant and from that point into the profession of accountancy. This illustration of necessity is greatly simplified.

If asked why he chose to become an accountant, he might respond by saying that he likes working with numbers and seeing things add up to their inevitable result, which gives him a feeling of security because it corroborates his comforting belief that the universe is governed by logic, which is in harmony with mathematics. It would never occur to him without analyzing his thoughts that it all began in primordial life when he wanted to retain his feces so as not to be severed from the filial cathexis to the external agent of absolute dependence.

At every major trauma of ego ontogenesis and the myriad assaults of tension producing stimuli in between major traumata, the ego guides behavior to respond with the aim of defeating sources of tension producing stimuli to reduce the tension they engender. The experience of earlier traumata and the ego guided behavior aimed at reducing the tension produced by the earlier traumata devolve to be employed to reduce the tension produced by later traumata in a concatenation devolving from the past to the present.

A given human behavior is advantageously understood by tracing its origins to the point in ego ontogenesis from which it arose. The oral stage trauma of weaning produces numerous behavior derivatives springing from the experience of weaning. The behavior of suckling upon objects such as fingers and toys during infancy help reduce decathexis tension produced by filial fears of abandonment. Subsequent behaviors aimed at reducing decathexis tension which are derived from the suckling practice of infancy might in adulthood include cigarette, cigar and pipe smoking; overeating, kissing and engaging in various forms of oral sex; loquacity; speechmaking; singing and acting in drama; reciting poetry; conversing; and numerous other behaviors of an oral nature. It is important to remember that tension-reducing behavior tends to be aimed at reducing tension provoked by stimuli impinging simultaneously from more than one source.

Biting the nipple during infancy in a futile attempt to defeat the weaning process for the purpose of reducing decathexis tension produces other examples of oral behavior derived from the trauma of weaning experienced during infancy. Emitting profane expletives, voicing biting remarks, expressing sarcasm, engaging in polemics, resorting to cynicism and employing satire are derivative behaviors in adulthood which may be derived in part from biting the nipple in filial hostility during weaning when the breast or bottle was being withdrawn. However, not all such behaviors in adulthood necessarily arose from these infantile sources, but many do. Biting upon objects in infancy during weaning may be provoked partly by the tension producing stimulus of erupting teeth as well as to reduce severation tension produced by withholding the nipple to facilitate weaning.

There are numerous common behavioral derivatives springing from the primordial experience of toilet training. The anal expulsive phase, which occurs ahead of the anal retentive phase, gives rise to many commonplace behaviors.[2] For example, playing with malleable materials, which in childhood might include modeling clay, finger paints, play dough and playground mud and in adulthood might include such culinary practices as preparing sauces, pureeing vegetables and making sausages, which may in part be derivative behavior aimed at reducing the ego tension produced by decathexis fears. These behaviors tend also simultaneously to serve other tension reducing purposes such as preparing food to ingest with the aim of reducing the tension of hunger. In infancy, the playing with feces was given up to please an admonishing parent, and the later derivative behaviors such as those just cited enable the individual to sublimate the wish to play with feces while ostensibly obeying the parent by giving them up.

The retentive phase is made possible by the development of sphincter control, which enables the infant to withhold feces and urine and release them at times of his choosing. By these means, the infant ego is able to guide behavior with the aim of frustrating the parent's toilet training effort for the purpose of retaining the filial-parental cathexis. Behaviors observed in adulthood which are in part derivatives of infantile resistance to toilet training through sphincter control include such actions as the obsessive retention of personal possessions, the hoarding of money, excessiveness in the collecting of objets d'art, the inability to complete a project because of an impulse to hold on to it, stinginess, constipation, lack of openness in dealings, as well as numerous others characterized by obtaining, holding on to and not letting go of.

It is the anxiety of decathexis fear triggered by a current experience, which arouses anew the anxiety first experienced during primordial life, which shapes current behavior. For example, the infantile experience of being manipulated by the parent to the potty chair may have devolved to the present in such a way that being manipulated by a parentified authority such as a teacher in school or supervisor at one's place of employment, provokes anew the anxiety experienced during primordial life, arousing the present

---

[2] For examples of oral and anal stage behavioral derivatives, see **Brown, J. F.** *The Psychodynamics of Abnormal Behavior.* New York and London: McGraw-Hill Book Company, Inc., 1940, pp. 204-206.

decathexis anxiety and evoking reshaped tension reducing responses such as procrastination. The response during primordial life of clinching the anal sphincter may have devolved into a tendency in the present to procrastinate, not to let go of, or to resist the direction imposed by an authority. These are counter manipulation behaviors which tend to be self-injurious. Procrastination tends to be self-injurious in that it may lead to failure of accomplishment or detrimental resentment by a supervisor, customer or colleague. The operation of self-injurious counter manipulation may be seen in the colleague who is unsupportive of managers and co-workers by putting off doing the work or providing the cooperation expected of him.

The Oedipus conflict tends to produce a richer load of impinging stimuli than weaning or toilet training from which the individual inherits derivative behavior in successive stages of ego ontogenesis. It adds to fears of filial severation and the fear of parental retribution because of filial competition and hostility. The ego tends to parentify objects of authority such as teachers and supervisors and to relate to them as to the parent of the Oedipus conflict during the primordial stage of ego ontogenesis. Parentification may be beneficial or injurious depending upon circumstances in which parentification occurs.

The student who relates to his teacher as a beneficent parentified entity may elicit a favorable response from a teacher who relates to the student positively. The teacher may give special attention to the student, which facilitates the student's academic progress. However, the student who relates to his teacher as a maleficent parentified entity may elicit reciprocated dislike from his teacher who will tend to ignore him in his studies so that the student progresses less well academically than he otherwise might have. Similarly, the employee who relates to his supervisor as a maleficent parentified entity may do less well in his employment and career than the employee who relates to his supervisor as a beneficent parentified entity. In any case, the way the individual relates to authorities in his life will tend to be a function of the outcome of his struggle with the Oedipus conflict and the derivative behavior it fosters.

To understand in detail the individual's way of relating to an authority in adulthood, it is helpful to retrace the succession of responses to authorities during the succeeding stages of ego ontogenesis back to the primordial experience of the Oedipus conflict. While no easy task, it might not be as formidable as it may at first seem. It is a matter of identifying the authorities encountered in life, analyzing the way in which they were related to—which ones were related to as beneficent and which were related to as maleficent—sorting out the characteristics of the related-to-authorities and the way in which the individual responded to them and tracing it to his response to the Oedipus conflict in primordial life.

For example, if the individual responds with a tirade of invective to direction given to him by an authority, it may be inferred that during the primordial Oedipus conflict period he responded with temper tantrums to directions from the parent which frustrated him. But the temper tantrum response may have been to parental directions of a particular sort such as to tidy his playthings. In adult life, the anger he directs at his supervisor may most often occur when the supervisor directs him to clean up something such as his desk, work bench or a report which the supervisor rejected as sloppy. The primordial child who related to his parent with fear and timidity may relate to authorities in adulthood with timidity, or if the child experienced a reaction formation of filial hostility he might relate to authorities with hostility, which tends to precipitate defensiveness and dislike from authorities. Because of its self-injurious character, such behavior may be traced in part to an infantile counter manipulation response to toilet training.

The adult who relates to his supervisor as a beneficent parental surrogate may elicit from the supervisor a relatedness which is positive with the result that the supervisor becomes a patron to the individual and assists him in his career. Such behavior may be traced back to primordial experience when the individual related to his parent as a beneficent parental surrogate because the parent lavished praise upon him warmly when he was obedient.

Adolescence, which tends to be a particularly stressful stage of ego ontogenesis, may manifest numerous behaviors derived from the Oedipus conflict. Adolescence is a time of individuation, whose origins can be traced back to toddlerhood when the infant employed his new found faculty of locomotion to move away from his parent so as to explore other environs such as the other side of the room or the next room before returning to his parent to reduce the tension of decathexis provoked by his brief physical separation from his parent.

As the adolescent tests his capacity to achieve a measure of filial independence, he begins to individuate from his parent, which is essential if he is ever to become self-dependent. From his initial experience of individuating during toddlerhood, he expands his wandering practices into the latency period, going off from his parent, often with play peers, sometimes into environs to which his parent would object if the latter were aware, but always coming back to the parent to reduce the ego tension produced by separation and dependency.

Individuating may be an important issue for an adolescent ego for whom parentally imposed restrictions upon his comings and goings during latency had been experienced as especially tension producing. The behavior of the adventurous, risk-taking adolescent may be traced back to latency age experience in which the adolescent bridled under restrictions imposed by the parent. Thus, in adolescence he may venture into dangerous places such as abandoned factory structures, old warehouses or vacant residences, or riding on motorcycles, or taking up Para jumping, or swimming too far from shore, or seeking out questionable peers to socialize with, or experimenting with street drugs and engaging in petty crimes. The infantile counter manipulation response to toilet training may in part explain these risky behaviors.

The particular vector which individuation assumes in a given case will depend upon variables experienced earlier and the circumstances in which the ego finds itself at the moment. For example, if the parent's occupation were that of carpenter and the parent were striving to impose the occupation of carpenter upon his son, the latter might choose carpentering as an avenue of filial rebellion and take up music as a career choice, knowing that the parent was unmusical and not an admirer of musicians. Behavior chosen by the ego to reduce tension tends to be fortuitous and is chosen out of the available options perceived and evaluated by the ego at the time as having the capacity to yield a net tension reduction or a minimum net tension increase.

If an adolescent daughter of a socially prominent mother believed that to obtain the approval of her mother, which would reduce the ego tension of the ego worth deficit, she might pursue social prominence herself and do so with a dedication aimed at eventually surpassing the status achieved by her mother. She might in this way facilitate her additional aim of establishing an identity separate from her mother. Such behavior would be aimed at serving the dual purposes of establishing a separate identity and reducing the tension of the ego worth deficit. The multiplicity of avenues which might be pursued by the adolescent during individuation is extensive and tends to vary from one culture and socioeconomic class to the next.

Filial rebellion is an important avenue employed by the adolescent to individuate by establishing his separate and unique identity and his independence. Adolescent rebellion encounters special problems: if the adolescent rebels too strongly, he might alienate the parent and lose the parental protection and support he enjoys, but if he does not rebel adequately he may fail to individuate with the result that he is pulled back into the parent's orbit so strongly that he cannot separate, achieve self-dependence and go his own way.

He must choose an avenue of rebellion which achieves individuation without causing parental alienation. He may do this by choosing an object of rebellion in the form of a parental value such as religion, or life style, or choice of career and then balance any of these by adopting a parental value or array of values which gratifies the parent to an extent that the parent will be able to continue to identify with and introject the child, which preserves the parent's capacity to continue to protect and support the child until the latter reaches adulthood and becomes self-dependent within the context of his society.

Or the adolescent may pursue individuation by choosing a parental value to exceed his parent's devotion to it. Thus, he may become far more openly religious than his parent, or a much greater supporter of the parent's political values than the parent himself, or prepare himself to take up his parent's occupation with much greater success than the parent achieved. By this means he can separate himself from his parent by surpassing the parent but without alienating the parent who may applaud him for his zeal, giving a boost to his ego worth.

The adolescent is impelled by tension producing expectations placed upon him by his parents, by the extended family, by society and by his own need to reduce the ego worth deficit, to choose a career in life, including a means to obtain a livelihood. He must seek to establish a persona which others will abide if he is to be accepted into their company and which others will admire if he is to attain status among them. He must work toward obtaining a skill that he can sell in the marketplace as a means of livelihood or to cultivate entrepreneurial propensities which will one day enable him to succeed in business or learn how to gain a livelihood.

The adolescent must progress toward acquiring the social skills which will enable him to obtain a mate and a place in the social milieu and be able to propitiate colleagues in a bureaucracy or employers as an employee or customers as a businessman. Much of this he achieves by observing the ways in which others have succeeded and by learning from trial and error experience. If he inherits substantial wealth, he must be able to preserve and invest it if he is to rely upon it for his sustenance.

Many of the sources of impinging stimuli experienced in adolescence and the patterns of response to them will follow the ontogenesis of the ego into young adulthood. Problems of individuation such as filial decathexis tension produced by separation from the parent necessitated by striking out on his own will continue to plague the ego in young adulthood as it did in adolescence. Leaving home to attend college, or to enter the armed forces, or to seek employment in a different city or to establish his own residence will precipitate tension producing stimuli in much the same way with many of the same response patterns as it did during adolescence when the individual struggled to go his own way by such means as staying out late against the parent's wishes, or socializing with peers whom the parent regarded as unsavory or engaging in reckless behavior such as riding a motorcycle or speeding on the highway in the family automobile.

In young adulthood the ego may find itself intimidated by social encounters if this had occurred during adolescence, which could impede the young adult's progress toward finding a mate, obtaining employment and establishing himself in the community. Or contrariwise, if the young adult had been socially skilled during adolescence, this proclivity may assist him in achieving employment, finding a mate and obtaining a place in the community. The particular socializing predilection of the young adult will tend to have been inherited from earlier stages of ego ontogenesis. If he had been bold and confident during latency, those proclivities would likely have followed him into adolescence and thereafter into young adulthood. They may have been established during the resolution of the Oedipus conflict when his sense of worth was not impaired by filial fear or a hostile reaction formation to authority.

However, if the ego had been intimidated during the resolution of the Oedipus conflict and responded to it with a hostile reaction formation to filial fear, these propensities might have followed him into adolescence in ways which impaired his effort to acquire social skills, which in turn may have followed him into young adulthood, impairing his efforts to obtain employment, a mate and a desired place in the community. However, it is possible that the young adult through focused effort can defeat impairments in young adulthood which trailed him from earlier stages of ego ontogenesis. The earlier propensities may remain but be kept suppressed by the effort to defeat them.

When the young adult enters middle adulthood, the various propensities in force during earlier stages of ego ontogenesis will likely be brought with him, and impairments not defeated earlier may or may not be overcome in middle adulthood. Consider as an example the middle age judge who was active in the local political party while practicing law after graduating from law school which he had entered to earn the approval of his father. The father had an older brother who was an attorney of whom he had related to with the ambivalence of pride and envy which he hoped to propitiate by having his son become a lawyer.

During latency the father had exhorted his son greatly to do well in school, which the son had struggled in vain to do, and during adolescence had striven especially hard to qualify for college and then law school. But the son had been a mediocre student because of academic insecurity owing to his own parents' lack of education and his Oedipal fear of surpassing his father.

The son's academic success was barely adequate to enable him to enter college and later law school from which he graduated with a mediocre record. He eventually went into politics because he did not do well as a lawyer and subsequently was chosen by his party to run for a place on the court. As a judge he continually experienced envy and hostility toward the often clever, more affluent attorneys who appeared before him. Thus, he spent his middle adulthood years in an occupation he did not enjoy and was barely adequate to perform. He was the product of factors inherited from the vicissitudes of the vector of ego ontogenesis into which the succession of circumstances of his life impelled him to follow. The content of his primordial experience from which the outcomes at each stage of ego ontogenesis were rooted may be traced back from the derivative behavior observed in the present.

In another example, consider the cinema actor in middle adulthood whose career had faltered. He had survived the Oedipus conflict by pitting his domineering father against his mother who exercised a strong hold over the father who related to her as he had to his own remote and unsympathetic mother. The father held great expectations for the son and urged toilet training upon him, but the son relied upon his mother to ease his path. When the father was at work, the mother would allow the son to evacuate his bowel at a time of his own choosing. The father had himself pursued a career which led to his becoming the head of a large manufacturing corporation in which he intended his son eventually to succeed him.

During latency, the son displayed little interest in the factory but began to attend the movies with his age mates with a frequency which disturbed his father. The son took to reading about actors and following their careers, rejecting his father's repeated pleas for him to visit the factory with him. The son did well in school, which placated the father, who was gratified that the son was still on track to take over the management of the corporation one day.

This pattern continued into the son's adolescent years in which he graduated first in his class from his preparatory school. The son pursued a social life, participating in the most exclusive social clique at school. In college, he completed his degree in three years, graduating with highest honors. But to his father's displeasure, the son became active in the theater club at school. Following graduation, the son and the father clashed in a great and defining conflict when the son declared that he intended to travel to New York City and take up a career in theater. The father refused to support his son financially in this career path, which enabled the son to rebel openly against the father and to individuate by going his own way. The mother secretly sent money to the son after the latter succeeded in joining a theatrical company for meager pay.

Opportunities in the theater were so sparse that the son decided together with a newly found theater friend to move to Hollywood and seek a place in motion pictures. The son surprisingly succeeded in short order and began a career as a cinema actor. He acted in many motion pictures as the years passed but was never able to achieve the degree of celebrity he craved. His comely appearance and upper socioeconomic class confidence and manners had shunted him into society roles in which he typically appeared in formal dress at swanky soirées as the unsuccessful rival of the leading man for the affections of the leading lady. Now he was too old for the sort of role he was usually cast in, and work came less frequently. The celebrity he had aimed for would have enabled him to appear victorious to his mother in his rebellious competition with his father and would also have appeased his ego worth deficit and assuaged his narcissistic appetite.

In middle adulthood, the ego is left to do the best it can to achieve its aims with what it has accomplished by that point in ego ontogenesis. Typically, middle age is the apogee of individual achievement, and is that time in the course of life when the individual has attained the greatest power, worth, status and economic acquisition likely to occur during his lifetime. For great achievers, the power, wealth or status attained may be of great magnitude, for others it may be substantial but not extraordinary, but for most it will be modest but gratifying even if it does not elicit more than passing admiration of others in similar circumstances. Essentially, the middle age individual has by that time made his life into what it became and must enjoy it to the extent he is able or have no joy at all.

The numerous problems of his offspring, now in adolescence or young adulthood, may require him to come to his children's rescue or to the rescue of his grandchildren. If he chooses, he may become active in his community or on the state or national scene if he has attained a place in those loftier venues. The middle age individual tends to experience greater power, prestige and moment than others of his sort who are younger. Whether in a working class lodge, or as a member of the local school board, or a volunteer in prominent charitable organizations, state commissions or national organizations—whatever his walk of life—in middle age he tends to regard himself as more substantial than he does younger individuals of his kind, and he is usually ready to raise his voice to make his views known.

The walk of life in which the middle age individual finds himself tends to have been shaped by the promise or limitations of his native capacities in combination with his responses to tension producing stimuli during adolescence and young adulthood. The career chosen or into which he gravitated was likely determined by a combination of the fortuity of circumstances and the aim of reducing ego worth deficit tension by pleasing the parent. It is often the case that the middle age individual is able to recognize that the walk of life in which he journeys would meet the approval of his parents or at least of the parent who mattered most to him or of parentified entities to which he had transferred his filial relatedness.

Toward the end of middle age the individual tends to become increasingly aware of the limited time left to him in the course of life and begins to look more to the past than to the future when confronting the everyday stresses of living. Impinging stimuli of daily living pale before the magnitude of life's impending finality.

Old age and death follow middle age and bring with them their own set of tension producing impinging stimuli. The impact of derivative behavior upon the old age individual tends to be cumulative, the unresolved stress of a lifetime. But coping skills and capacities of a lifetime also typically are available to the old age ego to deal with accumulative residue of past struggles with the tension producing stimuli of tension sources which persist over a lifetime. These may include the undertakings of a lifetime aimed at reducing the tension of the narcissism, power and worth deficits, which for most individuals never achieved the ideal toward which the ego struggled.

Principles of Ego Ontogenesis

The ego arises epigenetically from the earliest state of conscious aware-ness experienced by the human organism and evolves into what it becomes. The ego is not created full-blown but evolves through the experience of its ontogenesis and is different at every stage of the individual's progress through the course of life. Although the ego of the elderly person tends to retain ves-tiges of the ego of the primordial child, it is no longer the same ego as the ego of the primordial child, even though the former evolved from the later, just as the mature oak tree, although it contains vestiges of the seed from which it grew, is no longer the acorn from which it derived. The human ego arises from the biology of the organism and does not survive the demise of the organism.

The ego's response to the tension producing impinging stimuli experi-enced at a given stage of ego ontogenesis becomes a shaping constraint upon the response of the ego to the tension producing stimuli experienced at the succeeding stage of ego ontogenesis in a concatenation of effects from stage to stage which devolve from the past to the present.

Ego tension is the experience of unpleasurable disquiet ranging from mild and tolerable to extreme and intolerable. Ego tension abides in that realm which the human mind has not been able to fathom, which is the same province in which consciousness lies. At this moment, the mind of man has not solved the question of what is consciousness and what is its physiologi-cal basis.[3] But most are convinced beyond doubt that they experience con-sciousness. The experience of ego tension is like the experience of conscious-ness in that the human mind recognizes when it experiences disequanimity but cannot explain its physiological basis except to recognize the presence of such concomitants as contraction of chest muscles, disturbed breathing, heart palpitations and the exuding of perspiration. There are many things in human experience which the ego cannot explain but nevertheless is impelled to press on in its tension reducing endeavors without ultimate knowledge of what the things are in substance and process. Ego tension and consciousness are two of these.

The ego adjusts to impinging stimuli by integrating their effect with its existing capacity to defeat tension-producing stimuli. When it encounters the

---

[3] For a discussion of the difficulty of establishing the biological basis of con-sciousness, see *Brain in the News,* Randy Talley, Ed., The Dana Press, Jane Nevins, Editor in Chief, Editorial Office: 5335 Wisconsin Avenue. NW, Suite 440, Washington , DC. 20015, A publication of The Dana Foundation, 745 Fifth Avenue, Suite 900, New York, New York 10151, Vol. 9, No. 10, pp. 2-3, *A New Thinking Emerges About Consciousness by* **Shanker Vedaniam** reprinted from *The Washington Post*, May 20, 2002, p. A9.

tension producing impinging stimuli of a subsequent stage of ego ontogenesis, it tends to resist at first, but then if unable to resist fully, it integrates into its tension reducing capacity the portion of impinging stimuli which it cannot resist. For example, the infant who cannot successfully resist the tension of weaning eventually incorporates the process of taking nourishment by means of the cup, bowl and spoon into its means for reducing the tension of hunger and to reestablish the filial-parental cathexis which was severed when the breast or bottle was withheld. The result is a change in the tension reducing means of the ego, which continues into subsequent encounters with impinging stimuli. Thus, over time the ego evolves into something different from what it was before it encountered the impinging stimuli in a process which is repeated at each encounter with major sources of tension producing stimuli throughout ego ontogenesis.

The ego ontogenetic process is fortuitous. Consequently, what the ego becomes is the result of chance encounters with impinging stimuli. At each encounter with impinging stimuli, the current capacity of the ego to reduce tension produced by the particular impinging stimuli is fortuitous. The way in which the ego will guide behavior to respond to a particular tension producing stimulus in, say, middle adulthood may be substantially different from the way it would respond to the identical stimulus during latency. For example, during latency the ego might respond to a painful fall by guiding the individual to run to the parent crying for relief, but during middle age the ego will be more likely to guide the individual, who meanwhile has become self-dependent, to go to the medicine cabinet for medicine and a bandage and to treat his wound.

A given behavior guided by the ego contains elements from earlier stages of ego ontogenesis which have continued into the present because they survived the earlier effects of tension producing stimuli to remain an element of the ego's response means when encountering subsequent tension producing stimuli. Earlier response patterns of the ego devolve from the past to the future often in a form reconfigured as a result of the ego's conflict or encounter with the earlier impinging stimuli.

At each stage of ego ontogenesis, human behavior is determined by the discrete factors of that stage for the individual concerned aimed at reducing ego tension, which in turn when taken in aggregate for all members of society determines the organizations and institutions of society. Human beings as a species determine the organizations and institutions of society as a consequence of tension reducing behavior practices arising from ego ontogenesis. The organizations and institutions of society are formed for the purpose of reducing the ego tension of their members.

The past is transmitted to the present in ego development by the derivative relatedness transference devolution concatenation process in which the experiences, responses and adaptations of the past to earlier tension producing stimuli are carried forward in succession to be employed by the ego in dealing with later tension producing stimuli. It is by means of the derivative relatedness transference devolution concatenation process that primordial experience is transmitted to the post primordial ego and thence to the ego at subsequent stages of ego ontogenesis throughout the remaining course of life.

The derivative relatedness transference devolution concatenation process is the process during ego ontogenesis by which the relatedness of the ego to an object, including its response pattern to tension producing impingements perceived as emanating from the related-to object, is adjusted and adapted for use in a later circumstance during ego ontogenesis in a procession which leads to a series of subsequent modifications of the original relatedness and response pattern so that at later stages the original relatedness and response pattern has been reshaped by the ego to deal with the later tension producing impinging stimuli.

For example, the technique of crying as an instrument of power employed by the newborn to impel the parent to intervene in order to reduce the infant's tension eventually becomes verbal complaining in the child, and later in the adult responding to parentified others it becomes more creative and imaginative verbalizations which may include satire, derision and caustic wit, and still later in, say, the political process it may become declaiming, and thence haranguing and demagoguery as it is reshaped from one circumstance to the next to respond to changing tension reduction requirements.

In the derivative relatedness transference devolution concatenation process, the ego relates to perceived sources of impinging stimuli, either tension producing or tension reducing, whether the source of that stimuli is the parent or a parentified entity or stimuli impinging from the natural environment such as heat, wetness, cold and the like. Relatedness is having an attitude or disposition toward a perceived source of tension producing or tension reducing stimuli, expectations about how one will be affected by that source and ways in which one is accustomed to interact with or respond to stimuli impinging from that source. Derivative relatedness is relatedness derived from earlier relatedness and reshaped by the ego to deal with later circumstances. The most important relatedness is relatedness to the parent of infancy and childhood and relatedness to parentified objects.

The ego distinguishes between sources of stimuli coming from the natural environment and the same sort of stimuli coming from an individual such as the parent or a parentified entity. For example, the rain as a source of tension producing impinging stimuli is perceived as a different source of impinging stimuli than would, say, the parent spraying water from a garden hose on a hot summer day or from a shower nozzle in the bath. The rain may be related to as neutral and without intention, while the spray from the garden hose or shower nozzle will tend to be related to as a form of parental hostility, or contrariwise, as a form of parental ministration depending upon the intentions of the parent as perceived by the child.

Virtually anything may function as an object of relatedness, but for the infant the most significant object of relatedness is the parent, and for the older child and the adult, parentified objects as well as the parent tend to be the significant objects of relatedness. When one relates to the parent, he tends to relate also to all ancillary objects associated with the parent. Therefore, when filial relatedness is transferred to another object, it is also transferred to all ancillary objects of relatedness perceived as associated with the object. For example, the child tends to relate to the parent as his protector and may regard ancillary objects such as the family ménage and objects within the family ménage and surrounding garden as beneficent.

After becoming an adult the child may parentify government and expect protection from government as he once did from the parent, and he may relate to ancillary objects of government such as governmental functionaries in the persons of policemen, firemen and schoolteachers also as objects of parentification. He may relate to these objects variously as benevolent parental surrogates or maleficent parental surrogates depending upon the fortuity of the circumstances in which he parentified these ancillary objects and displaced bifurcated filial ambivalence upon them.

For example, a considerate teacher comforting the child after a painful fall on the playground may become related to by that child as a benevolent parentified entity, and a policemen threateningly ordering a child to cease riding his bicycle on a pedestrian sidewalk might become related to as a maleficent parentified entity. Consider the example of the parent imposing toilet training. The child ego is aware of the decathexis tension experienced and the source of that tension as a determining force (the parent) who ejects the child from the connection to the protecting external agent upon whom the child is dependent absolutely.

This experience is one of terror and of being abandoned to all of the tension producing stimuli impinging ubiquitously, which the infant ego is helpless to defeat. As a consequence, the relatedness to the toilet training will tend to have elements of relatedness to the parent. For example, an odor which the child detects emanating from the parent may be associated with the odor of fecal matter experienced during toileting supervised by the parent and be related to with repugnance or pleasure depending upon which is tension reducing at the time the experience first occurs.

The question arises as to how the experiences and responses to stimuli of primordial life are passed on to influence the ego's response to impinging stimuli at later stages of ego ontogenesis without the ego's knowledge that this is happening? It is by means of the derivative relatedness transference concatenation devolution process that the experiences and responses to stimuli in primordial life are passed on unawares to influence the ego's response to impinging stimuli at later stages of ego ontogenesis. The transmission of primordial experience evolves over time rather than being conveyed instantly as a straight cut over from primordial life to post primordial life. The post primordial ego has been furnished with primordial experience so that it relates to objects in post primordial life as it related to them during primordial life.

For example, fecal matter is odorous and repugnant, but for the infant it may also be attractive and desirable. The repugnance inculcated by the parent continues to dominate the ego's perception of feces, but the ego's liking of feces, which became sublimated in primordial experience and transferred to surrogate fecal objects such as play dough, playground mud or foodstuffs which are acceptable to the parent, may be further transferred to objects in post primordial experience which are associated with pleasant objects.

It is by means of the derivative relatedness transference devolution concatenation process that primordial sublimations are transferred to new sublimated objects in post primordial experience. The post primordial ego may not recall the experience during primordial life when it first dealt with the tension producing impinging stimuli of being required to regard feces with repugnance and to give up regarding them pleasurably. But it remembers that it favored them and that favoring them was wrong, and to reduce the tension of filial fear of severation, it took up the practice of relating to them as repugnant.

The more that the latency age ego sublimated feces, the more is was able to suppress its favoring of them and to accept its awareness of their repugnance. When it leaves primordial life and enters post primordial life, it brings its relatedness to sublimated surrogate fecal objects as pleasurable along with its relatedness to actual fecal objects as repugnant. Thus, in post primordial life, the individual regards feces as repugnant and at the same time regards sublimated surrogate fecal objects, which he no longer consciously recognizes as fecal objects such as foodstuffs and plastic play materials, as pleasurable and acceptable. This is also the way in which relatedness to oral objects and objects of the Oedipus conflict are transmitted from primordial life into post primordial life.

The whole of primordial adjustment to the impinging stimuli of the oral, anal and Oedipal severation traumata and the tension reducing response techniques adopted to deal with the stimuli of those traumata is transferred unawares by the ego during primordial experience to post primordial experience. Consequently, the filial antagonisms of the Oedipus conflict, which are suppressed during primordial experience, are transferred to post primordial life in their suppressed state and are kept suppressed by the ego thenceforth.

Upon each occasion when stimuli threaten to unearth the antagonisms of the suppressed Oedipus conflict, the ego suppresses the conflict anew, but response patterns to Oedipal tension adopted during primordial experience will tend to be reshaped by the ego as it copes with stimuli which threaten to unearth the primordial oedipal experience. For example, the latency child who during primordial life suppressed great filial hostility, which provoked a reaction formation of filial fear, will transfer that suppressed filial fear and hostility in its suppressed state into post primordial life along with the behaviors fashioned in primordial life to reduce the ego tension of filial fear. If, say, the Oedipal child during primordial life adopted the practice of running away to hide when he heard his father voicing anger, he may in post primordial life tend to cower when in the presence of parentified authority figures such as a teacher or employer fuming with displeasure and seek to absent himself from the scene.

It is by the foregoing process that present behavior is influenced by past tension reduction tactics of which the present ego is unaware. Considerable analysis would be required of the present ego to reconstruct the concatenation of tension producing experiences and associated tension reduction techniques fashioned by the ego to respond to them which were first employed during primordial life and subsequently refashioned in response to later tension producing stimuli to create the armory of response techniques at the disposal of the of the ego currently.

The only thing unconscious about these tension reduction techniques is the history of their development and use, which the ego is only likely to uncover through the application of a form of psychoanalysis (not necessarily Freudian). Even so, recovery of primordial experience is unlikely because it was transferred to post primordial life refashioned in the form of sublimations, displacements, projections and reaction formations. For example, the post primordial latency ego may recognize his liking for handling play dough, but he will not likely remember when he sublimated his liking for fecal matter during primordial life into a liking for plastic substances approved by the parent as acceptable playthings.

There is no unconscious parallel mind controlling the conscious mind and determining present behavior unawares. There is past experience transmitted to the present by the process of derivative relatedness transference concatenation devolution and guiding current behavior by the application of ego-guiding techniques created in the past and reshaped by experience with the aim of dealing with tension producing stimuli in the present. In the present, the ego chooses the tension reduction technique from the array of techniques it has acquired throughout ego ontogenesis perceived as most appropriate, correctly or incorrectly, to deal with tension producing stimuli in the immediate present. The tension reducing technique chosen tends to result from the fortuity of the juxtaposition of the particular impinging stimuli and the response pattern it suggests to the ego from the reservoir of response patterns available from past tension reducing experience.

Therapeutic intervention requires the reconstruction by such techniques as psychoanalysis or hypnotism of the concatenation of ego ontogenesis which brought the individual to his current unhealthful state and adopting new practices which are in concert with the demands of reality. Such an undertaking is not easy and is at great risk of going astray and leaving the subject no better off and possibly worse off. The accurate perception of reality is elusive, and the reconstruction of memory of the individual's ego ontogenesis is a formidable undertaking.

Most individuals pass their lives being guided by derivatives of tension reduction tactics established earlier which were originated during primordial life. Most human behavior is derivative behavior, i.e., tension reduction behavior determined by the application of tension reduction means established in the distant past of which the individual is not aware and which he does not undertake to retrieve from the distant memory of the time it was initially established and the concatenation through which it has developed from the past to the present. Most behavior is derivative behavior because it is a response aimed at reducing ego tension by employing means shaped during previous tension reducing responses.

Ego mechanisms are stratagems invented by the ego to reduce tension produced by impinging stimuli which the ego cannot find a means to deal with effectively in concert with reality. Ego mechanisms take the form of illogic in conflict with reality which tricks the ego into accepting as in concert with reality. Ego mechanisms always fail ultimately and must be repeatedly refashioned and reapplied because reality always returns to vitiate them.

All tension reducing behavior is not comparable. There is a hierarchy of tension reducing behavior in which various tension reducing behaviors compete with one another for precedence. Sex may be a powerful tension reducer, but in a given circumstance may not be as powerful as, say, escape from an impending lynching. The various sources of tension producing stimuli are not equal in quality or intensity.

The ego is continually subjected to competing sources of tension increase and tension decrease whose reduction tend to have different qualities and degrees of necessity. For example, the tension increase of hunger when great enough will displace the tension increase of sex, and the tension increase of thirst when severe enough may displace both sex and hunger as sources of ego tension. The individual stranded in a desert and parched with thirst would likely eschew both sexual intercourse and food in order to obtain thirst-quenching water. But in the absence of thirst, he might prefer sex to ingesting a fine meal, especially if he has been eating regularly and has been deprived of sex. All manner of tension producing sources impinge continually upon the human ego competing in strength and urgency, which the ego sorts out in choosing which direction to guide behavior. Sources of ego tension always present themselves in a hierarchy of importunity which the ego must sort through to decide which to strive to reduce first. Prioritizing tension reduction needs is a continuous occupation of the ego.

Pleasure is the reduction of ego tension, but different sources of tension reducing stimuli produce different experiences of pleasure. Sexual pleasure is different from the pleasure of ingesting an haute cuisine meal, and the ego identifies and distinguishes between them when determining the behavioral guidance with which it determines human behavior. When the ego is confronted by impinging stimuli, it determines whether they are tension reducing and pleasurable or tension producing and unpleasurable. From its previous experience of these impinging stimuli it identifies them and determines whether they are tension producing and to be avoided or tension reducing and to be welcomed. And in the case of competing stimuli, the ego prioritizes them in terms of which are to be embraced first or which are to be overcome first. Normatively, the more severe stimuli are dealt with ahead of the less severe, although occasionally lower priority stimuli are dealt with ahead of higher priority stimuli when the ego has been unable yet to find a way to deal with the latter.

No verifiable pattern has been discerned by the mind of man to justify a belief that there is a controlling intelligence determining the arrangement and interactions of objects and their constituents. Everything appears to be unplanned and fortuitous. The patterns which are formed result from the properties of things which cause them to interact with each other in the way that they do. The mind of man, by analysis, by sorting and comparing, is able to discover the various properties of different things and the processes with which they interact when brought into proximity or contact with each other so that man can understand reality and create (invent) functioning objects which would not come into being without man's purposeful effort.

But there is no mind which functions like the mind of man to orchestrate objects not created by the mind of man. These objects come into being accidentally because of the interactions forced by processes and properties engendered within objects which come into contact in the absence of a planned action. The interaction of objects in mutual contact or proximity results from the properties of the objects themselves and the way in which the properties of interacting objects affect each other. Their contact is fortuitous and the outcome of their interaction is unplanned by a controlling intelligence. The human ego, impelled by the will to explain its environment, devises explanations in the form of theories or myths to explain what it does not know. For the cosmologist the universe came from the big bang; for the believer it was created by God in seven days. Neither has irrefutable proof of these explanations.

About the Author

Kenneth Jerold Comfort was born in Lawrence, Kansas, July 5, 1927, and received his elementary and secondary education in the Lawrence public schools. He left high school in 1945 during his senior year to enter the United States Maritime Service and served aboard the *U.S.S. Lafayette Victory*, which circumnavigated the globe. He returned to Lawrence nearly two years later to complete his high school studies. He entered the University of Kansas at Lawrence in 1947 and enrolled in the School of Liberal Arts and Sciences. In his academic studies he focused primarily upon the disparate fields of psychology and geography, the latter inspired by his maritime travels. Graduating in 1951, he entered the United States Marine Corps, serving during the Korean War era. In 1953 he returned to the University of Kansas and began graduate studies in political science while undergoing psychoanalytic therapy at the Menninger Clinic in nearby Topeka, Kansas.

In 1955 he moved to New York City with his wife and infant son and continued his graduate studies at Columbia University, which awarded him a master's degree in 1959 and a doctorate in 1970. At Columbia he focused principally upon American political institutions, international relations and political theory. He also began to search for ways to combine his interest in psychology with his interest in political science. During part of his time at Columbia he was employed by the erstwhile New York City Department of Social Welfare as a social caseworker.

In 1967 he moved his family to Albany, New York, where he became a New York State Public Administration Intern. While employed by New York State and serving in numerous state agencies variously as a public planner and in administrative capacities, he taught political science at Rensselaer Polytechnic Institute in nearby Troy, New York. He served as the Director of the Public Management Institute in the former New York State Department of Social Services during the last ten years of his government service.

In 1995 he left government to devote full time to research and writing. He is the author of *Power, Politics and the Ego* of which the first edition was published in 1998 and a revised edition published in 2002 and *The Ego and the Social Order* published in the year 2000. In 2003 he published *The Ego and the Pursuit of Happiness.* He is currently readying for publication a forthcoming volume entitled *National Security Policy and the Development of Tactical Nuclear Weapons: 1948-1958* to be published in 2005.* His favorite pastime is traveling the world over visiting historic sites, museums and architectural monuments. He currently resides with his family in the New York State Capital Region.

* To request information about purchasing these volumes, write to The New York State Public Administration Institute, Inc. at P. O. Box 74, Cohoes, New York 12047.

APPENDIX

GLOSSARY

Terms and Their Meanings as Used in this Volume

Acrobatics Coordinated physical self manipulation ranging from simple movements of daily living such as walking, eating and dressing to the spectacular virtuosic movements of gymnasts. In this book, acrobatics refers principally to ordinary movements of daily living.

Admiration Attributes Personal characteristics, features, qualities and possessions which elicit the admiration of others toward oneself. These include such items as one's house, family, children, education, social station, occupation, wealth and possessions.

Adolescent Individuation Precipitated by the onset of adolescence, the ego strives to separate from the parent by gaining filial independence, of being the child of one's parent and by establishing an ego ideal which contains some elements unique to oneself as well as retaining elements introjected from the parent.

Advocate See political advocate.

Aims, Stated and Unstated and Unrecognized See under separate headings.

Ambivalence Simultaneous love and hate for an object, particularly one's parent or a parentified object.

Appeasement A foreign policy of pacification or yielding to the demands of a potential enemy rather than opposing him by force.

Autobiographical Memory The ability to recall with a degree of continuity one's experience throughout the course of one's life. Autobiographical memory tends to begin at about age four.

Axon Nerve fiber that conducts impulses away from the body of the nerve cell.

Behavior The actions or reactions of persons or things in response to internal or external stimuli. See human behavior.

Behavior Formation A characteristic action or reaction of a person in response to similar stimuli which endures through time. A coprophilic propensity established during ego ontogenesis in response to toilet training may serve as an example. Such a behavior formation may evolve over time into conduct such as culinary pursuits as the sublimation of the coprophilic propensity.

Beneficent Parentified Entity or Beneficent Parental Surrogate

See parentify.

Bifurcated Filial Ambivalence The love-hate ambivalence toward the parent divided into two moieties, one of love and the other of hate, with objects of filial relatedness then segregated into objects of warmth or objects of hostility. In political behavior the government may be related to with warmth as a beneficent parental surrogate, but the head of state related to with hostility as a maleficent parental surrogate.

Bifurcation See bifurcated filial ambivalence.

Bladder Pressure The experience of ego tension because of a full bladder.

Bond A compelling attachment to an object involving identification and introjection whose severing would produce great ego tension.

Bowel Pressure The experience of ego tension because of a full bowel.

Cathexis The same as bond.

Cathexis Severation The severing of the attachment to the parent or a parentified entity.

Cathexis Withholding A practice in which the parent strives to control the child by threatening to sever the filial-parental bond or by diminishing its perceived strength. The practice also is used by parentified others to strive to control filified others.

Checks and Balance A constitutional structure in which sovereign power is divided among several parts of government so that they act to check each other in the use of sovereign power, creating a balance of power which tends to prevent any part from overpowering the others.

Communications Paradox The failure of two parties to understand the true meaning of the message each communicates to the other because of mutual mistrust or disdain.

Conscious, Consciousness The ego's awareness of its ongoing experience.

Conspicuous Consumption The prominent display of possessions as a testament to wealth, and therefore to power, status and worth.

Continuations Tension reduction behaviors in which earlier ego adaptations to tension-producing impinging stimuli continue in modified form. For example, kissing may be a continuation in adulthood of oral suckling during breast or bottle feeding in infancy.

Counter Manipulation A response of the infant ego to the parent's forced manipulation of the child to accept weaning and toilet training. By spitting out the forcefully spooned food, knocking over the food bowl, withholding the urine and feces and releasing them at untimely moments, the infant counter-manipulates the parent. When the parent withholds warmth and affection in disapproval of the child's behavior, the child may counter-manipulate the parent by self-injurious behavior. Cathexis-withholding by the parent is counter-manipulated by the child by self-injury which may take the form of neglecting the self, failing at self care, failing to make progress toward self-dependence, not protecting oneself from injury or sickness, neglecting one's health and hygiene and the like. The infant ego's resistance to manipulation by the parent is a forerunner to the adult ego's resistance to power and authority of all kinds including that of the state, its laws, officials and coercive functionaries such as the police and the military.

Counter-Transference A phenomenon in which one who is an object of transference by another person is provoked to transfer his own relatedness to other objects to the one who relates to him. Counter transference was discovered by Freud in treating patients whose relatedness to him provoked a transference in him to the patient. This phenomenon is commonplace in political behavior as political participants provoke relatednesses toward each other arising from the transference of filial aims and expectations established in childhood ego ontogenesis toward the parent, siblings and family. An example is parentification. The adult citizen parentifies the public official, and the public official through counter-transference filifies the citizen and treats him as the condescending parent treats the child.

Course of Life Begins with birth and ends with death. See life cycle.

Curiosity The ego's concern to understand the external world in order to deal effectively with the tension-producing stimuli which assaults it. Curiosity is presumably a biologically based propensity.

Cutaway In video graphic editing, material spliced into the video tape and presented as if current but actually from another source, often with voice-over commentary.

Decathexis/Discathexis Severation from the object of cathexis, usually the parent or parentified entity such as spouse, employer or nation. The threat of decathexis is highly tension-producing.

Deficit, Ego Deficit A deficiency in the amount of something needed by the ego to avoid tension increase. Deficits are created by traumata occurring during ego ontogenesis which set the ego on an unending quest for the means to reduce the deficit by making up the deficiency. Because the deficit is irreparable, it is never made up. Behavior aimed at making up for it is never abandoned, but never succeeds.

Denial The suppression by the ego of an idea, thought or perception which is tension-producing as a means to reduce the tension produced.

Depended-Upon Others External objects depended upon to reduce ego tension. They may be the parent or an employer, or other authority which provides tension reduction means such as income or food, shelter, clothing or protection from threat. The depended-upon other tends to be parentified by the ego.

Derivative Behavior Derivative behavior is a behavior pattern derived from a behavior pattern established at an earlier stage in ego ontogenesis. For example, withholding from a cathected other is a tension reduction technique established in response to toilet training which tends to be practiced throughout the course of life but expanded from the withholding of urine and feces to the withholding of a broad range of objects including love, financial help, and in the political process the withholding of such valuables as political favors, campaign contributions and even one's vote. See derivative relatedness transference devolution process.

Derivative Relatedness Transference Devolution Process The process during ego ontogenesis by which the relatedness of the ego to an object including its response pattern to tension-producing impinge ments perceived as emanating from the related to object is adjusted and adapted for use in a later circumstance during ego ontogenesis in a procession which leads to a series of subsequent modifications of the original relatedness and response pattern so that at later stages the original relatedness and response pattern has been reshaped to suit the later circumstances. For example, the technique of crying as an instrument of power used by the newborn eventually becomes verbal complaining in the child and later in the adult respond ing to parenti fied others becomes more creative and imaginative verbalizations which may include satire, derision and caustic wit, and still later in the political process becomes declaiming, and thence haranguing and demogoguery as it is reshaped from one circumstance to the next to respond to changing tension-reduction requirements.

Displacement The transference of relatedness to another object from the object initially related to. For example, the relatedness to a parent may be displaced upon a parentified object.

Displaced Filial Ambivalence The contradictory filial love-hate relatedness toward the parent displaced upon another object such as a candidate, official, political party, governmental entity, one's nation or foreign nation.   See bifurcated filial ambivalence.

Displaced Filial Hostility The hostile moiety of filial ambivalence displaced from the parent onto a different object. This commonly occurs in the political process when a political participant such as a voter transfers filial hostility to a candidate or other political entity which is then related to as a maleficent parental surrogate.

Displaced Filial Warmth Love for the parent displaced upon a parentified entity such as one's spouse, child or government, nation, political party or government official.

Display Advertisement   An advertisement in a publication such as a news paper which takes the form of a box which may consist of many column inches of space and featuring pictures, graphics and a mixture of type fonts and sizes.

Dogma   Theory acted upon as if it were reality.

Economic Process   The economic process is that societal activity having to do with the creation, distribution and consumption of products and services and with the ownership and exchange of property. It is within the economic process that people gain their livelihood.

Ego   The ego is that function of the human organism in which the organism experiences its own existence. It is the "I" which experiences the continuous multiple, overlapping cycles of the increasing tension of unpleasure followed by the decreasing tension of pleasure and guides behavior to defeat the tension-producing stimuli of unpleasure.

Ego Actual   The ego as it actually is as distinguished from the ego ideal and the ego real. The ego actual is unknowable to the ego but is conceived as how the ego actually is when not perceived as ideal or real.

Ego Ideal   The ego ideal is the introjection by the ego of an imagined idealization of the self. The ego-ideal is composed of all the attributes perceived by the ego as needed to reduce tension from all perceived potential sources. The ego ideal if realized would possess properties which reduce the ego worth deficit such as comeliness, talent, status, achievement, wealth and fame. It would possess properties which deal with powerlessness such as wealth, high office, and physical prowess. It would contain attributes which defeat the threat of severation which may take the form of a loving dependent family, membership in groups and organizations and devoted followers and supporters. It would contain validations of surety in the form of corroboration by the applause of those who share or can be persuaded to share one's views. And it would contain reassurance about indviduation and identity in the form of acceptance by others of one's established imago validated by one's being related to in terms of that imago. It would include verification of one's independence and self-dependence in terms of one's ownership and possession of the means of survival whether it be wealth, physical prowess or intellectual capacity.

Ego Mechanisms   Tension reduction techniques in which the presence of the source of tension is rejected with the result that the tension is reduced, but only temporarily reduced because the impingement of reality inevitably returns and the tension resumes. Mechanisms operate by means of self-deceiving logic. For example the mechanism of denial simply dismisses from thought the presence of a tension-producing source which continues to exist in reality and can be expected once again to penetrate the curtain of denial.

Ego Ontogenesis The course of development of the ego characterized by a series of major traumata in the form of severations of the ego from depended upon others. The ego's adaptive response to these overwhelming tension producing impingements give shape and structure to the ego which in turn determines the response pattern by which the ego guides behavior to deal with all other impinging stimuli which assails it.

Ego Power Deficit A perception by the ego of a deficiency in its power to deal with tension-producing impinging stimuli. The ego becomes aware of its power deficit following the onset of the trauma of weaning when its formerly perceived omnipotence is revealed as having been illusory. Thereafter to reduce the tension produced by the power deficit, the ego sets upon an unending and fruitless course aimed at restoring its formerly perceived omnipotence.

Ego Real The ego as it perceives the self when it is unable to perceive it as ideal. The ego's self perception fluctuates continually between the ideal and the real. The ego real is the ego's pessimistic and tension-producing perception of the self and the ego ideal is its most optimistic and tension-reducing perception of the self. The ego actual is the true ego situated at an unknown locus between the ideal and the real.

Ego Tension   See tension.

Ego Worth Perceiving oneself as valuable in the eyes of significant others such as parents, lovers, spouses, siblings, employers and colleagues.

Ego Worth Assets Possessions, qualities, attributes, capacities and characteristics which gain admiration for their owners.

Ego Worth Deficit A deficiency of ego worth which first appears as a consequence of weaning during ego ontogenesis. Weaning presents the infant ego with the reality of its dependency upon an external provider for the reduction of tension such as hunger. The infant ego places great value upon the object of absolute dependency and desires that the external object of dependency place great value upon the infant ego to assure its preservation. The deficit can never be re moved because the ego will forever experience dependency, first upon the parent and thereafter upon parentified others and the functionaries, organizations and institutions of society.

Ego Worth Needs Ego worth assets perceived by the ego as necessary to achieve worth.

Electoral Process   The process by which candidates are nominated and elected to office.

Elements, The   In this volume, the elements refers to the forces which constitute the natural environment such as the weather, and in par ticular severe weather.

Enteroceptors   See proprioceptors.

External Agent   An entity outside the ego upon which the ego depends for the reduction of tension. During childhood the principal external agent relied upon is normatively the parent, and in adulthood tends to be parentified entities such as spouse, societal organizations and institutions and their functionaries.

External Agent of Dependence   See external agent.

External World   Everything which exists beyond the boundary of the ego.

Executive Budget   A lump sum government budget proposed by the executive, appropriated by the legislature and segregated into objects of expenditure and spent by the executive. It denies to the legislature and gives to the executive the authority to determine government expenditures in detail, thereby enhancing the power of the executive over the legislative.

External Object of Dependence   An external object, usually the parent during infancy and childhood, or in adulthood a parentified entity such as an employer or government, upon which the ego relies for the reduction of ego tension whose source it is unable to deal with successfully.

Fantasy   An ego mechanism in the form of a narrative created by the ego in imagination in which the ego's tension-reduction needs are satisfied. The mechanism offers only temporary respite because the tension-producing impingement of reality always returns.

Familify   To relate to an object as if to one's family.

Familified   An object related to as if to one's family.

Feelings   The body responds physiologically to ego tension accompa- nied by various sensations such as elevated temperature, perspira- tion, muscle contractions in the thorax, accelerated breathing, more rapid heart rate, gastrointestinal pain, and the like. These sensations are felt physiologically, and lead the individual to experience ego tension as "feelings," hence such expressions as feeling depressed, feeling fear, feeling angry, feeling discouaged; and when tension reduction is experienced, feeling happy, feeling elated, feeling suc- cessful, feeling optimistic and the like.

Filial Ambivalence   The child ego's simultaneous love and hate for the parent.

Filial Counter-Manipulation   See counter-manipulation.

Filial Hostility   Hostility directed at the parent or parental surrogate. Filial hostility is a reaction-formation to filial fear produced by the Oedipus conflict in which the child fears retribution from the same sex parent he believes he has enraged by competing for preferment with the opposite sex parent.

Filial Independence   A state in which behavior occurs without the control of the parent.

Filial Manipulation   The child's manipulation of the parent to control parental behavior in ways which reduces ego tension for the child.

Filial-Parental Conflict   Same as filial-parental relatedness.

Filial-Parental Interaction   See filial-parental relatedness.

Filial-Parental Relatedness The interaction between the parent and child which consists of filial ambivalence toward the parent, the child's struggle for independence, the parent's insistence upon the child's achieving self-dependence, and the practice of both parent and child of manipulating each other to gain their desired ends which is the reduction of ego tension which each experiences be cause of the other.

Filial Rebellion   The process by which the child struggles to separate from the parent by rejecting selected parental values and practices. Filial rebellion tends to be a tension-producing experience for the parent, but a mixed experience for the child because rejection of parental preferences while it reduces the tension of the individuation imperative, it increases filial fear and consequent tension. The child's resistance to parental self-dependence training should not be mistaken for filial rebellion.

Filial Relatedness Transference See filial relatedness transference process.

Filial Relatedness Transference Process   The process by which the ego transfers relatedness to the parent to a parentified object such as a spouse, teacher, supervisor, employer, public official, political candidate, head of state or nation.

Filial Self-Dependence   See self-dependence.

Filification   To relate to a person or object as a parent relates to a child.

Filify   To relate to as if to one's child.

Fraternification   Related to as if to a brother.

Fraternified   An object which is related as if to a brother.

Fraternify   To relate to as if to one's brother.

Gerrymander   To establish an election district in such a way that the population of voters in the district favors one's own candidacy or political party. The boundaries of such a district drawn upon a map may have a fanciful shape such as an animal or other imagined object.

Generalized Parent A condition in which the child relates to the parent without distinguishing whether the parent related to is the father or the mother. In adult political behavior, the generalized parent phenomenon may be present when the individual relates to government as a generalized "they" as in "They are preparing us for war."

Good Offices Usually provided by a head of state or his emissary to other states in mutual conflict in order to facilitate the effort of the contending nations to find a settlement of their dispute.

Human Behavior Anything whatsoever done by a human being that is guided by the ego. All biological processes of the human organism including autonomic and involuntary actions are of concern to the ego psychologist but do not constitute human behavior unless and until they impact the ego by producing ego tension.

Id The ego creates the id as an object of projection to separate itself from responsibility for dangerous wishes. "It made me do it" is the infant ego's defense for its filial hostility, "it" being the "id." The id is offered up as the cause of actions whose authorship the ego desperately wishes to disclaim because of the tension-producing fear of parental or societal retribution. In adulthood the ego tends to accept the blame for a large range of wishes and behaviors including those arising from biological imperatives which it disapproves in itself.

Idealize To perceive an object as possessing absolute perfection. See ego ideal.

Identification An ego mechanism which powerfully keeps reality at bay. The ego takes the object of identification into itself and relates to it as if it were itself, but simultaneously recognizes the object of identification as a separate external object. The ego vicariously enjoys and suffers the pleasure and unpleasure attributed to the identification object which it cathects. Severation from the identification object is highly tension-producing and painful for the ego.

Identification Object An external object with which the ego identifies.

Identify The introjection by the ego of an external object which it relates to as if it were itself.

Identity The ego's perception of the self as distinguished from everything else.

Identity Crisis The crisis occurs during adolescence when the child struggles to separate from the parent and to establish an identity different from that of being the child of his parent.

Identity Loss The diminution of identity strength suffered by the individuating adolescent as he reduces his reliance for identity upon being the son or daughter of his parent.

Imago The same as persona.

Individuation The process by which the infant acquires the capacity to cope with cathexis deprivation tension when voluntarily leaving the parent's side to wander beyond sight of the parent. The infant's moving away from the side of the parent is a response to the tension of curiosity and requires a capacity for cathexis object constancy which is belief that the parent is still present even when out of sight. See adolescent individuation.

Impinging Stimuli Any agent, action or condition that elicits or accelerates a physiological or psychological activity or response. The agent may be a physical sensation or a thought, memory or idea.

Instrument of Power A means employed by its user to exercise power. It may take the form of authority, wealth, physical weapons, persuasiveness, information, ideas, status, or the media of communications. In the political process the sovereign power of the state is the premier instrument of power. Important instruments of power for the infant include crying and sphincter control of elimination processes.

Introject To incorporate into the ego an object external to the ego. For example, the infant while subjected to weaning may figuratively take into it the mother from whose breast it suckles the milk. Thus, the infant can relate to the mother as a part of itself rather than as an in constant external object.

Introjection An ego mechanism by which the ego figuratively takes into the self an external object and then relates to it as if were a part of the self.

Judgmental The practice of projecting one's superego failings upon an external target, typically another individual whose superego failings are patently manifest in his behavior. Those who are viewed as non-compliant with prevailing social mores are particularly attractive targets for the exercise of judgmentalism as are the poor, who are regarded as lazy and feckless and the authors of their plight, as well as are criminals, who are seen as deserving of their punishment.

Kinesthesia The undifferentiated complex of sensation which when conveyed to the brain gives the ego an awareness of the soma and which produces ego tension or the reduction of ego tension when the soma is stimulated.

Latency Period A period during ego ontogenesis typically between the ages of six to twelve beginning with the resolution of the Oedipus conflict and ending at the onset of puberty.

Legislative Structure The distribution of power within a legislative body whether to strong leaders, for example, or to the chairpersons of legislative committees. The distribution of power is strongly shaped by whether the government's executive power is assigned to the cabinet which increases the power of the chief cabinet officer or prime minister and weakens the power of committees, or whether executive power is assigned to a separate executive outside the legislative body as in a presidential system, a structure which tends to strengthen committees. However, a presidential system with executive budget tends to strengthen legislative leaders as the principal negotiators with the executive and to weaken legislative committees and committee chairpersons.

Life Cycle From the time of birth to the reproduction of and rearing of offspring to maturity. Differs from the course of life which begins with birth and ends with death.

Lobbyist A person employed by a client to persuade legislators, their staff employees, the chief executive and executive staff employees, governmental agency heads and personnel, and sometimes rank and file voters through the communications media, of the virtues of the client's legislative and administrative aims, which are usually self-serving. See political advocate.

Locomotion Physically moving from one location to another. The infant and child moves by pulling itself along, crawling, toddling, walking and running. The adult employees draft and riding animals and machines.

Maleficent Parental Surrogate A parentified entity to which filial hostility is transferred. For example, the individual unaware of the cause of his hostility, perceives a political entity such as a candidate, public official, political party, municipality, head of state or the nation as maleficent and a deserving target of hostility. See bifurcated filial ambivalence.

Manipulation Acting to shape another person's behavior to one's own purposes by physically moving him or by affecting his motivation through techniques of subterfuge, trickery, threat, enticement and the like. The manipulator may or may not be aware that he is engaging in manipulative behavior.

Mastery Command of the requisite knowledge, skills and abilities to defeat sources of tension producing stimuli. In political behavior mastery refers to the capacity to succeed at one's role in the political process, whether public official, candidate, bureaucrat, pundit, lobbyist, or rank and file voter.

Maternification An object related to as if to the mother.

Maternify To relate to an external object as if to one's mother.

Mechanism Mechanisms are techniques employed by the ego to reduce tension, particularly when other means fail. Mechanisms are based upon self-deception by the ego. By tricking itself into believing that the impinging stimuli has been defeated or does not exists, the ego gains temporary relief. However the reality of the impingement repeatedly assaults the ego so that the effect of the mechanism is repeatedly broached, accompanied by the return of tension and conesquent unpleasure.

Multiparty System   A political system in which three or more major political parties compete for control of the sovereign power of the state. Typically in a multiparty system two or more parties are compelled to align themselves together in order to control the instruments of government in which sovereignty resides. Multiparty systems tend to operate in parliamentary structures and are incompatible with a presidential system in which only one political party can hold executive power.

Narcissism   Self love. The ego's cathexis to the self and manifested in tender, affectionate, protective regard of the ego for itself. Narcissism suffuses with all ego-guided behavior and all ego experience.

Narcissism Deficit   The loss of narcissism resulting from the infant ego's extension of primary narcissism to the external agent of dependence, normatively the parent, initially as a consequence of the trauma of weaning in response to which the ego identifies with and introjects the parent as the means to restore the severed filial-paternal cathexis.

Narcissistic Gratification   The ego experience of being the object of love as manifested for example in the devotion of another, in admiration, in the granting of indulgence, special favor, applause, celebrity and the like.

Need An object or activity identified by the ego as imperative for the reduction of ego tension.

Net Tension Decrease   A result when an activity or circumstance creates ego tension in the near term but decreases it over the longer term. For example, cultivating a garden is tension-producing in the near term, but the food it produces will reduce the greater tension of hunger over the long run.

Net Tension Increase   An increase of tension resulting from activity which increases tension on balance less than it reduces tension. For example, drinking seawater to quench tension-producing thirst would lead to even greater thirst and greater tension.

Neuroleptic   Antipsychotic drug.

Neuron   Nerve cell.

Neurotransmitters   Chemical substances which transmit nerve im pulses across synapses.

Object   An entity perceived by the ego as increasing or decreasing its experience of tension.

Object Cathexis Deprivation   The loss of an entity to which the ego experiences a compelling bond such as a parent or parentified object. Such a loss is tension-producing.

Object Constancy   Belief that an object which is out of sight nevertheless continues to exist. A capacity for object constancy is necessary
for the infant to leave the parent's presence without experiencing
increased ego tension.

Oedipus Conflict   During primordial ego ontogenesis, a state of affairs
in which the child desires the opposite sex parent and competes with
the same sex parent for that object, then coming to experience great
fear of retribution from the same sex parent. The Oedipus conflict
becomes a lasting major shaping force in filial-parental interactions.

Object Cathexis Deprivation   The experience of attenuated cathexis
object attachment which occurs at each transition from one stage of
ego ontogenesis to the succeeding stage and is reexperienced in
adulthood when the bond with a parentified object becomes attenuated. Persons alienated from their homeland may experience cathexis deprivation as may persons who have lost a parent to death or
who suffer from home sickness.

Ontogenesis   See ego ontogenesis.

Over Compensation   Behavior aimed at reducing ego tension which
exceeds what is required to defeat the source of tension-producing
stimuli. For example an individual who suffers ego worth deficit
tension which he attributes to his small size and physical weakness
continues to train his body even after he has gained muscular
strength and power which far exceeds the average individual.

Parental Manipulation Manipulation of the child by the parent to reduce ego tension of the parent. Examples are forcing the child
against its wishes to take nourishment by means of cup and spoon
and to use toilet facilities for bowel evacuation and bladder voiding.

Parentify   To relate to a person or other entity as to one's parent.

Parliamentary System   A legislative and administrative structure in
which the executive function is incorporated in the legislature.

Party Leader The individual recognized by party members as having
the responsibility to manage the party's affairs, particularly in
establishing and pursuing public policy in the name of the party. The
leader has charge of patronage in the broadest sense and determines
its distribution to party members. The party leader may or may not
hold elective public office.

Parental Surrogate   An object related to unawares as if it were one's
parent. Authority figures such as teachers, police officers, spouses,
employers, public officials, political candidates, governments and
nations are examples of entities which may be related to as parental
surrogates.

Paternification   The process or relating to an object as a paternal surrogate.

Persona   The factitious image of oneself which one presents to the external world.

Personality   The unique combination of tension-reduction techniques acquired and practiced by the individual ego in response to a combination of impinging stimuli which is unique to each individual.

Physical Pain   Unpleasure in the form of ego tension produced by stimuli impinging upon the nervous system of the human organism accompanied by sharp physical sensations. Non-physical unpleasure is produced by stimuli impinging upon the ego without sharp physical sensations.

Pleasure   The experience of tension reduction through relief from tension producing impinging stimuli. Rapid tension reduction is experienced as heady exhilaration.

Political Advocate   The political advocate differs from the lobbyist in that the lobbyist's political aims tend to serve the interests of a paying client, while the advocate alleges that he serves the public interest or a noble purpose. The advocate tends to make his aims public through the communications media and by means of rallies and other public demonstrations. The lobbyist tends to function quietly in private meetings with public officials and their staff employees and in many cases would rather the public not be aware of his aims and methods.

Political Behavior   Human behavior in the political process.

Politicized Issue   A societal issue which is injected into the political process usually by advocates who seek access to and use of the sovereign power of the state to support their position with respect to the issue. A societal issue may become politicized unintentionally when its presence confronts the political authority with a problem which it cannot ignore without risking a loss of votes in the next election. The abortion issue may serve as an example of the first, and widespread drug abuse as an example of the second.

Political Party   An organization within the state which acts to gain control of the sovereign power of the state to achieve the aims of its members. In a democracy the party operates through an electoral process. In non-democratic societies, a political party may exploit the   electoral process or resort to violence and other illegal means to   gain   control   of   the   sovereign   power   of   the   state.

Political Power   The sovereign power of the state.

Political Process   The political process is the activity by which individuals seek access to and use of the sovereign power of the state to achieve their aims.

Political Value   An entity concerned with the political process to which worth is attributed. It includes such entities as preferred form of government, degree of importance attached to rectitude in the political process and the proper role of government in society. See value.

Power Power is the capacity to get one's way even in the face of impediments. It is the ego's main reliance to defeat tension-producing impinging stimuli.

Power Base The resources which can be drawn upon to access and use the sovereign power of the state to gain one's ends. It includes such items as the authority of office, the control of patronage, the capacity to obtain campaign funds and particularly the votes one can command upon behalf of his political aims.

Power Deficit The ego's perception of its loss of power following it's discovery as a consequence of the weaning trauma that its former omnipotence was an illusion and that it is dependent upon an external agent, the parent or care giver, to defeat tension-producing stimuli. The ego never ceases its striving to rectify its loss of omnipotence, but it never succeeds in making up the deficit.

Presidential System A political system in which the sovereign power of the state is separated into competing branches of government which check each other, the executive power being assigned to a president forcing a political structure consisting of two major parties which vie for a majority of votes in order to gain control of the executive power. Ordinarily voters who support minor parties cannot hope to share in executive power.

Primordial Ego The ego as it exists prior to the beginning of autobiographical memory. It is during the primordial period that the ego experiences and is shaped by its response to the traumata of weaning, toilet training and the Oedipus conflict.

Primordial Power Deficit The ego's discovery of the power deficit occurs during the period of its primordial existence.

Projection An ego tension-reduction mechanism, perhaps modeled upon the spitting out of food in response to weaning. In projection the ego attributes to an external object its own unwanted, tension-producing attributes to rid itself of them so as to avoid the tension and resulting unpleasure which they invite. The ego's first major act of projection is the creation of the id or "it" upon which blame for the ego's unwanted urges are projected to free the ego from the potential retribution which the exercise of those urges might invite.

Proprioceptors Sensate impinging stimuli arising within the soma and to the ego via the brain increase or decrease tension indicating the condition of the intestines and the location and condition of limbs and organs. Bladder and bowel pressure and cramped legs or arms are examples.

Psycho-Political Focusing Sorting out various political behavior options and choosing the option which maximizes net tension reduction or minimizes net tension increase. The rank and file voter engages in psycho-political focusing when deciding which candidate to cast his ballot for.

Public Policy   The principle, criterion or precept against which government action is tested to assure its appropriateness. It is a guide to government action sanctioned by the sovereign power of the state. It is embodied in law, in rules and regulations, in administrative directives, in court decisions and dicta, in governmental practices and in the attitudes and the daily performance of government employees.

Public Policy Process   The public policy process is embodied in the political process. It is the activity by which individuals seek access to and use of the sovereign power of the state to establish, implement and maintain a public policy intended to achieve their aims.

Rationalization To make rational through self deceiving illogical thinking a tension-reduction action which is actually irrational. For example, interest in prurient literature condemned by the superego might be rationalized by excusing it on the basis of protecting others.

Reaction-Formation   An ego mechanism in which a tension-producing experience is replaced by its opposite. For example the tension-producing experience of filial fear is replaced by the tension-reducing experience of filial hostility displaced upon a maleficent parental surrogate.

Reality   The totality of all that actually exists.

Reality Testing   Behavior aimed at verifying or correcting one's perception of what actually exists. See surety.

Rectitude   Rectitude is right behavior, and right behavior is behavior which conforms to the demands of reality as defined by the super ego. The content of the superego is passed down from one generation to the next but is subjected to modification as the ego in a succeeding generation changes to adapt to tension-producing stimulation unique to it. The particulars of rectitude may change from one generation to the next and differ from one culture to the next.

Reengulfment   The reversal of individuation.

Refueling   A behavior in which an individuating infant returns to its mother briefly to reduce the ego tension of severation before toddling away again to play or explore.

Regression   The return to immature response behaviors of early stages of ego ontogenesis to deal with tension-producing impinging stimuli experienced in later stages of ego ontogenesis.

Relatedness   A condition in which the ego has assumed aims and expectations with regard to an object.

Relate To   To assume aims and expectations with regard to an object.

For example, impelled by tension-producing impingement of the Oedipus conflict the child ego attempts to reduce tension by seeking to possess the opposite sex parent, an aim which itself produces further tension in the form of fear of retribution from the same sex parent. Subsequently as an adult this same ego may relate to authority and depended-upon figures with the same ambivalent expectation he/she related to the same sex parent during the ascendancy of the Oedipus conflict.

Response Repertoire   The full array of mechanisms and techniques acquired by the ego to deal with tension-producing impinging stimuli.

Romanticize   To make into an object of romantic love. To displace filial infatuation upon an external object.

Security   Total protection from or the capacity to defeat all actual and potential tension-producing impinging stimuli.

Self   The individual within which the ego functions as the experiencer of tension and the guidance means for reducing tension. Normatively the internal-external boundary of the self tends to be the epidermal sack which contains the body of the human organism. But the use of such mechanisms as projection and introjection blurs the boundary.

Self Dependence   The capacity of the individual to provide for his own tension-reduction wants and needs independent of his parent or of a parental surrogate. See filial independence for contrast.

Self Image   A perception of the self created by the ego.

Self Neglect   A form of self injurious behavior. See counter manipulation.

Separate Identity   A unique identity. The ego strives to establish a separate identity during adolescent individuation as a part of the adolescent's struggle to separate from the parent.

Separate Identity Conflict   The filial-parental conflict caused by adolescent individuation which impels the adolescent to seek a separate identity from that of being identified as the child of the parent.

Self Injury   In this volume, self injury refers to behavior in which the child subjects itself to injury in the form of physical damage or harm, neglect of its health and neglect of its progress toward self-dependence and the like. The child is unaware of its self-injurious behavior whose purpose is to counter-manipulate the controlling parent who identified with and introjects the child and thus suffers vi cariously from the child's self-injury behavior. If the child were aware of the aim of its self-injurious behavior, it would be unable to continue with it. Examples of self-injurious behavior in adult politi cal life are extreme civil disobedience, political martyrdom, terrorism and armed rebellion.

Sensate Stimuli   Stimuli which produce sensation.

Separation-Individuation   The process by which the adolescent ego establishes a separate identity from the parent and becomes self-dependent in the context of society.

Separation of Powers   The division of the sovereign power of the state into separate branches of government which compete with and check each other's use of sovereign power. Separation of powers tends to produce a government characterized by indecision because of the difficulty of negotiating agreement among the several branches to which sovereign power has been dispersed.

Severation   Condition of being severed from the object of cathexis.

Severation Experience   The experience of increased ego tension produced by severation from a depended upon external agent and the process of adaptation to the severed condition.

Severation Trauma   The overwhelming stress produced during ego ontogenesis by being severed from the primary external agent of dependence, usually the parent.

Siblification   To relate to another person or object as if to one's sibling.

Silent Stimuli   Stimuli not accompanied by sensation. The ego may be unaware of silent stimuli when they impinge without the ego's direct knowledge as in the case of hormonal secretions which cross the blood-brain barrier, or the ego may be aware of the source if it is deliberately self administered as, for example, in drinking an alcoholic beverage.

Societal Issue   A concern within a society which is disputed by two or more salient groups. If the sovereign power of the state is sought by a party to the dispute to help it prevail, then the societal issue becomes also a political issue.

Sorofication   The state of relating to a person or object as if to one's sister.

Sorofy   To relate to a person or other object as if to one's sister.

Sound Bites   In television broadcasting, brief spurts of information of dramatic character, often taken out of a larger context, and intended to grab the viewer's attention and hold it long enough so that he will still be watching when the next revenue-producing advertisement is aired.

Sovereign Power   That power within the boundaries of the state which knows no greater power. Sovereign power is usually possessed by the state alone.

Sovereign Power of the State   That power within the state which knows no greater power.

Sphincter Control   Contracting the muscles of the bladder and anal sphincters to control the release of urine and feces. Sphincter control is an instrument of power employed by the infant during the anal stage of ego ontogenesis to manipulate the parent to serve his tension-reduction desires.

State A defined territory upon the surface of the earth presided over by a sovereign authority.

Stimuli See impinging stimuli.

Stress Ego tension which persists for which an effective avenue of reduction is not achieved.

Sublimation Sublimation redirects a tension-reduction aim from one which produces a net tension increase to one which yields a net tension decrease, at least temporarily. For example, the infant child may sublimate his forbidden love of feces to modeling clay whose products tend to be approved by the parent. In adult political life the voter resentful of paying taxes for national defense may sublimate the resentment by elevating military spending to the lofty purpose of providing the means to maintain world peace.

Superego   The superego is formed as the means to gain relief from the tension produced by the Oedipus conflict which the ego accomplishes through filial capitulation to parental supremacy. The superego contains the prescriptions and proscriptions which the child regards as parentally imposed and tends to function as the self-regulator of behavior for individual members of society.

Suppression The application of denial to the importuning tension-producing stimuli of reality.

Stated Aims Formally stated purposes which the ego intends that others accept at face value.

Surety Surety is the experience of being "sure of oneself," confident in one's judgment, of being correct in one's decisions. The quality of surety is essential to the ego's tension-reducing guidance function because the ego must accurately assess reality if it is to seek and find the source of impinging stimuli which it must deal with to reduce tension. The ego's surety is its conviction that what it perceives as real and accurate is indeed real and accurate, that it can rely upon what it understands of the world around it to be valid.

Surety Deficit The surety deficit is a consequence of the trauma of weaning and from the time of its onset lasts throughout the remaining course of life. Prior to weaning the infant ego customarily did not experience doubt about the reliability and accuracy of its expectations regarding reality and how effectively to gain relief from tension-producing stimuli. After the trauma of weaning its expectation about reality and how to satisfy its wants and needs becomes confused and uncertain and it looks for advice from parents and later from parentified external entities such as church, government, science and academe.

Surety Aims The means adopted by the ego to achieve validation of its surety. In the political process the means adopted may include seeking to gain and to use the sovereign power of the state to impose surety views upon others to reduce the ego tension of uncertainty.

Synapse The junction across which a nerve impulse passes from an axon terminal to a neuron, a muscle cell or a gland cell.

Tension The experience of disequaminity which may range in intensity from mild disquiet to overwhelming panic. It is in response to tension that all human behavior arises.

Tension Producing Impinging Stimuli Stimuli which impinge upon the ego resulting in increased ego tension and unpleasure. Such stimuli can be physical or silent, imposed or self administered in form or take the form of thoughts, perceptions, ideas or memories.

Tension Producing Impingement A particular stimulus identified by the ego as the source of tension increase and unpleasure experienced by the ego.

Tension Producing Trauma A profound tension-producing impingement upon the ego which results in a reworking of the ego's tension-reducing capabilities and practices.

Tension Reducing Guidance Function The function of the ego to seek and identify sources of tension-producing stimuli and to act to defeat them.

Toilet Training Trauma A profound injury to the ego produced by the impingement of toilet training which has a lasting effect upon the ego's capacity to deal with tension-producing stimuli.

Transfer To shift relatedness from its original object to a different object.

Transferred To An object of transference, usually perceived to have attributes of the parent.

Transference The propensity of the ego to shift a relatedness from its original object to a different object and then to relate to the second object as if it were the first. For example the ego's relatedness to the parent may be shifted to a political candidate, an official, a political party, a government or a nation.

Transference Relatedness Devolution The transference of relatedness to current objects to objects subsequently encountered in a devolving chain from the present into the future. This is the process by which, as an example, the infant-child's relatedness to the parent is transferred first to other family members, then to teachers, and thence to authority figures encountered later such as employers, government officials and to the state and the nation.

Two Party Parliament A parliament dominated by two major political parties.

Two Party System A political system dominated by two major parties in which third parties when present play no more than a minor role usually because of their ability to align with a major party. In elections minor parties may effect the outcome by drawing votes from the major parties.

Tenure A condition of service in which one cannot be removed without cause and due process.

Undoing An ego mechanism in which a tension-producing impinge ment is treated as if it never occurred.

Universalize A mechanism employed by the ego to reduce tension by attributing its tension producing behavior to others in general. For example, a candidate for public office who accepts and spends illegally obtained campaign contributions strives to reduce the tension produced by a punishing superego by attributing the same illicit behavior to others as a universal principle.

Unpleasure The experience of tension-increase resulting from the impingement of tension-producing stimuli. See physical pain.

Unrecognized Aims Purposes of the ego not recognized by the ego because they have not been analyzed and consequently not disclosed.

Unstated Aims Purposes of the ego not formally presented because of potential tension-producing negative consequences.

Values A value is any physical or non-physical object, or idea, thought, memory, activity, belief, viewpoint, sensation, experience, attitude, perception or any entity which reduces ego tension for the individual who ascribes worth to the valued entity.

Will A biologically based force within the organism which is experienced by the ego as a compulsion to reduce tension by whatever means the ego can discover.

Voice Over Video tape presentation in which a commentating voice is heard but the commentator not shown.

Worth See ego worth.

SELECTED BIBLIOGRAPHY

Ackerman, Nathan W. *The Psychodynamics of Family Life, Diagnosis and Treatment of Family Relationships.* New York: Basic Books, Inc., 1958.

Adler, Alfred. *Understanding Human Nature.* New York: Garden City Publishing Company Inc., 1927.

Almond, Gabriel A. *The American People and Foreign Policy.* New York: Harcourt, Brace and Company, 1950.

Albrecht-Carrié, René. *A Diplomatic History of Europe Since the Congress of Vienna.* New York: Harper and Brothers, 1958.

Allport, G. W. *Personality: A Psychological Interpretation.* New York: Holt, Rinehart, and Winston, 1937.

Axelrod, Donald, *Shadow Government: The Hidden World of Public Authorities—And How They Control Over $1 Trillion of Your Money.* New York: John Wiley and Sons, Inc., 1992.

Bailey, Thomas A. *A Diplomatic History of the American People.* New York: Appleton-Century-Crofts, Inc., 1955.

Beard, Charles A. *An Economic Interpretation of the Constitution of the United States.* New York: Macmillan, 1913.

___________ *The Supreme Court and the Constitution.* New York: Macmillan, 1912.

Berelson, Bernard, and Steiner, Gary A. *Human Behavior: An Inventory of Scientific Findings.* New York: Harcourt, Brace and World, Inc., 1964.

Bettelheim, Bruno. *Freud and Man's Soul.* New York: Alfred A. Knopf, 1983.

Blos, Peter. *On Adolescence, A Psychoanalytic Interpretation.* New York: The Free Press, A Division of Macmillan Publishing Co., Inc., 1966.

__________ *The Adolescent Passage: Developmental Issues.* Madison, Connecticut: International Universities Press, 1989.

Bowlby, J. *Attachment and Loss.* London: Hogarth Press, 1969.

Brown, J. F. *The Psychodynamics of Abnormal Behavior.* New York and London: McGraw-Hill Book Company, Inc., 1940.

Cardozo, Benjamin. *The Nature of the Judicial Process.* New Haven, Connecticut: Yale University Press, 1921.

Carr, Edward Hallett. *The Twenty Years' Crisis 1919--1939: An Introduction to the Study of International Relations.* London: Macmillan and Co. Ltd., 1956.328

Cheever, Daniel S., and Havilan, H. Field, Jr. *Organizing For Peace: International Organization In World Affairs.* Cambridge, Massachusetts: The Riverside Press, 1954.

Coutu, Walter. *Emergent Human Nature: A symbolic Field Interpretation.* New York: Alfred A. Knopf, 1949.

Décarrie, Therésè Gouin. *Intelligence and Affectivity in Early Childhood: An Experimental Study of Jean Piaget's Object Concept and Object Relations.* Translated by Elizabeth Pasztor Brandt and Lewis Wolfgang Brandt. New York: International Universities Press, Inc., 1965.

De Tocqueville, Alexis. *Democracy in America.* Translated by Henry Reeve. Henry Steele Commanger, ed. New York: Oxford University Press, 1947.

Dinerstein, H. S. *War and the Soviet Union.* New York: Frederick A. Praeger, 1959

Djilas, Milovan. *The New Class An Analysis of the Communist System.* New York: Frederick A. Praeger, 1957.

__________ *Profit in the Ruins, Fall of the New Class: A History of Communism's Self-Destruction.* Vasilije Kalezic, Ed. John Loud translator. Knopf.

Ettin, Mark F.; Fidler, Jay W.; and Cohen, Bertram D., eds. *Group Process and Political Dynamics.* Madison, Connecticut: International Universities Press, Inc., 1995.

Erikson, Erik H. *Childhood and Society.* New York: W. W. Norton and Company, Inc., 1963.

Farrand, Max. *The Framing of the Constitution.* New Haven, Connecticut: Yale University Press, 1926.

Foner, Eric, *The Story of American Freedom.* New York: W.W. Norton & Company, 1998.

Foner, Eric, *The Story of American Freedom.* New York: W.W. Norton & Company, 1998.

Freud, Anna. *The Writings of Anna Freud. Vol. II: The Ego and the Mechanisms of Defense.* Revised. Translated by Cecil Bains.

Freud, Sigmund. *The Standard Edition of the Complete Writings of Sigmund Freud.* Edited by James Strachey. London: The Hogarth Press, 1971. 24 Vols. Index Vol. 24.

Fromm, Erich. *Escape From Freedom.* New York: Farrar and Rinehart, 1941.

Greenspan, Stanley I., and Pollock, George H., eds. *The Course of Life.* Madison, Connecticut: International Universities Press, Inc., Vols. I - VI. 1989.

Hartmann, Heinz. *Ego Psychology and the Problem of Adaptation.* New York: International Universities Press, 1958.

Hilsman, Roger. *To Move A Nation.* New York: Doubleday and Company, Inc., 1967.

Hitchiner, Dell Gilletter, and Levine, Carol. *Comparative Government and Politics.* New York: Dodd, Mead and Company, Inc., 1970.

Hofstadter, Richard. *The American Political Tradition.* New York: Knopf, 1951.

Holborn, Hajo. *The Political Collapse of Europe.* New York: Alfred A. Knopf, 1959.

Horney, Karen. *Neurosis and Human Growth.* New York: Norton, 1950.

Ignatieff, Michael. *Isaiah Berlin A Life*: New York: Metropolitan Books Henry Holt & Company, 1998.

Jennings, Ivor. *Cabinet Government.* Cambridge: Cambridge University Press, 1959.

____________ *Parliament.* Cambridge: Cambridge University Press, 1957.

Jones, Ernest. *The Life and Work of Sigmund Freud.* New York: Basic Books, 1953.

Keir, David Lindsay. *The Constitutional History of Modern Britain 1485 - 1951.* London: Adam and Charles Black, 1955.

Kennedy, David M. *Freedom from Fear, The American People in Depression and War, 1929-1945.* New York: Oxford University Press, 1999.

Kent, Frank. *The Great Game of Politics.* Garden City, New York: Doubleday, 1923.

Key, V. O. *Politics, Parties, and Pressure Groups.* 5th ed. New York: Crowell-Collier, 1964.

Kissinger, Henry A. *Nuclear Weapons and Foreign Policy.* Garden City, New York: Doubleday and Company, Inc., 1958.

Klein, Donald F.; Gittelman, Rachel; Quitkin, Frederic; and Rifkin, Arthur. *Diagnosis and Drug Treatment of Psychiatric Disorders: Adults and Children.* Baltimore: Williams and Wilkins, 1983.

Kohut, Heinz. *Analysis of the Self.* new York: International
Universities Press, 1971.

Konner, Melvin. *The Tangled Wing, Biological Constraints on the
Human Spirit.* New York: Holt, Rinehart and Winston, 1982.

Lasswell, Harold D. *World Politics and Personal Insecurity.* New
York: The Free Press, 1965.

Lindzey, Gardner, and Hall, Calvin S., eds. *Theories of Personality:
Primary Sources and Research.* New York: John Wiley and Sons,
Inc., 1968.

Lorenz, Konrad. *On Aggression.* New York: Bantam Books, Inc.,
1967.

Lubell, Samuel. *The Future of American Politics.* New York: Harper
and Brothers, 1952.

Luethy, Herbert. *France Against Herself.* New York: Meridian
Books, Inc., 1958.

Mahler, Margaret S.; Pine, Fred; and Bergman, Anni. *The Psychological Birth of the Human Infant: Symbiosis and Individuation*
New York: Basic Books, Inc., 1975.

McKean, Dayton David. *Party and Pressure Politics.* Cambridge,
Massachusetts: The Riverside Press. 1949.

McKenzie, R. T. *British Political Parties, The Distribution of Power
Within the Conservative and Labour Parties.* New York: St.
Martins Press, Inc., 1955.

Morgentthau, Hans J. *Politics Among Nations, The Struggle For
Power and Peace.* New York: Alfred A. Knopf, 1978.

Munroe, Ruth L. *Schools of Psychoanalytic Thought.* New York: The
Dryden Press, Inc., 1955.

Murphy, Gardner. *Personality; A Biosocial Approach to Origins and
Structure.* New York: Harper, 1947.

Neustadt, Richard E. *Presidential Power.* New York: Wiley, 1960.

New York State Division of the Budget. *The Executive Budget in
New York State: A Half-Century Perspective.* ed. by Robert Kirker.
Albany: The New York State Division of the Budget, 1981.

Packard, Vance. *The Status Seekers.* New York: David McKay
Company, Inc., 1959.

Palmer, Kenneth T. *State Politics in the United States.* New York: St.
Martin's Press, 1972.

Parrington, Vernon L. *Main Currents of American Thought.* New
York: Harcourt, Brace and World, 1927—30.

Pervin, Lawrence A. *Personality: Theory, Assessment, and Research*
New York: John Wiley and Sons, Inc., 1975.

Piaget, Jean. *The Grasp of Consciousness: Action and Concept in the
Young Child.* Translated by Susan Wedgwood. Cambridge,

Massachusetts: Harvard University Press, 1976.

Post, Seymour C., Ed. *Moral Values and the Superego Concept in Psychoanalysis.* New York: International Universities Press, Inc., 1972.

Eissler, Ruth S.; Freud, Anna; Hartmann, Heinz; Kris, Marianne; and Lustman, Seymour. Editors. *The Psychoanalytic Study of the Child.* New York: International Universities Press, 25 Vols.

Rangell, Leo, and Moses-Hrushovski, Rena, Eds. *Psychoanalysis at the Political Border, Essays in Honor of Rafael Moses.* Madison, Connecticut: International Universities Press, Inc., 1996.

Rapaport, David. *The Structure of Psychoanalytic Theory.* New York: International Universities Press, 1960.

Riessman, David; Glazer, Nathan; and Reuel, Denney. *The Lonely Crowd: A Study of the Changing American Character.* Garden City, New York: Doubleday Anchor Books, 1953.

Rogers, C. R. *Client-Centered Therapy.* Boston: Houghton, 1951.

Rogers, Lindsay. *The American Senate.* New York: Knopf, 1927.

Rosenthal, Alan. *Governors and Legislatures: Contending Powers.* Washington: Congressional Quarterly, Inc., 1990.

Rossiter, Clinton. *1787: The Grand Convention.* New York: Macmillan, 1966.

Sarnoff, Charles. *Latency.* London: Jason Aronson, Inc., 1989.

Simon, Herbert. *Administrative Behavior.* 2d Ed. New York: Macmillan, 1957.

Sorauf, Frank J. *Party Politics in America.* Boston: Little Brown and Company, 1968.

Spitz, Rene. *Rene Spitz: Dialogues From Infancy.* Selected Papers Edited by Robert N. Emde. Madison, Connecticut: International Universities Press, Inc.

______________ *A Genetic Field Theory of Ego Formation.* New York: International Universities Press, 1959.

Sprout, Harold and Margaret. *Foundations of National Power.* New York: D. Van Norstrand Company, Inc., 1951.

Schuman, David and Olufs, Dick W. *Public Administration in the United States.* Lexington, Massachusetts: D. C. Heath and Company, 1988.

Schuman, Frederick L. *International Politics.* New York: McGraw-Hill Book Company, Inc., 1953.

Sears, R. R.; Rau, Lucy; and Alpert, R. *Identification and Child-Rearing.* Stanford: Stanford University Press, 1965.

State of New York Management Resources Project. *Governing the Empire State: An Insiders Guide.* Edited by Jane Zacek. Albany,

New York: Management Resources Project, Rockefeller Institute of Government, 1988.

Stern, Daniel N. *The Interpersonal World of the Infant, A view From Psychoanalysis and Developmental Psychology.* New York: Basic Books, Inc., 1985.

Sullivan, Harry Stack. *The Interpersonal Theory of Psychiatry.* W. W. Norton and Co., 1953.

Thompson, David. *Democracy in France: The Third and Fourth Republics.* London: Oxford University Press, 1958.

Weber, Max. *The Theory of Social and Economic Organization* Translated by A. M. Henderson and Talcott Parsons. New York: The Free Press, 1947.

Spitz, Rene A. *No and Yes: On the Genesis of Human Communication* New York: International Universities Press, 1957.

Veblin, Thorstein. *The Theory of the Leisure Class, An Economic Study of Institutions.* The New American Library, 1953. Copyright by the Macmillan Company, 1889, 1912.

Wilentz, Joan Steen. *The Senses of Man.* New York: Thomas Y. Crowell Company, 1971.

Williams, Philip. *Politics in Post-War France. Parties and the Constitution in the Fourth Republic.* London: Longmans, Green and Company, 1958.

Wilson, Woodrow. *Congressional Government: A Study in American Politics.* Boston: Houghton Mifflin, 1885.

Winnicott, D. W. *The Maturational Processes and the Facilitating Environment.* New York: International Universities Press, 1965.

Zimmerman, Joseph F. *The Government and Politics of New York State.* New York: New York University Press, 1981.

INDEX